'*Acid Alex* is quite simply on ... ve
ever read. It is also well-written ...
... uy

'Heartbreaking! Entertaining! Int ... ns Grundling, *SL* magazine

'Nothing I have read has sketched the scorched social landscape of South
Africa's last half-century with such intensity and honesty. Read it.'

— Charles Thesen, *Marie Claire*

'There are elements of Hunter S Thompson, Herman Charles Bosman, William
Burroughs and William Wharton. But in the end it is an amazing story told in
a unique voice. A voice moulded by pain, a voice honed by a government
reformatory ..., whetted by the SADF, and sharpened by Pretoria Central.

It is the story of a man who went to hell and came back, a morality tale, a
Bildungsroman, the narrative of a fuckup who found redemption, and the
anthem of a lost generation.' — Caspar Greeff, *Sunday Times*

'Truly, as Koos Kombuis says, this is "an astonishingly breathless story" ... Besides
being a great read, *Acid Alex* is an invaluable record of a type of mania that
gripped a certain type of South African in the last quarter of the 20th century.

It's a book that's going to appeal to many young South Africans who
currently have to turn to the United States for their myths of pointless excess,
and it's going to inspire them. Not necessarily in a particularly savoury way.'

— Chris Roper, *Mail & Guardian*

'Lovejoy's debut literary work is nothing if not a compelling read. It's a trip
beyond your wildest imagination – but not for the faint of heart.'

— Peter van der Merwe, *Business in Africa*

'This at times disturbing book is always readable and will not fail to move you.'
— Garth Johnstone, *Mercury*

'*Acid Alex* is not the type of book you dip in and out of, put down, and then
forget. It's a tough, gritty read which gets under your skin and stays there long
after turning the final page.' — Serai Ogle, kalahari.net

'Lovejoy is a good storyteller and a gifted writer with a keen insight into what makes people tick.' — Luke Stubbs, *Cape Times*

'*Acid Alex* is bar, reguit, onbeskof en blatant. Dit sal die boek 'n onreg aandoen om dit tot 'n spesifieke genre te probeer beperk. Dis outobiografies, maar dit het ook die spanningselement van 'n speurverhaal en die emosionele stamina van 'n uitstekende roman. Dit verloop byna soos 'n dokumentêr waarin talle instansies en individue onder die skrywer se skerp tong moet deurloop, en hy raak plek-plek besonder kleurryk in die uitdrukking van sy misnoeë. Maar die boek is ook openhartig, gevoelvol en aangrypend.

— Sophia van Taak, *Die Burger*

'Al Lovejoy ... recounts a life so extraordinary that just reading about it will shock you, challenge you, excite you, scare you, make you angry, make you sad, make you laugh out loud and most of all make you completely unable to put the thing down.' — Daniel Friedman, JHBLive, jhblive.co.za

'[T]he most relevant and freshest piece of South African literature I have come across. It speaks like the author speaks. It is written with bleeding passion and brutal honesty in his charismatic and conversational prose – exposing parts of the past 30 odd years of SA underground culture. *Acid Alex* will have you turning chapters late into the night.' — Daev, Alternative Eye, alteye.co.za

'Alex Lovejoy's *Acid Alex* is probably the best biography that I have read in the last decade ... It's a "ware" South African story of a life lost in the darkness and eventual redemption, about what happens when the monkeys call the tune and Shylock comes calling for his pound of flesh. It's in short one of the great South African rock 'n roll stories ever written and if there is any justice he should win a literary prize ... Highly recommended.'

— Benjy Mudie, Rock of Ages, rock.co.za

'In terms of popular culture and understanding a couple of generations of white South Africans, this is the most important book ever written about South Africa. In terms of what it does and tries to do, it may still make the list of most important books in total about South Africa. Regardless, this is a book that demands to be read.' — Dave Chislett, The Chiz, thechiz.co.za

Acid Alex

AL LOVEJOY

Nominated for the Alan Paton
& The Bookseller's Choice Award(s)

2005

lovejoytrust@yahoo.co.uk

www.acidalex.com

First published 2005 by Zebra Press

ISBN 1-4392-4940-7

Library of Congress Control Number 2005447642

THANK YOU SANDY

This is for Tash & Robbie,
Chinas and our Family
&

Those in that Great Crowd who watch us …

Some of them being:

Ash, Joe'a, Bernard, Kevin, Ma-oes
Johnny, Michelle, Stuart
Phillip
Jurgens
Llewellyn
Fabian, Alzaan, Gerhardt
Frazier
Kerkorrel
Yuri
Schalk
And you my darling Christine …

Contents

Foreword

In your hands, you are holding a book which is about to turn South African literature on its head.

Congratulations on buying it. Or shoplifting it. Or getting a signed copy from the author's website. Or whatever. By owning it, you have just become a cutting edge reader. That is, if you read it. But you will, you will.

Once you have started on the first paragraph, this book will be impossible to put down. That is a guarantee.

I knew Al. I knew the drug scenes he is writing about. And he writes about those scenes so vividly, so compellingly, that after reading a page – any page – of *Acid Alex*, my lungs start hurting, my chest starts wheezing, and my eyes fill with tears. To me, reading this manuscript is like peeling an onion. A very large onion. It is like peeling an onion with a very sharp knife. It is a harrowing experience, because it is the truth.

Yes, I am the 'mal ou' who lived in Al's kitchen. I have written a bit about that experience in my own autobiography, which I haven't read for a while for the very same reason, but if I remember correctly, I subtly altered the setting and some of the facts in order to protect certain people. Since Al has now told everything exactly the way it was, there is no longer any need for secrecy. Yes, I stayed in Al's kitchen while I planned my cultural revolution. I later pulled it off, by the way, but that is another story.

This is Al's story, and in many ways it is even more surprising, more shocking, more far out than my own. Compared to Al's story, my own life seems rather tame. I am thankful for that. At least, in Al, I have one person whom I can point to and proclaim: 'Look, this guy was more wasted than I was.' Or: 'Look, this man went further than I ever did, challenged more conventions than I did, dared more than I did, and actually survived to produce a better book than I will ever produce, and in better English, too.'

Al Lovejoy, as a writer, is very difficult to define. I would guess he is a kind of mixture between Herman Charles Bosman and William Burroughs, but that doesn't quite say it all. There are bits of Walt Whitman, here, and bits of Haruki Murakami, and bits of Kafka, and Kerouac, and Zappa, and even Courtenay. But, most of all, Lovejoy the author is his own person. He bounces from page to page like a fireball, he wraps sentences and images and events together like sosaties and then braais them. He undermines, he jokes, he preaches, and most of all he tells his story, his astonishingly breathless story, one of the strangest stories ever to come out of Africa. If Mandela topped bestseller lists with *Long Walk to Freedom*, this book could just as well have been called *Dizzying Rush to Jail (and back)*. Boy, what a literary turn-on. God, what a trip.

The repercussions that will be caused by a story such as this will, for obvious reasons, hit far and wide. This book is more than just an innovative literary experiment: together with its subject matter, it will do for South African culture what *Trainspotting* did for modern Scottish consciousness. The social implications are staggering. There were, and are (today more than ever), many people like Al in our society. Al was very much a part of the so-called 'lost generation' of South African kids who grew up under a repressive regime, and also suffered under apartheid. Al's essential problem – and this was my essential problem – was finding legitimacy in a seemingly hostile adult environment. Since birth, he was surrounded by idiots. He was an intelligent child caught in a hopelessly dysfunctional world.

This was the reason why I squatted in his house back then, this was the reason we became friends, this was the reason why we landed up in street fights together, why we did drugs. I have always known about Al's potential writing talent. I knew, even back then, that if he wrote his life story, he'd have a bestseller on his hands. The problem was to find the time and patience to finish it. The problem was: how the hell do you write a full-length novel AND hold down a steady job as an international drug smuggler at the same time? Luckily, a few things counted in Al's favour: his expertise in the IT industry, his basic willingness to do the right thing should the right thing prove profitable enough, and his brutal honesty as an author.

Of course I cannot vouch for the absolute truth of every incident in this book – to do that, I would have had to be with Al right from the start of his life – but I can vouch for his sincerity as a person, his odd insistence on street ethics, and his sense of fairness which, as he explained to me during countless late-night conversations, came from looking after himself and his buddies during bad times.

Thank you, Al, for completing this book, and thank you for letting me stay in your kitchen all those months. Oh, and I'm sorry I never cleaned up that shattered tequila bottle I flung against the wall in a fit of rage. Or was it you? Never mind. What's done is done. I wish you the best, my bra, now, henceforth and evermore ...

Koos Kombuis

Acknowledgements

✶

An official hearty thanks goes out to Comrade Smirnoff, Messrs J. Daniels and J. Walker and Senor José Cuervo – all whom spring to mind and bounce off the liver as ever-present and faithful companions to this task. The rest of you can all piss off until somebody pays me for the zol.

I *know* I owe someone for the tequila ...

No, jokes aside – scribbling out the chronicle of a scratched and dented life as a form of therapy, learning to write my own valid expression of African literary art, and simultaneously daring to complete my first book has been quite a wild life-experience ... or is that ... wildlife experience?

Buckets of tears were shed over it. Bank accounts were bankrupted. Everything not nailed down got pawned. Sleepless nights were spent wide-eyed in local pubs fighting large immovable slabs of Writer's Block. Pain, sickness, bad zol, misery, hunger, no booze and depression were rampant – and of course, you do realise, we are *not* talking about what the author had to suffer through here ... *veral jy Talette.*

I want to thank each of you as an individual and all of you as a group, including everyone whom I can't fit into print, those unwitting muses who put up with me and my shit, and cheered me on during *Acid Alex*'s long, arduous breech birth.

I especially thank my champions. Those who not only took the time to read my scribblings and sketches of this very *Acid Alex*, but seriously encouraged me to keep going and finish telling his story. So, in no particular order:

My high-school English teacher, Suzette Conradie, who taught me to love the poetic drama nestled in well-flavoured English through enacting Shakespearean plays— running around stoned in the Knysna woods. A good teacher's influence can be infinite. Koos Kombuis, thank you for supporting and encouraging this barmhartige krimineel, you old boemelaar you. Safety, shot china, you gave me peace of mind, the inspiration to push it to the finish and dared me to flavour it in a unique South African way – lekker. Gina, my first sharp-eyed and productively critical proofreader, wherever you are – thank you. Meiring, Lombard, Heinrich, Stoffel and all the wives, rugrats and staff. Without your help and support, *Acid Alex* would not be an electronic book – especially you, Stoffie. And all you okes' moral and multifaceted support definitely helped me pull it off. Fonnie, Francois and Karen. Then Bobby Boy and K-woman of course. Thanks for everything and everything my brother. Few men have friends like you. Liezel, Nicola, Vicky, John-john, Diana and Gabriel. Ja, Ridley and my boetie The Hobbit – not forgetting all the bras and the seriously sexy chicks next door. Jackie-boy, Dave, Kabous and all the hot babes at Mystic, Bohemia and Springbok. Wouldn't have made it without you girls. Oudste, Joey Evil, Rasta Allan, Rasta Neville, Rasta Paulus and every single other *boom*-roeker in the Bos.

Ja, and all the rest of my chinas, Family and Dr's Hilda and Irene.

I skiem ol' Joe Dog did a very gnarly cover, *al moes ek zol blare byvoeg!* It sure as shit ain't flattering but it certainly does the job.

Vat hom Fluffie—

Lastly, hats off to my editor, Robert Plummer, because he made losing my literary virginity as painless and as much fun as possible, and he's only mentioned last because he watched my back until the last word.

Thanks R.

I'm goofed right now, so if I forgot to mention you in person, china, don't be all goeters and make it a matter of pride – rather smoke a spliff with me when you see me again. You know I love you like I love these other mense on top here anyway. Especially Brian Miller! Viva!

Of course you do ...

So, there we go, cousin – shot, inkosi, kwaai, one-time, salut – lekker. I am feeling most South African today—

AL LOVEJOY
Stellenbosch
June 2009

Author's Note

There is (at least) *one* untruthful statement in this book. Stands to reason, then, that I can safely assert that I am only randomly irresponsible for events as portrayed within. Being a good bullshit artist, I've also changed names and invented contexts for myself and others – to protect the identities of mense I smaak and create a legal nightmare for those strangely misguided individuals who might not smaak me. Because of the very dubious nature of my sanity, the rest errs suspiciously on the side of what I reckon might be tentatively described as ... uhhhmm ... mostly non-fiction?[1]

Now, just in case you are under eighteen, or not a nice cousin, I must warn you:

[ENTER AT OWN RISK]

Because: Multilingual Obscenity, Widescale Offensiveness, Murky Scandals, Straightforward Defamation, Pantheonic Blasphemy, as well as Racial, Linguistic, Religious, Sexual and several badly defined Prejudices aimed at both Individuals and Institutions are discussed volubly within. If this might possibly offend you in the tiniest of ways, then: *Put Down My Book ... Go away.*

No, this is NOT reverse psychology – *put down my book and piss off.* If you don't, you probably want to think seriously about seeking professional help.

If you're one of those mense (like me) who kinda always skiems, ho ho, what the fuck, and simply jumps in— then rapidly goes on to explore *any* or all: Recipe, Instruction, Formulae, Advice, Ritual, Narcotic or Nasty Sexual Practice – as contained within, and YOU consequently find a big angry horn up YOUR ass – then, my dear cousin – it's all on YOUR own world.

Oh, and TRUST ME ON THIS ... you will most definitely *need* professional help. Lots of it.

---

1 I think I hear a lone Dewey number wailing away miserably in a corner somewhere, obscured by Abnormal Psychology, Dangerous Religion and Organised Crime. While over in the Science Fiction & Fantasy Section one can hear badly muffled sniggering – coming directly from a scruffy-looking rack of dog-eared Pratchetts. The kind of sniggering *meant* to be heard.

This book is for consenting adults only. It's kinda like a cyberspace psycho-club with a groovy hardcopy ink-job. See, I reckon it's highly possible that this laddie might become a mite *more* than the sum of his pretty cover and inky bits, so – in my capacity as his loving old man – I designed and co-wrote him a psychedelic, roeker-bookclub in cyberspace @ www.acidalex.com. Copies of this book can be bought there.

The club's for all roeker-style storytellers, jellymentals and more obscure readers to get together and kick together a forum and storyboard that really rocks! There's no cover charge to get in, but right of admission is reserved for adult members only. Music trivia, mutual petty crime yarns and sexual availability statistics will be avidly collected, edited and posted by a Facebook gang of reprobates. Look for the link ...

Hey, and post cool, fun shit, like – pictures of you and your friends taking off your bikinis for his very personal, highly encrypted, seriously password-protected collection. And send him lank cool trippy stories and photos to publish on the site. He's into collecting freaky tales like his own. He's got a bunch already that never made it into print. The author had to cut just over a standard-sized novel from *Acid Alex*.

I am a shameless digresser and the World's Worst Bogart. In some strange way the two go hand in hand. Especially if one of them is clutching a joint. In this book I will digress—

Before I do, let me tell you that *Acid Alex* is a book about child abuse and how it leads directly to crime. It's about spiritual abuse as an opiate of the masses and drug abuse as an opiate of the senses. It explores selling God as a drug and taking love as a pill. In a weird way it tries to prove that we do not inherit the earth from our ancestors – we are currently only borrowing it from our children, and, loving them is *our* spiritual healing.

Ag, in my opinion you will enjoy *Acid Alex* much better if you first close him. Then thoroughly roll some nice ... smelly ... sticky ... hairy—Mary Jane on the naughty bugger's face. Get him between your knees, swaai a fat number on his nose and toke – then, if you still haven't lost track of what you're doing – spread that bad boy back open and give him a lekker good read.

Enjoy, cousin ...

And Noah began to be a farmer, and he planted a vineyard. Then he drank of the wine and was drunk, and became uncovered in his tent. And Ham, the father of Canaan, saw the nakedness of his father, and told his two brothers outside. But Shem and Japheth took a garment, laid it on both their shoulders, and went backward and covered the nakedness of their father. Their faces were turned away, and they did not see their father's nakedness.

So Noah awoke from his wine, and knew what his younger son had done to him. Then he said:

'Cursed be Canaan'
GENESIS 9, 20–25

TO HIS *GRANDSON* ...

Prologue

*P*ing!

The seatbelt light above my head goes off. I snap open my belt, take a deep breath and stand up.

Jesus, I need a drink.

From this point onwards I will have to remain perfectly in character. Breathe slow, breathe slow – relax. Remember it is ALL about body language.

I glance over at Brother E.

He tosses back his beautiful rock star hair, using that weirdly feminine gesture of his, the 'hey girls look at me' move, then flashes lots of teeth and slips me a surreptitious wink. Ugly bastard. I hope nobody saw the wink. That's one of the things They look for. Suspicious conspiratorial acts. Breathe slow, breathe slow: no tension, no drugs.

There isn't much tension in me anyway. I've been busy doing my slow breathing exercises since the cabin movie screen showed us to be 500 kilometres from Paris. I was deep in my safe meditation place even before the pilot announced our descent towards Charles de Gaulle. And I've been consistently working on my airport persona for days now. Body language. The breathing helps relax my muscles. My muscles construct my body language, and that tells Them what They want to know about me. If I can make my muscles lie credibly, all will be well.

Ready or not – I cannot back out now. Oh sweet fuck, I need a drink sooo bad.

Breathe slow, breathe slow: relax your shoulders and neck, Al. Hey, this is the first time you're doing it into France! That's it! Happy and excited! Positive. On holiday!

I had better act better than Bobby de Niro. And remember, folks, it won't be a golden statue I lose out on if I fuck up. I will be staring at the business end of the bars in a French jail. But that's ridiculous. I can't end up in a French mang because I have – breathe slow, breathe slow, tummy light – no drugs in my possession.

Liar, liar, pants on fire.

I don't.

But still, it isn't the zol we are both carrying that troubles me. It is the fucking computers. I am re-entering the European Union – illegally. I have to pray They don't know that the Belgians expelled me from re-entering the EU when they released me from Leeuwen three months ago. I had better pray to all the gods They don't know. The problem is, *I* know. Fuck, I saw Inspector van den Linden of the Belgian Airport BOB enter me into their intelligence database when they arrested me and Fuckhead at Zaventem in Brussels back in '97. I wasn't nervous then, but I am now …

Bastard.

My cover is well and truly blown. Interpol, the DEA, De Belgiese Rijkswacht and our own local SANAB – all know about me now. I just have to hope that I haven't been red-flagged and that the EU Point of Entry computers are not linked between participating countries. They can't be. I mean, I am travelling on a Benelux visa – *in your own name, you prick* – happily issued by The Netherlands five days ago, dammit. Benelux is *tog* Belgium, The Netherlands and Luxembourg – and if the Dutch don't know that the Belgians are on my arse, then the Frogs sure as hell can't. Surely not? Fucking Frogs. What was it that the Flemish okes in jail called them? Oh ja – *verdomde kikkervreters*. Fucking frog munchers.

Oh shit I'm panicking. Breathe, breathe – shake hands with the kikker- vreter koffiemoffie. He's attended to you the whole flight. He is your friend – *Very nice flight m'sieu. Merci beaucoup!* Keep breathing. Don't sweat. Whatever you do, don't sweat.

Get objective, Al. Now!

Project yourself.

What's ahead?

Okay let's see. Their first line of defence will be at the aircraft door itself. Probably about three of them. Somebody tall, ugly and serious in police uniform. Some bland, middle-aged nobody in civvies, and somebody else wearing a bright orange vest with neon reflective writing all over it and carrying a rasping radio handset. Being Europe, neon vest will probably be a woman. The uniform and the vest will be there to draw the attention of each passenger disembarking – the civilian nobody will be the seriously dangerous one. It is his job to watch each person coming out the gate and gauge his or her reactions carefully. Remember, it works on very simple psychology.

Systems check, Al – teach yourself.

Case study: You are [NOT!] carrying anything – diamonds, industrial espionage, stolen art, money, High Grade Marijuana, whatever. You are [NOT!] guilty and You know it. They obviously don't know anything but you think they do. You think They can see it written all over you. Well, you know something – you're right. They can. As you step off the aircraft you will react to the three people standing there whether you want to or not. Your reaction is triggered at a subconscious level and you will show that reaction in your body language. The people who are standing there are simply trained to recognise it and pick it up. They are also chosen for certain skills in this regard. C'mon Al – you know this because you studied it on the Internet. If you are [NOT!] carrying a burden of guilt you will definitely react to the police uniform first and to the orange vest second. That is what gives you away. The tiniest of flinches, the path that your eyes – *especially your eyes* – take, and the position of your body and head. These will tell the civilian that there is something wrong. You should have noticed the neon colours first. That would be normal animal psychology. Stare at the cop six tenths of a second, stare at the vest three tenths of a second, stare at the cop six tenths of a second and you are busted. The key here is the civilian. He will have been recruited because he – it's almost always a he – is naturally curious. He will also be deeply empathic, which gives him the ability to project, to feel, the emotional mindset of his marks from their facial micro-expressions. He will also have been trained in grooming habits, gestures and clothing displays. He will especially look for passengers who avoid eye contact, surreptitiously stare at the cop and sweat. He looks for sweat in the cool static air-conditioned environment like gold. That is his bread and butter. Sweat.

But, of course, I know this stuff. I'm Airport Alex, the ou formerly known as Acid Alex, also alternatively known as Skollie Papillon or secretly known as Alexander-Bitch-Born-Bastard-Blikkieskos-PuddlePirate-Asterix-Yster-Lix-Douglas-Goulding.

I am a professional international drug smuggler and wholesale distributor, or so I am telling myself. I'm a Das. I'm not carrying anything.

And here we go … Just like I thought. Be (Look) relaxed. Give the orange vest eye contact. Actually there are two of them. Nod at the civilian staring at you. *Ça va*, Frog. Look forward with cool determination. Do NOT look again. Don't even fucking peek. Okay, so far so good.

Now Big Brother is watching you. Forget the visible cameras. They are all dummies. You cannot see the real ones. Walk next to Brother E. Do not follow each other; they will know you are planning something. Take it easy, relax. Remember the pen is in your shirt pocket. Breathe, breathe, relax. Everything is going as planned.

Okay here we go. Luggage. Relax, bra. Anti-terrorism is watching. Cool. Be bored. You've done this before. You have already beaten the dogs, X-rays and spectrographic scanners.

Okay here comes the luggage. Right, let's go. Next to Brother E. Okay, here it is. Match Point. Time for Brother E to pick a fight. Christ I hope this good-cop bad-cop thing works out for us ...

[!!!]

... Jesus these padda mapuzas are aggro. The one Brother E swore at looks like he's going to shoot him.

Right, whip out the pen.

M'sieu, I'm sorry, here is a pen for my friend. I'm sorry, we are tired; it was a very long flight. My friend did not mean what he said.

Brother E, Shut Up!

And fill in the form ...

These people are just doing their job.

I'm very, very sorry officer, we had some problems travelling – our luggage got lost by Customs at Johannesburg and we almost missed our flight. Thank you, my friend did not mean what he said.

APOLOGISE BROTHER E!

Yes, we will be careful.

Thank you.

Thank you.

And we are through!

Stupid fucks got so uptight about Brother E they didn't search us. One more to chalk up to the books. Stupid macho freaks. Won the pissing contest and lost the pak. Yeeehah!

Oh God, now I need to drink. Brother E is going to get mad at me but I can't help it.

I Have To Have Alcohol.

Any fucking alcohol. And spliff too. But that will have to wait till Amsterdam.

No shit, I have to have it. Now. Brother E had better never find out how bad it is; I barely want to think about it myself, so he will fucking freak. I am in shit. Fuck it is so bad that I almost hoped we got caught back there so I could dry out again inside. How's that for fucked up, dude? Even more fucked up is me being an ex-missionary and theology student ... and I can't talk about it. I probably won't ever be able to talk about it. Not after Christine.

What the fuck am I gonna do?

I can't go to rehab. Jesus, I'm a fucking drug makwera. We run the whole eastern seaboard between Cape Town and PE. PAGAD is hunting us. They already shot Chad and that other ou on our payroll. The various flavours of the so-called Cape Town mafia want to know who the fuck we are and when they can break our legs. Michel reckons the Amsterdam Big Boys want a sit-down with us when we get there – and that has to be a deadly serious business proposition in the making. And, Oh Yes, Boys and Girls, just for shits and giggles, the happy little pitbulls from SANAB visited us for a chat the other morning. They came all the way from fucking Wynberg for breakfast. I can't go to rehab. It will be a hilarious fucking joke that would make all the Wrong People horribly nervous.

Oh, God, what am I gonna do? I'm buggered. Well, actually Not Quite Enough is kind of the point at hand, Al.

Fuckit, let's go get a dop ...

PART I

Thumbsucker

1

The Big I Am

∞ Uncreated ∞

I am
I am One.
I am in the Spirit.
I am the only begotten of the Spirit and my Father.
I am male and I am nameless.
The breath, wine, bread, fruit and meat
Of the Spirit are all within me
And I sleep,
Perfect in Her darkness ...

*

I was born to tell a story.
It all began on a Wednesday morning.

At 04h20, 3 April 1963, I entered the light, got my first hiding, and joined the human race.

Africa.

The local general hospital of a large town named Bulawayo, in a beautiful, bitter country, once called Rhodesia. The girl who brought me into the world was apparently a mere fifteen years old, and I can only imagine that back there in her day and age it must have been a very long, lonely and difficult experience to have gone through. My father? I don't know. I heard various accounts. First he was a soldier. Then, one of three men. And, last but not least, no one was quite sure who he was.

In any event he has always meant nothing to me.

The wildly clashing accounts of my biological mother's virtues varied over the years, but one thing that remained fairly consistent was that she was a laatlammetjie from a fairly well-to-do Afrikaans Rhodesian family.

A very rare breed indeed – *if* I took any stock by it.

To this day I don't know who either of my biological parents were. From my outward appearance however— I seem to be a white man.

Her Majesty's Government placed me in a Home run by the Roman Catholic Church as a Ward of The Crown. Evidently my biological mother's parents and grandparents were not up to the moral rigour of raising me.

Oh, and someone named me John.

The time I spent in the Catholic Home was uneventful, except for an accident that occurred one terrible afternoon just after my first birthday.

I was on the back seat of a car being driven by two nuns from The Home, when a drunk driver ran a red light and hit us side-on, instantly killing both of the sisters and somehow flinging me right out the rear passenger window and underneath the drunk's vehicle. The impact fractured my right arm in three places, near tore my left ear off, crushed my left leg and gave me multiple head and internal injuries. I apparently lay there trapped and unconscious for almost an hour before someone noticed a third victim. The drunken man was completely unhurt. I was then rushed to hospital and very nearly did not make it because I flatlined on the OR table three times and only pulled through because of the extraordinary effort made by a dedicated young ER surgeon. It appears he was too young and idealistic to realise that he should have given up and let me go.

I am quite certain about The Home and the accident because I saw an old black and white photograph of a small serious-looking kid with the right side of his body all done up in plaster, his right arm pointing out all white and stiff. The kid is me standing in the courtyard of The Home – I recognised him easily from a memory in the mirror a long time ago ...

Denise Eve was the only daughter of Audrey and August Nesbitt.

She was their eldest child and helped to raise her two much younger brothers. The Nesbitts were a quietly prosperous, very colonial family who owned the Cecil Hotel in Fyfe Street, Bulawayo. Denise did not see much of her father as a young girl because he had left to join the dark war against Hitler in North Africa. At eighteen she met a much older man of wealthy German/Afrikaner descent and against her horrified parents' objections—she married him.

Leo, it transpired, was a psychotic despot who beat her, humiliated her and performed sick, sexual acts with her as the live prop in his ugly little marquis. One of them related to her severe arachnophobia. He would strip her stark naked, tie her to a horse and then chase the animal through thick bundu infested with bird spiders the size of small soup plates.

He got off on it. And she fell pregnant ...

At some time during the pregnancy, he flew into a routine fit of rage, and in the beating that followed— he kicked her swollen belly, whereupon she lost a tiny boy whom she buried painfully as Michael. At this heart-rending juncture, with no real qualifications or means to escape to the outside world, she began realising just how badly stuck she was in a twisted and very dangerous marriage.

Leo played club rugby with a mate named Walter Douglas Goulding. Denise met him at a rugby club braai on their farm. He was a shy man – among women at least – who hid behind brute strength and a prematurely balding tough-guy image. He grew up the middle son in a family of seven kids. His pa was a real old-time, white, Southern Rhodesian gold and emeralds prospector who staked and panned a shallow mine in their backyard until he died from the Black Lung when Wally was fourteen. Wally had been too young to work down the family mine and too old to sit around doing nothing while his sisters ran the house – *under Old Ma Goulding's Iron Fist* – so his job was to take their battered .303, go into the bundu and poach for the pot. His ma, an Apache-Mexican woman, took over the reins after the old man died and moved the family to a big mining town. He left the little schooling he had behind and began an apprenticeship with the local asbestos operation to help his brothers support his mother and sisters.

Wally and Denise found themselves strongly attracted to each other ... *But* ... they were only able to declare their dangerous secret after she had finally divorced Leo. Wally apparently took his share from a grave robbery, bought a ring and proposed. It was not that untoward on Wally's part because his family apparently originally hailed from a long line of coalminers and gravediggers in Wales. They had touched down a hundred years or so earlier and started off by prospecting for gold and shooting ivory in the Knysna forests. Thereafter they gradually followed Rhodes' wide route northwards to the bigger strikes – digging minerals, burying miners and happily introducing the Golding/Goulding name into the emerging bastard southern African mulatto community.

Under the cold, angry disapproval of August and Audrey, they married. This time they objected to her marrying beneath her class.

The nuptials were barely over when Denise discovered that Wally drank like a fish, got really mean and only took his marriage vows as seriously as the price of the next tart. What made it worse was that doctors told her that the brutal termination she had suffered at Leo's fists and feet completely ruined any chances of her safely falling pregnant again. And of course added to that was her own stubborn pride, which simply wouldn't face a second divorce or her parents' haughty scorn. Instead she paid homage to the louder sages of that era's pop-psychology pundits and twisted Wally's arm into adopting a kid to prop up the seriously floundering marriage.

That is how, one fine day, some six months after my accident, I stopped being a toddler whom someone had named John and became Alexander Douglas Goulding.

One of my very earliest memories is of waiting in the car outside The Home while Denise fetched Yvonne Rhoda – my new little baby sister. Her nicknames became Cookie Wooks and Chinkie. She had ever so slightly oriental features and I loved her.

My nickname became Bitch-Born Bastard after I scratched the car one afternoon with my tricycle and Wally took a serious crack at beating me to death with a buffalo-hide belt. Denise saved me by running out into the driveway screaming at Wally:

– *Stop* WALLY! *Jesus Christ Stop.* STOP!! *He's had enough! You're going to kill him.* STOP!! *He's only a bloody baby for Christsakes* JEEESUSS WAAALLLY STOP! –

From then on I knew to be *very* frightened of Wally.

There was another thing that constantly incensed Wally – my thumb-sucking. I would take my shirt or sheet, twist it around my fingers, and suck my thumb while smelling the fabric. The scents of certain types of cotton cloth were somehow just right and I would inhale them while sucking my thumb – my little head drifting off in pacified toddler world.

Wally kept on telling me to stop bloody chewing.

He never realised the reason I held the fabric to my face was to *smell* it, not chew …

I'm lying in bed sucking my thumb when for some reason I try to see why I mustn't chew. I bite a small hole in my sheet and try to chew but it isn't very nice. It makes my sheet wet and that doesn't smell right. Denise comes into the bedroom and sees the hole.

She calls Wally.

This time he does not hit me. He drags me to the kitchen and grabs a bottle of pickled red chillies. I get force-fed most of them until it feels like I am burning alive. I desperately try to scream, beg and cry for him not to any more until the pain becomes too much and I start choking:

– *I'll teach you to chew. Chew You Little Bitch-Born Bastard,* CHEW!! *Now Swallow Damn You! Swallow!! More!! ... Now Chew! I told you to Fucking Chew!!* –

Eventually satisfied, he drags me off to the bathroom, runs a scalding bath directly from the hot tap and throws me into it, holding me down while I burn up in bubbles and pyjamas. EVERYTHING is burning now. The burning claws into my brain like a bright hot chewing thing that is so bad, I cannot scream. I am so strangled up in agony I can barely breathe when he lets me up for air. But I want to scream though – I NEED to scream so badly ...

Denise was on the Pill. One fine day, very soon after Yvonne arrived, she discovered to her extreme consternation, that she was, in fact, a little bit pregnant. As her term progressed and she became very pregnant, she found it increasingly difficult dealing with a hyperactive little boy and a near year-old baby girl, so it was decided that I would go and visit an uncle and aunt who lived near Victoria Falls. A lift was arranged with acquaintances of Wally and Denise, and so, with a little suitcase and a five-shilling note, I left home on my own for the first time. I was three.

On this excursion I experienced my first hunt.

My uncle decides we need a bit of biltong and elects to take me along. We load up a Land Rover with a rifle clipped to a rack in the cab behind us, my uncle driving and me riding a small animated shotgun next to him – so thrilled I simply don't know how to keep my backside on the seat. As we reach the kill zone he orders me to settle down and spot game. I scan back and forth, peering around wildly and spotting things everywhere. My uncle just chuckles paternally, ruffles my hair and encourages me to keep on looking.

Suddenly he stops the Land Rover in a low growl of dust. The two farm munts on the back immediately crouch down – dead silent. There is no sound except the subtle enveloping screech of hot cicadas and the low cry of a single bird. He quickly, but very quietly, unclips the rifle, clicks open his door and swings out – gently slipping a round into the breech.

I slide over to his side and follow. My quickened breathing is pounding in my ears. He steps around the vehicle and begins raising the rifle's stock to his shoulder but I stop him silently with my hand on his arm. In a careful low voice I ask him if I can shoot the buck. He looks at me with a bemused smile, which becomes disbelieving as I go on to explain that he must put the butt of the rifle against the side of the Land Rover at my height and hold it there while I sight and pull the trigger.

He snorts a disbelieving grunt, swears under his breath, pulls the stock back to his shoulder and, after a breath-taking pause— fires off a shot.

It's the LOUDEST SOUND that I have ever heard!!

As the shattering shock waves roil from my ears I find myself in a bright world of no sound at all. For a long moment everything seems to stop moving except the slowly coiling gun smoke ...

Then the munts burst into action with two deep-throated *ye-heh* shouts. They leap off the Land Rover, laughing and jabbering away to each other and run crashing off into the nearby bundu – where now I suddenly see a big buck lying on its side. I had wanted to shoot but had not even spotted it!

I dismiss this embarrassing thought immediately, shake my ringing head in denial and run to keep up with my uncle. As I arrive, one of the munts lifts the buck's head by the horns.

It's still alive!

It is huge and very pretty to see close up, but it also has a big steaming hole in its side near the slowly moving back leg. Big coils of bright red, wet, wormy things stick out everywhere around the hole and blood is coming out all over its leg and tummy. A lot of it. It kicks feebly, making a sort of grunting *huuuka-huuuka* sound. Snot and spit drool out of its mouth and nose, and its tongue lolls out in the dirt. Its eyes blink and roll crazily. The steaming wormy things jiggle with its kicks and more ooze bright red out the hole.

The munts yell, whistle and grab it tighter – containing its weakening thrashes. My uncle pulls out a big knife from his sheath and, while the munt at its head pulls the horns right back, he cuts its throat with a single satisfied grunt. A jet of smoking dark red blood comes gushing out and the buck makes one, two more little jerks, then a rude *uuurp* sound comes from its ruined throat, and it goes into a long shiver until it's completely still. Round little droppings start dribbling from its bum and it makes a long wee-wee.

The munts drag it to the Land Rover, leaving a trail of dark red mud and droppings trailing in the dust. They load it up on the back with its head hanging over the tailgate – still dripping, and we drive back to the farm slowly.

I am quiet.

It had been an overwhelmingly intense experience. I couldn't stop thinking about the steamy glistening wormy things. Also its eyes, and how they suddenly didn't move crazy or blink any more after it shivered and went still. They just stared. Empty, stiff and shiny. Like water that wasn't really water but was dream water and did nothing if you drank it. If you made the hole in the buck's side go away and stitched up its throat and washed off all the blood— it would be a dream buck.

There – but not really. Not behind its eyes any more.

We arrived back at the farmhouse and took it to where two poles were planted into the ground near the sheds. The munts tied it hanging upside down from a crossbeam that spanned them. Then they gutted, skinned, dressed and cut it up into biltong and their share. I watched the whole process in silence. Later I asked my uncle about the wormy things and he said they were its guts coming out of the exit wound.

Eric Walter Goulding's entrance into the world was marked by a difficult Caesarean section. Denise was very happy but utterly exhausted and in a lot of pain. Eric turned out to be a noisy, fretting baby who made maximum use of his very healthy lungs. It vexed Wally so much having a squalling baby in the house that he threw Eric and Denise out on more than one night, telling her to take her noisy bloody brat and sleep in the goddamned garage. The thing was, Yvonne was such a quiet baby that one never heard her, as opposed to Eric, who yelled non-stop about eighteen hours a day.

I remember wetting my bed during this time and living in raw terror of Wally finding out – which he always did through Denise. These incidents were punctuated by strappings to cure me. Wally was not going to have a bed-wetting, thumbsucking little bitch-born bastard living in his bloody house. He would fix me – *by Christ he would fix me!*

Denise had her hands full. The little ones took up all her time, so I was largely left in the care of Sam.

One day, years before, a skinny little picannin had appeared on the doorstep of Audrey's house in search of work. She looked him up and down, decided he appeared honest enough, named him Sam and then told him to report to the Chief Garden Boy. Audrey soon decided he was being wasted there and promoted him to No. 2 Kitchen Boy, where he worked under Cook. He had become No. 2 Cook Boy by the time Wally and Denise celebrated their nuptials. August and Audrey duly gave Sam to the happy couple as one of their wedding presents, and he became our House Boy or munt – as the white Rhodesians would say. Wally simply called Sam *Kaffir* and maintained that the only Good Kaffir was a Dead Kaffir. This worried me deeply because Sam was my friend. He taught me to ride a bicycle and plant a garden, and we played together with the new squiggly, squirming, licking little bundle of joy that came into my life – my doggy Candy. Sam lived in his Kaffir khaya behind the kitchen where I would often go sit, watching him while he cooked his sadza. He would smile at me and sing softly.

Denise did not like it …

– *There is a place for Kaffirs and there is a place for us and Sam's khaya is not a place for you. You stay out of there and you stay out of his toilet too, I don't want you getting Kaffir Germs on you –*

Sam had a funny toilet. It was just a hole in the ground. Denise said that was because Kaffirs couldn't use a toilet properly. None of them Knew Any Better. She never found out that I secretly ate sadza with Sam, from the same pot, in true Matabele style, using my hands, and never died from his Kaffir Germs. I defiantly told Denise I loved Sam and that he was my friend.

I was too shy to tell him this myself.

– *You can't love him, you stupid little bugger. Kaffirs are different to us. They are Black for God's sakes. And as I've already told you: They Don't Know Any Better. But it's okay kid, really, I quite understand why you say that about Sam. See, he is one of the Better Ones. He's not stupid, cheeky and lazy like most of them are. He's a Good Kaffir. And he seems to know His Place, but you better forget about him being your friend or you'll get a Bloody Good Hiding. Even if he is a Good Kaffir he will always be a Kaffir. But you are not! You understand me? We are Better Than Them and don't you ever, ever forget it! A good dog is only a good dog until the day it bites the hand that feeds it –*

I thought Sam was a Good Kaffir too, and stayed secret friends with him because he was better than me in lots of things. He wouldn't bite me. I was scared Denise might find that out and give me a Bloody Good Hiding.

When I started going to nursery school, Sam would take me – holding my tiny hand in his massive one – and walk with me all the way there, smiling and singing as I skipped along next to him. Many times during the long hot afternoons I would be playing in the garden with Candy, and the Sugar Cane Man would walk past hawking. Sam would procure a tiekie from Denise, lead me out into the street and whistle for him. I loved sugar cane. I would bite off a piece, chew and let the sweetness explode into my mouth. Chew and spit. Bite, chew and spit, with syrup running down my chin while Sam and the Sugar Cane Man spoke softly together about Kaffir stuff, both grinning openly at my unbridled delight.

It was so mush. *Mush* is a word white Rhodesians used and it comes from the word *mushile* in Sam's language and means something is nice.

Unlike the day I fell off the swings at nursery school and into a nightmare afternoon of pain and fright that ended with a couple of stitches in my hairline. Or the terrible afternoon when I was expelled from nursery school for pinching another kid's yo-yo.

Wally did not like it. No – not one little bit.

I remember other, happier events, like when it rained. In Zimbabwe there is a summer rainfall. It comes mostly in the form of late afternoon thundershowers which erupt suddenly into dark, pelting wet electrical storms that last a short while and then abruptly stop ... leaving everything bathed in a strange yellow light and the smell of rain and gently rumbling thunder. It produced deep mud patches in the garden, which Yvonne and I got filthy in. We would make ourselves a mud bath and get plastered from head to toe. Funnily enough, Denise did not mind this, as long as Sam cleaned us up before we came back into the house.

I had Special Places.

One was the big tree behind the kitchen and the other a rock in the garden shrubbery. I would sit there and think after hidings or just because I wanted to. I talked to myself a lot. And while I was regretting some misdeed or other, I would usually rail away at myself. During these long bitter monologues, I called myself The Big I Am.

It came from Denise ...

– *You think you're such a clever little Bastard don't you? Who the hell do you think you are? The Big I Am?* –

I wanted sweeties one day.

I knew that sweeties could be obtained with money. Problem was – I didn't have any. *Denise did.* It was in her handbag but I knew she wouldn't give me any. No problem. I got hold of her handbag and took some coins from her purse. *I knew, that she knew, that I had no money* – so I hid them under a few particular rocks in the garden. Then I called her and asked her to come and play with me. While we were ostensibly playing, I *discovered* all the coins. Denise was at first mightily puzzled but then very quickly twigged what was going on and made sure that I understood clearly – *Stealing is Wrong*. Backside first.

The Big I Am had a lot to think about.

I entered school at the age of five. I was a little too young but Denise wanted me Out Of Her Hair. That year Neil Armstrong would walk on the moon. Sam walked me up to the bus stop every day and made sure I boarded the school bus safely. When I wasn't in the garden or with Sam, I watched TV and listened to the radio as much as Denise would let me. There was a lot of stuff about The War. I didn't like it, though. I preferred watching *The Jetsons*, *Casper the Friendly Ghost* and *Batman and Robin*. On the radio they spoke about another place called Vietnam where they also had a War, and a man named Tom Jones sang 'Those were the days'. He was my favourite.

Wally spoke about the Kaffirs a lot. Actually, he spoke about The Kaffir. Singular. An Entity. As in:

– *The Bloody Kaffir is going to take everything in this country You Mark My Words* –

Wally spoke about The War and The Bloody Kaffir with his brother Cocky, his mate Ron Wood and all the wives. They argued about it. Wally declared emphatically that he would never live under Kaffir Rule.

– *Ian Bloody Smith is running this Poor Bloody Country into the ground and they will never win The War* –

Around that time we went to Mozambique for a holiday. It was the first time I had ever seen an ocean. I immediately loved the sea. The beaches were beautiful and the water was warm. Much later I realised that Wally and Denise were not just holidaying. They were scouting for a place to get away from The War.

Around the age of five and a half I had my first sexual encounters.

I knew that girls and boys were different. Boys, said Denise, had Lollos, and girls had Fannies. Cocky had two children – Linda and Clive. One day they were visiting us. Linda and I sneaked off to the garden in the block of flats next door. There we stripped off and played show-me-yours-and-I'll-show-you-mine in the shrubbery. Unbeknown to us, we had been seen by an old lady who lived upstairs. We tired of the game quickly and put our clothes back on. On our way back the old lady confronted us. We looked at each other in instant panic, thinking that we were going to get a terrible hiding, but she was a sweet old dear who took us up to her apartment and fed us milk and chocolate. She called us dear little children and then sent us home with a kiss and a pat on the bottom.

The second one was a Very Big Mistake.

I opened the door to Denise's room one day and found her stark naked. She was putting powder on her body and looked funny with white blotches all over her skin and hair between her legs. I stood staring at her hair in absolute shocked amazement until she broke the spell, screaming in a sudden furious rage that I was a Filthy, Dirty Little Bastard and I was to go to my room NOW! She was going to Lambaste The Living Daylights Out Of Me. I went, terrified that when she eventually did come, she was going to drag me to the bathroom and bash my head against the washbasin until my teeth came spewing out. In my head I had washbasin and lambaste all mixed up. She just beat me with a belt until she was exhausted and my throat was raw from screaming.

Wally had been making serious plans since our holidays.

– *We are going to lose The War and I'll be damned if I am going to live under a bunch of Goddamned Filthy Kaffirs* –

He decided that we were going to see what South Africa had to offer. We took a holiday. After four days of driving we reached the Cape. Wally and Denise liked what they saw. Wally did a little hunting around and found a job. After that holiday, Wally and Denise made short weekend treks from Bulawayo to Messina, just over the border. The purpose was to get money out of the country. The government had restricted the amount of cash that each person was allowed to take across the border, to curtail the flow of white people leaving and to prop up the war effort. Every weekend Wally and Denise, and Cocky and his family, would load two cars and pop over to salt away the cash limit in the bank.

On 11 April 1969 we packed up the car for the final time and left for the new life Wally had arranged for us in South Africa.

The Big I Am was heartbroken.

Part of leaving the country was saying goodbye to television, my little doggy Candy, and my secret friend – Sam the Good Kaffir.

Sam was given back to Audrey, who put him back to work in the hotel. A few years later, I'm not too sure how many, he had worked himself up to Head Chef of the hotel. During a security sweep he was caught with a box of grenades and two landmines hidden under his bed in the hotel's Kaffir Quarters. He had been part of the Resistance. It was a great shock to the family. Everybody had thought he was a Good Kaffir. Without a doubt. The police charged him under the Rhodesian Terrorist Act and he was hanged.

Lala gashle madala baba ...

2

Khayas and the Treks

We retraced the route we'd taken during our holiday and found our way back to the town of George in the Cape Province. George lies at the foot of a peak in the Outeniqua mountain range, a peak that looks like a huge winged sentinel leering down at the town. It was to become a fixture in my mind and my dreams, but I didn't know it then.

Our first house was near the verdant lakes and forests that lie between George and Knysna, in a resort named The Wilderness. We lived in what we kids called the Piccaninie Khaya. It was not really a house as much as two dilapidated, thatch rondavels connected by a couple of rough walls with a tin roof. It had no electricity, so we relied on paraffin lamps and a wood stove. The structure had once been the old Kaffir khayas that housed servants of a rich man who owned a mansion over the hill next to the lake.

We children loved it.

At first.

Wally had found employment with a vegetable-packing plant in the industrial area of George. Being of school-going age and having already attended kindergarten in Bulawayo, I was duly enrolled at George Preparatory School. In those days there was no bus service for kids who commuted to school in the town, so I had to leave home early in morning with Wally. School did not begin for a couple of hours, so I'd go to the old caretaker's office and sleep on a little bed that was placed there for me. I had a small lunchbox that Denise packed and a little plastic bottle of tea. My feet were always cold. See, there was no money for shoes, so I went barefoot. Beyond these mild discomforts, I loved school and made friends quickly.

Denise did not have a good time of it. *When we were Rhodesians*, we had Sam, food from the hotel and an active social life. In South Africa we had nothing. Denise had had an absolute ball during our first whirlwind visit – feasting on chocolates, wines and other delicacies that were simply not available in war-torn Rhodesia. But that holiday was Very Much Over. The furtive weekend treks across the border had only managed to salt away what was left of Wally's railway cheque after rent and expenses. This was not a lot. Denise had been used to servants and a high social standing all her life – and she was a very proud woman – so it was immensely difficult for her to adjust to her new lifestyle as a penniless, *classless* immigrant. She had to live in something Kaffirs had once lived in and she had to do everything Herself with only the amenities of a Kaffir. She complained bitterly about this to Wally, who did not take too kindly to what sounded like a criticism of the exhausting efforts he was making.

Fights broke out. Bad fights. Usually about money. Yet, I never saw him beat her.

I think it had something to do with what Wally knew Leo had done to her before. Wally was violent, sometimes very violent, but that was mostly only towards Yvonne and me. The one thing he did not spare on Denise, however, was his tongue. He had a filthy, foul, abusive mouth and he used it like a club in an attempt to batter submission and subjugation into her. It was frightening to us kids – we could not understand why Wally and Denise were so upset all the time. Him, I knew more or less how to steer clear of, but her rages and beatings over even the smallest things escalated dramatically.

She was fair in that she beat Yvonne and me equally, but Her Eric was another story. Squonkhead lived in a constant state of highly strung panic and clung to her desperately. He'd get punished too, but it was on a different scale. The hard truth of the matter is that Eric was for Denise what she had wanted in her foetus Michael. She had chosen me at The Home, but I had never been a baby for her. Yvonne had been a baby but she was the wrong sex. Eric was perfect. Yvonne and I were emotionally difficult children who bickered a lot. I think that at that point Denise began to regret having to feed and clothe two kids who were Not Her Own. Wally simply became much nastier in his efforts to cure me of my *thumbsucking, bitch-born bastidness.*

Yvonne and I still sucked our thumbs, to the constant agitation of Wally and Denise. Wally had fashioned a lash out of a piece of hosepipe, about two feet long and cut lengthways into four, with a taped handgrip at one end. This would come out at the drop of a hat. A sense of dread started to come over me, and wouldn't go away, even at school or when he wasn't there. So many things qualified for a hiding with Wally. A simple one was being cheeky or backchatting. Breathing wrong at the right time was backchatting. Denise got into the habit of storing up all my misdeeds to infuriate him with at the end of the day. It was around then that Yvonne and I began comparing the marks on our backs and legs. The four flogs of the hosepipe made bruises and cuts that bled.

We moved to George.

Wally and Denise were at each other all the time now, and he started bringing wine back from work, although I would soon make my own private discoveries in this regard ...

One day I was riding my bicycle up and down our road when I saw a furniture truck parked in the empty lot next door. The big side doors were open and a few men were sitting around a gas bottle cooker and a bubbling pot. I rode up and, being of friendly disposition – as well as being majorly bored – I greeted them.

They were speaking a language that I was learning at school called *Afrikaans*. A friend from school, whose mum was the librarian, told me that Afrikaans people were called Rockspiders and Afrikaans was called Rock. The same kid taught me swearwords in Rock and other useful stuff like all the other words for Rockspiders – Crunchies, Hairybacks, Clutchplates, Planks, Ropes, Boneheads, Dutchmen – *Afrikaners-vrot-bananas*. They in turn called us Soutpiele and Rooinekke. Most of the other kids at school spoke Rock. In fact, there was only one English class for each grade – all the rest were Rockspiders.

Before then, the only people I'd met who weren't white were the very dark Matabele people, who spoke a language called Ndebele. There was another big tribe of black people in Rhodesia called Shonas, but when the grownups discussed it they agreed unanimously that the Mashonas were all a rotten bunch of Bad Kaffirs – The Whole Bloody Lot. None of them ever worked in the hotel or at Audrey and August's house because they always fought with the Matabeles.

The men in front of my bicycle were neither black nor white – but *in between*. Wally had told us these people were called Hotnots, and some of them were even Worse Than Kaffirs. They spoke Afrikaans funny. I did not understand enough words of the language yet, but I could tell it was different from the way the other kids at school spoke. I spoke English to them and they answered in a heavy accent, using strange words. They called me Little Larney. I didn't know who Little Larney might be but I guessed he must be like Richie Rich or Little Lotta in the comic books. They were drinking from an enormous bottle of yellow stuff, which they poured into a glass and passed to each man in the circle, who would then gulp it all down. I asked them what it was. Appletiser, they told me – for when they eat, indicating towards the pot. I asked them for some.

They laughed.

Then the one with the bottle poured me a glass. I knew of course that I was doing about a hundred things wrong. First, I was drinking from the same glass as Afrikaans people who looked halfway to Kaffirs. Denise would have an absolute fit if she knew I had gotten Kaffir Germs on me – even if they were only halfway germs. Secondly, as I tasted it I knew that what they called Appletiser I called wine. It's just that I had never seen a bottle of wine so *big*. But I drank it anyway. Just like them – two or three gulps and gone.

They all whooped, laughed and applauded as I gave the glass back. I had just drunk about four times the amount of wine we kids were allowed with lunch on Sundays! They asked me questions in their strange English and I answered. The glass went around. When my turn came up, I asked for some more. They laughed and said no, it was not good for me to have too much. I insisted and they argued among themselves in Afrikaans, but then gave me some more – but not as much as the previous round. I hung around and tried for a third time, but they flatly refused. I said goodbye and they wished me well. I rode off up the road – with a lovely, buzzy, dreamy feeling flowing all over and in me.

It was the nicest feeling that I had ever felt.

Wally brought Aunty Thelma home.

As a man, I understand now what adult issues were involved, but at the time it felt like our own personal war had broken out with its ugly theatre confined to our little house.

From early on in their marriage Wally had reserved himself the right to bring other women into the mix, or at least to attempt to. This may have remained a latent desire until then, but it burst to the fore that night. Thelma was some woman he had picked up, or maybe he'd been seeing her – we didn't know. But the fact of the matter was that he brought her to the house and invited Denise for a ménage-à-trois. Denise thought it the sickest, most despicable act he had ever committed and, losing it completely, flew into a rage that utterly terrified us. The sound of screaming and things breaking was so frightening that all three of us children hid under our beds crying.

One day I had a fight after school. A group of boys teased me because I didn't have shoes and because I sucked my thumb. In the melee that followed I received a blood nose, which stained my shirt, and a tear in my school pants. That afternoon one of the boys came to our house – on his mum's orders – and apologised to Denise, saying that he was sincerely sorry for what had happened. Denise was not amused, and showed my torn pants to Wally when he came home. He beat the shit out of me, which was to be expected, but the next morning he did something else. I woke up to his voice in my room—

– *You don't want to look after the clothes that I buy with good money. Which I work my* ARSE *off for! Little bitch-born bastard, you treat your clothes like a Kaffir. Well if you want to live like a Kaffir and be like a Kaffir, I will treat you like a Kaffir and* ALL *you'll get from me is what any bloody Kaffir deserves. Now get undressed and put this on* RIGHT NOW. *This is how you are going to school today –*

He had taken a hessian sack and cut three holes in it, which he forced me with a few good hard clouts to put on – yes, without underpants. There was a hole for my head and two for my arms. It was dirty and stiff, and scratched horribly. Once I was dressed in it I was sent out the door – yes, without breakfast either – crying and pleading. No use. I went out into the street and around the corner, where I hid in a bunch of bushes. I waited until Wally had left for work and sneaked back to the house and begged Denise to help me. She obviously thought he had been a bit heavy-handed, because she made me a quick breakfast, gave me the mended pants and wrote a letter for my teacher because I was a little bit late. Nothing was said, and the next day I went to school as usual.

We left George and moved to Mossel Bay. This was probably the worst time of my entire childhood. Besides being bullied silly at school by a huge Rockspider named Blackie Swart, I had a teacher with sadistic tendencies. He had a special plank he used to hit us with that had stuff written all over it. On top of this, there was Wally's ever-present ultra-violence to deal with.

Suppertime always follows the same routine. We sit down at the table at exactly seven o'clock every night. There is no television in South Africa, so we listen to the radio. Always – Springbok Radio, with the news at seven and then a serial: *The Avengers* or *The Mind of Tracy Dark*. Tonight, instead of the next episode of John Steed and Emma Peal's derring-do, the station is tuned to Radio South Africa, which broadcasts classical music and other boring programmes. I ask permission to leave the table and change it to Springbok Radio instead. Wally looks up from his plate – his nose goes all white and his eyes freeze thin and hard. He pushes back his chair, strides to the sideboard and picks up the radio. In one quick movement he grabs me and proceeds to smash it into smithereens on my head. He does not utter a single word. The only sound is his grunting and the radio shattering. I am too shocked, too frightened and in too much pain to scream. The others are just as terrified – Denise included. I end up concussed, with little gashes all over my head, and completely bewildered as to what I'd done wrong.

I started going to the library fairly often. I liked sitting at a little desk reading books of my choice. Especially the easy ones like *Tintin*, *Asterix* and *Lucky Luke*. I read some of the more difficult books because I had found that with story words I could make pictures in my mind. I could go away anywhere. The librarian was the mother of a nice girl in my class named Jenny. One day I was drifting around selecting books when I noticed Jenny's mom staring at me. This made me nervous. I hadn't done anything wrong – had I? Not that I could think of anyway, so I went back to my business. She came out from behind the stamping desk and asked me if I would please come along with her for a little chat. I felt sick inside. What had I done wrong? I could not remember – I might have done something bad, but I really didn't remember what it was. It couldn't be my books. I always treated my books very carefully and I had never handed one in late.

We went into a little office where another lady was working, and Jenny's mom shut the door. She must have seen the scared expression on my face because she told me not to worry, she just wanted to ask me something. Nothing was wrong. I relaxed a little, very relieved. Then she asked me to take off my shirt. I looked at her, confused, and then it dawned on me – something was Very Wrong. She told me that nobody was going to hurt me and that all she wanted was just to see something better. I could hardly refuse. I was faced with two gentle but very firm adults, and so, with great reluctance, I removed my shirt. The other lady gasped, put her hand to her mouth and started blaspheming quietly in Afrikaans. They made me lift my arms and turn around. Jenny's mom thanked me and told me to put my shirt back on. Then she sat me down and asked me, in a very kind voice, to tell her where the marks came from. I said they came from playing rough at school. She told me that, in her opinion, this could not be true. She had a son a year above me and she had never seen him ever get hurt like I was – no matter how rough he played. Where did I get hurt like that? I said I didn't know. She asked me if somebody at home was doing this to me. I panicked. I told her no. Images flashed through my mind. Wally. I told her I was okay and could I go now – please? No, she said. She was going to get to the bottom of it. I knew, I just knew, that somehow Wally was going to find out about this, and he was going to think I had started it, and then it would be bad – *Very Bad*. He hated other people *interfeeering* – as he called it. It was too much for me and I burst into tears and started begging them to please leave me alone – I had not done anything wrong – *please*. The more they asked me, the more I cried, and after a while Jenny's mom came and put her arms around me and told me not to be scared and promised that nobody would say anything – *nobody*. Promise. I calmed down eventually and left, but I didn't take out any books that day and I never went back to the library again.

Wally found another moonlighting job. It meant travelling on weekends to the little seaside town of Witsand, along the coast towards Cape Town. There was a small ramshackle hotel there, and Wally was contracted to build two refrigerated storerooms. We trekked to Witsand every Friday afternoon, and stayed there until late on Sunday while he worked on the job.

The hotel had an Olympic-sized swimming pool filled with salt water. One weekend we arrived to find the pool drained for cleaning. It was a steep slope from the shallow end to the deep end, and covered with algae. I decided to slide down. If I did it standing upright, I reckoned, I wouldn't get my clothes dirty. I went for it. Halfway down, my foot hit a deep crack. I flew through the air and hit the bottom head first. I sat up with a very sore face, spitting out gore and pieces of my two front teeth. They were shattered almost to the gum line. Raw nerves suddenly started screaming in agony. I had to remain in closed-mouthed misery for the rest of the weekend until we could reach a dentist the following Monday. The dentist looked at the damage and announced that there was nothing he could do except make a covering to place over the broken remains and wait until I was about nineteen or twenty before crowning them. He took a cast of my mouth, and a few days later fitted a big squarish chunk of silver over the stumps. The effect was devastating – I looked hideous, like the Jaws character in the James Bond movie, with a mouth full of steel. The kids at school howled with laughter and called me Blikkieskos, which is Rockspider for tinned food. My humiliation was complete. I began to utterly loathe school. According to the dentist, I still had to go through at least ten years of that kind of ragging.

I started shoplifting, and sometimes I cut myself on purpose with stolen razor blades.

Wally started coming home late. He was working overtime, he said. That was great with me because it meant I would be in bed by the time he arrived home. He usually wouldn't wake us up to hit us unless he thought it was necessary. Denise became suspicious. Late-night fights started breaking out. Then she found out: Wally had started *an affair* – as she called it – with one of the secretaries at Irvin & Johnson. Her name was Swallow, and she was married. My beatings dropped dramatically as the rest of the household turned into a constant screaming war zone. Denise began taking all sorts of pills again and had hysterical fits, so I started preparing supper for the family almost every night. This continued sporadically for a while, until one night Wally came raging into the house drunk as a lord, went to the bedroom and returned with the gun.

His .38 Special.

He started screaming threats and waving it around. Yvonne and Eric disappeared into their rooms and under their beds – fast. I was preparing supper and was trapped between the sink and the kitchen table. I remember watching that gun – not Wally: the gun. That deep dark hole in the front of it held cold icy dread for me. Never in all of Wally's most terrible beatings had I ever been so terrified. I knew then that he could commit murder.

It was in his heart.

The only reason he wouldn't do it was retribution. He would go to jail and hang. But that didn't stop him running out the door and driving off to his girlfriend's house to threaten and scream at her and her family – mainly the two boys who wanted to beat the shit out of him for trying to interfere with their mother and their family. It was not the last time that the gun came out, but I wised up and learnt to run like hell whenever he got like that.

That incident became the straw that broke all the camels' backs. I'm not sure, but I think Swallow's husband moved out at that point, or thereabouts. At the time, Mossel Bay was a very small town, and Irvin & Johnson was the biggest employer. Word went out that a serious scandal was brewing. Wally and Swallow could lose their jobs.

We got out of Dodge City again – fast. This time we headed west, down the Garden Route to the little town of Paarl in the Boland, about sixty kilometres from Cape Town.

Paarl derives its name from the Dutch word for *pearl*. It lies in a luscious vine-filled valley at the foot of a very large hill. That hill is almost one single rock, and from the shimmering distance of Cape Town, it looks as if there's a huge glazed pustule bursting out of its crown. Erected on top of this is the *Afrikaanse Taalmonument*. I've always wondered vaguely whether Paarl Rock was the reason why the Afrikaners were called Rockspiders.

Wally started working for a company that canned fruit and vegetables and manufactured jams, chutneys and tomato sauce. Also, by Wally's proud account, a United Nations sanctions buster. He showed us cans with labels printed in a weird assortment of foreign writing. They all clearly stated, in small Roman lettering, that the contents had been produced in the country associated with whatever language was displayed. These were affixed to the cans, then carefully smuggle-exported to Taiwan, Algeria, or wherever, and sold there as if the food had all come from *there* in the first place. Wally spoke of ships' names being repainted in the middle of the night, vessels being *apparently* lost at sea and a host of other interesting shenanigans to place the stuff in the target countries. Right under the bloody UN's nose, Wally added smugly. It was the first time I had ever seen Chinese, Arabic and other foreign writing. To me, it was as if a Chinese label on a can made the peach slices inside— Chinese peach slices, even though I knew they were simply the ordinary All Gold brand that was grown over the mountains. Just the idea made it more exciting. I wasn't very clear what sanctions and boycotts were exactly, except that Wally said they had to do with the rest of the bloody world *interfering* in things that they knew absolutely bugger all about.

Wally dumped us in a tiny little semi-detached house in a small poor-white area of the town, called Daljosephat. He and Swallow moved into the upper-middle-class suburb of Courtrai, under the shadow of Paarl Rock. We never saw her, and in fact I had only been in her cold, disdainful presence on two awkward occasions before.

Eric and I were enrolled in Paarl Boys Primary, and Yvonne in La Rochelle Girls School. We saw Wally very rarely. He would come round, drop off some foreign or blank cans from the factory and sometimes leave Denise a little money. This always turned into a screaming match between them. Wally said he had no bloody money. Denise accused him of being a lying bastard and wanted to know how he had managed to buy a new car – a Citroën – and new clothes, when his family had bugger all and he and *That Bitch* were living it up in The Lap of Luxury. Denise was in a constant state and started going everywhere with her pills in a handbag that she never put down. She ranted at Yvonne and me, saying that we had chased Wally away because we were so bloody naughty.

For a while I believed it.

Things fell into a miserable routine. I began doing science experiments with chemicals and nearly burnt down my bedroom. Well, I did scorch the paint on my chest of drawers. Denise went quite berserk. Once the fire was doused, she grabbed me. I tore loose and ran, but she managed to catch me just as I got out the front door. An almighty white light exploded in my head as she roundhouse-slapped me into the wall. She spun me around and tried to pin me on the floor by grabbing my inner arms and digging her nails into the flesh, making four moon-shaped lacerations in each arm. The pain was dreadful and made my knees buckle, which is exactly what she wanted. She pinned me down with her knees on my shoulders and upper arms, grabbed me by the hair, and began slamming my head against the veranda floor, screaming incoherently. Her skirt had rucked up high around her thighs, and every time she pulled my head up I was forced to stare right into her crotch. There were bunches of pubic hair sticking out on both sides of her panties. The sight of it made me want to vomit, and I closed my eyes and tried to protect my mind from the sledgehammer strobe exploding as my head hit the concrete again, and again, and again.

The headache and dizziness lasted two days, and the half-moons healed into deep black cuts with a purple-green halo around each incision.

Because we lived in a very poor white neighbourhood, many of the people nearby were in the same boat – pretty much drowning in debt and poverty like we were. For the very first time, Denise found sympathetic ears. She began spending extended periods at our neighbours' houses recounting over cups of tea her long tale of woe. She had lost everything, her husband was a lying cheating bastard, she couldn't cope with three hungry kids on her own, she hadn't worked since she was eighteen, she was qualified for nothing except being the dutiful wife of a lying cheating BASTARD, and so on and so forth …

We reached the point where we didn't even have food for the next couple of meals – not even the smuggle-export Chinese or Arab tins from Wally.

He hardly ever came round any more.

Denise went looking for help and approached the minister of a Methodist church nearby. He politely informed her that while he did sympathise with her plight, the church was *not* a welfare organisation and she should rather approach the local Department of Welfare. It was the policy of the church *not* to support solicitors of personal aid, especially when they didn't actually *belong* to the church. She did as the vicar suggested, but was informed by a lady at the Welfare that her husband made more than enough money to support her and her dependants. Denise explained that Wally was living with another woman and that he gave her nothing. She was told that this was a marital issue and that she needed to sort it out with her husband or seek a divorce.

I know all the details because Denise had the lady from next door over and told her that story, with much repetition, weeping, explaining, cursing and shaking of her head. I understood it all because the lady next door happened to be Afrikaans, and Denise had to explain the big words to her. Mrs Naude spoke very broken English, but Denise refused to speak Afrikaans to her even though she had learnt it at school. It had to do with That Bitch being Afrikaans, and also because whenever Denise had tried speaking the language, she was laughed at because of her accent. Most of the folks in our small neighbourhood were Afrikaans. We found sympathy among them, and so somebody gave us a few potatoes, another a cabbage from the patch in their backyard, a few tea bags from someone else, a cup of sugar here, two eggs there, a miraculous bit of pork, and so we had something for a couple of days.

As if by magic, there was a knock on the front door the day after all the food ran out. Two ladies stood there with magazines under their arms. They were Jehovah's Witnesses. Denise invited them in, eager for the company and a sympathetic ear. Over numerous cups of tea she relayed her desperate plight. Soon enough – immediately – we had more than sufficient to eat and even greater provisions of reading material. Our house turned into a Witness Sanctuary overnight. Then the Jehovah force-feeding started. I put my foot down and refused to participate. I quickly developed a loathing of Jehovah, and most especially for all the little books Mr Russell his Special Prophet had written. I very carefully staged my balk in front of the ladies and Denise. I could see that Denise was mightily irked, but she kept up her front for the JWs' sake. I was excused after saying that I did not really care much about Jehovah thank you very much. Eric and Yvonne had no such luck, and had to sit in on the endless Bible Studies.

The JWs had another version of the Bible because apparently the King James Holy Bible that Denise owned was an incorrect interpretation and only the Jehovah's Witness Translation of the Holy Scriptures was The Truth. Apparently there was a Conspiracy by The Church to subvert Jehovah's Will. Jesus was not God like the Sunday school teacher in George had told us – he was just a Prophet like Mr Russell. The ladies went on about this at length. They looked up verses ALL the time and used these to prove their arguments, although it was not terribly clear to me exactly who they were arguing with. They spoke about The Church but I could not make out which one. Roman Catholic like my friend Pascal's Mass in George, or Presbyterian, or maybe the local Methodist church that Denise swore she would never set foot in again even if she were stone dead. I didn't know much about churches. I was just glad to get away and stay away. Denise became weird again, and violent. I realised she was scared that the JWs would stop helping us. I nursed dizzying headaches and sported more black half-moons on my arms and neck. She had taken completely to her new way of disciplining me and terrorised me with threats that she would use her nails more often. She had a very healthy, very sharp set of talons.

Denise went off and consulted a Lawyer. I didn't know exactly what a Lawyer was, but according to Denise she needed one for her Divorce. I didn't know exactly what a Divorce was either, but I did understand that it meant they would be splitting up on Divorce Papers because of Summonses, and The Supreme Court, and stuff called Affeydavids or something like that. It all sounded very complicated. Denise swore that she was going to fight him tooth and nail. I wondered about this. Wally was much stronger than her, but she knew how to hurt with her nails. Divorce became an ugly word in the house. It had been used as a threat between them for years, but now it seemed very real and very serious.

One fine day they fetched us from school and took us to court. We were taken into an office and asked some questions by a man in a black dress. Then we raised our right hands, swore our allegiance and were duly pronounced naturalised citizens of the Republic of South Africa. On the way back to school, Denise informed me that it was not a dress that the man was wearing – he was in fact a Judge, and the black robes he wore gave him the authority to Judge. I had been born under Her Imperial Majesty the Queen, become a Rhodesian after UDI, the Unilateral Declaration of Independence, and had now legally become a South African in front of a Judge. I had just turned eleven and pondered on all of this.

A short while later I arrived home from school and Denise told me to pack my bags, because I was going to live with Wally and That Bitch. Apparently the Divorce had gone through uncontested, until it came to the custody hearing for us children. Both Wally and Denise wanted full custody of Eric. Neither of them wanted custody of Yvonne or me. They had a bitter fight in court, which the Judge resolved by awarding custody of the little ones to Denise and sending me to live with Wally. The Judge had awarded Denise child support to the tune of R100 a month per child under her care. Wally was asked if he wished to give Denise maintenance of his own free will, since the court was not going to force him to do so. Wally agreed to pay her one rand a month. Denise had her victory – Eric – and she said so to the lady next door. I was sick with fear and apprehension. I could not do a thing. They – Wally, Denise and the Judge – had all decided already.

I hadn't even been to the courthouse to see the Judge.

Wally and Swallow moved out of their house and into a flat in the centre of Paarl. I followed reluctantly. Denise took the little ones and moved to Fish Hoek in Cape Town. Initially it was not as bad as I thought. Wally and Swallow went out almost every night partying and I was left on my own. Wally was his same old dangerous self, especially when he was drunk, but he did not hit me as much or as badly as before. I spent most of my time in my room being careful not to mess up my bed and stayed out of their way. I was so damned lonely that it was driving me crazy. I took to spending my afternoons walking around town as in Mossel Bay, and the shoplifting and smoking started again. I did it all alone.

Swallow's food was different to Denise's but there was more than enough to eat. She also said grace in proper Dutch before eating. She wanted nothing to do with me beyond being coldly civil. She had never planned to live with one of Wally's brats and I think she took him to task for not finding a legal alternative.

Swallow was a proud Rockspider. She could virtually recite her family line all the way back to the Groot Trek. What I could not understand was why she had hooked up with Wally, who could only swear brokenly in her precious Moedertaal while she harboured barely concealed resentment towards the English. This was a close-up enactment of something I had been dimly aware of since arriving in South Africa. The white people in the country were generally either English- or Afrikaans-speaking. In some Afrikaans households, marrying an *Engelsman* was considered as thoroughly evil as your favourite youngest daughter marrying a Jewish Communist Kaffir behind your back. It was simple – Rockspiders and Soutpiele did not like each other. With a real Rockspider, it did not matter whether you were the best person on earth, they would always hate and despise you secretly for not being like them.

Then Denise phoned Wally with the news that Audrey had contracted galloping abdominal cancer and did not have long to live. Audrey had asked to see us kids one last time before the end. Passports were arranged, tickets bought, immunisation shots given, and then Denise and us three kids left for Rhodesia once again.

We arrived to find her bedridden in the local hospital's oncology unit. The War was very visible outside. There were soldiers on the streets with guns everywhere. At almost every shop, people were searched. Security sweeps and police checks were the general order of the day.

The husband of one of Wally's sisters – Gordon – had got two bullets in his back and a slight disability, which made him unfit for combat but otherwise okay. Another cousin was also out of it with a bullet through his chin and two in his arse from a hot pursuit that had gone wrong, but he had to go back into the bundu when he had healed up. Denise's oldest brother Ian miraculously survived tripping off a terrorist anti-personnel mine, which threw him into a pile of rags thirty feet away, knocked him windless and left him concussed and deaf for a couple of days – YET unbelievably without a single scratch on his person. Suddenly I was surrounded by war stories. It was all the grownups ever spoke about. I also wanted to go into the bundu and fight Terrs and be a hero. I promised myself that as soon as I was old enough, I would join the Army.

Ian showed me how to strip his carbine. It was a Belgian Fabrique Nationale (FN) 7.62 mm FAL. I could soon field-strip it blindfolded – *something I endeavoured to do diligently* – and on one occasion I broke it down into every single individual component, right down to the firing pin, cleaned the whole lot, and reassembled it. Ian took us to the shooting range and gave us kids protracted shooting lessons with it, so that if – *God Forbid* – we ever got caught up in *A Situation* we would know what to do. The FN is an overpowered rifle and is very difficult to handle, but that didn't stop me from loving every moment of it. Ian helped me to begin a collection of bullets. He even gave me some captured Russian ammunition that the Terrs used in their AK47 carbines and warned me that it was illegal to have it in my possession.

Ian was an intelligence officer and he showed me pictures of what the Terrs did to other Kaffirs. I had nightmares over those pictures and can still see some of them in my mind. One of the worst of them depicted a rural Batonga village chief up in Binga who had refused to assist the Terrs. They came into his kraal when the Security Forces were out of the area and grabbed him. Then they made the rest of the kraal sit down and watch his re-education. They stripped him stark naked and tied his hands behind him with barbed wire. Then they took a tent peg, shoved it into the wire between his hands, forced him to his knees, and hammered the peg into the ground behind him. This kept him completely immobilised in a sprawled kneeling position. Crude wire tourniquets were tied around his upper arms and legs. They then ordered the villagers to bring them beer, lit up dagga pipes – *I had no idea what dagga was* – and started teaching their revolutionary lesson. Each one of the Terrs took turns at stabbing him with a bayonet, the idea being that the one who killed him lost the drinking game. According to the villagers, he screamed for about an hour until one of the Terrs carefully stabbed him in the larynx, after which he remained mostly silent until he died some horror-filled hours later. I haven't seen animals that rip up something to kill it like that. Not even leopards. Animals try to kill quickly and cleanly and only rip up flesh after the kill to eat it. They only ever rip flesh to feed. These things were Acts of Terrorism, and Atrocities, as Ian called them. It was his job to catch these people and send them to the Gallows. He told me that not all Kaffirs in The War were terrorists – only the evil ones. These animals weren't freedom fighters – they were war criminals.

The pictures seemed to back this supposition.

He had another picture of a baby girl who had been killed by her mother. After the mother had smothered her, she cut the poor mite open and removed all her internal organs. Then the cavity was packed with Russian plastic explosives, steel ball bearings and a detonator. Her little body was stitched back up and dressed. The mother then strapped the bomb to her back in a blanket African papoose style and boarded a bus to go and plant it. A security sweep caught her at a roadblock.

We visited Audrey. She did not look good.

I was sent into the ward alone – she was only allowed one visitor at a time. What confronted me was not Audrey at all. She had always been a big robust woman, but she was reduced to a skeleton and had lost most of her hair. I barely recognised her. I told her I loved her, said goodbye and left the ward. She died immediately afterwards and I was the last person to speak to her.

Arrangements were made and we left the hospital. A solemn group of grownups gathered in August's house to pay their respects, give their condolences and offer him support. Somebody was lamenting Audrey's death loudly when I decided to voice my opinion and declared that I was very glad that she was dead because it meant she did not have to hurt any more. This just poured oil onto an already smouldering fire. They were all incensed that I was the last person to see her alive because, although I was Denise's brat – *one of her bloody mistakes* – I certainly was not Family in the Blood sense, and that morbid privilege should have gone to a Nesbitt. It was decided that I was *In The Way* and would remain *In The Way*. More arrangements were made. A day later and in the midst of a filthy catfight between Denise and her two brothers' spouses over who had claim to which and what of Audrey's possessions (she had not even been cremated yet), I was bundled onto a train and packed off to the town of Wankie on the north-western border of Zimbabwe.

3

Sandy

I stare out at the darkening bundu trundling clackety-clack past the train. I'm in one of those old wooden coaches with pictures of wild animals on the walls and the upholstery and curtains all done up in deep green. I like it. Much better than the bare aluminium and grey of the South African Railways. I'll be arriving in Wankie soon. I wonder who this Uncle Sandy is that I am being sent to. Damn I feel lonely. Well, I suppose this Uncle Sandy is going to be able to Handle me. Why else would they send me to him? Shit. Another grownup who likes to hit kids. I'll have to be careful and hopefully it won't be too bad. I don't know though.

They wouldn't send me to just Anybody. Shit, I am truly in trouble. Ah, fuck it – I'm tired. Let the Conductor wake me up when we arrive. He knows I'm a kid travelling on my own and I must get off at Wankie and be handed over to this Uncle Fucking Sandy.

It's starting to get dark now. I'm sleepy …

His wife was with him. They greeted me warmly.

He was adamant that I call him just plain Sandy, while she insisted very firmly on the full Aunty Dorothy. I was aware of the reasons why I had been packed off to them, and during the drive home I made my usual polite grownup small talk while wondering what sort of an ordeal I was in for. When we got there, Sandy showed me to my room.

He had prepared it in advance for me.

At supper Sandy asked me if I would like to go to work with him the next day. My choice. He suggested offhandedly that I might have some fun. I agreed, not even knowing what kind work he did. I asked, but he evaded the question with a twinkle in his eye. I gathered it was something to do with the Railways.

He was being nice to me. Really nice, but it made me nervous and a little scared. I didn't trust grownups.

Next morning at 05h30 we left for the station. Sandy introduced me to a Matabele man named Chivassa, and led us to what I later learnt was a 15 Class Garret Steam Locomotive. It was a huge black loco crawling with shiny copper pipes, a massive water tender up front, the boiler and piston assembly after, and the driver's cab and large coal bin behind it. Steam hissed gently out of her sides, billowing like white petticoats as we set about preparing her for the journey. Chivassa stoked effortlessly, singing softly in Ndebele, until his skin glowed like black silver in the dull red roaring heat.

Dawn pinked its way quickly into the sky, and the lights on our line turned green. Chivassa leant out of his side, waving a torch back and forth until he turned and nodded to Sandy.

We slowly pulled out of Wankie.

I stood next to Sandy, beside myself with happiness. The sky was turning a rosy blue and the bundu passing us was fast changing from dark purple to green. I asked Chivassa if I could stoke. A dazzling white grin tore across his nodding black face, indicating that I could go right ahead. Sandy smiled at me and winked at Chivassa. I stepped up to the coal bin, pulled out a shovel and tried hurling it into the coal as Chivassa had done. This did not happen. What *did* happen was a painful shock bit into my palms and slammed into my wrists and ran up to my elbows. Sandy and Chivassa roared with laughter. Sandy told me I would break a wrist trying to do it like that. He got up from the driver's seat and showed me how, by bucking the shovel. I gave it a go but there wasn't quite enough strength in my arms. I also tried tossing it in as nonchalantly as Sandy had done, but being left-handed I had to twist the wrong way to the steam pedal to reach the grate and dropped most of it. The next shovel was almost better, and soon enough I started to figure out how to hit the pedal and stoke in an ordered rhythm of movement. I was beginning to get filthy from coal dust, and it irritated my eyes, making the edges of my eyelids burn, and more so when I rubbed them. Somehow Sandy and Chivassa didn't seem to be getting dirty.

Sandy showed me a hose and I washed. It was freezing cold but I felt much better. The black residue left me looking more like Chivassa than Sandy.

The sun rose onto a simply beautiful African day. The bundu was lush and deep green. Flocks of birds flew up before us, and vervet monkeys and chacma baboons scampered in alarm across the tracks ahead. A herd of impala grazing a way off all lifted their heads and stared at us as we thundered past. The feeling I felt inside me was something too lovely to describe, too strange to understand. The awesome splendour of the panorama had overwhelmed me. There is, in my opinion, nothing more beautiful than the African bundu just after sunrise. I asked Sandy where we were heading. He told me we were on our way to Victoria Falls, one hundred miles away. We would arrive there in about three hours' time. I settled in, explored the cab and asked Sandy questions about everything I didn't understand. He explained it all and asked me questions to ensure that I had completely understood. My knowledge, dirtiness and utter exhilaration increased exponentially.

We arrived in Victoria Falls and washed up, and Sandy took me to a local marimba bar for a Coke and a chat ...

– *Alex. I am a very straightforward man. You were sent to me because down in Bulawayo they think you are trouble. I only met you last night on the station, but I have been watching you very carefully. Here's how it is. I like you – I like what I see. You did well today and you catch on quickly. I am not going to treat you like a kid ... like the rest of the grownups you know. I don't think that is what you want. If you want to swear, swear. If you want to smoke cigarettes, smoke. Just remember though, if you fuck with me then I will fuck with you, even though I'd never want to. I personally don't think that you are trouble. Just talk to me, okay? Then we will get on just fine –*

It was the most shocking conversation I'd ever had with a grownup. I stared at him, speechless, and then – I couldn't help it – I grinned and stuck out my hand. Sandy grinned back, winked at me, took my hand and shook it. He then said he figured I needed a few things, so after we had finished our drinks he took me to a store and found a brand new set of blue overalls and a pair of gumboots. It would be my work uniform from then on.

Sandy didn't work on weekends, and when Saturday came he called me to his study. He unlocked his gun cabinet, removed a rifle and handed it to me. It was a beautiful Czech pellet gun. He plonked a big box of pellets in my hand.

Be careful with it, he warned, and NEVER point it at a human being, even when it isn't loaded. It was mine as long as I stayed with them, and I could store it in the cupboard in my room.

I was in awe. I spent the rest of the day in the bundu looking for targets to shoot. I found some old rusty cans and spent hours plinking away at them. There were some other kids in the neighbourhood who were more or less my age. Two girls and a small boy. One of the girls was very pretty and I wanted to impress her. I loaded up and took a pot shot at a grey dove resting on the telephone wires in the street.

I could see from the burst of feathers that I'd hit it, but its wild ragged flight away told me that I had only wounded the poor beastie.

Far from being impressed, the girl I was trying to woo turned on me and yelled that I was stupid, mean and cruel, then ran off to our home. She returned with a grim-looking Sandy. I wasn't even aware that Sandy knew her. Apparently he knew all the kids in the neighbourhood and they all loved him. This I only found out later.

He took me to one side and asked me what had happened. My heart felt like it was tearing out of my chest – I was so scared. This was it. This was where he would beat the shit out of me. I told him I had shot a dove but it hadn't died, and then I waited. He nodded his head gravely, and told me that carrying a gun meant I had the power of life and death, and that was an adult responsibility. He wanted me to know that he considered me adult enough to carry a pellet gun but he expected me to live up to its *demands*.

– *It's easy to threaten or pull the trigger, Alex. Son, any stupid fool can. It doesn't make you a man, it just makes you a dangerous, stupid fool. Only, this time* YOU *are that dangerous fool. I don't mind you shooting that bird. I think you acted stupidly shooting it in front of the girls – they don't like that sort of thing – but all the same, I don't mind. What I do mind, though, is that you did not kill it properly. Because you were only out for some self-centred amusement and weren't willing to stalk and make a clean kill, there is an animal out there in a nightmare of pain, slowly bleeding to death. Okay, so this is how it is: You are going to take that pellet gun and you are going to find that dove and then you are going to kill it. This time you will do it right.*

One single shot.

Then you are going to bring me the carcass, and remember one thing – I will KNOW *whether it is the same bird or not, so don't try and be clever and shoot some other dove. I will be able to tell which of your shots wounded it and which one killed it. Now, remember, I am not forcing you to do this. You can refuse right now – but also remember that if you refuse to finish this, then we will just lock up the rifle and agree that you are not adult enough to carry it –*

I spent the rest of the afternoon climbing over fences, being chased by dogs, grownups and houseboys, and every time that poor dove saw me it flapped drunkenly out of range. I kept praying that a cat would not get to it first. Eventually I was able to get close enough for a clean shot and I ended it. I retrieved the carcass and could see what Sandy had meant about the difference in the wounds. The killing shot was a clean hole with very little blood, but the botched wound was messy and had soaked its feathers with dried black blood and gore. It made me feel stupid, mean and cruel, just like the pretty little girl had said, and I made a solemn promise to myself never to do something that dumb again.

After three weeks of working on the line, Sandy announced that he was taking some leave from work and asked me if I had ever been fishing before. Hah! Of course I had. I had lived in Mossel Bay for goodness' sake. Sandy nodded. He told me we were going fishing in the morning.

We left early and stopped the car so near to Vic Falls that the endless thundering roar of the water hurtling into the gorge made conversation difficult – IT WAS SO LOUD! We loaded Sandy's boat with camping equipment, guns, ammo, fishing tackle, food and drink. I cast off and jumped on. The boat chugged and burbled backwards, and Sandy turned us away from the falls and brought the engine up to full throttle. Spray and a strong breeze blew into my face as the sound of the Great White Thunder gradually diminished behind us. I was in seventh heaven. In my wildest dreams I could not have imagined this! I had to be the luckiest kid on the planet!

We passed a number of other boats on the massive, island-scattered expanse of water, and plenty of hippos and crocodiles. There were a couple of flat-bottomed, touristy, sightseeing ferries. Nervous European croc-watchers with cameras among olive green patrol boats bristling with guns, sandbags and very serious-looking men with black painted faces. Sandy explained that this area was heavily protected for the sake of tourism. Zambia was on the distant shore and crawling with insurgents. I asked if he thought we could win the war.

– *Son, that is the most adult question that you have asked me. I am not going to answer you now, but I will later on. Okay?* –

Okay.

After travelling upriver for some time we headed for the bank of one of the large dense islands, and secured the boat to a crude log quay. We took some things and I followed him to an opening in the forest, where there was a small wooden cabin. It had a fireplace and everything. Sandy explained that he and a couple of his cronies owned the place jointly and used it whenever they wanted to go fishing. We made camp and ate. Tinned baked beans, sardines, thick slices of bread and butter, and steaming mugs of hot coffee. I munched it all down in blessed contentment.

We took the boat into a nearby creek to start fishing. Sandy selected two rods, fitted the reels, fed the gut through and tied on a couple of spinners. He asked me if I knew how to cast with a coffee-grinder.

– *C'mon Sandy, I've fished before. Okay? There are some things I do know how to do, you know … –*

Okay, okay, he was going to fish off the stern and I would fish off the bow.

Funny thing was, I was actually lying. I had caught fish with worms, fillets, chokka, redbait and mud-prawns, but I had never caught with a spinner before. I figured I wasn't that stupid and watched Sandy out of the corner of my eye, trying to imitate him. A few minutes later he yelled out that he had one. I watched him fight it in. It was a lovely two-and-a-half pound yellow bream. We grinned at each other, popped it into a keep-net and went back to our fishing. Some minutes later he had another one, and a while later yet another. As he hauled each fish in, my bright mood darkened. Sandy picked up on this and asked me why my bottom lip was dragging on the deck. Was something bugging me? I rounded on him:

– *Yes Sandy, there is something bugging me. It's strange how you took the bottom of the boat and left me with the top. You know where all the fish are and you won't let me catch any –*

He shook his head, seeming amazed and amused, and offered to swop places. Damn right we swopped. I sat fuming at his lack of fairness and fished off the stern. After a few minutes Sandy hooked another from the bow. And a few minutes later – ditto. I sat steaming with an odd anger that I could not place properly. I mean, who was I actually angry with? Sandy noticed this too, and asked if everything was okay. I said I was quite fine thank you. He nodded and went back to his fishing. At the end of the day he had bagged a dozen two- to three-pound yellow bream. Enough supper for a great gang of folks and of course one very sullen, fishless, eleven-year-old boy. As we made our way back downstream and back at the camp, Sandy ignored me – whistling to himself while he cheerily fried fish for our supper, which we ate with boiled potatoes and tinned sweetcorn. He swilled his grub down with a beer and I sulked through a Coke. I grumbled goodnight and huffed off to bed early. I was being absolutely stupid but I didn't know how to stop myself.

The next morning I awoke to the smells of Sandy making breakfast. Fried eggs 'n bully beef, bread and butter, and steaming coffee to follow. I tucked in and, after the night's sleep, felt slightly better about not catching. Sandy cheerfully asked how I had slept and I told him well. Neither of us mentioned my behaviour from the previous day. We jumped into the boat and headed upriver. Lo and behold, Sandy took us to exactly the same spot. He noticed the dismay on my face as I dropped the anchor per his orders.

– *What's chewing you up, Alex? Time for you to talk to me, son* –

– *There are no fish here, Sandy* –

– *Then what the hell do you think I caught here yesterday? Old boots?* –

– *You know where all the fish are* –

– *Alex, let's stop this bullshit right now. Okay? There are fish all around here, everywhere. This is one of the greatest rivers in the world to fish in* –

– *So why didn't I catch any* –

– *Aaah, now I understand. So what you are actually pissed off about is that I know how to catch fish and you don't? Is that right?* –

[Silence]

– *Is that right Alex?* –

– *Alright, yes* –

– *Son, do you want me to teach you how to fish in this river?* –

– *Yes Sandy* –

– *Well, come and sit here next to me and get rid of your fuck-you-jack attitude. I don't understand you. You missed a whole day of fishing because you were too snotty to ask for my help. Alex, I have been fishing in this river since I was a little older than you. That's forty-odd years. If this was a competition, which it isn't, then I would beat you blindfolded. What the hell is wrong with you? You've been doing fine up until now. Smile, son. I'll teach you everything I know. Now watch carefully. You must trawl your spoon as if it is a small fish swimming in the water and not just toss it out and drag it in. You must fool the fish* –

. . .

– *Yes, like that. And let it stop a little every now and then to rest. Yes, like that – easy does it, you're not in a rush* –

About five minutes later I hooked one! And then another! The really great thing about Sandy was that even though I had made a complete and utter fool of myself and wasted my own precious fishing time, he did not rub my face in it.

As the days passed I started identifying and naming landmarks. Gunfire Rapids, where I had to lie on the bottom of the boat in case we got shot at; Scarface's Territory, the domain of an enraged bull hippo who'd had a bad run-in with a boat propeller; a nameless wide, long stretch full of dense verdant islands; and on to what I first called Gunfire II Rapids but later renamed Landmine Rapids.

Here the river narrowed considerably. We moved through a series of branching channels that Sandy seemed to know very well, clearing the Zambian side, and after heading quite a way down one stream, he pulled up to the bank. I jumped off and tied us to a bush. Sandy passed me the rods, a bucket of worms, a small toolbox containing tackle, and the FN, which I slung over my shoulder. Then he joined me with the rest and led me over the low sandy embankment. Suddenly I understood why the river had narrowed. Before us lay a small grassy lake. Sandy explained that the Zambezi was a flood river. In other words, every rainy season it overflowed its banks. The pool in front of us was a normal part of the river during the rainy season and, as he further explained, was packed with ravenous fish for the rest of the year once the water had subsided and trapped them. NOBODY fished there. The whole area for miles was marked on maps as a military red zone. Sandy led us to a nice spot. We set the weapons down, propping them on forked sticks which we pushed into the sand. The fish we caught would be tossed into a big open keep-net.

Sandy pulled a worm from the bucket, broke off a small piece of it and threaded it onto the hook's barb. He winked at me.

– *Take a butcher's at this, son* –

He cast a short way into the lake. The float hit the water, bobbed for all of five seconds and disappeared. He struck and brought in a plate-sized silver bream. Quite a fierce little fighter too! I put a piece of worm on my hook as Sandy had done, cast in and – bang! – I had one. Just like that! As it turned out, our only real problem was a possible shortage of worms.

We fished furiously, stopping only for sandwiches and cold drinks. Sandy spoke:

– Alex, do you remember the question you asked me the other day? –

– What question was that, Sandy? –

– The one about the war –

– Oh ja, I remember. So what's the answer? Are we going to win it? –

– See, that's why I said I'd only answer you later on. It is not that easy to answer. First of all, you answer me a question. Do you know WHY there is a war going on? –

– Ja, Uncle Ian told me. The Kaffirs want everything in the country. The Shona Terrs have the Red Chinese Communists giving them guns and the Matabeles have Russian Communists giving them guns, or something like that, and Ian Smith is trying to save us from them all –

– Uncle Ian told you that, hey? Well, that is an oversimplification and I wouldn't quite agree with his politics, but it's a more or less correct statement. Let's try and look at it another way completely. Picture your class at school. Okay. Now let's pretend there are two blokes in your class and that together these two bully all the smaller blokes and take their milk money every day. Nobody can stand up to them. Have you got that? Now, let's give them names. The one bully is very big, so let's call him Makhulu. The other one is smaller, so let's call him Piccanin. Now, Makhulu always gets Piccanin to take the other kids' milk money to make the poor little bastards feel even worse. How would you feel if a titch took your milk money and you could do bugger all because of his huge mate? Do you get the picture? Now, imagine what would happen if Makhulu had to move away to another town. He would leave Piccanin in deep shit, right? Piccanin would be all on his own. All those poor bastards that Piccanin helped to rob are going to want their milk money back. Do you understand what I am talking about? –

– Sandy, I don't know what the hell you are talking about –

– Okay, let me try and explain it like this. Makhulu in our pretend picture is England. Piccanin is most of the white folks here in Rhodesia after we separated from England, and the smaller kids are the black folks. Now do you get the picture? –

– … I thiiink so. England and the white Rhodesians have always bullied the Kaffirs and now that England is gone the Kaffirs want their stuff back from the white Rhodesians? –

– Exactly –

– But Sandy, does this mean that we are going to lose the war? –

– What do you think? –

– I dunno, Uncle Ian says we have the best bush fighters in the world –

– Think of it this way, son. What is the biggest problem facing Piccanin apart from having to pay the money back and maybe getting clobbered by the other kids? –

– I don't know, Sandy. What? –

– Do you think Piccanin has any friends? –

– No, of course not –

– See, that answers your question. After all is said and done, Piccanin has no friends and Makhulu lives in another town. And let me tell you, in this world, if you have no friends, you have nothing, and that is what losing is all about –

Sandy liked to tell me stuff in stories that explained other stuff. It usually made it easier to understand. He also liked to pick me out about stuff he thought I needed to think about too. He next decided that it was the time for one of those Chats, and it turned out to be one of the most important talks we ever had. He continued.

– Son, what is a Kaffir? –

I looked at him in disbelief.

– What do you mean what is a Kaffir? Black people are Kaffirs, Sandy –

– Okay. I accept that you say that. But why do you use the word Kaffir? –

– I dunno. I suppose because a Kaffir is a Kaffir? –

– Come on, Alex, what the hell does that mean? –

– I don't know, Sandy, and I don't know what you want from me –

– I'm trying to get you to think, son. Alright, leave that, and answer me this: What does the actual word, Kaffir, mean? –

– I don't know, but you're going to tell me, right? –

– Sarcasm will get you nowhere, boy, but I'll humour you. The word Kaffir comes from a black language called Swahili, which borrowed it from Arabic, and it means that a person is not a Mohammedan. Do you know what a Mohammedan is? –

– No –

– You've been to church, haven't you? –

– Ja –

– Well Mohammedans have a church too, but they don't believe in God and Jesus – they believe in Allah –

– Who's Allah? –

– Allah is the name they give God, and anybody who does not worship

Allah they call an Infidel in white man's language and a Kaffir in the black man's –

– Wow. So all the Kaffirs are infidels. But Sandy, I don't go to Allah's church and I'm not a Kaffir –

– Exactly. Now you're starting to think. No son, you're not a Kaffir and neither am I, and guess what? Neither is Chivassa. Chivassa goes to a Christian church. You didn't know that. If you interpret it like that, you can't call Chivassa a Kaffir either –

– Then what is Chivassa, Sandy? –

– Chivassa is a Matabele man, son. And he is a good man. I've known and worked with him for fourteen years. You are still a bit young, but as you grow up I hope you will learn that who or what a man is comes from inside him. People are good or bad from inside themselves, son. You will find bad men and good men in your life ahead of you. Some might be black, some might be white, some might even speak other languages or pray to God in a different way, but what will hurt you is when you give them a bad name before you give yourself a chance to know them. Once you get to know a man, you will know whether he is good or bad. Good men live and give to the world from inside themselves; bad men complain about it and try taking whatever they think the world owes them. Resist bad men and avoid them, but remember, if you judge a man because he is different to you, you might lose out on a friend. And remember what I told you just now – if you have no friends, you have nothing –

– But Sandy, why does everybody else call Chivassa a Kaffir? –

– Son, you are going to have to answer that one for yourself, and––

At this point we were interrupted by a slight noise behind us. Glancing over our shoulders, we found ourselves staring into the barrels of six guns and, behind those guns, twelve very surprised and serious-looking eyes. The faces were all blackened, and one of them started swearing profusely in a low voice – the patrol leader. They all lowered their weapons and clicked the safeties back on. He asked us, amidst a string of really hot, angry, hissing expletives, what exactly the fuck we thought we were doing there. Fishing, replied Sandy. This only made him swear worse. Were we possibly aware that we were right in the middle of a free-fire zone and that two Terrs had just blown themselves up planting landmines not five clicks away from there? (Of course we weren't aware, idiot.) No Sergeant, we hadn't heard a thing.

Fucking idiots – we had to get the fuck out of there – right NOW!

Sandy told him to keep his hat on. We began gathering our kit. The other boys in the patrol helped us carry the big sack of fish back to the boat. We dished out fish to all of them for their supper, and left, with the Sarge still swearing as only a really livid trooper can.

I resumed working with Sandy on the line. One afternoon we were preparing for the trip back to Wankie. The passenger train was hooked up. Sandy was down on the station platform speaking to the Chief Conductor. I was up in the cab chatting with Chivassa and stoking. Sandy appeared.

– *Son, I want you to do me a favour* –

– *Sure Sandy, what's up?* –

– *The Chief Conductor and the Head Steward on this train are good mates of mine and they've invited me for a game of cards. Will you take us home tonight?* –

– *You mean drive us home?* –

– *Well, how the hell else are we going to get there?* –

– *Jeez Sandy, okay, sure, no problem* –

Sandy disappeared. I looked over at Chivassa. He just grinned at me. I grinned back. The lights turned green. I leant out of the driver's side and signalled. The Chief Conductor and the guard waved an all clear. I spun the direction wheel into forward, released the brake and slowly opened the regulator. Long shrieking whistle and *Chooof, chooof, choof, choof* ...

We gently left Vic Falls. I did not spin the wheels. I did not spill soup in the dining car.

We were up on the escarpment and thundering along nicely when I hit a bomb. It was a small round cap explosive that had been laid on the tracks and detonated very loudly when the loco hit it. It was used as an emergency signal to the driver that he had to stop immediately. I stopped. Up ahead I could see a group of Army personnel all over the tracks. A huge black sergeant dressed in bush cammo strolled down towards us. He carried a pump-action shotgun and was festooned with red shotgun shells sheathed in leather bandoliers criss-crossing his chest. I thought he looked like something I had seen in a war movie. He came up to the cab and asked to speak with the driver. I informed him that I was in fact the driver. He didn't bat an eyelid – he probably saw coal-blackened eleven-year-old kids driving passenger trains all day, I'm sure – hah! He ordered me to wait. They'd discovered landmines under the tracks and the Army engineers were busy clearing them. He would come back and tell me when we could continue safely. After some time we resumed our run home. At the station back in Wankie I stepped down from the cab feeling like Roy Rogers, Audie Murphy and John Wayne all rolled up into one. I swaggered over to Sandy, expecting him to laud my magnificent performance, but he popped my bubble instead.

– *What the hell are you goggle-eyeing at? What? Do you expect a Noddy badge or something? Come, let's go home and have supper and see if you can beat me at checkers afterwards. But you better watch your head going through that door, son, it looks so swollen it might not fit –*

Inevitably a day dawned when I had to board the train back to Bulawayo. Saying goodbye to Sandy on Wankie station was the hardest thing I had ever done, and I cried most of the journey back.

Travelling by train only made it so much worse.

*

I arrived back in Bulawayo to a loud, bitter and unhappy Denise. The two little bitches her brothers had married had spitefully connived to cart off the lion's share of Audrey's earthly goods, and on top of it all— the Kaffirs had all suddenly become Too Bloody Cheeky. They wouldn't even get off the pavements and out of Your Way in the streets any more. She was unhappy and remained unhappy and extremely volatile all the way back to Paarl, where a surprise was awaiting me. In the period during our absence, Wally had arranged new accommodation for Denise and had found a place about four kilometres outside of Paarl on the road to Franschhoek. Swallow had in the meantime also put her steel foot down and I was no longer welcome to live with them. Good riddance. I found myself back with Denise and the little ones.

Wally came around from time to time, and sometimes they would scream about money. Denise became most violent after his visits. She wanted him back from That Bitch. The shock that I felt leaving Sandy and being plunged back into the nightmare of living in Denise and Wally's world broke me emotionally.

Things quickly took a turn for the worse at school too. I had missed out on a lot that year. I found myself in the headmaster's office more and more often for tardy schoolwork. One day, I brought my precious bullet collection to the school for a class oral. My teacher considered this dangerous, failed me and sent me to the office. Mr Terreblanche – Tebbie – gave me a long speech in his fractured English about dangerous illegal ammunition, flapped me and confiscated my bullets with a satisfied smirk. I had everything in that collection: military (ours and theirs), hunting (everything up to elephant), various pistols, etc. Not only that, but I had very carefully prised all the projectiles out of their casings and emptied the shell's cordite into a special tin that I had hidden away at home. I had polished each bullet until it gleamed like gold. I thoroughly despised Tebbie – those bullets had all come from Ian and most especially from Sandy.

Something happened to me after my time with Sandy. All my life, Wally, Denise, teachers and bullies had made my life a misery, and along came somebody who never hit me or swore at me, and he made me feel completely different about myself, and then he went away and it ALL started again. It caused me massive emotional turmoil. I stopped feeling scared all the time and began to feel angry, especially when I was sent to The Office some time later and saw my burnished bullet collection lined up in Tebbie's trophy display cabinet. Why was it dangerous and illegal for me but not for him?

Fuck Wally, fuck Denise, fuck Tebbie – FUCK THEM ALL!

The nightmare lasted until I was packed off to boarding school at the end of the year.

*

The man I left behind in Wankie was the only real father figure I have known in this world. His name, like mine, was Alexander, but he was known to all by his other handle.

Sandy ... is not with us any longer. My *baba* quietly went off some years ago and joined the Great Fisherman and his Fishing Buddies.

It is he whom I thank in the dedication at the beginning of this book.

Thank you again Sandy.

I love you, you beautiful old man.

4

Asterix and the Rockspiders

Wally dropped me off at Worcester High School's hostel the day before the start of Standard 6. It was the first time I had ever owned a brand new blazer, tie and long pants. Kids had the option of being day boarders, weekly boarders or term boarders. I was going to be a term boarder.

Wally muttered something about me bloody behaving myself, then awkwardly slipped me a two-rand note and disappeared with Swallow. I was on my own again for the first time since Sandy – very nervous and somewhat excited.

[**Score 0-0**]

With me were seven other okies. A few of the bigger okes in the corner seemed to be completely at home and were already making their beds. One of them, next to the window, was the biggest boy in the dormitory. He was tall, well built, with Gallic good looks and a mop of jet-black hair. He ordered quiet and introduced himself as Jean-Pierre du Toit – JP. Our dormitory captain. Apart from JP's cronies – Bokkie van Wyk and Jannie le Roux – the rest of us were new to the hostel and the school. Two of us weren't Afrikaans. I realised this might be a problem when I introduced myself. Bokkie looked at JP in horror:

– *We gotta fokken soutpiel, JP!* –

Oh fuck, don't tell me they have all that Rockspider/Soutpiel shit …

JP grunted noncommittally and gave us a rundown on dormitory rules. We were to understand that *he* was responsible to the prefects in Matric, who were in turn responsible to the hostel onnies, and severe punishment would be inflicted on our persons if we happened to fuck up and get him into trouble.

– *Did you fokken sotte unnerstand, Soutpiel?* –

Oh, I understand you, Rockspider. You're that little Lord Muk on toast, aren't you?

I hadn't quite reckoned on *living* with prefects and dormitory captains. With this came a slight stir of unease. The bell went and JP informed us it was time for supper. I followed the others out, teaming up with a German boy named Anton Grossman. Supper was quite nice, although I found that the food wasn't shared out very fairly. The table prefect would take as much as he wanted from each serving bowl – nobody was allowed to touch anything until he did – then there followed a pecking order decreed by him. After supper a huge boy stood up and banged his table with a knife for silence and said a prayer of thanks for the food. Then he ordered all the *sotte* to report to the smoking sheds immediately. Catcalls, whistles and laughter broke out. My table prefect pointed a meaningful finger at me and two other lads.

The smoking sheds were long bicycle sheds for the day scholars behind our hostel. I found myself in a large group of other nervous-looking Standard 6s. A bunch of big okes all sat down on benches against a wall and began lighting up cigarettes. The boy who said prayers remained standing in front of the smokers. He shouted for quiet and introduced himself as Paul Conradie, then informed us – *sotte* – that we were about to undergo *doop*. It would last for a week. During *doop* we were to address all the Matrics as *Meneer* and all the girls in their class as *Mejuffrou*. Each of us would be seconded to an *Oupa* in Matric. He finished and pointed at me:

– *You! Soutpiel with de teef. You and jour pêl with you, you is my sotte. Okay?* –

Anton and I went over to him a little nervously. The others were rapidly seconded to various oupas in a similar fashion. Paul took us off to one side and asked where we came from. We were to remain his personal sotte for the remainder of that year, apparently. First order of business would be the allocation of a nickname each. I was given the moniker *Asterix*, and Anton was designated *Wingnuts*. Anton had buck ears, and I was small, probably the smallest and youngest.

I was twelve.

Paul eventually called a halt to the traditional merry hazing to make one last announcement. Smoking was only permitted among the Matrics. This was policed by the Matrics, who had been known to develop short-sightedness in the presence of smoking— *gifts*. I was slow on the uptake, so Anton had to clarify it for me: *If we wanted to smoke, we would have to bribe them.*

Cool.

Anton and I followed the flow of boys in other grades to the back, where we sat down, lit smokes and I met my first partner in crime. An oke with Belgian parents from Rondebosch named Digre. With him was a cat named Lucky from Somerset West. Anton, I discovered, was from a farm near Worcester.

Digre was the eldest and seemed to be worldly beyond any of us. He fascinated me no end.

I decided I wanted to be friends with him.

Eventually we went back inside. I grabbed my pyjamas, changed in the bathroom toilets because I was very shy, and slept badly in my strange bed, tossing around in the dark night full of snoring, farting, grunting strangers.

After the first day of school, lunch, study and sports, I walked innocently into the showers to wash and got a big shock. The okes in the showers all had ball hairs.

Shit! I didn't!

I couldn't undress in a crowd like that, so I figured to wait until the bathrooms were empty and quickly grab a shower in private, but by bedtime I still hadn't made it. I jumped into my PJs in the bogs. I felt dirty and uncomfortable and, because I was stressing, I started sucking my thumb. JP walked up to my bed with a look of utter incredulity on his face.

– *Sot, is you still a fokken baba? Why're you chewing your donnerse hand and why haven't you showered? –*

I lied, saying that I hadn't had time to shower.

– *Sot, dere is one thing I kannot take an dat is a dirty arse vuilgat – you mus' fokken shower! –*

Next afternoon I nipped downstairs to the primary school kids' bathrooms and washed. It also conveniently saved me the embarrassment of changing in the dormitory, but I hadn't counted on JP. He took me to task again, although I told him I had washed. He informed me darkly that he was watching me very carefully.

The following day I bathed downstairs again. Later, back in my dormitory, I found JP, Bokkie and Jannie waiting for me.

– *[JP] I mos fokken warned you, sot! I hate a dirty arse vuilgat. An' doan try tork kak, you didn' fokken shower and now you goana kak –*

They dragged me to the showers.

I tried explaining about downstairs but they wouldn't listen. They started slapping and hitting me. I pleaded desperately as they ripped my clothes off, then lost it and started yelling. JP grabbed me by the hair and

47

slammed my head into the wall. Hard. Once I was concussed and naked, they tossed me into a bath and switched on the cold tap, taking turns with floor-scrubbing brushes, hitting and scrubbing as I cried harder. The pain of it was terrible and the shame of them discovering and screaming with laughter at my hairless crotch made me feel like I had died and gone to hell, especially when they started viciously scrubbing me *there*. Eventually they left, sniggering, nudging each other in the ribs. I sat crying alone in my shame and horror, with my nose bleeding, my skin raw, my crotch and arse on fire, and my poor head hurting like it did after one of Denise's worst rages. By some horrible miracle nobody had heard my muffled screams. JP reappeared and informed me coldly that if I ratted on them, that would be me – *stone dead*.

The nightmare had begun.

JP and pals picked on me all the time, and I began living in a hell of casual slaps, unsuspecting *lammies*, knuckle 'n collar clouts and ugly insults, because I was poor, had horrible metal prosthetics on my teeth, sucked my thumb, spoke English and was basically too fucking small and way too frightened to do anything about it.

[Asterix-0 : Rockspiders-3]

Our beds all had big square bed boards. It was a standing hostel rule that every morning they had to be removed and packed against the wall next to the window. Why? I don't know. I also had a problem with sweaty feet. If I did not change my socks at least twice a day, my feet would smell vile, and I developed rashes and scabby skin between my toes. All our laundry was done by the hostel staff, but I did not have enough pairs of socks to last the whole week – so I simply washed them by hand myself and then hung them up to dry in the dormitory.

This irritated JP.

One grim day, about a month into the new term, I was hanging my socks over the bed boards to dry. By some stupid error of judgement I happened to hang them over JP's boards. Too late, I heard him sneaking up behind me, and he lashed out with his foot, kicking the boards hard – mashing my hand between them. Agony exploded in my trapped fingers and I spun around in shock. JP stood there, grinning at me lasciviously.

Deep, deep down inside me something snapped.

My eyes fell upon the nearest bed. Lying on it was a heavy wooden tennis racket. In one fluid motion I snatched it up with my good hand and hit him with the thin edge as hard as I possibly could, right in the middle of his forehead. All the bottled-up pain, shame and terror came gushing out of me, and I put everything I could into the blow. I shattered the racket and blood ran instantly from his hairline. His eyes snapped back (*lights*) in his head, and he went down (*out*) like a felled tree, crashing to the floor, with one of his legs twitching – unconscious.

The hostel father gave me six cuts and a written expulsion warning. Apparently JP had a proclivity for bullying, which the hostel father could not deny, because of a string of prior incidents – not involving me – and he was expelled. I was just a scared twelve-year-old kid who had stood up to a strapping sixteen-year-old bully. I cried from the cuts and the pain in my hand. I felt horrified about JP, but I was glad he was gone and could not hurt me any more.

[**Asterix-1 : Rockspider-KO**]

I found that I had made an instant friend in Digre. He demanded that I tell him the saga over and over. Digre hated Rockspiders. I loved the attention I was getting, and when the hostel father transferred me to his dormitory, I felt that the tide had turned for me at last. Digre took me under his wing and I met his other friends in Standard 8 and 9.

They were just the coolest okes around, and introduced me to their music. I had never really been a fan of any particular rock group, although I had my favourite songs on the radio. But these okies were all hardened rock fans and it wasn't music that I had ever heard on the radio before either. There was a band called Led Zeppelin that blew me away instantly, and another called Pink Floyd that made a sort of weirdly melancholy rock and synthesiser mix, full of freaky sound effects, which I fell in love with the first time I heard it. There were other bands like Uriah Heap, Bachman Turner Overdrive, Bad Company and Fleetwood Mac. I was suddenly In and Turned On, Bra!

I loved having an older friend and protector in Digre, but there were a few strange things about him. For one, he did not give a damn what other people thought. I would often wake up in the morning to the sound of him pulling his wire, only he called it *wanking*. I asked him repeatedly to have some decency, but he would just tell me to shut up – he was trying to concentrate! He did it using a sock over his member, which I thought was disgusting, but I tolerated it because he gave me many other things in our friendship. He said nothing about my teeth or thumbsucking, and he caught on quickly that I had no tuck and that I received little or no pocket money.

The first thing Digre did was to begin completely redefining my vocabulary by teaching me slang words for everything. For instance, cigarettes were called *entjies* and stealing stuff was called *scaling* or *slukking goeters*. He also said *eksê* a lot *eksê*.

With Wally and Denise, I'd been able to keep my shoplifting carefully hidden, but that was not so easy to do now, living in close proximity to four other okies. They soon discovered that I had very sticky fingers. Digre was the first to catch on, and far from finding it objectionable, he extolled and encouraged my dubious talents – pressurising me into scaling goeters for him. His parents had opened accounts with various shops in Worcester to take care of his immediate needs, but of course that did not cater for any of his wants. The stuff he bought on account he shared with me equally – but because I was consequently always at the wrong end of the balance of trade, it became my given task to sluk various goeters and make up the deficit. My shoplifting reached brazen new heights. I saw it as a challenge and the means to gain greater acceptance among my newfound friends.

Digre was a charismatic oke and managed to draw acolytes and smitten chicks, but he was always very, very careful to remove himself from any immediate danger to his own person. I felt uneasy about this, but my need for a friend and protector was greater. I placed myself in the position of number one disciple. I needed to, because Bokkie and Jannie had not taken lightly to JP's expulsion. Digre had a fearsome reputation, even in Standard 7, because he had actually beaten up a Matric! Not a Matric in the hostel – that would have been his downfall – but one at the school. They had had a fight over a chick and Digre hit him in the face, then threw him down the stairs in the science building.

He was not afraid of violence on his own terms.

One night he took me across the road to a ruined property and we beat a spiritsuiper half to death. We arrived back in the hostel breathless and I saw that I had blood all over my takkies. I was terrified that we had killed him. I did not sleep well that night, nor the next or the one after that, and only after about a week did I slowly start relaxing as I realised that the police were not about to come and arrest us both for murder. I crept over to the building alone one afternoon with my heart firmly in my mouth, and poked around in the dense bushes that he had crawled into. I found nothing. I never let on to Digre that the fear and apprehension were making me sick with worry. I knew he would only interpret them as signs of weakness.

They know I did it. They are watching me. Soon … They are going to come. It's the rope for me. It's The Rope.

[**Asterix-1 : Spiritsuiper-dead?**]

I spent two weekends at Digre's spot in Cape Town and was utterly appalled to discover that he had absolutely no respect for either of his parents, swearing viciously at them and cursing them in vile, filthy gutter language whenever he thought they were trying to defy or control him. He actually slapped his mother in front of me and bragged that he had kicked his dad down the stairs and broken both his legs.

Why on earth his folks tolerated him doing that mystified me. I had never ever even so much as *tried* to defy Wally to his face.

He would probably kill me.

Strangely, though, I found myself willing to sacrifice my scruples in the face of Digre's evil indulgences because I genuinely thought he was the best thing I had going for me at the time. We spent that entire weekend playing marathon games of chess and drinking brandy in his room until we were too drunk to see the board properly, whereupon we passed out, woke up and simply repeated the process again.

The second weekend I spent there, we decided to try smoking some *dagga*. I had heard a lot about dagga but didn't know exactly what it was, except that it was a drug.

Drugs were illegal and made you brain-damaged.

Digre told me *That* was a load of kak invented by the boere and the boneheads to stop okes from getting on a pluk. He also had other names for dagga like gunston, zol and *boom*. We arrived at his spot late that Friday afternoon and immediately went up to Plumstead High School. Digre said the one coloured oke who worked there was also a dagga merchant. We found the ou and announced we wanted to buy two rand-baalle. The coloured cat refused, telling us that we were laaities. Digre retaliated hotly that he had no choice – he was a merchant, we had money and we would piemp him to the boere if he didn't score to us. The ou swore a thick blue streak but nevertheless sold us two sticks wrapped in brown paper. We figured that we would wait until after supper that night to try them out. As we were leaving, Digre's dad called out cheerfully:

– *Where're you boys going?* –

– *[Digre] We're going to the park to smoke dagga* –

– *Okay, okay, there's really no need to be sarcastic. I was only asking a question* –

That was typical Digre.

We arrived at the park and hunted for an empty bottle, which we promptly smashed for the bottleneck. Digre said we needed to roll a *girrick*. This we did by taking the silver packing paper from a packet of entjies, after removing the thin transparent paper, using a match to melt the gum holding it to the foil. The metal was folded into a long thin strip about a quarter of an inch wide. This was then rolled into a spiral, which fitted neatly into the back of the neck where the bottle cap went. Digre tore off a piece of entjie about a half an inch long and put the tobacco from it into the pipe. This was called a *backstop*. Finally we opened one of the rand-baalle. Zol looked exactly like the herb oregano, except it also had little green and brown pips and small stalks in it. It was the first time either of us had ever seen it – I don't know where Digre had learnt his smoking lore, or his slang for that matter, considering he knew all the words but had no actual experience. He tore open the rest of the entjie and put the tobacco in with the gunston. This was called *mix*. He blended it in, poured the whole lot into the pipe and *stopped* it down.

Right, we were ready!

We were both a little apprehensive about what would happen to us, so I was elected to bust it and try it out first.

Again, typical Digre.

I held it in the special two-handed grip that he had demonstrated, and he lit two matches held in a slight V to fire me. I puffed and puffed and made myself blue trying – but I simply could not get the damn thing going. Digre took over, and half a box of matches and a headache each later, we finally managed to get a little bit of smoke into our lungs. Eventually we called it a day and threw the pipe and the other rand-baal away. Wasted money. It had done nothing to us. We argued as to why on earth mense and the boere made such a big fucking jol about it. We had, of course, prudently stashed a bottle of brandy in Digre's room, and so, without much further ado, we headed back to his spot and broke out the glasses and the chessboard.

Digre's move – me to pour.

[**Asterix-0 : Dagga-0**]

Back at school I had two very close calls shoplifting and lost my nerve. Previously I had always had nerves of dropforged tungsten steel. Nothing rattled me. All that changed. I simply could not do it any more.

I was too scared, and trouble appeared in paradise.

Digre couldn't understand that I needed pluk to do what I did with my adhesive hands, and it had evaporated into thin air. He yelled at me, and when I yelled back he kicked me in the face, making a big gash in his foot from my metal front teeth.

Digre did not like being confronted on core issues.

On Sunday mornings we were supposed to attend a church of our own particular denomination. Our crew conscientiously avoided attending church, and usually took off to a nearby shopping arcade instead, where we sat smoking and having fat splabs. We splabbed about anything and everything. Chicks, sex, rock music trivia, urban legends and our own dubious exploits. Basically whatever was controversial and far-fetched enough to pass the time until returning to the hostel for lunch.

One such Sunday we were sitting splabbing when somebody noticed that a louvred window above us was slightly open. Anton and I checked it out. I figured that if I stood on Anton's shoulders I could reach the window and would easily be able to remove two of the slatted panes. I did exactly that, and slithered through. I found myself in a receptionist's office and scooted around the desk, quietly opening drawers with a scrap of paper from the wastepaper basket so as not to leave fingerprints. In the first two I found nothing of value except a Parker pen and an ornamental letter opener. In the bottom one I hit pay dirt. It contained a little red cashbox and a carton of Chesterfield. The carton of entjies had eight packets and the unlocked cashbox had seventy-odd rand in notes and change. This was a small fortune, considering a pack of Chesterfield only cost twenty-eight and a half cents at the time. I stuffed my blazer pockets and opened the door. Only Lucky and Anton were still around. The others had removed themselves promptly – Digre first. We searched the other two offices but came up empty-handed. So we left and caught up with the others, who were slowly sauntering back to the hostel. Digre immediately demanded to know what goeters I had scaled. I showed him the Parker pen. He appropriated it and that kept him quiet. Then I gave everybody else a packet of entjies, not really so much to share as to seal lips. I kept my mouth shut about the money. I didn't want Digre having everything. I would bullshit him that I had received pocket money from home and then share it with him bit by bit.

[**Asterix-1 : Office-0**]

That first break-in set a precedent. We began using our Sundays to explore every alleyway and back entrance in town to find other soft targets. Once we discovered some outdoor fridges belonging to a restaurant and broke into one of them. All we could really carry away were three cases of Coca-Cola. I mean, what the hell would we do with a crate of lettuce or a catering-sized bucket of mayonnaise, for instance? We found some other offices another week and called these break-ins 'jobs'. I was usually the one who did the actual deed, with Anton and sometimes Lucky assisting. Digre of course kept his distance until the job was over, and then asserted his right to distribute the goeters.

During weekdays we were permitted outings downtown in the afternoons after study – provided of course that we did not have any sport or extramural obligations. There was a kafee opposite the police station that we almost always frequented for the purpose of playing pinball and smoking freely without being seen by teachers.

We were all dedicated pinball freaks, wasting every spare cent we had on the game, and the Pinball Kafee was our favourite hangout.

One Friday night Digre, Lucky, Frank, Anton and I were sitting together in study. We were all majorly, *majorly* bored. A quietly whispered conversation began among us concerning the boredom factor. I made the clever suggestion that we plan a job on the Pinball Kafee. Digre thought this was a *befucktaaa* idea! First we had to decide who would be part of the crew. At this point the idea went to the dogs. Nobody wanted to risk slipping out and breaking into a kafee right next door to the boere station! I accused the rest of being *meid*, which of course was kind of like throwing down the gauntlet. I thereby placed myself nicely on the spot. If I didn't do it, then I would be exactly what I accused them of. *That came from Digre.* Hah! I would simply do it alone! I realised, though, that I had better plan it very, very carefully. We started sketching a rough draft. This was about ten times more fun than the actual deed!

First, open an exercise book and write down:

The Great Pinball Kafee Job – by Asterix (Okay, okay AND Digre):

Tools needed: Small iron bar and towel to break window, socks for fingerprints, Laundry bag for goeters, Entjies and matches to mark time, dark clothes and takkies – Guts.

01h45 – Leave the hostel via Frank's route. i.e. climb out the window of our dormitory, scoot along the concrete ledge – without falling into the Krismisrose – onto the roof of the entrance to the front-portaal and slide down the corner drainpipe.

02h00 – Arrive at Pinball Kafee and go into yard of old Catholic church next door. Smoke entjie and listen for activity in boere station.

02h10 – Break small window high up on church side by placing towel over it and giving it a good hard thump, then run and hide in bushes next to church. Smoke entjie and wait.

02h20 – If no activity from boere then go and clear out glass from window and go back to bushes. Light another entjie. Wait.

02h30 – If still no activity from boere then assume coast is probably clear. Climb into kafee. Start collecting goeters starting with watches, entjies, pipes, Ronson lighters, biltong, salami, chocolates, sweets, etc. Toss watches and meat into laundry bag and throw out through burglar bars of toilet window at the back. Throw out all other goeters. Burglar bars too small for full laundry bag.

02h50 – Open bolts of side door next to boere station charge office and see what duty boere are doing inside. Slip out very carefully. Go collect goeters behind toilet, toss in laundry bag quickly and get the fuck out of there!

03h00 – Arrive back at hostel. Climb back up drainpipe ...

03h10 – Have midnight feast!

The plan worked perfectly, except the window didn't break on the first thump I gave it. Only on the third crack did it shatter. Also, while I was still inside gathering all the goeters, I was forced to dive to the floor three times because of boerevans pulling in and out of the station next door. Their fucking headlights shone right into the shop and illuminated everything like daylight! When I finally arrived back at the hostel, it was only five minutes outside of the original plan. I made one small insignificant mistake though. I accidentally left the iron bar that I'd used to break the window on the counter inside the kafee. I found this out when we went to have a look at my handiwork – ostensibly smoking and playing pinball as usual. The whole place was full of embarrassed, angry-looking boere, and the Greek owner was spitting in rage at their inefficiency. I was starting to live up to my nickname Asterix. I was the smallest and youngest but I had the most guts out of anyone in our crew.

I needed it that way.

[**Asterix-1 : Pinball Kafee-0**]

The next Saturday morning Digre and I made a quick excursion to Cape Town by catching the earliest train through. Once in Town we took off to the Grand Parade. We strolled around expectantly. Eventually what we were searching for found us. A very scaley-looking coloured ou flashed a watch at me. Digre grinned and called him over.

– *Eksê my broer, we don't wanna buy that watch, we wanna talk to your baas* –

We gave him a quick peek into the rucksack with all the watches from the previous Friday night's job. His eyes widened. He took a good look at us, decided we were obviously not undercover boere and told us to hang ten. While we were waiting, we haggled with each other to set our going price. We eventually decided one hundred and twenty rands would do nicely – thirty watches @ R4.00 each. The scaley ou arrived back and told us to follow him. He took us off to a big, black Mercedes Benz with tinted windows and informed us that only one of us should get in. We both suddenly felt uneasy. It all looked like something straight out of a mafia movie. Digre thrust the bag of watches at me.

So utterly fucking typical.

I opened the door, climbed in and found myself next to a huge fat black man dressed in a zoot suit with a natty Fedora on his head. I introduced myself:

– *Hi, I'm Asterix* –

– *[Deep bass laughter] Sawubona Asterix, I'm Zulu. Whatchoo got fo me?* –

– *Thirty watches. Here, have a look* –

– *Uh-huh, Uh-huh. Right, you tell me now where you steal them and doan lie to me, I get very cross* –

– *We stole them in Worcester, Mr Zulu* –

– *Uh-huh, Uh-huh. Whatchoo want for them? Imali?* –

– Er ... we, er, want one hundred and twenty rands for them –

– Uh-huh, Uh-huh. Okay I give you thirty rands –

At this point he rattled off something in Zulu to the driver. The driver turned, gave me thirty rands mirthlessly and opened my door. I peered at Mr Zulu, but he just grinned.

– Hokay, you go home now Asterix my fren', and next time you got stuff, you come to Zulu. Hamba gashle –

Caveat Emptor?

Digre was livid with me because I had not gotten the agreed price, but he cooled down quickly enough when I hotly suggested that he go and renegotiate with Mr Zulu himself.

[**Asterix-30 : Mr Zulu-120**]

The two-week Easter Holidays arrived. Digre and Lucky had plans to go camping in Hermanus for a few days with an acquaintance of ours in Standard 9. His name was Zonnies – a Dutch oke from Holland. I still had a good chunk of the seventy rand from the first office job hidden away from Digre, as well as five cartons of entjies from the Pinball Kafee job. Digre had taken the whole thirty rand Mr Zulu had given me for the watches as his share. He reckoned that if I had gotten a hundred and twenty like we had agreed, we could have split it evenly, which meant that I in fact, *seriously*, still owed him thirty rand from his missing sixty split!

I slung Denise a bullshit story about spending time with Digre at his parents' house, then packed my share of the pinball goeters into a rucksack with some warm clothing and my sleeping bag. I managed to hike through to Hermanus without any trouble and arrived in Piet se Bos late that night. After a miserable night on Grotto Beach, I gratefully bumped into Digre at the beach kafee the next morning. He was piss-pleased to see me and took me up to where he, Lucky, Zonnies and another oke named Thomas were all camping in the bushes. After enthusiastic greetings, I asked them what the plan for the day was going to be.

Zonnies looked at me slyly.

– Eksê Asterix, do you smoke boom? –

I glanced over at Digre but he just grinned mysteriously.

– Ja Zonnies, me and Digre tried it but it was a lot of kak. I prefer to suip brandy eksê –

– [Zonnies] Come my broer, let ME *make you a pipe, and then if you still*

*don't smaak it eksê, then kwaai, we'll score you some dop and go for a jol
on the beach –*

*– I'm kwaai with that, Zonnies, but I'm telling you now my broer, it
doesn't graft on me –*

Digre laughed his *Wah-ha-ha* laugh. I looked over at him, but he kept
it tight and mysterious.

Zonnies took out a fat roll of bundled newspaper. He opened it and I
saw a huge pile of light-green dagga. He told me that this was a poison skyf
– Cape Town Cietas – that grew on the slopes of Table Mountain. It was a
type of seedless skyf also known as sensimielia. He went through the
familiar motions of mixing it and *stopping* it into a bottleneck, and then
tossed a box of matches to Digre and told him to play fireman. Digre fired
and Zonnies bust the pipe. I immediately noticed a difference between the
way that he smoked and the way we'd tried to. He seemed to suck the smoke
straight into his lungs without pulling it into his mouth and then inhaling
like a smoker does with an entjie. He passed the pipe to me and told me
to pull it like him. I tried to but my grip wasn't quite right and I just sucked
air. Zonnies told me to try again. I did, only this time when I sucked, my
lungs instantly filled with thick harsh burning smoke. The sudden fire
in my throat caused an uncontrollable spasm in my chest and I started
choking as I vainly tried not to cough. Finally, after swallowing what
seemed like most of it, I managed to hack out the great white clouds that
were smothering me. Molten stinging tears poured into my misty eyes, and
somewhere outside I heard the crew whooping and laughing. I burped and
another huge cloud of smoke came out my gut. I blinked and gaped at
Zonnies – mildly asphyxiated.

*– [Zonnies] So I thought that you and Digre were old boom-roekers. What?
Were you talking kak to me eksê? Huh Asterix? Come on bra, you don't look
like you smoked any of that, it all went to waste. Take another hit eksê –*

Determined to show Zonnies how wrong he was, I forced my breathing
back to normal and hit the pipe again. This time I choked even worse. He
told me not to drag in so much air, but I had already had *more* than enough.
I passed the pipe to the left-hand side as instructed. The other okes all had
a hit and I saw to my shame that Digre took one without coughing.
Suddenly I noticed that there was something happening to my head in a
hurry. I was starting to feel an overpowering dizziness and my eyes were
kinda pulling funny and felt muzzy. I burped and more smoke came out.

I was still full of it! Zonnies announced that we were going to hit the beach for a jol. Something was definitely happening to me. It was nothing like feeling drunk – and much, much worse. And it was getting stronger. I stood up and burped again. More smoke. I stumbled down the path to the beach below us. I felt sick. Not just a little queasy, but full-blown-horrible-I-can't-stand-from-nausea sick. The other okes wanted to know what my problem was. I told them thickly that I felt pukey. They all laughed, and then Zonnies initiated a game of hide and seek among the rocks. I summoned every ounce of willpower and attempted to join in, but after about two minutes I just collapsed on the beach retching violently. After a while, Zonnies and Digre came over to me.

– *[Zonnies] Eksê Asterix, are you okay eksê? Do you feel kak my broer?* –

– *Ja Zonnies* –

– *Listen my broer, you gonna be okay eksê. You just had too much and it's making you feel kak-gerook. Los playing with us and sommer just park off here and chill out. We'll come check you out in a while. Are you kwaai with that eksê?* –

– *Ja Zonnies* –

I was not kwaai with it – I was not kwaai with anything eksê. I lay there for an hour of hell, utterly convinced that Zonnies didn't know what he was talking about and that I was about to die. People simply didn't feel that bad without dying. Eventually I recovered enough – more or less – to go staggering down the beach to a tap. I soaked my head for ages, washed my face and drank a whole lot of water. This I puked out into the bushes immediately. I drank some more and found I was starting to feel immensely better. My stomach had finally settled. The intense, raging-out-of-control, buzzing dizziness had settled down to a gentle comforting hum and my eyes felt all wonderfully dreamy. My head started to feel much clearer and wild startling thoughts went hurtling through my mind like beautiful fiery rainbow comets. I wanted to grab hold of these pure awesome revelations, but they slipped out of my reach and new ones instantly distracted me. I found my mind able to lock in and focus on the finest details of the amazingly bright world around me. I slowly lazed back down the beach in transfixed wonder. The whole beach leapt out at me, and I knew then that I could focus in on any micro-detail and magnify it a thousand times in a flash. Vague stunning realisations exploded out of this into myriads of glowing absolute truths and I knew then that if I collected these chains of thought and wove them together into a necklace I could hang it around Mother Nature's neck and solve all her problems. I had discovered the secrets to all the mysteries of the Universe!!

I was suddenly jolted out of my splendid reverie by Digre, who leapt off a rock somewhere above my head and landed next to me with a wild yell.

– *AASTERIIXX eksê!!! Howzit my broer! You look like you're enjoying your pluk at last. So bra, what do you skiem? It's lekker eksê, hey?* –

I nodded at him, very stoned and a little irritated that he had just chased away all the secrets to the Universe. I wanted to explain this, but somehow I could not fit mere clumsy words around the vanished revelation. I grinned and it ALL suddenly seemed very, very funny— *eksê*. I started giggling and Digre joined in. Just giggling was suddenly hysterically funny. Raging giggles boiled over inside me like shaken champagne and we both collapsed down onto the sand howling with laughter at absolutely fuckall in particular.

—*eksê*

I was lekker dikgerook.

We found Zonnies, who was happy to see me feeling better, and we all proceeded to attempt building the biggest sandcastle that we possibly could. It became so big that people from all over the beach strolled over to take a look. Later that afternoon we made another pipe and I was blasted out of my senses once again. I just lay there semi-comatose on my sleeping bag listening to the muted roaring applause of a vast audience in the wind-rustled Port Jackson bush all around our camp. The beach kafee proved sympathetic to our cause and swopped us packets of pinball entjies for little five-cent white-chocolate Lunch Bars. We needed these quite often, because as the zol started wearing off, the craving for sweet food became unbearable. This was happily called *the munchies.*

[Asterix-TKO : Dagga-1]

By the end of that week I was smoking pipes as hard as Zonnies and Thomas. The morning of my thirteenth birthday, Zonnies sat gazing at me with a bemused expression while I was smoking. Then he made a profound prophecy:

– *Asterix, I'm going to tune you something hectic and you might lag, but years from now you are going to check back and know it is true. Out of all of us you are going to turn into a regte ou-roeker* –

Zonnies didn't know how accurate his words would become. But I wasn't alone because we both became international zol smugglers as men.

However, back on my thirteenth birthday, I romantically imagined that I had joined the ranks of those who crossed over that invisible blue line called The Law and defied it by smoking dagga.

It made me feel like I belonged.

It made me feel like an equal.

It made me feel I was fighting – *at what?* – back at last.

It made me feel stuff that I thought of while I was gerook

… but I always seemed to forget.

It made me feel gerook.

I arrived back home in Paarl with a little less than five days left of my holiday. I started smoking entjies at home and Denise did nothing about it. She just warned me that she never wanted to see me smoking and the only place she would permit it in her house was in my bedroom with the door closed. She also warned me that if Wally ever caught me it would be on my own head.

The afternoon of the next day Wally came around. Denise was in town shopping. Yvonne and I were bickering over something in the kitchen when it got ugly and I slapped her. She screamed and Wally came roaring in.

Yvonne fled.

Wally seized me by my shirt, grabbed a carving knife and aimed an underhand blow at my midriff. I realised with horror from the sounds he was making that he intended killing me and I tore myself out of his grip by ripping the shirt right off my body. The knife missed me by a whisker and slammed into the cupboard where I had been pinned a fraction of a second before. The force of the blow pierced the wood so deeply that he could not extract the blade to try and stab me again.

I fled.

Glancing over my shoulder I saw that he had his hand on a huge solid two-pound glass ashtray. This he hurled at my head. I ducked and darted through the flying shards as it exploded against the wall. By now I knew I was in mortal danger. I tore out of the house, pissing my pants from fear, and headed up the driveway for the gate. He came sprinting out after me, jumped into his Citroën, started it and – engine howling – immediately fishtailed up behind me in a roar of gravel and dust to try and run me over. I managed to make it out of the gate, across the road, and dived straight over the fence into the roses. I didn't even feel the thorns. I picked myself up and ran dodging and moaning in dread – waiting for the shot. It was my luck that he didn't have his revolver with him that day.

Much, much later, I slipped back down to the house and Yvonne helped me run away to Cape Town. I went straight to Digre and stayed there for three days. I called Yvonne and she told me it was safe to come back. She was also sorry that she'd caused me so much trouble.

[**Asterix-1 : Yvonne-0**]

[**Asterix-0 : Wally-3**]

In the new term we drank brandy, played chess and broke into places. I took up rugby for fear of being a moffie. To my immense surprise I excelled at the game. I also managed to break the school record for getting cuts both at the school and from the hostel onnies. One amazing day I found I had started sprouting ball hairs and underarm fluff. I finally stopped shooting blanks and my voice abruptly broke.

I proudly began taking showers with all the other okies.

[**Asterix – Bushy : Voice –** *Falsetto*]

The year eventually drew to an end. I passed Standard 6 and Digre left the school. The reason completely escapes my mind right now.

5

Asterix and the Boere

The new school year started on cue, and with it came a bunch of new faces among both the boys and staff. The first of these was our new hostel father – *Dokter* Gerber. It transpired that he was both an educationalist and a clinical psychologist. Wally and Denise had decided that I needed to see a shrink. Surprise, nasty surprise, it was the dear *Dokter* Gerber. This meant traipsing off to his consulting rooms to suffer through everlasting fifty-minute Friday afternoon sessions. *Dokter* Gerber turned out to be a *spare-not-the-rod-to-figure-out-the-child* kind of guy. Our sessions started that very first week.

Yuck.

There were three new hostel residents in our Standard 7 class. The first was a boy named John Ripley, who was to become my new best friend and partner in crime. The other two were both Jewish – a boy called Harold and a six-foot giant named Andrew who was nicknamed Spotty. John and I were in the same dormitory. I was no longer a sot, so on the first day I joined everybody behind the smoking sheds to watch the new sotte going through doop. It was a lot more fun watching it from the other side of Standard 6.

Trouble reared its ugly head three days after the new term started. Rockspiders, like elephants, simply never forget. Bokkie van Wyk and Jannie le Roux were back, meaner and both in Standard 9. The first time I saw Le Roux, he sneeringly asked me where Digre was. I ignored him but realised instantly that I'd better tread very carefully because those two would be out to get me. They had not forgotten JP.

When the incident occurred it was a sheer mistake on my part. An accident. It happened outside behind the bicycle sheds in front of all the other smokers. I was standing peeling an orange with my fingers and had almost managed to tear the entire skin off in one big chunk. Anton, Lucky and John were with me, smoking and chatting. John didn't smoke though; he was just there for the company. I finally tore the peel loose and unthinkingly tossed it over my shoulder. I immediately heard a violent outraged voice:

– You fokken klein POES! *I'm gonna bliksem you dead! –*

I spun around to see Le Roux advancing towards me. The chunk of orange peel had hit him square in the face. My heart did an elevator drop to my knees and bounced back hard.

Oh shit! I didn't do it on purpose. I would never antagonise this idiot. Fuck him! Fuck him! He's not going to hit me. He's not...

What I did next was a reflex action that was utterly foreign to my experience. Instead of running away, which would have been the sensible thing to do, I stepped in and hit him three times as hard as I possibly could. Southpaw. Very fast. *Bam-bam-bam!* I never dreamt I possessed speed like that. Or power! Neither did he, I could see from the utter disbelieving shock in his watering eyes. Blood came gushing out of his nose and his lip started swelling up. I stood my ground, with my fists cocked, as if I was ready to go again. In my head and terrified heart I knew that not in a thousand years would I be able to release that explosion of cornered rage again, and if he had so chosen, he could have calmly pounded the stuffing out of me, blindfolded and with one hand. Instead he turned and walked away in silence, holding his face, trying to staunch the flow of blood and tears.

Some kinds of badly brought-up brats *love* seeing displays of cruelty being inflicted on anything other than themselves. The kids in my hostel were no different. Fights were events that were relished and treated like gladiatorial sport, with the merits of the bout being measured by the flow of blood and the physical size and ages of the combatants. The loser was generally thought to be the one bleeding the most. The other okes loved what I had done to Le Roux, especially the smaller okies who had fallen foul of him. Young Asterix immediately became something of legend. Anton and Lucky seemed quite proud to be my friends. A small Standard 7 had taken on a big Standard 9 and beaten him fair and square – without fighting *dirty*. I discovered something else about bullies. They enjoy hurting others but cannot take the same punishment themselves. Van Wyk slunk away behind Le Roux and they never confronted me again.

[Asterix-2 : Rockspiders-0]

Athletics and swimming were on our sports card, so we started practising furiously for the upcoming competitions. The annual swimming gala was quite a to-do and the event traditionally ended with a heavily chaperoned disco-dance.

I needed a date and was secretly keen on one of the chicks who hung out in our break-time smoking group named Vanessa, but she was really pretty and unapproachably in Standard 8. I was terribly self-conscious about my teeth and thumbsucking, but in a fit of bravery, boosted by my victory over Le Roux, I hesitantly asked her to accompany me. To my utter amazement she agreed. When the day dawned I was more worried about that evening's festivities than I was about the competition. I had nothing to worry about though. I came second in the backstroke, and after the disco Vanessa kind of led me to the bushes in her hostel driveway and initiated me into the art of kissing. The bushes were stiff with other couples all doing the same thing, but I felt unique and Master of my Universe. It was the most incredible thing to feel the soft warmth of a pretty girl with her arms around me and the taste of her tongue dancing sweetly with mine for the very first time.

Even though she was a mite taller than me.

I had a girlfriend! I had a girlfriend! La lala la-la!

[**Asterix-TL : Vanessa-XXX**]

John, once he had finished laughing at me, was about the most intelligent guy I had ever met. Until Ness came into the picture, we were virtually joined at the hip. His hobby was electronics and he avidly taught me everything he knew. I was soon able to differentiate between capacitors, resistors, transistors and diodes, and was learning how to read circuit diagrams. I told him that I had done a lot of break-in jobs with Digre but that I hadn't done any new ones. John had a naughty streak a mile wide and liked the idea. We didn't actually plan anything but we did talk and fantasise about taking down really big scores. I began to realise that my friendship with Digre had been very unbalanced, but with John it was different – we were equals.

One fine day we vandalised some tiekieboxes because we wanted the microphones from the telephone receivers to make an intercom. After we had done the deed, we discussed stealing a *whole* tiekiebox for the coins inside, as well as the electronic components. We managed to damage a couple quite badly without any luck, but finally one day we worked out how to do it using a series of different tools. The phone unit we put into a suitably sized suitcase for covert transport. We took it down to the river and smashed it open. There was about fifteen rand inside. We also recovered the damaged internal electronics, but there wasn't much that we could salvage for our own use.

[**Asterix-1½ : Telkom-0**]

John invited me to come and spend a weekend at his parents' pozzie, where I met his two other closest chommies. The one was an okie called Jacquie and the other a complete nutter named Paul. Jacquie was a child genius with insanely strict parents. For some reason Paul utterly hated the old woman who was his next-door neighbour, and between the two ouens they had fashioned an FM transmitter that would break into normal radio reception for about fifty metres around Paul's house. They demonstrated it to me by setting it to the same frequency as Radio Good Hope and cutting into live transmission, making barnyard animal noises and swearing as vilely as they knew how. From the radio in Paul's room I could hear that it really worked! The old lady evidently kept on phoning the SABC to complain bitterly. Paul also fed weedkiller to her prize roses and laxatives to her yappy little lapdog. It was nuts but it was a feud he took great delight in.

That weekend I decided it was time for John to pull a job. He sort of agreed in principle. The next day we were walking around a shopping arcade when we happened upon an electronics shop. We both stood with our noses glued to the window – fantasising about what we would buy if we had the money. At the top of our list were two awesome two-way radios on display. As we stood there, an idea started creeping into my head.

– *John, why don't we pull a job on this place?* –

– *This place? Cantrell's? How are we going to do that?* –

– *I dunno eksê, I was thinking of a smash 'n grab* –

– *A smash 'n what?* –

– *A smash 'n grab, like the real villains in the British Underworld do for jools* –

– *Asterix, you're fucking mental and you read too many crazy books. Can't you see that this spot has a burglar alarm? Look at that silver strip in the window* –

– *Ja, I can see that, ou, but think seriously now. How long do you skiem it will take for the boere to get here?* –

– *What's that got to do with it?* –

– *Look, there aren't people's houses and stuff around here. If we come and go on bicycles we could be in and out of here in a minute,* LONG *before the boere pitch up. And we'll work out an escape route so they'd only be able to catch us if they were on motorbikes –*

– *I dunno eksê. What if something goes wrong?* –

– *Nothing can go wrong, bra. We'll just plan it very, very carefully. We'll wear socks on our hands and balaclavas on our heads and this afternoon we can ride around and work out the perfect escape route. Relax bra, I've done this before* –

– *You've done a smash 'n grab before?* –

– *Not a smash 'n grab exactly, but remember I was the oke who did a job on the Pinball Kafee* –

– *I dunno – do you really think it could work?* –

– *Yes bra, trust me* –

John was very skittish about the whole gedagte, but the more I worked on him, the more he grew into the plan. I had another surprise up my sleeve. I wanted him to be the one to toss the brick. I sensed that he had a bit of a yellow streak and I wanted to toughen him up a bit. That afternoon we worked out a perfect escape route, which the boere would never be able to follow in their yellow vans. We would have about twenty seconds of danger crossing the main road, but then we would be on a footpath and clear. John had his own bicycle and I was going to use Paul's Chopper. Jacquie was going to help us by listening to the boere on radios he had in his room.

That night we dressed in dark clothes, with balaclavas rolled up into beanies on our heads, and stuffed spare socks in our pockets. I took along a rucksack for the goeters and a half-brick from John's backyard. Then we rode down to Jacquie's house to wake him up. John was still as nervous as a cat at a door-slamming contest but I told him to relax, breathe, take it easy, and we rode around the arcade and surrounding streets a few times.

All was clear and dead quiet.

We pedalled up to the shop and carefully stood our bikes against the pavement for an instant getaway. I passed John the brick.

Truth or Dare, John?

He took a deep breath, drew his arm back like an American football player and, as he was about to throw— chickened out like a balloon deflating. He turned to me, very sheepish at my obvious irritation, and told me he just couldn't do it. He was too scared.

I took the brick from him, snorted in derision, and hurled it straight into the the glass. The window exploded like a giant fracturing bomb and the alarm started clanging furiously. John recoiled as if somebody had shot him, jumped onto his bike and took off like a bat out of hell. I ran crunching through the glass to the burglar bars, ignoring the insanely loud ringing, grabbed the two walkie-talkies, fished them through the bars and took off after him. He was riding so hard that it took me some time to catch up. I managed to cut in front and stopped. He stared at me, twitching, trembling – out of it. Eventually I convinced him that we had gotten away scot-free. Then he asked hesitantly if I had taken anything. I showed him the contents of the rucksack, and as he looked up I saw the fear leave his eyes and greed creep in. I nipped that right in the bud and pulled an anti-Digre right there and then. I informed him that I had done everything and that he had merely been a part-time spectator. If he wanted goeters, he would have to participate next time. The walkie-talkies were mine! We rode back to Jacquie's house, dropped the rucksack there for safekeeping and went back to John's spot to sleep.

[**Asterix-1 : Cantrell's Electronics-0**]

Back at school John and I had some real fun with the walkie-talkies. We called each other from everywhere and chatted all the time. I even gave one to Vanessa for the day once. I still wanted John to get his feet wet on a job though. We were bunking church as usual some Sunday a short while later when we happened to stroll past Quenet's Arcade. Charlotte Quenet was in our class and her dad owned the pharmacy that ran the length of the arcade. There were padlocked glass display cases along the passage, with various sporting goods and toys in them. In the box nearest the entrance was a giant Scalectrix set we wanted. At the back of the arcade was a public toilet we could use as an escape route. That night we returned at about 01h30. It looked to be a straightforward job. I left John in the arcade to work on the display case and moved off to a good vantage point with the other walkie-talkie so I could keep a lookout for the boere.

It was his turn to do the dirty work.

After a long time – too long – I heard the sound of breaking glass. I radioed John immediately to find out what had gone wrong. He said he'd bent the wooden frame of the cabinet's flap too much and the glass had shattered. I told him to pack the Scalectrix and get the fuck out of there. Now!

He did so.

A few minutes later I reached our rendezvous point. John was already there, white-faced and rummaging around in the rucksack. He looked up, started swearing and told me he had dropped one of the cars at the display case. He swore that he was gonna go back to fetch it, then put his balaclava and socks back on and left.

It was very dangerous.

I had a set rule that I never went back. A few minutes later John returned, all wild-eyed and panting. I asked him why he had taken so long. Some old toppie was there when he arrived and grabbed him! John skrikked and punched the toppie in the guts. When the geezer let him go, he bent down, grabbed the car and ran. We stared at each other, mortified. It was supposed to be simple. This wasn't supposed to have happened!

– *[Me, worried] Did he see your face eksê?* –

– *No* –

– *Did you look at him?* –

– *No, he grabbed me and I punched him. I didn't even think* –

[Long terrible silence]

– *[Me] Alright my broer ... I skiem we're okay. The boere will probably skiem it was a coloured laatie eksê* –

– *I fucking hope so* –

– *Don't worry, we'll hide this move away until it all cools down and then we can jol with it. And my broer, you are now officially my full partner. You've shown that you've got as much pluk as I have, so now we're even with everything* –

We hid the car set, balaclavas, tools and socks away very carefully. We would fetch them the following afternoon. The boere might already be patrolling around for suspects because of the old toppie! We kept the radios with us and quickly got back to the hostel.

I slept soundly but poor old John didn't.

[**Asterix-Formula 1 : Quenet's-0**]

We hid the Scalectrix in a safe place in the hostel and took it easy for a while. All we did were a couple of tiekiebox jobs for movie money and smokes for me. Then one day we decided to steal the hi-fi system from the school music centre. Jacquie had a similar one that he would swop us for – to make it cold. We did the job and John went through to Cape Town to make the swop. Along with the other hi-fi, he brought back a fat transformer that we made into a killer power supply for the Scalectrix, which we now decided was cold enough to start playing with. We told everybody that John's granny had died and left him the hi-fi and some money.

[**Asterix-1 : Worcester High School-0**]

Getting in and out of the dormitory at night to commit our nefarious deeds had pretty much become a simple routine. We had a long thick rope we'd knotted at intervals. We'd take it out of its hiding place, tie it to John's bed, and abseil down. The two of us became masters at doing it, although there was one small problem. On the wall below our window were dirty footprints. *Dokter* Gerber saw them and freaked out. There was no proof that either John or I had made the marks, so he couldn't flap us for it. He told us repeatedly to clean them, but we simply ignored him.

We didn't know how they had gotten there – why should we be held responsible? Sir. He ordered us again. We still ignored him.

One Friday afternoon John and I were standing down at the school gate organising something with a new bra named Dorrian. We all looked up to see *Dokter* Gerber bearing down on us with a cane. His eyes were steamed up behind his small rimless spectacles and his nose was flared out and white. He didn't say a word – he just started laying into John and me with the cane. We fled towards the hostel, but he managed to grab me and continued hitting me wildly. He yelled at John to come back, pointing at the now dark footpath on the wall and screaming and swearing incoherently in Afrikaans. He dragged me to his office, still thrashing me all over, locked me inside and disappeared. My back, shoulders, legs and arse – everything burnt like fire from the caning. Five minutes later he dragged a crying and struggling John in.

Same treatment.

He informed us heavily that – by God! – he was not a man to be trifled with. We were GOING to clean up the marks on the wall. And on top of it, he was gating us for the entire weekend, starting right then and there. He marched us upstairs to the study hall and locked us inside. When we'd both recovered a bit we took off our shirts. We were covered with stripes. John counted about twenty on me and I counted about the same on him.

– *John, this ou isn't allowed to flap us like this eksê* –

– *Asterix, he just did, in case you hadn't quite noticed* –

– *No, I mean he's not allowed to by law. I heard somewhere that onnies are only allowed to give you six flaps in one day* –

– *So what are you going to do?* –

– *Fuck him bra, he's supposed to be a shrink and everything. He can't just go mal like this. He's supposed to fix crazy mense, not go completely befuck himself. I'm going to the School Board* –

– *How are you going to do that, Asterix? He's locked us in, bra* –

– *John, somebody invented drainpipes for a good reason eksê* –

We managed to crawl down a drainpipe and hightailed it to the School Board. There, a lady behind the front desk asked us our business. We told her that we wanted to lodge a complaint about a teacher beating us. She looked at us sceptically and called someone on her intercom. A tall thin man with old chorb scars on his face ambled into the room, looking bored.

– *Yes boys, how can I help you?* –

– *[Me, rehearsed] Good afternoon sir, we want to lodge a complaint against Dokter Gerber at Worcester High School for illegal corporal punishment* –

– *Illegal corporal punishment? [Looking slightly amused] Why did Dr Gerber give you punishment?* –

– *[John] Marks on the wall, sir* –

– *[Me to John] They don't understand, bra. Just take off your shirt and turn around eksê* –

We removed our shirts and turned around. The immediate hiss of shock from both of them indicated the message had definitely got home. Suddenly they weren't bored any more and wanted to know when, where ... *all business.* We told them, smugly pulling on and tucking our shirts back in. The lady kept on interrupting with mutters of sympathy – *foeitog, foeitog* ... It was definitely Dr Gerber? Yes, definitely *Dokter* Gerber. Somehow I knew, whatever *we* had done wrong was *not* the issue any longer. The man led us out to his car, drove us back grimly and disappeared into *Dokter* Gerber's study. We ran upstairs and watched from the dorm. Soon he and a very subdued *Dokter* Gerber came out, got into the car and drove off. We didn't see him for the rest of the weekend, and on Monday there was a hurried announcement that *Dokter* Gerber was no longer our hostel father and Mr Brand (one of the hostel onnies) would be taking over until the end of the year. I popped into the Art building on the way to Vanessa the following week, and lo and behold his offices were also empty. It seems that the good *Dokter* was no longer allowed to look after kids or practise shrinking their poor pips any longer.

Lekker.

[**Asterix**–2 : un *Dokter* Gerber-0]

John and I were moderately wealthy. We had protection money, which I beat out of Spotty, and of course all the kosher tuck his mom sent him. He had turned out to be a big empty bully. We also had a beautiful Kenwood hi-fi, a giant Scalectrix and two walkie-talkies. I decided however that we needed more. *Much more.* I also decided that we needed to expand our crew. Anton was willing to join in on jobs, as were Lucky and Dorrian. They had seen me get away with it since Digre's time and now they wanted a piece of the action. Dorrian was a new ou in Standard 8 from Goodwood in Cape Town, but he fit in with the crew perfectly. He was a belt fighter. Any hassles from Rockspiders or whoever and he would whip off his thick leather belt and whale the offender with the huge buckle end.

We decided to take down a shop at the end of Quenet's Arcade called Blazer's Office Equipment. We would use the same escape route out the back of the public toilet, with one small difference – this time we would make sure we had our own key and lock the door behind us so that if the boere or the old man from the Scalectrix job came I could have my crew out of there before they even reached the entrance to the pharmacy.

I briefed them:

Me: Boss and coordinator – across the road on top of building for a
  wide view of boere/interference, in radio communication with John
John: Leader of crew at Blazer's front door in communication with me
Anton: Break glass above lock on door with steel pole
Lucky: Carry four laundry bags for goeters
Dorrian: Responsible for key to public toilets (tied to wrist)
Everybody: Dark clothes, socks and balaclavas
Everybody: Be fucking cool

We did the job on a Sunday night and it went like clockwork. The previous afternoon we'd visited Blazer's surreptitiously and tested the spare key I'd sent Dorrian to buy. Next, we took a good long look at the interior of the shop. I broke the floor up into imaginary sectors and assigned each crewmember a portion, to cut down on the time spent inside grabbing goeters. We opened the back window of the toilet, hid an iron bar outside in the alley and locked the door from the inside. The following night we penetrated the arcade from the quiet back alley, climbed into the toilet and unlocked the door. My crew gave me five minutes to position myself on top of a three-storey building across the road, and on my radio command they each did their job. From my vantage point I could see everything for three blocks. Not a car or soul to be seen.

We got four laundry bags of goeters. Like I said – it went like clockwork.

Back at the hostel we decided to hide the loot, but this was difficult as there was so much of it. Eventually we stashed the whole lot in trunks and suitcases in the hostel storeroom. We had slukked pens, tapes, calculators, tape decks and an assortment of other electronic gizmos – all very new and very expensive technology. I told the crew to sit tight, let it all cool off and then we would make the split or fence it.

Mr Zulu maybe? Only this time I will do it better. I won't let him rip me off again.

[Asterix-1 : Blazer's-0]

John and I went back to our normal routine, piss-pleased with ourselves. We broke our own rules though, and sold one or two calculators to okies in matric. I needed money because I had become responsible for my crew's needs.

It was a mistake.

In 1977 a simple digital calculator was cutting-edge technology. Kids at school didn't have them. John actually owned one (which wasn't stolen) but that was purely an exception. I also forgot that I had enemies (Le Roux *et al.*). Enemies who hated me, watched me and wondered why I always had masses of money. Why did I have a crew of ouens who answered to me as their leader when I was the smallest and youngest of them? What was Asterix up to?

Somehow, *somebody* found out …

The following Friday afternoon I was sitting restlessly in study when the okie on telephone duty informed the study onnie that I had a visitor.

A *visitor?*

Who on earth could be visiting me?

Definitely not Wally or Denise. Wally and Swallow had moved to a place called Krugersdorp up near Johannesburg somewhere. Denise wouldn't visit me unless it was a life or death issue, and then she would simply have phoned or only come after study.

Who on earth is visiting me?

I was still racking my brain frantically when I got to the *voorportaal*. A tall, freckle-faced stranger with a bushy ginger moustache stood waiting for me. Huh? He smiled with everything except his eyes and spoke:

– *[Afrikaans accent] Good afternoon, I'm Sergeant Labuschagne from the CID and you are Alexander Goulding, am I correct?* –

My heart exploded in my chest. I felt the blood gush down through my insides and run into my feet. Pins and needles suddenly attacked me all over and I felt myself wanting to turn into jelly. Painfully I held on for dear life, letting none of it show in my face (I hoped) and answered:

– *[Sweetly] Good afternoon Sergeant. Yes, my name is Alex Goulding. What can I do for you, sir?* –

– *Alex ...? You don't mind if I call you Alex do you? [No] ... Alex, I am investigating some thefts and I wonder if you could help me?* –

– *[Fuck, fuck ohfuck] No, Sergeant, I don't mind at all. What is it that you want help with?* –

– *Oh, nothing serious, I just want to ask you some questions. Firstly, I see you have a walkie-talkie [slung over my shoulder], do you mind if I have a look at it?* –

– *No Sergeant, help yourself* –

– *Very nice, Alex. National Panasonic. Do you mind telling me where you got it?* –

– *I bought it from a guy in a classified advert in the Argus* –

– *Mmmm ... Do you remember the man's name?* –

– *No I don't remember unfortunately and I lost his phone number too* –

– *You lost his phone number ...? How would you know that you lost it if you haven't been asked to look for it?* –

– *[Huh?! Fuck, this guy's clever] ... I dunno ... I think I looked for it but I couldn't find it* –

– *Mmmm ... Actually I want to ask you about something else. Do you know a shop called ... [flipping through a small spiral notepad] ... ah yes, called Blazer's Office Equipment?* –

– *It's that shop in Quenet's Arcade, isn't it?* –

– *Yes, that's the one. Well, it was broken into and a lot of stuff was stolen. I'm not saying that you broke into it but maybe you know something that you can tell me to help me find out who did. You don't mind helping me, do you Alex? –*

– *No, Sergeant , I don't know who broke in there –*

– *Well that's a pity, Alex. Do you mind if we take a look up in your room? –*

– *No, Sergeant [You stupid ape, I don't have anything up there], but I'm not sure you will find whatever it is you are looking for –*

– *Well, Alex, it's just routine. [Yes and I'm the King of Siam] Just a boring part of my job –*

– *Follow me, Sergeant –*

I led him up to my dormitory with my heart still sloshing around in my guts. Damn! How on earth had *They* found out? He searched my bed and locker and found nothing. Thank goodness he didn't ask to see my trunk and suitcase in the storeroom. We returned downstairs and he consulted his notebook once more:

– *Okay Alex, I am satisfied for now. There is just one more thing. I need to speak to a certain boy named John Ripley –*

– *No problem, Sergeant, I know who he is – I'll call him for you –*

– *No Alex, you don't understand, I want you to wait here while the boy on telephone duty goes to call him. You do understand don't you? –*

– *Yes, Sergeant [no Sergeant, three bags full Sergeant, aaaaaahfuck!!] –*

John arrived and went through much the same shockingly amiable conversation. I heard it all through the door of the visitors' waiting room. John admitted nothing. They disappeared upstairs and returned some time later. Sergeant Labuschagne called me out into the hall. I avoided looking at John and saw that the Sergeant had a tape deck and two Parker pens in his hands. *Oh shit no!!* He spoke:

– *Well, boys, I am nearly finished. John had these goods in his locker and although he says they come from home, you boys understand that I must check them out. It's my job. So what I am going to do is take them to the office and later I will return them. Then we will be finished. So you can go back to study now and I will see you later. Okay? –*

– *Okay, Sergeant, we'll see you later –*

He disappeared into a red car parked outside and took off. We immediately ran upstairs and I turned on John spitting with rage:

– *What the fuck were you doing with all that stuff in your locker you dumb cunt. You've just got us bust. That fucking pig is going to be back just now to lock us up!! –*

– I'm sorry Asterix, how was I supposed to know? –

– We agreed, you stupid dumb fuck, that we would leave every fucking thing hidden away until it fucking cooled down eksê –

– I'm sorry my broer. I didn't think that this would happen. And please don't swear at me like that –

– I'll do more than swear at you, you Stupid Fucking Poes!! I feel like fucking you up eksê –

– Asterix, let's stop fighting. What are we going to do? –

– Well, there's only one thing we can do. We must run away. I'm not going to jail –

[Thinking fast]

– Where are we going to run to? –

– We'll hike to Cape Town now and go to Dorrian's house tonight, then tomorrow morning we can start hiking through to Durban. We'll take as much goeters as we can with us to sell on the way and then we can find jobs in Durban later on. Okay go! Start packing eksê –

By the time the bell rang for the end of study, John and I were packed and ready to go. We waited for Dorrian and them to come up to the dormitory and got detailed directions to his pozzie. I also left instructions with Anton and Lucky to move all the rest of the goeters to a safer place later that night. The three of them were understandably rattled silly, but we assured them that the boere somehow (Le Roux?) only knew about John and me. We wished Anton and Lucky farewell and told them to make good use of the rest of the stuff and not get caught.

John and I left.

We decided that the boere would probably drive along the main road out of town to look for us once they discovered we had disappeared. Instead we would cut straight through the veld to the railway line and follow it to the N1 some five kilometres out of town. We didn't think they would look that far. Two and a half hours later we found ourselves hiking next to the N1. At the distant sight of any red cars we instantly dived into the bushes. We weren't taking chances! We concocted a story about camping with friends that weekend. My alias was Roger Matthews and John would be Paul Bradford. I also had a razor-sharp six-inch bush knife concealed on my person in case we were picked up by homos or something.

I felt exhilarated in a way. I was scared of boere in the oncoming cars but other than that we were free! We were free as the birdies and we didn't have to worry about homework and teachers and all that shit any more. Okay, I would miss Vanessa like crazy, but I could find another girlfriend. No more Wally. No more crazy Denise.

Asterix was free!

[**Asterix-1 : Boere-0**]

A non-red cabbie eventually stopped. We ran up, thanked the man and told him where we were going. He turned out to be a nice jovial fellow who easily bought our story and took us all the way to the Goodwood off-ramp in Cape Town. We eventually found Dorrian's rather dingy house and knocked on the front door. A tired and battered-looking lady who I took to be Dorrian's mother opened it. She took one look at us and began yelling hoarsely:

– *Youse two. YOUSE TWO!! You little naaiers. Fuck off from my house! Fuuuuck ooorff!! I've had the Welfare, the School, the Po-lies, and every other fucking Ou around here because of youse …* –

John and I fled.

The rasping fishwifey curses of Dorrian's mother (*mother?!*) rang down the road behind our pounding hearts and footfalls. What the fuck had gone wrong? And what a *siff* woman! We glanced at each other in breathless panic. What were we going to do next? Neither of us knew Goodwood at all. We were, for all intents and purposes— lost. I stopped running and stood gasping desperately for air. After getting my wind back I decided that we needed some semblance of practicality in our situation and that meant a place to sleep for the night. We trudged onward, thirsty, hungry and bone-weary, down the numerous nameless streets until we came across the deserted backyard of a service station. The gate was locked, so we jumped over it and took a look around. A stack of flattened cardboard boxes lay in an alleyway behind some filthy toilets. We took these and fashioned them into a kind of platform to lie on. Then we unpacked our sleeping bags on top and crawled into them. We lay sleepless and frightened, discussing our scary future. After splabbing for a long while, we convinced ourselves that we would be okay once we reached Durban. In our bags we had a couple of tape decks, calculators and expensive pens that we could sell off piece by piece. We just needed to get through the night and we would be fine.

Then it started raining.

We decided to call it quits and start hiking immediately. We could sleep in the cabbie that gave us a lift. So, with creaking bones and aching muscles, we jumped back over the gate and started walking towards where we thought the freeway might be.

Some time later we found ourselves nearing a high-rise hotel that very distinctly marked Goodwood's skyline. We knew the freeway lay behind it. It was still raining, and as we tramped along the block we saw two men run out of the hotel bar ahead of us and jump into a car. By the time we reached the vehicle they had started it and were about to pull away. Then one guy wound down his window and called us over as if to ask directions:

– *Hello boys, come here quickly ... Listen we are police officers ... [flashing an SAP badge] Tell me what are your names?* –

– *[Me, slightly shocked] I'm Roger Matthews and this is Paul Bradford* –

He turned, muttered something to the other oke in the (*red!*) car and pointed at me:

– *You with the black hair, open your mouth and show me your teeth* –

I knew the game was up, but I tried my luck anyway. I pulled down my bottom lip with a frown on my face but he told me that he wanted to see my top teeth. I tried looking confused, as if I didn't understand him, and at that point he yelled to his partner that we were their suspects! They both leapt out of the car to grab us. We were way too tired to run and just stood there meekly. The one who grabbed me pushed my top lip up roughly and confirmed that I had a huge piece of metal in my mouth. They looked at one another in utter disbelief and handcuffed us together. One of them put us in the back of the car and the other tossed our rucksacks into the boot.

They climbed in and took off.

It was either just plain dumb luck or Divine Intervention that we had been nabbed. Thirty seconds either way and we would have missed each other. Four people in the middle of a huge rainy city in the dead of night and our paths crossed at *exactly* the wrong moment.

We told them we were hungry, so they bought us a half-loaf of sliced white bread, a packet of viennas and two tins of Coke. We drove back over the mountain to Worcester, stopping once at the Du Toit's Kloof Pass Hotel so that our ecstatic arresting officers could have another quick Klippies and Coke to celebrate.

By the time we arrived back in Worcester it was already the early hours of the morning. Our two boere were still very much in high spirits (literally) as they frog-marched us into the charge office. They removed the handcuffs, searched us and paled when they saw my anti-homo knife. They hadn't bothered to body-search us before bundling us into the car. My wrist was sore from the cuff. So was John's. They also found my entjies and confiscated them. I begged for one but they laughed nastily and informed me that no smoking was allowed. Then they searched our bags and asked us where each of the items had come from. We answered truthfully. The only item that wasn't stolen was the calculator that really belonged to John. When he told them it was his own property they got ugly and one of them slapped him hard. I interrupted to confirm that it really was his and they told me to shut the fuck up. We either told the truth or they would donner us. They were drunk and getting mean, so John prudently apologised and *admitted* that we had stolen it. They nodded their heads knowingly and made some more dire threats about what would happen if we didn't give our *volle samewerking*. Eventually they finished laboriously writing down a list of all our belongings except for our sleeping bags, which they handed back to us to take to the cells. They finished off by making us sign some papers. Then, without further ado, they marched us off and locked us in cell 3C.

The cell was quite big but bare except for an open toilet and a washbasin in one corner. There was a stack of canvas-covered foam mattresses in the other corner and we took two each to sleep on. There were no pillows but there were some *miff* grey blankets. I took one, rolled it up and placed it under my sleeping bag as an uncomfortably hard pillow. Better than nothing. Right, we were ready for bed! But first we needed to inspect our surroundings. Besides the toilet, which had no seat and flushed via a button in the wall, there was a cage of bars around the outside cell door with its own gate and lock. We suspected that this was so that we couldn't overpower the boere when they opened up. Yeah, right. A narrow concrete ledge served as a bench along one wall. Apart from this there were simply the four walls and these were covered with graffiti.

We set about reading it all.

Most of it was just names, dates and crimes all gouged out in Afrikaans or pidgin English, but there were also badly etched pictures of crude penises dripping with semen and ugly drawings of hairy vaginas with base comments about *poes, piel* and *holnaai* and dark sexual desires. There were messages scribbled by previous occupants about the depraved and filthy nature of the boere and many terrible curses that the writers happily heaped upon them all. Someone had written that he had broken his mother's heart to please his friends. Many had engraved undying love for a girl/wife/mistress. There were pictures of crosses and numerals with hangman's nooses, hands, dollar signs and sunrises. The numbers 26, 27 and 28 appeared a lot. Many other writers cried out to God for mercy and some wrote little sermons in bad Afrikaans about Jesus. We found an open space and used a belt buckle to scratch:

ASTERIX AND JOHN WERE HERE – JUNE 1977.

[Asterix-0 : Boere-3C]

We went to bed and actually slept quite well, considering they left the light on the whole night.

The following morning we were woken up by a coloured constable and two white officers. The one with the most gold stuff on his shoulders was a Captain, and it turned out he was also the father of a kid in our class named Bradley McKenzie. Captain McKenzie asked how we had slept and if we were alright health-wise. We answered in the affirmative. He informed us that we were to be collected by members of the CID later that day for questioning. He also suggested that it would be in our own best interests to aid them in their investigation by getting everything off our chests and telling the whole truth once and for all.

A short while later the coloured constable came back with two sticky egg sandwiches and a couple of polystyrene cups of lukewarm coffee. He told us it came from the Pinball Kafee. I begged him for an entjie and at first he said no, but then relented and gave me two loose ones and a box of matches, with a dire warning that we had to be very careful not to let the Sergeant see that we had cigarettes or else he would be in deep, deep trouble. I thanked him profusely and hid them away. Thank goodness John didn't smoke.

We sat around splabbing for a while and then we heard the keys outside again. The detectives had come to fetch us. One of them was Sergeant Labuschagne. They handcuffed us together again, led us to the red car and drove us to their offices about a block away. There they took the cuffs off and then photographed and fingerprinted us. Sergeant Labuschagne took us through to his office. I took the initiative and apologised to him for lying the previous day. He looked mildly surprised and said he would be happy to hear the truth, *if* that was what we wished to tell him. I told him that it would be better for me to start because John had not been involved in all the things that I had.

That got his attention.

I began with the very first office job and then listed them as far as I could remember. At some point he stopped me and went to a filing cabinet. He removed a big pile of files and told me just to say yes or no. He then listed the address and date of each housebreak and/or theft and I simply nodded or shook my head. When it came to the Pinball Kafee Job, he laughed, and got up to call his colleagues in the other offices. Apparently it was a famous unsolved case. As they crowded into his office, he proudly pointed me out to them as his suspect. They looked a little disbelieving until I told them about my mistake (leaving the iron bar in the shop). They all shook their heads in utter amazement and made joking comments about a small one-man crime wave. Eventually Sergeant Labuschagne was satisfied. The big pile of files had been whittled right down. He had removed twenty-six dockets in total – including Blazer's. He went through these with John and separated six. At this point he phoned his Major to discuss what cases we should be charged with. After a long discussion he put the phone down. The big pile of twenty cases that I told him I had done on my own he took and dumped in his wastepaper basket. Those were all officially closed from that point forth – including the Pinball Kafee job. They weren't even going to bother with the Cantrell job – he would just make a phone call to close the case. The other six he was going to charge us both for. He asked me what I had done with all the goeters. I told him about Mr Zulu, swopping the hi-fi with Jacquie (stressing that he didn't know that it was stolen) and explained where we had hidden the stuff in the hostel (stressing harder that if it wasn't there any longer it was because other okes had stolen it all). He then told us that when we appeared in court it would be pointless to plead not guilty because he could prove that we had been involved in at least one of them. We assured him that we would plead guilty. We weren't going to lie any more. With that he thanked us, filled out two statements (which we signed), and we were taken back to our cell.

[**Asterix-6 : Boere-20**]

We sat, reread the graffiti, used the toilet uncomfortably (studiously *not* watching each other and trying hard *not* to make embarrassing noises) and waited. The coloured constable came to feed us again. His name was Konstabel April. This time he had brought us barely warm curry and rice with the same insipid plastic coffee.

We waited. I smoked one of the entjies. We dozed.

Suddenly the keys were jangling outside again and this time we had visitors. John's parents. John went over to the cage and spoke softly with them. His mom and dad kept on giving me evil looks. *I had dragged their baby into this mess.* His mother had brought a Bible and some tasty food. Eventually they left.

We waited.

The outside world seemed to announce its proximity and presence with the fickle sound of unseen keys. It had a Pavlovian effect on us. Tinkle, jangle, clink and we would jump up expectantly.

Knock-Lock – Who's at the door?

Now it was my turn. Denise. She was shocked, dismayed and angry. John got the same dirty-look treatment from her.

Wally was on his way. He was flying down from Johannesburg. Apparently he had to borrow money from That Bitch and he was not at all Bloody Happy about it. How could I have done this to them? They didn't have any money. Don't think that I would get any sympathy. I had brought this all on myself.

She had brought some biscuits, my little portable radio (*that I wasn't allowed to keep at school with me because it might get scaled*) and some playing cards. Eventually she left – still majorly pissed off.

Silence reigned once again.

We greedily ate some of John's mum's food. Roast chicken with ham, cheese and tomato sandwiches. Munch, munch – lovely lunch. I smoked the other entjie. The cell darkened. We heard the keys and it was Konstabel April with coldish pies and tepid pinball coffee for supper. He gave us two more entjies and a box of matches, warning us about the Sergeant once more.

Some time later the keys rattled again. This time it was the Sergeant. He asked how we were doing, gave us several more cigarettes and warned us not to let the Lieutenant find out or else he would be in deep trouble.

We played cards and listened to the radio. Around 21h30 we heard the familiar tinkle outside yet again.

This time it was the Lieutenant. He asked us if we had spoken to our parents, if were we okay and – true as fuck – gave us a *packet* of smokes, warning us not to let the Captain find out or else – yes, you guessed it – he would be in deep, deep shit!

There endeth the first day.

We had a radio, playing cards, loads of entjies, lekker food, a Bible, the lights on and silence.

We slept slightly better that night, but obviously neither of us could have a wank.

The next morning Captain McKenzie was back. He had told his wife that two of Bradley's classmates were in his cells, whereupon she insisted on sending us three meals a day. Konstabel April was dispatched to the McKenzies' house to collect them. He grumbled that his own wife didn't even cook meals like that for him. I'll bet she didn't. Mrs McKenzie went to town. The main course was always accompanied by an assortment of cakes, biscuits or pudding. A veritable feast. We gave a bit to Konstabel April. She also sent a Bible with a note of encouragement.

That afternoon a couple of our other friends – not crewmembers – came to visit us, as did Vanessa. She cried a bit, told me she loved me, and I never saw her again. Our bras brought entjies (which Konstabel April let us keep), biltong and another Bible.

By the end of the second day we had chow, entjies for Africa and two more Bibles.

Monday morning dawned.

After breakfast we were taken to the court building and locked in cells directly beneath the courts. In the cells around us were a bunch of very noisy hotnots and kaffirs all yelling and carrying on. The boere on duty kept telling them to *Shut Up* but they wouldn't listen. We were eventually taken up some stairs into a box and told to stand there. A lot of white people wearing black robes were in the court. The judge came in and everybody stood up and sat down again. The judge sat down facing us. One of the men in black robes stood up and said some things to the judge. He called the judge *Your Worship*. The judge then told us that we were going back to the cell for eight days. He didn't bang a hammer or anything like in the movies and we were promptly taken back to 3C.

Great! It meant we would be missing exams at school, although school holidays were coming up as well and that wasn't so great.

That afternoon Wally arrived. He didn't say much – he just wanted to know what the bloody hell I had gone and done this time. Somebody else sent another Bible – we now had *seven*. Tuesday morning John's parents came around again. They wanted us in separate cells, but Captain McKenzie refused to separate us. Apparently we had also made it into the provincial newspapers. Our names weren't mentioned but it stated that two white boys aged fourteen and fifteen were being held in connection with a string of housebreaks involving goods to the tune of R30 000. Somebody had seriously puffed up his or her insurance claims. A police spokesman said that they had been trying to catch the main culprit and youngest of the two for a year and a half. We had managed to set something of a landmark. In 1977 it was virtually unheard of that *white* children our age could be involved in a string of serious crimes like we were, especially in a small Afrikaans dorpie like Worcester.

The bail hearing came around. The police had initially not wanted us to be released on bail because we had run away once already. However, because we had given our full cooperation and also promised not to run away again, they were willing to release us into our parents' custody on a bail of five hundred rands each. Wally said there was no bloody way in hell he would give away five hundred rands. Said he didn't bloody have it anyway. During the bail hearing a strange thing happened. We stood in the box and the white men in black robes said all the things they needed to say. Then, just before the judge was about to tell John that he could go with his mom and dad, a man stood up in court and asked to speak to the judge.

It was Diane Wearne's father (Diane being the girl who sat behind me in register period). The judge told him to come up and stand in the witness box. He told the judge that he knew me (huh?), I attended the Sunday School where he was a Youth Minister (double huh?), his daughter also knew me very well and was in class with me at school (okay …), and that he and his family wanted me come and stay with them until the trial was over (what!?). He would personally post my bail and take responsibility for me. The judge looked somewhat astonished. He asked Mr Wearne if he knew that I had run away from the police. He answered in the affirmative, then turned and asked me from across the court if I would promise not to run away if I came and stayed with them. I gave the court my word. The judge deliberated for a moment, then thanked him and ordered John into the custody of his parents and me into the care of Mr Archibald Wearne. He further instructed that I had to *stay* in the care of Mr Wearne, I was not allowed to go home to Paarl or anywhere else, and should Wally or Denise wish to see me they would have to visit me at the Wearnes. He then bound us over for trial a month distant and the court adjourned.

[Asterix-1 : 3C-0]

We stood down from the Prisoner's box and John's family whisked him away instantly. Uncle Archie came right over, chuckled a little to himself and then, out of the corner of his mouth (*sotto voce*) – said that he hoped The Lord would forgive him for stretching the truth a wee bit concerning our relationship.

The Lord? Our relationship?

What the fuck was this ou talking about?

Wally and Denise drifted over and he promptly introduced himself. They looked slightly shell-shocked. I felt really, *really* strange. I kind of belonged to Uncle Archie at that point. I wasn't even allowed to stay with Denise. Good thing too. I could imagine – with icy cold dread running up my spine – what Wally would have done to me if I had gone back to Paarl with them that day.

[Asterix-Uncle Archie : Wally-0]

The next morning the Wearnes gathered for breakfast. They were extremely nice people except they freaked me out because they held hands when they said grace for meals.

Also, this *Lord* thing seemed to permeate *Everything*. After breakfast a big surprise awaited me in that regard.

The family gathered together in the lounge with their Bibles. Uncle Archie explained that we were about to have *Family Time*. It started off with Auntie Ellen picking out some Bible verses, which each of us read aloud.

I used one of the six Bibles I brought from 3C. No problem there.

Then Uncle Archie read a passage from a devotional text, which they discussed. I was not very vocal on the religious stuff and only answered direct questions – *Yes, No, I dunno.*

Then the horror began …

They prayed.

Out loud!

And everybody was supposed to join in.

Of course they had loads to pray about and the dread slowly rose in me as my turn inevitably came round. I sat squirming in mute dismay while the silence slowly congealed into a solid smothering mass. Eventually, a million years later, Uncle Archie seemed to sense my discomfort and said Amen.

I had never been more pleased to hear someone utter a four-letter word.

I enjoyed being with the Wearnes but I began to loathe Family Time. But I did eventually pray one day. I sort of mumbled something to the effect that I was sorry that I had stolen things and asked Jesus to help me not steal again. I felt that that concluded my most obvious business with God.

Amen.

[Asterix-? : *The Lord*-1]

The day of the trial arrived. The judge found us guilty of housebreak and theft and sentenced us to three months in prison to be suspended for three years. During those three years we would be on probation and would have to see a Welfare officer regularly.

Case dismissed.

[Asterix-0 : Judge-3]

I said an awkward goodbye to the Wearnes and drove back to Paarl with Denise. She informed me that Wally had bought a house in Krugersdorp and we were all going to move up there to join him. She and Wally were going to remarry. He had finally woken up and decided to leave That Bitch.

Two days later Denise and I clashed. I can't remember why, but I do remember her advancing on me with her face all twisted up into her hate rictus with her nails extended and ready to claw. She was going to do her lambasting *thing* again. I cocked my fists, stood my ground and spoke in a low, utterly committed voice:

– *You take one more step towards me you bitch and I am going to fuck you up* –

[!!!]

– *[Shrieking] What the* HELL *did you say to me!?* –

– *You heard me. You take one more step towards me and I will fuck you up* –

– *[Incoherently] You little* BASTAAAARD!! *Who the* HELL *do you think you're talking to?! I'm going to phone the Welfare!* –

– *Phone the Welfare. See if I care* –

– [Unsteady] I'm going to phone ... the POLICE!! –

– Phone the Welfare, phone the police and phone the fucking fire brigade for all I care. I'm just warning you that if you try and hurt me I am going to punch your lights out. Now fuck off and leave me alone –

– You filthy ungrateful little bastard. Just wait until your father hears about this –

– Get out of my room Denise, and leave me alone before I hurt you –

I shocked us both very deeply by standing up to her like that. I was just tired of all the hatred and pain and the years of having to take the full agonising brunt of extreme adult frustrations (which I barely understood). If I could stand up to an evil Rockspider and a big wimpy Jewish bully, then I could definitely stop her shit.

In its tracks.

[Asterix-? : Denise-0]

She got me into her car under some pretext the next day. When I asked her why we were going in completely the wrong direction she gleefully said she was taking me to Valkenburg Mental Hospital because I was sick and needed *help*. I waited until she slowed down to take a corner, flung open the door and dived out. I rolled along the pavement, tearing the skin off my elbows, back and knees, but I managed to get away without breaking any bones. If anybody was sick in the fucking head – it was her! I made my way home, in pain, but I knew she would have some other ugly thing waiting up her sleeve.

I took no chances and that night I ran away to Digre again.

Three days later I phoned and asked Denise if she was willing to stop her shit. She sounded tired. Her anger had deflated and she agreed to leave me alone. I returned to Paarl and a week or two later we moved up to Krugersdorp. She never ever tried to get physical with me again, but she did testify against me at my second court case three months later.

Check you lekker, ou Asterix – *bly wakker eksê* ...

6

The Stink-Gang Bomb-Bang

Johannesburg was like a foreign country to me. I vaguely remembered passing through there on the way to the Cape in '69, but my kid's eye perceptions had changed. It was flat, dusty, crowded and littered with dirty mine dumps. All the grass everywhere was dead. The house that Wally had bought was in the suburb of Silver Firs, just outside of Krugersdorp proper. It was like a dream to us. We kids walked around in it oohing and aahing – not quite able to actually believe that at long last we had our *own* place to live in. I even had my own room! Of course there was a snag. A horrible snag, we soon found out.

Two days before our arrival, Wally and Swallow were married in the Krugersdorp magistrate's court.

Denise was devastated. I watched her carefully, waiting to see what would happen. She appeared to absorb the news numbly, which was somehow scarier. No screaming freak-outs, no crying jags, just dark-ringed catatonia around her eyes.

I was enrolled in the local English school, Krugersdorp High. The principal – and *Grand Pooh-Bah* – Mr Branson, was a grim, humourless man, who clearly did not warm to the idea that he was being asked to admit a child on court probation into his school. He announced tersely that he would give me *A Chance* but I should be aware that he would be watching me carefully. *Very carefully.* We all stood up and shook hands, he adjusted the carrot up his arse and we left.

At school, my new best mate was an ou named Darren, who was originally from Manchester, England. Darren and I quickly perceived that we were soul mates and began bonding.

He taught me some Joburg slang. Girls were called *stocks*, china, and zol was still zol but you could only buy it in Munsieville from the bozies, who called it *nchangu.*

Through Darren, I met Laura. She was a short, fat, blonde girl who lived with her mother Sharon and her much younger brother Tony. Their father had died when they were young. Laura's pozzie turned out to be a sort of afternoon way-station for the neighbourhood high-school kids. Mostly guys. I also met Laura's best friend, and Darren's girlfriend, Carla there. She and Laura attended a girl's Catholic Convent.

We were always able to make a noise on the hi-fi at Laura's pozzie because Sharon worked. Everybody was into Rodriguez, Pink Floyd, Santana, Led Zeppelin, Deep Purple, and all the rest ...

Soon after I arrived, there was a disco at Laura and Carla's school. Darren was going with Carla but Laura didn't have a boyfriend so I was paired off with her. There was something about Laura that I couldn't quite put my finger on. Darren asked me how many (*none!*) stocks I had fucked. A couple, I told him. Yeah well, Laura would put out if I wanted. *Guaranteed.*

Really?

That night at the disco I danced with both Carla and Laura but mostly with Laura because Carla was obviously with Darren. I sat down with her towards the end of the evening and we started kissing and stuff. A great sense of well-being began settling over me. It was the start of a feeling that I had not had since Vanessa. I looked at Laura. Okay, she was fat but she had a spark of light in her or something. If her fatness chased you away her spark would bring you back almost more strongly. I had only known her a couple of days and I thought I really liked her.

Afterwards we went back to Laura's house. Her mother was asleep and so was her little brother. The four of us tiptoed into Laura's room. She had two beds so that a friend could sleep over. Carla and Darren climbed onto the guest bed and I climbed onto Laura's and she switched off the light. We started kissing. I put my hand up her blouse and fought my way through the rolls of fat to her bra. I wanted to see if she would let me touch her *koek* but I was way too shy. Eventually I plucked up enough courage to start fumbling with the top of her pants. She flopped over onto her back and snapped her legs wide open. Wow! I unbuttoned her pants, after struggling a bit, and pushed my hand inside and down. The shock of her – *bush* – hair in my fingertips – *under her panties!* – made the white flaming thing go flip-flopping around in my stomach, trying to tear its way out of my cock.

Carla and Darren were dark panting shapes on the other side of the room. I pushed my hand further down and into soft sopping wetness. I poked around and pushed my finger in and out. Laura was groaning and bucking around on the bed. It went on for what seemed like an eternity until I heard Darren whisper that we had better stop because we had to get Carla back home. Laura jumped up – *jerking my hand rudely out of her* – and switched on the light. We all sat blinking owlishly at each other, getting used to the glare.

I walked up the road to drop Darren off and on the way we sniffed each other's middle fingers. I was silently congratulating myself. I had never felt more like the king of the world. At home I wanked twice, still sniffing my finger.

I went back the next day. Laura was happy to see me. Other people were at the house. Guys. She was laughing and joking with everybody. They just sat around, not saying much. There was a really dumb British oke named Keebol and another okie named Titch. Titch was very short but he had dropped out of school and was working already. He also had his own flat. An ou named Greg was there too.

I couldn't quite put my finger on it but there seemed to be some sort of hidden tension in the air. Laura kept dancing around, touching and flirting with all the others. I felt a green snake awaken in my gut. I had come there to see *her*, not share *all* her time with these other fucking guys. I made a show of fucking off because *I didn't need that*.

She phoned me later and asked if anything was wrong. I told her that I'd wanted to visit her but she hadn't seemed like she really wanted to see me. She told me I was soooo wrong. Of course she'd wanted to see me. I mustn't get angry. She just had a lot of *friends*. I shouldn't mind *friends*. She had always had lots of *guy friends*.

I was placated. I went to her house the next day and she was there alone. We went into her room and lay on the bed. I touched her pants and she snapped her legs open. I made my finger wonderfully smelly again until Darren arrived some time later.

A few days later I took the plunge and asked Laura to go out with me. She was astounded. Did I mean it? Yes, of course I meant it. Did she want to be my girlfriend? Yes or no?

Yes, she wanted to be my girlfriend. No guy had ever asked her to be his girlfriend. Of course she wanted to!

I was ecstatic. I had a girlfriend again. Okay she was fat but she was friendly. She was friendly to everybody.

I spent the next week enjoying the novelty of the idea. I wet my middle finger three more times and even sucked on her breast once. At home I wanked furiously thinking about her.

I let myself fall in love.

When I managed to get away from home eventually the following Friday afternoon, I went looking for Laura and Darren. Darren was nowhere to be found. Neither was Laura. I found Carla at her house looking after her little sisters and she told me that Laura had said she was going to meet her mom in town and Darren had gone to Titch's house for a boys' afternoon. They had beers and stuff. I was incensed. Why the fuck had he left me out? I asked Carla how to get to Titch's flat.

I walked there and rang the doorbell. I could hear sounds inside but nobody answered. I rang again. Finally the door opened. It was Darren (*surprised!*). He looked at me funny.

– *Howzit china* –

– *Howzit. What's up broer?* –

– *Nothing much, just a couple of us hanging loose, playing Kerim* –

– *Well, what's the score? Can I come in?* –

– *Hey, I don't know if Titch would like that china. It's his place you know ...* –

– *Well fuck it broer, ask him ...*

Darren yelled inside saying that I was at the door and was it okay if I came inside. Someone shouted back that it was *up to me* so long as I kept my fucking mouth *shut*. I followed Darren inside.

I would keep my fucking mouth shut.

Darren's older brother Steve, Greg and Keebol were playing Kerim in the lounge. Beers lay around. It was four men to the game so I stood aside and lit a cigarette. Darren gave me some of his beer. Five minutes later a door opened and Titch strolled out of his bedroom tucking his shirt into his pants. He had a big shit-eating grin on his face and asked if anybody *wanted to go again for seconds?* He noticed me and suddenly his face fell flat. There was another movement in the bedroom doorway and Laura stepped out into the passage. All she had on was a small towel wrapped around her. She looked at me (*shocked!*) and I suddenly realised what Laura's definition of a *friend* was.

I felt sick. Titch asked her if she was *Okay* and *Did she want to take a bath?* She nodded wordlessly, not looking at anyone, and walked into the bathroom and closed the door. I felt absolute nauseating horror raging around in me. *Them. All* of them! One by fucking (*who wants to go again?*) one. Five guys. *Ohmyfuck!* I stood around trying to look like I was totally cool with whatever was cool with *them*. After what I thought to be a decent lapse of time I joked with Darren that I had wasted my whole afternoon looking for him and now I had to get back home.

What was I going to do about it? Wage war with all five of them? With her? With myself for thinking that a slut could be my girlfriend?

Everybody I knew had known?

Halfway home I puked.

I somehow managed to pick up and re-swallow my outraged pride, and after three weeks of Laura's crying, begging and telling me she was sorry, I accepted her back. I don't know why. I absolutely and utterly loathed myself for what it made me in their eyes. I was starved of something that I could only get from her (*spark*), and even though it made me a social fucking joke I would sacrifice myself to that comedy because my driven need (*tobespecial*) was stronger than my shame.

The local slut's boyfriend. He doesn't mind sharing her because he's such a pathetic soppy wanker.

I was a slut's wanking virgin boyfriend.

A week later I fucked her.

We weren't really going out any more (from my side at least), although she kept begging me to. She kept up the crying jags and moaned incessantly until I told her that I would go out with her again but only if she would promise me that what had happened in the PAST would stay in the PAST. She swore on all that she could think of that she would stay faithful. It would be like we were married. Just without papers.

Time passed. Darren and I got bust for bunking school and my second really serious bad mark went on my file. The Grand Pooh-Bah Branson declared that the Chance he had given me was up. He did not see Any Reason why he shouldn't Expel me. I told him contritely that I would Never Ever Do It Again Sir and blah be de blah ... I left riding on a little less than a polony skin of a Chance later – nursing six cuts.

Then I caught Laura with Greg and Keebol one afternoon.

I refused to speak to her for two weeks until her crying performances became too much and I had a make-up fuck with her.

She was there to fuck anyway ...

Then I stupidly let off a stink bomb in Assembly at school one morning after being dared. My gat got expelled and I was dragged off to my second bout in the Prisoner's Box – only this time Wally and Denise were the State's extremely hostile witnesses.

PART II

The Book of Iron

7

Iron into Yster

I awake –
I am on The Train,
That black iron Train …
Rattling and roaring
  down the dark starless night
Going to:
  bad the … bad the …
  bad the smoking dread …
I want to get off
And I dunno if I can,
I'm so afraid
Of nchonalanga man …

I awake –
Wally where's the high jump?
Pull up your stinking socks.
Bitchbornbastard just won't listen
Now you'll just find out.
Divorce the only answer
Please leave the only creed
Cure of your thumbsucking
They'll meat your every need.

Denise why're you doing this?
Why can you both not see?
Wally there's a SCHOOL *there*
That's going to jump INTO *me …*

I awake –
Man, that was some horrible dream. Shit, where am I? Oh. Denise. Train.
Fight. Welfare. Judge. Going to THAT *school in George – Die Bult. I didn't pull*
up my socks like Wally warned and now I'm for the high jump. Oh Fuck …

The train slowed and steamed into George station. Denise and I alighted wordlessly, a silent loathing hanging heavily between us. It had been a very bad journey.

I looked up behind me. The old, dark, winged sentinel that had haunted my childhood dreams had not changed. It still crouched there, leering over the damp and sleepy town.

Hello Demon Mountain – I'm back ... And this time I'm alone.

After a moment, a tall, freckle-faced man with red hair came up and asked if I was the new pupil for Die Bult. Denise happily switched into Brave Reasonable Denise mode and confirmed the fact.

I discovered that he was Mr du Plessis – one of two school psychologists. He led us to a canopied bakkie in the parking lot and locked me in the back. All of a sudden the realisation of where I was heading flooded me and in my gut the slumbering fear-reptile writhed in its murky nightmare, making me momentarily nauseous.

I perched on a wheel-well, swallowed hard and gripped my suitcase.

Soon enough we turned into the distantly familiar avenue of trees leading up to the school offices. As the engine stopped, the shrill sound of Denise's voice filtered through from the cab. Mr du Plessis was being volubly instructed in *The World According To Denise ...*

I cringed – she was already trying to mess it all up for me!

He unlocked the back and told me to leave my suitcase there. My things would be returned later. Much later, it transpired.

We were led into the building to a room with a high counter much like a police station charge office. Behind us was a closed door with the legend:

G.H. Krüger – Skoolhoof

A lady came bustling up, all smiles, and said that I must be the new boy. She asked Denise for the court file, which she fussed from her handbag. The woman perused it briefly and then beamed up at me. Mr Krüger would be with us shortly, she announced primly, a hard little gleam dancing in her eyes.

This bitch doesn't just do it for the money and perks – she likes locking kids up.

Denise still had Mr du Plessis firmly by the ear: *We Have Tried Our Damnedest With Him* and *My Husband And I Just Know That This Is For The Best* and *We've Only Heard Good Things About Your School*, etc....

I wished she would shut up. She could be so damned pornographic – *street-sluttish* – with her troubles and opinions.

Jesus, it's a goddamned government reformatory. What good things could you have heard about it? He fucking threatened me with it when I was a little kid for Christsakes. That stupid Welfare bitch that helped the two of you get me signed over to the State tried her damnedest to sugar-coat it into a holiday farm for happy teenagers.

Do you All think I'm a fucking Moron! Huh? And WAKE UP *Stupid!! He's* NOT *your fucking psycho alkie husband any more!*

Fear and rage. Rage and fear. I was so damned scared and angry. And there was bugger all I could do about it.

Swallow hard. Don't wake the snake up. Look cool, kid.

Eventually the door opened and a severe-looking man with greying blond hair and large steel-rimmed spectacles appeared. He studied me briefly with cold, pale blue eyes and introduced himself to Denise in laboured English.

Krüger.

He asked Mr du Plessis what hostel and workshop I had been placed in.

Hostel 4 / Electricians.

He nodded noncommittally and announced to Denise that she should say goodbye because I was about to leave. Denise looked a little nonplussed about being driven into the wings but recovered quickly enough to say her farewell in a sad put-on tone that tried to suggest she wasn't — *the same person who had vociferously testified to have me sentenced there in the first place, dammit.* I detested her fawning hypocrisy. Krüger told me that the court had placed me in HIS care and everything that happened to me from this point forth depended entirely on ME. He summed up ominously in Swartland Afrikaans:

– *MAAK GEBRUIK VAN JOU KANSE, SEUN* ... –

Make use of your chances ...

... He Steals, Your Worship. He threatened to Bash Me and he's run away from home Twice. I was trying to get him Help one day and he just Dived right out of the car. You should just See how he treats his sister too. I can't Handle Him Any More and nor can My Husband. We have tried our Very Level Best but we simply cannot be Held Responsible. I don't know what he's going to do next. We feel it's completely Out Of Our Hands ...

I was led to a long, low building next to the office, with the sign:

Electrician's Workshop. Inside I found five of my peers working at various benches with motors, wires and other electrical stuff. They were all dressed in grey. Grey shirt, grey shorts, grey socks and brown shoes. It looked weird. As Mr du Plessis introduced me to the teacher, interest stirred among the okes. It transpired that they were all in my class. Mr du Plessis left and the teacher turned me over to them. They crowded round, eyeing me up and down, all with semi-veiled hostility. They asked two questions.

What was I in for?

Where did I come from?

I felt stupid saying that I had been sentenced for letting a stink bomb off during Assembly at Krugersdorp High (*and I wasn't going to explain that Wally and Denise had absolved themselves of all responsibility for me by means of a legal court case, which they and the fucking Welfare speedily arranged after my expulsion – I got sent here because I was kind of un-adopted – yeah, right ...*) so I told them I had been bust for housebreak and theft. Twenty-six counts, I added for good measure. Better to sound like a real bad oke. They weren't very impressed, and one of them announced that I was a kleppie – a marrobaner. At first I couldn't figure that out until it dawned on me – *kleppie*: a kleptomaniac. What the hell a marrobaner was I had absolutely no idea, but I figured it must be slang for a thief.

I wasn't going to ask.

Instead I asked them why they had all been sent there. Three of them answered but the other two said aggressively that it had fuckall to do with me. From the moment they started speaking, shock began setting in. They all spoke like Cape Town gammats. English and Afrikaans mixed with weird (*Kaffir?*) words. The same accent and everything! Fuck. They were WHITE kids for goodness' sake.

One oke's crime stuck badly in my mind because it seemed so repulsive. MEIDNAAI.

He had apparently been caught screwing his mom's charwoman. That okie's name was Johan Dysel, and later on in the showers I would discover that he had the largest wop I have ever seen on another man. He was truly hung (three inches above his knee) like a proverbial donkey.

I was asked what Stronk had said to me. Stronk was G.H. Krüger – Skoolhoof. All the teachers had nicknames. The teacher in the Electricians Workshop (I don't remember his real name) was called Bols – from Bols brandy, because he always had a half-jack in his desk drawer. They asked if Stronk had instructed me to— *MAAK GEBRUIK VAN JOU KANSE ...* It was apparently his stock slogan and he said it to every new boy.

What hostel I was in? Four. Dysel told me to waai with him when the bell rang. We were hostel mates. Then they asked me if my escorts had used roller-skates on me.

Huh? Roller-skates?

Ja, roller-skates – handcuffs. Had they used handcuffs or had they been soft ous? I told them that Denise had brought me there. That really shocked them. After a heated discussion, they concluded that they had never heard of *anybody* who hadn't been escorted to the school by either the mapuza or the Welfare.

The mapuza?

Ja, the mapuza – Gattas, Boere, Po'lice, Kêrels – The Law. Somebody concluded scornfully that if I didn't know what the boere were called then I had to be a full-on skaap. Another ou commented that Denise must really hate my guts.

Bols ordered them to quit chattering and get back to work. I stood awkwardly to one side with my head spinning.

Marrobaner, kleppie, roller-skates, mapuza, gattas. Maak gebruik van jou kanse ... Stronk – Meidnaai? MEIDNAAI! *Dear God, what have I got myself into?*

Eventually a siren went off signalling big break. I followed Dysel.

Meidnaai?

Streams of other grey-uniformed boys were making their way in the direction that Dysel was taking me. On the way he cheerily announced that I was now a blougat and that I would remain a blougat for a full year, after which I would become a Das. The blougat thing I figured out easily enough – it was obviously the same as being a sot. I asked him what a Das was. He told me that all the ous in the school were known as Dasse by the mense in George, but among the boys being a Das was a privilege. I started figuring. *Dassie* was the Afrikaans word for a rock hyrax, and the school's name was Die Bult – so I supposed that rock rabbits lived in the hills, and that somehow made some kind of obtuse sense.

Fuckload easier to understand than meidnaai.

I looked at the crowd around us. Some of them sure as hell didn't look like boys. The magistrate said I would only be released upon completing Matric or turning twenty-one. Some of these buggers sure looked like they were sukkeling to make Matric. They weren't boys – they were fucking grownup men!

We arrived at the hostel and Dysel took me to a wooden building where all the boys-to-men were crowding. He announced loudly that I was a new rooinek blougat from Joburg who had been klapped for being a marrobaner.

A really big oke with an eleven o'clock shadow called me:

– *Eksê blougat, come here! Wot's yore gama, robie van Joburg?* –

– *Excuse me?* –

– *Wot's yore fokken name, thief?* –

– *Alex* –

– *Why is you so fokken gevrek? En wot's going on in yore bek? Did you fokken bite a dustbin? Hah?* –

– *[Me, hesitantly] No ...* –

– *HERE JESUS GOD, BLOUGAT!! You better fokken wake up vinnig! En with daai piece of iron in your donnerse bek, your gama is Yster from now on. How you laaik dat?* –

– *[Me, confused] Dis okay ...* –

– *Hear dis fokken ou. Dis Oakaaay ... Yore fokken piel is Oakaaay, Poeslappie! Looks like you IS fokken gevrek!! Where's dat ander blougat? Ferreira! Kom hier you fokken whorejaer. Take yore maatjie Ystertjie on his fokken handjie en give him dop en rogue* –

The boy who'd been told to give me dop and rogue was an oke named Gavin Ferreira from Cape Town. He had arrived six weeks before me, after being caught with dagga and Obex a second time.

Gavin told me the ou who had interrogated me in badly butchered English was the Headboy of the hostel. He was apparently sort of okay as long as you WOKE UP and didn't fuck up with him. Yeah right, like I was going to try that out. He was only the meanest-looking mutherfucker that I had ever laid eyes on in my life.

Probably a meidnaaier too.

Dop was bitter beige tea we drank out of stainless steel mugs. Many years before, Wally had wanted to clear some junk out of the backyard in Meade Street. He got two kaffir convicts from the local prison to help and they brought along stainless steel mugs like this one. I thought, at the time, that their kaffir germs had to be real bad because they weren't allowed to drink from any of our old kaffir cups that Denise kept under the sink. They were like ultra-kaffir or something.

Fuck, just look at me!

Rogue turned out to be two thick slices of plain brown bread smeared with horrible-looking reddish-pink fruit jam.

Gavin explained that the ous had words for everything and dop meant any hot drink – coffee, tea, whatever – and we drank it out of boepbekers. Bread was rogue and anything put on your rogue was smearies. Anything. This stuff looked like something that Swallow would give to a garden kaffir – *in a tin plate*. I politely declined and handed the rogue back to him. He wolfed it down gratefully. Then he took me into the small single-roomed wooden building called The Bungalow. Apparently each hostel had one and it was the only place that smoking was permitted on school property. He warned me not to flash entjies in front of everybody, so I didn't.

Then I got my second really big shock. Almost everybody was smoking loose tobacco rolled up in strips of newspaper and stuck together with spit – just like the kaffirs and hotnots did.

Oh God no, sis! They all speak like gammats. They eat rogue, drink dop and smoke like kaffirs and hotnots. Oh my fuck, What dark world have I fallen into? I'm never going to make three years and two months of this!

I carefully slipped out an entjie without removing the packet from my pocket. As Gavin fired me up he spoke loudly to no one in particular:

– *I'm pawning him on the drag and no pawning on the pawner* –

Huh? More Swahili. I asked him what the hell he had just said. He tried to enlighten me by explaining that he had verbally reserved the right to share my entjie by declaring a first pawn. He had also declared that nobody could share it with him – *no second pawn*. He wasn't actually allowed to do so as a blougat – he was taking a chance, because we weren't allowed to declare a *no pawning me* on a first pawn. Any Das could pawn a blougat on a first pawn if he hadn't been pawned already, but a blougat could only pawn a Das if the Das was willing. That meant that I wouldn't have been able to smoke my entjie alone anyway. Dasse were allowed to declare a *no pawning me*, but only if another Das hadn't said *pawning you* first. I looked at him utterly thunderstruck and asked him to repeat that – *slowly*. He laughed and explained again. It would be a while until I did get it, but I didn't want to look stupid, so I asked him what a drag was instead.

All entjies were called *drags*. The entjie that I was smoking (Chesterfield) was called a *private*. A drag made from loose tobacco and Rizla paper was called a *private Dassie-puff* and one made with check (telephone book or newspaper) was an *ordinary Dassie-puff.*

Shop-bought tobacco was called *snout* in English and *twak* in Afrikaans. Uncle Guvvie gave us evil, black, foul-smelling twak for free once a month – called *issue.* You couldn't give it away and only smoked it when you had absolutely nothing else. Sometimes Uncle Guvvie gave us good issue, almost like the offcuts of BB in the shops, but that was called *private issue.* The quality of issue depended on whether it was pawnable or not.

Issue Dassie-puffs usually never got pawned.

– *Last two questions. Who's Uncle Guvvie? And if a drag is an entjie, then what is inhaling a puff called? –*

– *Taking a puff is called a chestie, and taking two puffs is called a double clutch –*

– *And Uncle Guvvie? –*

– *My broer, all of us here belong to The State eksê. Uncle Guvvie is the Government and we are all Guvvie laaities. Everything we get comes from The State, from Uncle Guvvie, and my broer you better wake up 'cos Uncle Guvvie is fucking watching you eksê –*

Nice thought …

The siren went off again and everybody left for classes. Gavin told me to go back into the hostel and look for Tannie Mop. She was Jaamie's wife. Jaamie was our hostel father. His name was actually Mr Louw but he had been nicknamed Jaamie because of his resemblance to Jamie Uys the movie director.

Tannie Mop turned out to be a friendly bustling Afrikaans matron without an ounce of malice in her. She asked me where I came from and what family I had and so on and so forth. Nothing bad. Then she informed me that her husband would speak to me in more detail about everything, but for now I had to accept that all my personal effects had been locked away and would be kept for me in safekeeping.

She took me to a store full of clothing, bedding and toiletry supplies, and began stacking stuff on a table. Grey shirts, pants, socks, even underpants – old and newish-looking. Next, a pair of navy blue shorts, a light blue vest, ugly takkies and brown shoes. Then a white long-sleeved shirt, long grey pants and a tie. I tried on various threadbare suits and blazers until I had one of each that fitted passably. She added blankets, sheets, a pillowcase and a pillow to the growing pile, gave me a toothbrush, toothpaste and a light blue towel, and cut off a hunk of soap from a long red bar.

I sniffed it – *yes sir, kaffir soap.*

She announced that my number was 4/57 and that for the duration of my stay at the school it would remain my hostel and laundry number.

I was not to forget it.

Then she produced a bag with the number 4/57 on it and told me to take off all my clothing, underpants included, and put them inside. I was to get dressed in the grey clothes.

Finally, she led me to a bed in a dorm and told me to make it up and pack my stuff away.

I did so and lay down in Uncle Guvvie's clothes. I was still thinking about how much of me he suddenly owned when I drifted away. I was awoken by the sound of other boys. I went out nervously and found them all lining up at the entrance to what I presumed must be the graze hall. A dapper, grey-haired, bespectacled gentleman with a clipped silver moustache and a skull-like bald head appeared and somebody yelled – *Stilte!* The man had a clipboard and began calling out names. Each person responded by yelling – *Teenwoordig meneer!* I was surprised to hear my own name, and I called out, announcing that I was present.

I had just met Jaamie for my first roll-call.

Inside the graze hall the boys went to their tables and Jaamie introduced me to the hostel proper. One of the boys said a hurried grace and they all sat down. Jaamie led me to a table where a place had been set for me, and I ate my first lunch courtesy of Uncle Guvvie. Graze politics was similar to Worcester, although later I discovered something disgusting but quite funny about pudding days.

On Wednesdays and Sundays you got a bowl of pudding. The first thing you did was spit in it. Then you closed your eyes for Thanks, knowing it was safe from other unrighteous fingers and you weren't gonna piss off The Almighty by not praying with your eyes closed.

After graze we had a short smoke break and then it was time for study. Someone told me Jaamie wanted me in his office. I found him seated behind his desk. Jaamie turned out to be a no-nonsense, old-school Rockspider who only spoke Afrikaans.

He began …

I was now a part of The School. If I looked around I would see that there were no bars on the windows. This was an Industrial School – not a prison. Here I had the opportunity to better myself by learning manners and a trade to help me earn an honest living later in life. It was nobody else's responsibility but my own to procure that ideal. This was also my very last chance. The only place I could go from here was to Constantia School in Tokai – and TK had bars like a prison, so I wouldn't get away from there so easily. No, better to apply myself to my given tasks and display the correct gratitude to my Maker.

Die Bult worked on a Group System. If I misbehaved I would move down a Group and if I proved myself by merit I would move up. My privileges and freedoms depended on my Group.

Groups were listed from AA-Group to FF-Group. A new pupil was automatically placed into E-Group, meaning: no private clothes, no freedom and the privilege to take part in compulsory sport.

Every Monday afternoon a *Koshuisraad* would convene, made up of himself, the Assistant Hostel Father, the Headboy – *Fokken Poeslappie* (*HIM?!*) – the Secretary and the four hostel leaders. It had powers to decide Group placement up to D-Group. I would be on probation for six weeks, and after that could automatically be passed to D-Group. It depended on me. Then my suitcase, and bag 4/57, would be returned.

Smoking was not permitted until I turned fifteen and said up my Smoker's Rules in front of the Raad. He checked my file – fourteen years old.

– *Don't let me catch you smoking, Goulding* –

Not very nice sir. I must smoke.

– *Ja meneer!* –

There was also a *Leerlingraad*, composed of the Principal, Vice-Principals of the school and workshops, the school psychologists, Headboy, Under-headboy and all the Headboys of the hostels. The Leerlingraad convened monthly and had power to grant Holiday Permission as well as all other Group placements – *but Stronk and his staff retained absolute veto on everything.*

Holiday Permission began with approval by the Koshuisraad, provided you had no entries in the Strafboeke from the previous term. They listed when you got flapped, gated or given extra hostel duties. If the Koshuisraad approved Holiday Permission, it was passed to the school and your workshop. Finally, if it passed all three checks it went before the Leerlingraad for endorsement. From there it was sent to the Department of Welfare office nearest the address that you submitted for approval. Their agents would visit the address and determine whether you were welcome there and if it was a fit enough abode. Finally a train ticket had to be produced and then I could go on holiday. Uncle Guvvie would provide one free ticket a year.

The school ran on a Christian work ethic. All labour was done by the boys themselves. Weekdays started at 05h30 and each boy was allotted a portion of the hostel to sweep, polish and dust. This was called my *inside honk*. After morning Stiltetyd, Inspection and Breakfast came my *outside honk*. Then school.

There was no Study on Friday afternoons. Everybody worked on their outside honks or went to the doctor or dentist. Saturday mornings were spent working on outside or inside honks before Dorp. Saturday afternoon was Sport, Movies or Rest. Saturday night – Study. I would attend my own church in town on Sunday mornings and have Rest in the afternoon. On Sunday evenings there was a church service in the school hall.

There were roll-calls at set times and at random.

All work done in the workshops was remunerated by the State. Uncle Guvvie would pay me once a month and my wage was called Dassie-pay. It would be in the region of R5.00 (@ 25c per weekday) for an E-Group. It graded incrementally on a Group-dependent scale.

F-Groups received no Dassie-pay.

There was a tuck shop that was open Thursdays which sold drags, toiletries, writing materials, sweets (*lollies*) and cooldrinks (*collies*). I could buy things on credit, and the money would be deducted from my next Dassie-pay.

Smart way to keep cash out of our hands.

Walloping – *running away from the school* – was punishable by an automatic sentence of six cuts and F-Group. Wallop three times and I would be placed in FF-Group (lockup) awaiting transfer to TK.

– *Any questions?* –

– *Nee meneer* –

Jaamie led me to a passageway and told me it was my inside honk. He also extracted a battered leather book bag from a cupboard and informed me that I had to mark it and stash it in hole 57 of the long book bag cupboard next to the graze hall.

From there he took me to the garden and gave me a patch for my outside honk. Finally, he led me back into his office and made me sign a paper, which declared that he had explained all the rules to A.D. Goulding, Hostel 4 Hole 57 – and that I had understood them.

It disappeared into my File.

Then he sat down, tugged his waistcoat straight and folded his hands on the desk-blotter. Peering over the top of his bifocals, he capped it off with what I realised was a set speech.

He had NOT asked that I be sent there. He didn't even care WHY I had. All he cared about was that I understood that everyone got the SAME opportunities when they came through the gate, and it was ENTIRELY up to me to make use of them. If I did, it would benefit me, but if I didn't— it would be hard on me. VERY HARD. And ONLY on ME. I was not a new problem to him. He had been in the business of Dasse for a long time and there was nothing new that I could show or tell him. He knew everything there was to know about a Das.

EVERYTHING ...

Hello my Sssssson ... Welcome to the Machine ...

Yes Sir! Uncle Guvvie Sir!

Later, back in the bungalow, a couple of okes drifted over, all asking the same goeters.

What had I been gaaned for?

Where was I from?

Some, I could see, were trying to get a feel of who I was, but others clearly had baser intentions – large and small. They tried bumming drags off me but I told them I didn't have any. They all had one thing in common – a deeply etched fear, staring suspicion and a (*ratlike*?) aggression that seemed at a constant war in their mannerisms.

There was something weird about them all.

One oke seemed to offer a genuine welcome and commiseration at our mutual plight. His name was Robert Nienaber. He promised to help, and tuned me to waai with him – scuttling off and snapping his wrist at me to follow.

He took me to a tiny boiler room behind the kitchen and we bounced a drag. He asked me where I was from, wharrawharra.

I tuned him a slightly extended version, saying I'd been bust for marrobaning goeters and being expelled twice – the second time for letting off a stink bomb in Assembly at Krugersdorp High. I don't know why I trusted him enough to give him a closer version of the truth. He just seemed to have a vulnerability I kinda recognised.

He told me he was a weeshuislaaitie. He and his younger sister had been in St Michael's Home in Cape Town since they were both tiny after their parents pegged in a car accident. Nobody adopted them, so they eventually ended up in Norman House Place of Safety in Joburg. When he passed Standard 5, Uncle Guvvie automatically sent him to Die Bult and his sissie to Tempe School for Girls in Bloemfontein.

He told me blandly that he'd seen Fokken Poeslappie – *his real name was Colin Someone-or-other* – give me my welcome and in his opinion I really was a *skaap* and I really was *gevrek* – but I shouldn't take it too badly, because he, Nienaber, wanted to help me. He would teach me how Everything Worked. He liked me, and because of that he would make sure I had a bra who could sort out goeters. Lastly we were in the same class, which meant we were in for the same long ride in Uncle Guvvie's Poesplaas.

I didn't know whether to be very grateful or deeply insulted.

Later on, Gavin asked me what Nienaber wanted. I told him. Gavin laughed – Nienaber had tried the same stunt on him when he arrived.

He explained.

The whole school was divided up into where you came from. There were the Cape Town Ouens, the Joburg Ouens and the Durban Ouens. You stuck to your Ouens. Gavin was a Hostel 4 Cape Town Ouen, for instance. Nienaber was not accepted completely by either the Cape Town Ouens or the Joburg Ouens. Mostly because he had fuckall and was always trying to pawn everybody. The only good thing he had going for him was that he was a Das. More importantly, he also had no Company.

– *Huh?* –

– *Ja, Company* –

Each clan of Ouens was made up of smaller groups of ous in Company with each other. Say for instance your mense sent you pakkies full of lollies and another ou's mense sent him straight kroon – you and that ou could get together and put all your goeters together, pawning each other. You scored your drags and movie tickets with his kroon and he could *tand* your lollies and goeters with you. Sometimes ouens came to Die Bult from other places like Doerfuckoffontein, and the only way that they could survive was to be Company with somebody in one of the main clans. Then they would have protection and be sterkbene. It was also a good move to avoid all the weeshuislaaities. They always had fuckall so they would invariably scale anything they could lay their hands on and sooner or later it would get you into kak with the onnies and other ous.

I was automatically a Joburg Ouen and if I had kroon, goeters or whatever, I could shop for a Company among them. But I had nothing except the five privates in my pocket. Wally, Denise and I had not parted very amicably.

The Company issue was very serious and had a lot to do with the laws of pawning. If a blougat had a Das as his Company, he would have the protection of that Das from other Dasse on pawning issues. If somebody made a second pawn and didn't close the pawning, it could be taken to a third pawn. Third pawns were automatic between two ous in Company. Of course, if you had no Company and you were a blougat, anyone could pawn you on anything, although pawning didn't cover goeters issued by Uncle Guvvie. Pawning only extended to private goeters – the measure of our wealth and ultimate place in the general pecking order.

Gavin also gave me some very sombre advice. He told me that it would count for *EVERYTHING* in Die Bult.

Firstly, don't be a nackerball – someone who always runs off to the onnies to try and gain approval from them. It would get me fucked up.

Secondly, NEVER, EVER fucking piemp. PERIOD. Do it once and I would be ostracised *and definitely fucked up too (a pillowcase over your head and some serious knocks to it with a steam-iron one or another dark night when you wrongly thought you were dossing lekker)* and branded as the lowest piece of shit for as long as I was in there – and *beyond …*

It would never leave me.

Useless advice. I wouldn't do that kind of shit anyway. I knew what it felt like after (*Le Roux?*) did it to me.

Finally it was time for Stiltetyd. We sat next to our beds and somebody read from a Gideon's Bible. We prayed – *or didn't* – and waited. We were not allowed to sit or lie on our beds at any time between morning Inspection and the end of Stiltetyd at night.

Somewhere out in the night, two trumpeters sounded out Taps. It was an integral part of school life. Uncle Guvvie's Lullaby. Then it was Lights Out.

The long day was finally over.

Silence.

Then:

– *[Fk. Poeslappie] Eksê Rooies* –

– *Wat?* –

– *Time to show de new blougat ... Bingo* –

– *Ja!* –

– *Okay, youse is all fokken vuilgat, but youse know de rules. No ou plays meid, every ou mus' do it* –

– *Eksê blougat!* –

[...]

– *Yster!!* –

– *Ja ...* –

– *We gonna play Bingo. You know wot is dat?* –

– *No ...* –

– *Okay it's like dis. We all gonna skommel eksê, and the first ou what skiets must say Bingo and then the second ou, an' den like every ou what skiets mus' say Bingo eksê. En you must fokken doen it, hey? If you traai play meid, you kry sommer 'n paar lekker fat warm klappe* –

– *Okay ouens, laat waai!* –

Suddenly the dark was filled with furious thumping and rustling sounds. I couldn't tell whether they were really wanking or just fooling me, but I couldn't take that (*'n paar lekker fat warm klappe*) chance, so I started wanking for real. At last some ou gasped – *Bingo!* – then another, and another, and I realised that it was for real.

Then I – *Bingo!* – finished the game.

The ou called Rooies started describing what kind of spunk had come out of him.

– *It was mos'ly water but dere was a lekker big snotterige bit, like a pap spoon full* –

The other ouens hooted and laughed nervously.

I didn't know what to think (*disgustingdirty*) and fell asleep with the confused words of the day still ringing in my head:

Marrobaner, mapuza, pawning, Fk. Poeslappie, 4/57 – Meidnaai, Bingo! ...

*

I had barely begun dossing when the siren went off. I thought there must be some mistake. It was still dark outside, for goodness' sake! The other ous all jumped up and were scurrying around quickly, tossing on clothes and making their beds into perfectly square box shapes. I was still half asleep.

Fk. Poeslappie came over to me and asked in mangled English if I thought I had the whole day to myself – or maybe I wanted to lie on my arse and play with my piel while *he* made my bed and cleaned my fucking honk. He and the other ou, Rooies (*It was mos'ly water but dere was a lekker big snotterige bit, like a pap spoon full*), were our dormitory leaders.

The rest of us were blougatte.

I was trying to think of some kind of placating response when all of a sudden I found myself on the floor with a metallic taste in my mouth.

Almost as an afterthought, a blinding flash went off in my head.

– *YOU BETTER FOKKEN GET UP BLOUGAT!! I'M NOT GONNA NAAI YOU!! AN' YOU BETTER MAKE YORE FOKKEN HONK RIGHT! IS YOU AWAKE NOW POESLAPPIE!? –*

I jumped. I ran. Everything spun and hurt.

I had my clothes on and was busy making my bed when I noticed all the other blougatte scuttling out of the dormitory. Suddenly I was alone with only four other okes – Fk. Poeslappie, Rooies and two other okies who were grabbing cleaning materials from a cupboard. Rooies stopped chatting with Fk. Poeslappie and came for me. He had no expression in his face but his eyes told me he was going to … I bent over my bed, tucking the blanket in wildly—

Another white light exploded in my head.

This time it was a straight punch to the jaw. I looked up at him in utter shock and disbelief. He told me calmly that the klap was for being late for my honk. I got up and – *STROBEFLASH!* – found myself back on the deck again, my head ringing worse. And suddenly very SORE. The second klap was for making my bed in a way that would make him look like a poes in front of Jaamie during Inspection. He told me to observe – he'd show me – ONCE.

I carefully (*fuckingpoes*) memorised him. Then he strode out of the dormitory to take me to my honk. I followed blindly and was immediately beset upon by two large okies on their knees with polishing brushes. They jumped up and yelled at me to get off their fucking honks.

I stopped, startled.

WAS I FUCKING DEAF?? Get off their fucking honks!!

I had to follow Rooies but I couldn't cross their honks ...?

What was I supposed to do?

One oke came up to me – *I cringed* – and tossed down two shoebox-sized pieces of blanket. Use the fucking taxies blougat, and ask permission to cross his fucking honk. I did so. Go! – he warned – but do that kind of kak again and I could look forward to getting fucked up. I put the taxies under my shoes and shuffled on, in pursuit of Rooies. At the border of that ou's honk I had to leave his taxies behind and climb onto the next ou's taxies, *after* asking permission to cross that honk too ...

I caught up with Rooies.

He pointed me to a floor-polish brush, a battered broom, a few pieces of blanket and torn Guvvie towel. I was to get on my knees and take hold of the brush, *like so* – as if I were about to give the floor heart-massage – and polish the surface in a rhythmic, seesawing motion. It was hard work and – after another klap – I found out that I had to keep my feet up while doing it. My fucking shoes dragged on my fucking honk making fucking marks and they would make Rooies look like a fucking poes in front of Jaamie during Inspection. After a few minutes I had shooting pains in my shoulders, arms, back and – most of all – my knees, which were rubbed raw from the floor. It took a short while to figure out I should put taxies under them too.

Rooies' system was simple. You did something wrong and he klapped you. You counted a few stars while he very placidly explained (*fokken gevrek*) your error. Then he showed you how to do it right. Once. If you did it wrong again, he klapped you twice. The first time for doing it wrong and the second time for taking him for a poes by not listening to him the first time.

I was crying in open misery by the time the siren rang for Stiltetyd. I got klapped for that too. My mouth was bleeding inside and my face felt hot (*snottysore*) and battered. My top lip was swollen and damp. Another klap and Rooies calmly told me to hurry up and stop snivelling. There were NO fucking crybabies in Dassie Bult. The lowest piece of living shit that I was permitted to be was a worthless blougat. I had obviously mistaken Rooies for the visible part of a lady's reproductive organs quite a lot that morning.

During Stiltetyd, Fk. Poeslappie warned me in an ominous, low, singsong voice that I better get my shit together before Inspection. Jaamie was coming, and if he and Rooies looked like poese in front of Jaamie, then what had happened to me so far would seem like satisfying group sex compared to how fat they would kick me in my poes next. I dried my eyes and wiped my slimy lip with my arm.

It was mos'ly water but dere was a lekker big snottery bit, like a pap spoon full.

The leaders had to make sure that we shaped up to Das standard. This was accomplished by inflicting physical violence on us any which way they pleased. They were expected to do this without obvious evidence of their handiwork, so mostly they avoided the face and concentrated on other areas. Fist to the solar plexus, knee in the kidneys, kick to back of the head. Inventive klappe. Rooies had reddened but not *blackened* my face. He'd given me a mouthful of blood, made my kidneys ache, and caused my ribs to creak horribly with every breath I took, but if I had a good look at myself in the mirror I would see that I had been worked over by a master. I was in a world of real pain, from my gut to everywhere, but you couldn't really see it. My reddened face was for Jaamie's benefit. Rooies was just showing Jaamie that he had things under control. A new blougat had come in (*It was mos'ly water ...*), but he was showing me (*a lekker big snotty bit*) how things worked.

Inspection.

Jaamie walked in with a clipboard and somebody yelled:

– *Kamer 2 gereedfo' Inspeksie!!* –

– *[Jaamie] Môre manne, Klagtes en versoeke?* –

Everybody remained quiet. Jaamie exchanged a glance with Rooies and Fk. Poeslappie, then gazed expressionlessly at me.

– *Complaints or requests?* –

(*Piemp, Poeslappie ...?*)

None sir.

– *Mooi* –

Jaamie inspected the dormitory while we all stood to attention at the foot of our beds.

Breakfast started off with grace and a good gagging for me. I sat down to eat my mieliepap, sugar apparently not included, feeling lumpy and sore. As I was eating I noticed something suspiciously (*worm!*) like a worm in my plate. To my absolute horror it was. A curled-up, well-boiled worm embalmed in a lump of mieliepap. I put it on the side of my plate. Sis! It made me paranoid, so I started trawling through the tasteless white mud for more (*worms!?*) suspicious-looking lumps. To my absolute nauseating horror I found about five more. It suddenly dawned on me that I had quite possibly (*boiled worm!!*) swallowed one already. That's when the snake woke up writhing and I nearly lost my breakfast. I clung to the thin green edge of nausea and was about to push my plate away when Rooies calmly ordered me to eat my fucking pap blougat. Shaking, I pushed the image of (*slimywormshit*) worms out of my mind, scrunched my eyes closed so that they could only just see (*faintfurryroundwhiteblob ...*) the plate, picked up my spoon and strangled the snake.

... like a pap spoon full of wormsssslimysssnotteryness.

I went through pretty much the same shit with Rooies on my outside honk, and I was not allowed to smoke in the bungalow, but before I knew it, Flag Parade had ended and classes began. All the lectures were in Afrikaans, seasoned mildly with a little English. I was to take English, Afrikaans, Maths, Science, History, Electrician's Theory and Electrician's Practical. School was still school, even in Rock, and I found my way back into the work.

Fk. Poeslappie and Rooies discovered I sucked my thumb. Klappe rained down and the snotrag stayed damp. The old snake no longer managed more than a catnap and it twisted around in my gut, fretting constantly all day. I figured that a good one was a day when I didn't cry. I had only scrambled through one of those so far. I detested myself for crying, but I couldn't help it. There was nothing I could do. Even if I were big enough to defend myself, it wouldn't help a bit. Touch one of the leaders and the rest would tear you to pieces. Cut one and they all bled. Miserable could not even begin to describe how I felt. I clung to one hope:

HOLIDAY PERMISSION.

I only had to get through two endless months of Uncle Guvvie's Blougat (*Poesplaas*) Farm before the school holidays started.

Every morning, the last blougatte to make it out to their honk got klapped. The old blougatte were fast, so it was left to a few at the bottom of the heap to fight their way out of the door. By the third day I managed to overtake an oke called Koosklutch who only had half of one foot. The other half had been lost in a bad accident. The nickname had to do with his limp making him look like a car with clutch trouble. He had a huge, ugly old prosthetic boot that he thumped up and down with.

Bingo tournaments were staged almost every night, and Fk. Poeslappie and Rooies roamed the dormitory, checking that everyone participated. Klappe were dished out if you didn't.

I learnt that the worms in the food were called taragoppies. And one didn't look good protein in the eye. It was best to eat with a minimum of chewing and as little imagination as possible. Everybody did. The side effects were painful boils, which Tannie Mop sorted out with boil plasters and black ointment from a big tin. I saw ous suck the etter out of ripe boils with five fat white heads in one hole.

Before I knew it, the end of the long nightmarish week had arrived.

On Fridays we were issued a boepbeker full of aapies an' mangorries as an extra protein supplement to our diet. That stainless-steel mug full of peanuts and raisins was the only gift from Uncle Guvvie that was a constant and highly tradable commodity. From the very beginning, I lived from week to week waiting for it.

My privates were finished, mostly pawned by Robert Nienaber, but he told me to hang onto my aapies. He would smokkel them for a knoesie of snout and some check for me. And not to worry, he wouldn't sluk me out. I decided to trust him, and so it transpired that I descended to kaffir level and smoked my first Dassie-puff.

The only safe place to silent-puff was in the boiler room behind the kitchen or behind the bungalow at night. My snout slowly petered out from a sizable knoesie to a feeble, two-thirds paper, toothpick drag, and I was left to scratch surreptitiously inside the bungalow for any long tappies that I could find on the floor. There were very few of these, and they were mostly issue. I was not alone. Nienaber, Koosklutch and another ou called Doom were my usual rivals. I began to despair. I had been bribing myself with the promise of my next silent-puff to put up with the (*fokkengevrek!*) klappe and other shit all day. Nienaber helped me a little but he maar also sukkeled for everything. He and Koosklutch were allowed to smoke because they were old enough, so they always went into the bungalow and tried to pawn from the other ouens. Doom and I were too young. Doom was in my dormitory and got his name from being a total vuilgat. The ous reckoned that any insect that made the dumb mistake of landing on him would peg right then and there. He was a walking talking *non-perfumed* contact insecticide.

On Sunday morning I dressed in my shit-brown crimpelene suit. After breakfast I followed the rest of the ous up to the workshops to collect my two cents for church collection. We marched to our various churches in crocodile under the watchful eyes of the leaders. I was listed as Presbyterian.

Going into town was like stepping into a dreamscape. My focus had narrowed to that of a blougat, scratching around for tappies to silent-puff or a spare piece of rogue to pawn, and I had forgotten that there was a (*private*) real, ordinary, even familiar world out there. It seemed I had been gone for so long...

That evening I was introduced to the Sunday supper tradition. After a meal of banana, boiled egg, dop and rogue, we gave Thanks, and then Fk. Poeslappie would bang on his table with a knife for order, and to enthusiastic handclapping and hooting, the winners of the previous week's awards would stand and take their bows. Once the applause died down, they would announce the next week's lucky winners.

Mock fanfare.

It was the Grand Awarding of ... the Vuilgatbeker, and the even less sought-after ... Poesbeker!

As each happy contestant went up to accept his well-earned prize he was pelted with banana skins and eggshells. This continued until he had – *Speech! Speech!* – completed his hasty acceptance.

As the lowest blougat in the school, I was, as tradition demanded, awarded both trophies.

It wasn't so bad, really. Just a few slimy peels and eggshells.

That night we had a church service in the school hall. There was only one onnie on duty. We sang a few hymns and the ouens gave it absolutely everything they had. Each hostel always sat in their own set of seats and they all valiantly tried to out-sing each other. Hostel honour was at stake, and klappe were dished out afterwards for apathetic participation. Then the duty onnie would pray and we would roar out a few more hymns. Finally he read a long passage from the Bible and we would have one last go at tearing off the roof. Old favourites like *In Berge en in Dale*, *Oom God van Jakob* and *Onward Christian Soldiers* must have made even God stuff his fingers in his ears.

Then it was time for Blouesaand.

Blouesaand began thirty seconds after the onnie on duty had left the hall and ended just before the Opkoms roll-call twenty minutes later. In essence it was a massive game of hide and seek, with the bloues hiding and the Dasse seeking. The thirty-second gap was to give you a small head start.

Run and hide …

The Dasse hunted in packs, and being caught meant continual klappe from multiple sources all the way back to the bungalow. The bloues were all kept there until the last one had been found. Then the real fun started.

If we had all been winkled out before roll-call, we were subjected to a takkie party by the whole hostel, leading out from the door of the bungalow. This would entail (*ekis-eerste fokkof-ekis*) trying to grab a first place in the row of blougatte inside the bungalow, then diving for the door and crawling in between the legs of all the other ous in the hostel standing in a long line. They in turn (*fokkenblougat!*) flailed your back and arse with shoes, floor brushes and unidentifiable nasty hard things – as you (*gevrektepoeslappie!*) scrambled through. Most of the blougatte would be trying to hide their tears by the end of it.

If one or more of us managed to stay hidden, we were rewarded with no takkie party at all, and instead the ouens would play bok-bok in the quad with us bloues against the Dasse until Opkoms. But that didn't mean that you wouldn't get a klap for singing apathetically in Church either way.

The following Sunday, as reigning trophy-champion, I awarded Fk. Poeslappie the Poesbeker, and Rooies the Vuilgatbeker. They expressed their deep depreciation to me later by cutting me a dripping wet snotrag full of klappe on some (*fokkengevrek!*) excuse.

It was worth it though – seeing the shock in their eyes that I had even dared. It was no small business either. The Poesbeker and the Vuilgatbeker were serious open theatres. Everyone in the hostel treated anybody who walked onto that stage the same way and no one gave a flying fuck who you were when you stepped up.

By then I was starting to get used to all the klappe and learnt a strange lesson. It is something a boxer learns. You are going to get hit. Fact. The only thing to do about it is to learn to roll and move with the punches. In boxing it is an essential skill because it cuts down on your quota of pain and tires out your opponent.

Nienaber called it ducking and diving. He also told me it was much harder to be a poes to somebody who laughed the leaders' shit off. I tried that but it didn't get me very far. To master it, you had to reach a place in yourself where you simply didn't give a fuck any more, and I couldn't do that. Yet. Every day in that hole made me trade deeper and deeper into something called Payback where nobody fucked with me for free.

Then Doom walloped. One night after Bingo we all fell asleep as usual. The next morning he was gone. Jaamie had caught him silent-puffing the day before and took away his Holiday Permission. Doom decided that he wasn't going to make it without a break, so he took off down the walloppad. It made Fk. Poeslappie and Rooies look like big hairy menstruating poese in front of Jaamie of course, and that made it so much worse for all the rest of us.

Snotrags for everybody! Line up!

Doom was caught by the mapuza in Knysna, still wearing his Guvvie kitters, and that evening he was back in the hostel. Jaamie gave him six cuts, with F-Group to go, and Fk. Poeslappie and Rooies cut him his own special snotrag full of klappe in the bungalow afterwards. From then on he was in F-Group and spent most of his time on outside honks with one of the leaders watching him and keeping the snotrag wet. He took the pressure off the rest of us a little.

I received letters from Denise and Laura.

Denise's letter rambled on about bitter family scandal – *Poor old Uncle Ian, Aunty Gerry went and ran off ...* – and convoluted money troubles. I marvelled at her ability to mould truth into her own realities. She spoke to me in the letter as if the court case and all the shit with her and Wally had never happened. She was simply taking up the reins of a concerned parent with a child in a school quite far away. In my desperation for money to smokkel for snout I thought about her divorce settlement. Wally had to give her R100 a month for me until I was eighteen. I no longer cost her a single cent of that money and she couldn't even send me five bucks of it. Some concerned parent. The money troubles were a smoke screen to fob off any hints I might throw out. Wally owned the house, so she didn't even have to pay rent. All she had to pay for was food for her and the little ones.

Bitch.

I could completely forget about getting money or letters from Wally.

I wrote back neutrally (*I'm sorry to hear about ...*) and asked if I could submit her address for Holiday Permission.

Laura's letter was the prize. She gave me the low-down and dirty on Darren, Carla and the rest of the gang. Nothing much had changed. She was being FAITHFUL! She loved me and missed me, blah-be-de-blah. They were going to Cape Town for Christmas and she had asked her mom if I could come on holiday with them. Her mom had said yes!

Being faithful? I wondered. Going on holiday to Cape Town, Befuck! I wrote back straight away and explained how Holiday Permission worked. I figured her mom would know what to do, because she raised money for Boys Town for a living.

Waiting for Laura's next letter took me to a circle of hell deeper than the one I was already purgatorising in. At last, one lunchtime, Jaamie gave me a letter and, surprise upon surprise, he told me that I had received a PAKKIE! I didn't know which piece of mail to be more excited about.

Pakkies were given to you during afternoon study. Jaamie would call the ous with pakkies one by one, and then you went to his office. He cut the parcel open, searched it and removed all the contraband. You were not held responsible for stuff that was sent to you. Jaamie just confiscated it wordlessly. Because everybody else was in study, you had the chance to stash the goeters away in your locker before any of the other ous could see them and try to pawn them.

You couldn't pawn what you couldn't see.

Laura's pakkie had smokes, which – *aaaah shiiiit* – Jaamie took out and put to one side. There were also home-baked cookies and lollies, which I hid in my locker, but I couldn't help gulping down a cookie or two quickly. Mmm ... I slipped some more cookies and some lollies into my pockets and went back to study. I had kept her letter to read after my pakkie was opened so that if it was bad news, at least I'd have something sweet to swallow it down with. She started with the usual:

Hi, howzit, she missed me. She was still being The Big "F" Word. I was the only one for her blah-be-de-blah ... *wait* – Sharon had actually spoken to Stronk and given our holiday address to the Welfare in Cape Town! We would be staying with her Uncle in Kalk Bay. Her mom would stick me for the train ticket. Aah ... fuck, that was so good, that was so damned fucking cooool!

I couldn't contain myself. I grabbed Nienaber after study and told him, crazy with delight. It was only when I noticed the dead expression in his eyes that I realised it wasn't something that he would even pretend to be excited about because he never bothered with Holiday Permission anyway. WHO the fuck would he go to? I gave him a cookie and let him pawn me on another one. That got him excited. He smokkeled a fat knoes of snout for me with some of the lollies and I let him pawn me on most of it too.

There was a Pom oke in Hostel 4. He was hard and wiry, and rumour had it that he could piss all over Fk. Poeslappie if they ever had a fight. Rumour also had it that Fk. Poeslappie was too scared to ever start one. His name was Nick Noble and he was a real strange fucker. At the end of the year, Uncle Guvvie was going to deport him back to the UK. One of the freakier things he did was sign every piece of paper Uncle Guvvie gave him with the word FUCK. He also suntanned in every spare second and he smoked dagga.

The leaders would fuck up anybody that they caught smoking dagga. Nick Noble smoked zol. Sucks to Uncle Guvvie and sucks to the leaders. Apparently another ou named Webster also smoked with Nick but that was only a rumour.

One night, just before Opkoms, I slipped out to silent-puff in the boiler room. I found Nick Noble and Webster hitting a pipe. They hadn't expected me and I didn't expect them. Silence reigned for a few long moments as we stared at each other, then Nick spoke:

– *Do you smoke grass mate?* –

I nodded.

– *'Ave a chestie mate. But ya only 'ave one, And you better keep your fucking gob shut, Aw'right?* –

– *Of course, Nick* –

– *I don't want you blabbing to your blowkat mates about me or Webster, understand?* –

– *I understand, Nick, this never happened* –

He let me have three hits with them.

Later, after Bingo, I lay in my bed goofed and wide awake. I savoured my gerookness like a fine larney meal. It was gooooooood …

In fact it was the best I had felt since arriving at Uncle Guvvie's Poesplaas. Nick Noble was a real cool dude to have made me feel like that. For free. He was a Matric and he had been nice to a *blowkat* like me. What a MENS.

I thought ahead to the holidays. I had my Permission. All I had to do was stay out of (*silent-puffing*) trouble. I was going to Cape Town! To Laura. I started fantasising about Laura.

In my fantasy she was nowhere near as fat as I remembered her. She had (*darren.steve.greg.keebol.titch.who.wants.seconds …*) never fucked anybody. I was her first. Long before Darren and all the others. I tried hanging onto that fantasy but it kept wobbling out of shape, and the images of *that* afternoon in Titch's flat kept swirling in. Darren fucking her. No, Steve. Steve would have been first. Then Darren. Then Greg, Keebol, and Titch last. I wondered how it felt to put your cock inside another man's spunk. Sis. It was like being a fucking homo or something. The look of shocked surprise when I saw her walk from the bedroom to the bathroom – after Titch had come out. I felt bad thinking about her in that flat. It was a dark box that I only went into sometimes when I played Bingo. Her, lying on her back all spread out, and them in a line with their cocks all out and hard. I hated the image of other cocks in my mind. Pushing into her. Harder, harder, making her wet. Slippery. Not MINE.

Stop! STOP!!

I got carried away sometimes. Fucking homo stuff. It was a strange thing. We played Bingo almost every night, otherwise Fk. Poeslappie and Rooies would fuck you up. You knew when you did it that the other ouens were all doing it too and that made sick fucking nongie thoughts try and get into your head. Sis. Nongalosh was the prison word for an arse bandit. A homo. If Fk. Poeslappie and Rooies suspected for one second that there was anything nongie about you — they would kick you deep in your poes. Good and solid. Not just a little klap either.

There were no fucking nongies in Dassie Bult.

Moffies got fucked up.

I slept.

Two weeks before the holidays, I made it to D-Group. It meant that I got my private kitters back and I also had a Dorp or Movie privilege on Saturdays. No longer would I have to stand in the Dorp roll-call knowing I wasn't going anywhere. A lot of ouens in the school were in D-Group. E-Group was the biggest group. You were only supposed to stay in E-Group for six weeks, but if you were put on any of the Strafboeke they held you back for another six weeks and you lost Holiday Permission. Almost all the leaders and most of the Matrics were C-Groups. One oke had made it to B-Group in the last five years, and in all recorded history there had only been one ou who made it to A-Group – back in the sixties.

There had never been an AA-Group Das.

It had to do with the politics of running the school. The leaders were chosen carefully by the onnies. In return for their loyalty to the System, they were rewarded with leadership responsibilities. They had to keep school discipline tight and the wallop rate down and apply everyone to their honks. Succeed as a leader and you were rewarded with higher Group privileges. It gave you incentive and helped you to achieve the Administration's objectives. Stronk answered to Uncle Guvvie, and that was what it was all really about.

Pleasing Uncle Guvvie ...

The nature and shape of school discipline was left for the leaders themselves to define. Outside of that they had a set of written and separately *understood* rules to uphold. The onnies stayed out of it. As long as there weren't too many visible injuries, they had a free hand in procuring their mandate any way they saw fit.

That's the way it had always been. That's the way Uncle Guvvie wanted it.

The school was actually an important national monument in the area. It had an ill-lustrious past that stretched all the way back to the time of slaves. Stronk loved propagating the grand tale of its history – *Krügerganda*. It had begun as a slave-trading post. After the slaves were emancipated it was used as a place for orphans and the children of the indigent. Eventually it became a school for wayward boys who were introduced to the rigours of a Reformed Protestant work ethic and the fundamentals of acting like good Christian Gentlemen. One of the earliest trades taught there had been wagon-making.

Uncle Guvvie was actually very, very old. He was like a Groot Oom Kwaadraad or something.

Hostel 4/Hole 57, D-Group.

I had no money for movies, so I went for a walk into town for my first Dorp. Robert had no money either so he came along. It was the first little taste of freedom that I'd enjoyed since arriving there. I zoned Robert out as we wandered the familiar streets of George. That's all we could really do. We were only allowed in two of the kafees in town, and there were always leaders there to make sure that only a certain number of selected Dasse were allowed inside. We weren't allowed in any other shops because of shoplifting. Nobody in town trusted or liked us. That's where all the bad stories I'd heard about the Dasse as a child had come from. Wally had used them to threaten me with Die Bult.

Still, it was wonderful pretending that I was free.

The last two weeks flew past and then dragged forever on the final day. I was leaving Uncle Guvvie's Poesplaas.

I was about to die and go to heaven …

I left on the school bus with the rest of the Cape Town Ouens, all dressed up in private kitters. A box of padkos lay on my lap and the news that Johnny Killian was Headboy for next year sat uneasily in my head. Rooies was to be his subordinate. They had been chosen, as always, by the Administration. Killian had a bad reputation. He hadn't klapped me yet, but then again he had no compunction about klapping a Das if he thought the need had arisen.

I had seen it.

He and Rooies were both in Standard 9, and had been that year's under-leaders for Hostel 4. Soon they would be running the whole show. It destroyed my joy in seeing the back of Fk. Poeslappie. They were both ecstatic when told the news. I tuned them out of my brain.

Next year's worries. Time to go to heaven …

The train journey was an experience. We were all placed in the last two coaches. In the third coach was an extra contingent of conductors to try and maintain control and keep us away from the rest of the train. We stopped at Hartenbos and then it all went out the windows. The train went on to Mossel Bay and then returned, before continuing to Cape Town, so a small crew jumped off and went to the local bottle store with orders. When we got back into Hartenbos they were waiting at the station. Everybody got fucked. One oke, Thomas, was Out – a free man – and feeling generous. I was in his compartment. He made us pipes and shared a six-man can of Lieberstein with the other three of us. Thomas sadly only had two weeks to live before drowning while trying to dive for crays fucked on Mandrax. I remember passing out and sleeping with my head halfway out the window and waking up in Paarl the next morning with only an hour before our arrival in Cape Town.

And Freedom …

I was heading into the city alone. It was the only place that I had ever gone to alone by choice. Mostly to Digre but also to John. I still had to make it to Kalk Bay on my own steam.

I wasn't in a hurry.

Freedom …

*

The train pulled into Cape Town station and I stepped off. I had just walked into God's waiting room …

I stood looking at the metro timetable. I had enough kroon for a packet of privates. There was no way I was going to smoke issue Dassie-puffs in front of the private mense on the street. I could also seriously use a beer. But then I wouldn't have enough for a ticket to Kalk Bay.

Fuck that! I'll hike and buy privates and a spark on the way.

I bought a pack of Chesterfields on the Grand Parade and headed towards Main Road. I reached the Good Hope Centre and put my anchors down to hike. Nobody stopped. I smoked. I hiked.

After a while, a Morris Minor pulled over. I ran up, thanked the oke driving and told him I was heading to Kalk Bay.

– Yes … he breathed. *I go that way –*

The ou had a puffy round face, black glasses and a bald head. Slightly fat. Mid-twenties. He asked my name and where I came from.

From school. In George. Gonna join my girlfriend in Kalk Bay for Christmas. Oh, and my name – Alex. And him?

– *[Pom accent] I'm Martin and I'm what you would call a freelancer. Ha! Ha! Ha! I'm surprised you say you're still in school – you look like a bit of an Army lad to me –*

– *It must be my hair. We wear it quite short –*

– *That's a pity. I was going to ask you if you wanted to pop into a pub for a quick beer … –*

– *Well, I'm not actually in a big hurry, so if you want to, let's go –*

– *Alex, Alex. If they found out you were under age they would arrest me. You don't look like you're old enough to have been arrested, but trust me, you want to avoid that like the plague –*

Little he knew.

– *I have another idea. Why don't we just pop into my flat on the way. We could have a beer and I'll make us a quick bit of grub. How's that sound to you? –*

– *Geez, you mean that? Thanks man, that would be kwaai –*

He reached across and (*friendlylike*) squeezed my knee, just a bit (*it felt*) too long. He asked me to tell him about school. Fuck, I didn't want to talk about school! He looked like a larney straight ou. He would probably freak if he heard I was in one of those places. I tried to steer the conversation somewhere else. He seemed to sense that, because he stopped prying and put on some music. Pink Floyd – amazing! We reached his block and went upstairs to his flat. He went straight to the fridge and came back with two beers.

Cheers Alex!

Cheers Martin!

We drank. I lit a drag and chatted. This stuff, that stuff. Twice Martin asked if I wanted a bath but I told him it was okay. I downed my first beer and he fetched me another. I started to feel amazingly like the snake was untwisting itself from Poesplaas Die Bult and getting ready for a nice little snooze on the beach at Kalk Bay.

Martin said he liked me. I didn't act my age and I was good to talk to. I finished the second beer. I was feeling seriously fucking kwaai. I told Martin he was a kwaai dude too. He came back with two more beers and told me we should slow down a bit and enjoy them.

I had kind of gulped down my first two.

He suggested we play a game of cards. Cool. We started playing Rummy. After a couple of hands and another beer I was getting to be exactly like I wanted to be—

Alexander Douglas (Bitch-Born Bastard, Blikkieskos, PuddlePirate, Asterix, Yster) Goulding wants to get fucked, folks …

Go away Poesplaas! GO AWAY!

– [Martin] I'm getting rightly fucking bored playing a game of chance without betting for something –

– I agree, but there's one small problem. I don't have any money to gamble with, and if you gave me money then it wouldn't really be gambling, now would it –

– You're so right –

I lit another smoke. We drank.

– [Martin dis-seriously]Do you know what would be really nuts and a big laugh? –

– What? –

– If we played Strip Poker just for the fun of it –

– Strip Poker? But that's no fun without girls –

– Yeah, I know, but it would be a bit nutty and a bit of a lark, don't you think? –

I was sloshed. It seemed like a totally dumb thing to do, but what the fuck. There was no harm in it. We could play to underpants and then stop. Game over.

I couldn't sit there all day getting fucked.

He cut. I dealt.

Stud Poker. Queen high with one-eyed Jacks wild.

I lost.

I pulled off my ring and put it on the table.

He tossed a hand.

I discarded some trash and picked up a low straight.

Martin took something off.

We swopped hands back and forth.

I lost to my underpants.

– [Me] Well, that's the end of the line. Time to quit the game –

– Yeah, you're right. It wouldn't be fun to put our clothes back on and play again, but don't worry, I've got a better idea. Why don't we play for Penalties? If I lose, you have to tell me to do something, and if you lose then I'll tell you to do pushups or a dare or something nutsy like that –

[Weird]

– Okay, that doesn't sound too kak, but only for a couple of hands, and then I must hit the road –

We played.

I think I had an idea (*back in the car already*) that there were a lot of (*homo*) things that I didn't know about Martin. I was nicely drunk and having a good time but I wasn't really accepting the truth of my situation.

I beat him with my hand.

He did twenty pushups for his Penalty.

We played.

His hand took mine.

I went into his study where he couldn't see me and beat my one-eyed Jack for my Penalty.

He came in to see if I was Cheating.

(*homo*)

I was all soft.

Soft was (*homo*) Cheating.

He would show me how …

That was the great dawning of the exact (*homo*) situation that I had feared in darkness, although I had never rightly understood what to fear for, until Now – then I suddenly saw it in all its stark and lurid detail. There was a couch in the study. He kind of (*homohomohomo*) pushed me down on it, panting like a steam engine. He looked all porky but he was actually fucking strong. Like a big rock in a sack of mielie-meal. He open-mouth kissed me. His beard scratched my face (*tongueslimy*) and the fat of his face smothered me. There was fuckall I could do.

Afterwards Martin took pictures of me. He wanted me to lie with my legs open, so I did. I was still in Mental Defences mode until I walked out of the flat (*it never happened*). I put my hand over my eyes so nobody would see me and he took his pictures.

splay ...
[!click ...!click]
bend over ...
[!click]
splay ...
[!click]
splay more ...
[!click ...!click ...!click]
pretend you're coming ...
[!click]
bend your finger over and make like you're putting it into yourself ...
[ohgodyes !click ...!click] ...

After I had thrown on my clothes, I told Martin that I had to go (*it never happened*). He too put his ugly scarred little genitals back into his pants and then did something that threw me completely off balance. He sat down, told me I had been a real good sport and gave me eighty fucking rands. Just a little way of saying *Thank you*. I had been so sweet.

He dropped me off. My arse throbbed and felt slippery and hot (*it never happened*). I decided to reward myself (*it never happened*) by splashing out with my newfound wealth and buying a lekker chow. Eighty fucking rands. I could buy any fucking chow I wanted. I found a bakery and bought some cream doughnuts and a chocolate pie.

I was still very pissed.

I didn't want to open the door on what happened back there.

Not now.

Not fucking ever.

All that worried me were the pictures. Who would see the pictures?

Back on the road I stuck out my thumb. I needed to get to the station and catch a train.

The guy who stopped told me he was heading to Tokai. He would drop me at the station. Kwaai, I jumped in. He was tall and thinnish, thirty? Dirty blond hair. Wiry muscles in a cowboy movie. English oke. He started driving and pulled onto the freeway.

He reached over, put his hand between my legs and asked me if I had ever done it with a man. The absolute shock of it froze my brain. I simply could not believe that I had just managed to get away from Martin and already some other FUCKING HOMO had his hands on me. I must have looked paralysed because he started rubbing my crotch, panting – I liked it, I liked it, didn't I? I managed to unstrangle myself and tell him that I only liked girls.

Don't fucking lie to him! There was NOTHING *wrong with it and I liked it – he could* SEE.

Suddenly there was a lot of Fk. Poeslappie in his voice.

A horrible lot.

I didn't want to make him angry so I said (*when he stops I'll jump out*) I didn't mind but I still liked girls much better. He didn't seem to listen to me, but kept on panting about how much I liked it. My head was starting to figure things out again. He hadn't touched me proper. He was busy masticating my poor balls and cock through my pants. He wasn't actually touching me. I just had to wait till I could grab my rucksack from the back seat and jump out.

So I just sat there and let him do it …

He pulled off the freeway and turned into a forest road. I asked him why we were going in the wrong direction. He just kept on driving and panting that *I would like it. I had* TOLD *him that I didn't mind.* I said I really didn't want to go anywhere but he just kept on panting – not listening. The road we were on was absolutely deserted. He had opened his pants and had himself out. I tried not to look but he was fucking big and hairy (*uncircumcised*). And hard.

He stopped, opened the door and pulled me out. His grip was like steel. I kept on saying *please* I didn't want to but he wouldn't listen and pulled me into the forest. He pushed me to my knees and tore off my jeans and undies. I couldn't get out of his grip and I couldn't move my legs. Then he did something to himself behind me and I thought that I was going to be able to get away when he suddenly pushed my face down into the pine needles. Hard. Then my arse turned into a world of tearing hot pain. With Martin it had hurt like a very big hard shit stretching me, but this was like he had put a solid bar of white pain in me. The agony was so bad that it took me a moment to realise that my whole face was squashed into the ground and I couldn't breathe. Even then it didn't matter because the pain in my back pushed everything out of its way. All the strength went out of my legs. And it went on and on – and crescendoed like an orchestra hitting everything together. Again and Again. I desperately tried to find the centre of the pain and breathe. I managed to twist my face sideways into the pine needles and they poked and tore at my screwed-up eye. I wanted them to hurt my eye so bad that they would overcome the OTHER. I was making a small moaning sound that I couldn't help when I was very badly hurt somewhere. I could taste soil in my mouth decayed and musty.

Rotten.

One day I'm going to have a million bucks and I'm going to be in love and when this stops I am never going to remember it.

I sang it into the pain until he stopped. He collapsed on me when he stopped, jerking and making groany barking noises. He got off and let me go. I turned to look at him. His face went fucking hard (*bad!*) and he turned it (SNAKEBAD!) away:

– [HISSING] *You liked it. I SAW YOU PANTING. You liked it! You better fucking say YOU LIKED IT!* –

Somewhere deep, deep down inside me a much older, colder wisdom awoke and kicked in, pushing the hot demands of the pain away.

THIS IS NOT FUCKING OVER YET ... *WAKE UP!!*

What I said next could get me a fuckload more than an angry poephol. It could buy me witbene. This ou was fucked in his tree and he was insanely strong. He wouldn't sukkel doing it to me either. I had to get him to look at me and talk to me.

I managed to convince him I was just very shy and begged him to let me suck him.

We eventually walked back to his car.

A couple of times he started flipping out again but I kept on telling him that I actually liked it and maybe he should give me his address so that I could come and visit him and then we could have more time and do it slower.

Strangely, he drove me to the station as promised. I watched him fucking carefully the whole way and kept on blabbing about how I didn't want Them to find out I liked this stuff. I did like it, but it's just that I didn't want Them to find out. They could be so horrible if They found out you liked it.

He gave me some tepid water from a water bottle on the back seat.

It didn't take the taste away.

I didn't relax when he dropped me. I only allowed myself to begin thinking about it when I was on the train. I couldn't look anybody in the eye. I was certain they could see it in me. In my eyes. His spunk running out of my ears. My arse was a deep throbbing almost numb agony with deeper burning fires reaching into my gut. I smoked badly to get the shit taste out of my mouth. I hadn't even found out his name and he was going to make me witbene. I felt it. I had actually fucking felt it. Somehow, I had said all the vuil stuff he wanted to hear. Fuck. I was lucky. I was so fucking lucky. That ou back there was sickfuck twisted and he had let me go. I started shaking uncontrollably.

NONE OF IT EVER FUCKING HAPPENED.

I arrived at Laura's uncle's house trying to walk normal. He told me his name was Neil and I was to relax and make myself at home. In the toilet I found my underpants were soaked in blood at the back. Blobby, snotty, blackish-looking blood that had dried into the cloth. It had soaked into my jeans and on the blue side looked like a dark grease mark. It hurt trying to wipe myself and took a long time. I bathed carefully and there was a lot of blood in the water. It hurt to sit. I tried not to think how much it was going to hurt to take my next shit. After my bath I carefully spread my legs and bent over. I folded some toilet paper into long squares and padded myself dry. There was still blood in amongst the wetness. Shiny red blood crawling through the wet tissue paper. I folded myself a thick poeslap with a piece of toilet paper and bent over to get it to sit on my hole properly. Then I straightened and carefully pulled on clean underpants. It sat badly and it felt like hot sandpaper on me but it would keep me dry. I half wished that Laura were already there because I definitely needed a real (*softer*) poeslap.

I smuggled the bloody underpants out of the house and threw them away in a bin on the street.

That was that. As soon as I stopped bleeding and the deep hurt had gone away – it would be over. I would never ever fucking think of it again. NEVER.

I cried very badly that night. I hated myself for getting all crybaby in the dark but there was nobody to hear me, so it was okay. I was all fucked up inside. I had to seriously rage with myself to forget. *It never happened!* And I just bawled like a baby when I had to take a shit.

Stupid fucking blougat poeslappie. You fucking did it to yourself both times. If you had kept your fucking rucksack on your fucking knees, you could have jumped out the car. And with Martin don't tell me you could NOT *have walked out with your clothes on if you hadn't been so fucking keen on drinking all his beer. What? Are you a fucking nongalosh? You certainly* ARE *a fucking skaap. Everything Fk. Poeslappie and Rooies said about you is* TRUE. *You had better make some hard choices blougat. Some very* HARD *choices my friend. And you had better get your forgetting hat on too. Just now you are going to think into it back there, and think it wasn't so bad, and skiem and skiem and the next thing you know you will be beating your one-eyed Jack to get Queen High over it. Are you a nongie or are you a Das –* BLOUGAT MET DIE POESLAP?

The deep bruised fire in me died out. I only had spikes of pain when I parped my shit muscles, which I found I did unconsciously for all sorts of fucking dumb reasons I had simply never noticed before. Like coughing. Coughing was like getting reamed out by a jerky little midget with a strap-on rough wooden stake. Crude humour, like this, was a way of closing the door.

IT NEVER HAPPENED.

Laura arrived, the pain faded and two weeks into the holidays Uncle Neil approached Laura and announced that he had a Special Friend who was in the Army. The young man had a few days' pass and was coming to visit. Would Laura mind standing in as a date for one night and go clubbing with him? She told Uncle Neil no problem. I had a heated argument with her and afterwards snubbed her with the silent treatment. She had told me Neil was, you know … queer, only he called it being gay.

In light of recent events, this obviously disturbed me fucking deeply.

The Army moffie arrived and he and Laura went out for the night. Afterwards Laura fucked him. That was it – I wanted nothing to do with her any more. I found myself in a house full of strangers feeling utterly horrible with nowhere to go. I ambled down to the beach every day and hung around the rock pool feeling indefinably shit – drinking half-jacks of brandy from the slowly dwindling gintu money Martin had given me.

Father Christmas came and went without leaving much trace of his passage. A week or so after New Year, Laura came to me.

– *Alex, I need some help* –

– *You want my help? Why don't you ask your moffie?* –

– *Alex, please don't be mean. I beg of you. I'm in trouble and I need your help* –

– *Okay Laura, what can I help you with?* –

– *I'm late* –

– *What?* –

– *I'm late. You know, my period* –

– *Oh …* –

– *I'm always exactly on time and it was supposed to start last week* –

– *So what must I do?* –

– *Will you help me get rid of it? I know a way to do it* –

– *Whose is it? Your Uncle's Army bum-chum fuck buddy or mine?* –

– *Alex, please, you promised* –

– *Laura, I didn't promise you any fucking thing. Whose is it?* –

– *It's not yours, the last time we did it was at the beginning of the holidays just after my mom came down and my last period had only just stopped so I was safe. It's got to be his* –

– *So why don't you ask him for help? Why the fuck come to me?* –

– *He's half-gay and he's in the Army anyway* –

– *So he can't help you because he's half a hol-bunny but he can fuck you and get you pregnant, is that right?* –

– *Alex, please, I beg you* –

– *Okay, okay, what is it I must do?* –

She wanted me to take a Tampax tampon, cut it in half and then fill the empty space in the application tube with Epsom salts. Then I was to insert the whole lot inside her, standing up, with the tampon keeping the salt plugged up against her cervix. At that stage I had no idea what a cervix was. I read the illustrated instructions in the Tampax box, getting slightly horny, and did it. By nightfall she was white as a sheet, feverish and crying from pain. A day later she was admitted to hospital for an emergency partial hysterectomy that left her with a badly scarred uterus and only a part of one ovary. She could never have children again.

We both killed much more than we had bargained for.

8

The Blougatboek

I was not terribly happy to see my peers back on Cape Town station. The journey back to George steamed from Uneasiness and thundered onward to Downright Dread. The experienced blougatte all knew there were serious political issues at stake. We began each year with an election for the new Das leadership in each hostel. Johnny Killian and Rooies were already Stronk's incumbent executives for the school.

Nominations would be declared by the corpus. The leadership would be elected from those nominations by a free and fair democratic process. The Blougatboek would be amended at an informal inauguration of the new heads of the corpus. What the actual face looked like on that body of government we would discover soon enough.

Thing was, upon admission to the school, your name and the date of your arrival were entered into the Blougatboek. This book was presided over by the Headboy and kept by the Under-headboy. Ostensibly you were to remain a blougat for a full year. However, the new Das executive rewrote that book annually.

In your favour – *possibly*.

Us blougatte all entered into the round table indaba and examined each of our cases in detail, not forgetting that we couldn't do anything really except speculate about each ou and try and tell him what he wanted to hear.

After much palaver I drew a conclusion based on their experience that I would be declared a Das at best at the end of the third term.

Things back at school had not changed.

Hello Uncle Guvvie! Anyone home? Yster's back ...

Rooies was now the new dormitory leader. He seemed in a casual, almost jovial mood, which was difficult to interpret. He hadn't had reason to dish out klappe to the ragged-looking bunch of new blougatte – yet. Jaamie welcomed us all back at graze. After voting, Uncle Guvvie had a movie for us in the school hall.

The election began immediately after graze. Jaamie came in with ballots, which were dished out to everybody. Nominations for new leaders had to be announced verbally and seconded by someone else from the floor. Most of the nominations were made by Johnny Killian and seconded by Rooies. Then the nomination list was closed and we all voted. The election was secret, so after we had made our list of seven candidates we folded the ballots and they were given to Jaamie. He disappeared and came back five minutes later and read out the names of the new leadership.

Johnny Killian's exact list of nominations.

We went to the hall for the fliek.

Yul Brynner and a bunch of funny, tough, convict GIs escape from a military stockade and steal a shitload of gold from some hairy Nazis but they give it all away to save Yugoslavia for Yul's new chick in the Resistance at the end.

Dumb fucks. Kwaai fliek.

None of the new leaders watched it. Johnny Killian and Rooies took them all into the toilets at the back of the hall for a meeting. Being Headboy and Under-headboy meant you had absolute loyalty from your exalted brethren in running the school. It was a pat on the back and a special squeeze of encouragement to be chosen by Uncle Guvvie to belong to that special group.

Movies were always noisy, as all the ous cheered on the hero of their choice – usually the bad ous. Sometimes arguments and small scuffles broke out between opposing supporters. When the movie finished, the lights went back on. Johnny Killian came in leading his team. The Blougatboek was under his arm. They paraded at the front and the duty onnie left discreetly.

Johnny started off by saying he wasn't gonna piss about. The reason why school was shit was because *we* made it shit. By doing that, we made it shit for *him*. So, during his term of office— all F-Group offences would appear before the Studenteraad. Secondly, there would be a river of snot for every wallop.

Did we understand?

Ja Johnny!

His announcement puzzled the whole school. This *Studenteraad* was a new thing. There was the Koshuisraad and the Leerlingraad, but nobody could figure out what this Studenteraad was all about.

His other declaration was a clearly understood shocker though. If ANYONE walloped he would be rewritten into the Blougatboek on the date he was escorted back to the school, and there would be no annual clemency for such a re-declared blougat. You would serve the full term. Regardless of who or what the fuck you were before you walloped – Matrics included. The same applied to ALL F-Group offences.

This was insane. He was saying that even if you were an old Das and you got gaaned for an F-Group offence, you would be written back into the Blougatboek. There was rumbling among the Dasse, especially the Matrics.

Johnny ignored them and made a rambling speech about Rugby and School Spirit that went on for five minutes and said bugger all. That done, he opened the Blougatboek. All the blougatte who had been charged for F-Group offences during the previous year had their dates frozen. I would be a Das at the beginning of the third term. All the new blougatte from each hostel had their names written in.

Meeting adjourned.

Over the holidays I had forgotten just how bad it was being a blougat, and soon desperate thoughts lay siege to my mind. I got klapped every day. Over and over. Johnny and Rooies both had an insatiable appetite for it. I loathed myself for crying most times and was starting to go crazy from living in constant terror. The only way to stop the pain and unspeakable loneliness would be to wallop. I couldn't see any other way out. Going to a teacher was a certified sentence worse than death.

As it turned out, there was an ou named Michael Silvey, who by weird coincidence lived next door to Digre, who told me he was planning a wallop with another blougat called Riff-Raff. I wanted in and he tuned he would talk to Riff-Raff.

They were planning to leave that Friday morning, and I had to be at the bottom of the rugby fields at 01h00 sharp. They would wait exactly fifteen minutes and then waai without me. Problem was, Rooies kept a close eye on changes in the behaviour of individual blougatte, and he could spot wallopers before they had even decided to wallop. Klappe dissuaded you from this folly. I had to be careful, very careful.

As a D-Group I had all my own private kitters. That Friday, I hid a big plastic bag away in my hole. Next, I complained about a bad stomach ache and was sent down to Tannie Mop for medicine. She gave me some utterly vile muti, told me to lie on my bed until lunchtime and disappeared. I quickly packed private kitters into an old khaki rucksack and stashed it in the plastic bag under a bush in the foof.

I thought about walloping right then and there, but common sense prevailed. The mapuza would search the roads leading from George, and in broad daylight I would get bust immediately. Besides, I had no food.

Giddy excitement started rising in me but I knew I'd better hide it. Properly. Having airs like I was about to go on holiday would just attract Rooies' unwanted attention. I also decided not to tell Nienaber. When Johnny and Rooies discovered I was gone they would fuck up all the blougatte and anybody else they thought might have aided me. He was a good bra and I didn't want to test his loyalty or put him in unnecessary jeopardy.

That night it started raining. Damn! After Lights Out it was still pouring, but I realised this was to my benefit. The noise of the rain would cover any sound and make me invisible once I was out in the night. But this didn't stop me from being almost stupid from fear.

Eventually it was time to go. The dormitory was a colony of snores, groans and farts. I quietly rolled some blankets into a fat bundle to fake the shape of my body, all the time listening carefully to the sounds of sleep and rain. My mind jumped from snore to grunt to snore, skittish and terrified that the gentle thrumming on the roof was masking some horrible surprise.

Tinkling thick silence.

I took a breath, grabbed my takkies and ran lightly to the graze hall. I opened the door, praying the hinges wouldn't squeak. They didn't. I slipped inside and squeezed it shut. At the far end of the hall I knelt down and put on my takkies. If anybody saw me now I was 100 percent bust. I carefully slid open the window nearest me. It made a hollow sound, which skidded hideously among the empty tables and chairs in the dark. I held my thumping breath.

Silence.

I slid over the sill, dropped down lightly into the cold wet night and ran into the foof. I looked for the plastic bag in the dark, and eventually found it. Then I ran back to the bungalow, where I quickly stripped off my sopping PJs while my naked flesh gibbered in protest, and got dressed in most of my clothes. As a clever afterthought I bit holes in the bag and pulled it over my head as a makeshift raincoat. It made it awkward to carry the rucksack but it seemed like it might help. I headed back into the rain and made straight for the rugby fields, avoiding the yellow security lights cut by silver ribbons of rain, and skirted along them in deeper shadows. It was fucking cold. All too soon I felt icy water trickling down into my shirts, and I moved faster, trying to warm my body.

Rendezvous point.

At first I thought I was alone, then a shadow detached itself and came towards me. It was Silvey – very, *very* glad to see me. He reckoned Riff-Raff had chickened out because of the rain, and we left without him.

First we had to cross the foof.

The foof was thick tangled vegetation that grew on either side of the small mountain river that bled endlessly from the black winged Outeniquaberg behind us and flowed through the school, creating a little valley that twisted down towards the sea, and cut the school off from the town. That little valley was a lush jungle riddled with masses of thorny bramble, utterly impenetrable in places. It hid a layer of dead vegetation covering evil-smelling black mud, and it was infested with insects.

About 150 metres across.

Twenty minutes later we were both torn bloody, but we'd managed to cross it. Then we started fighting our way through wet heather towards the distant road. I'd quickly lost the excitement I'd felt earlier for escaping Poesplaas. I tried to not think at all, and clomped on behind Silvey, sullenly – hating the night. Eventually we reached the Cape Town road and crossed it into a small forest. The forest floor was a mat of pine needles, and under the really big trees it was bone dry, so we made a moerse fire to dry our kitters. While we waited, we spoke:

– *Eksê Silvey* –

– *Ja my broer* –

– *Do you skiem we gonna make it or what?* –

– *I'm starting to hope so. I lost a lot of pluk back there in the foof bra* –

– *Ja, fuck that was blind eksê. Pity about Riff-Raff hey* –

– *Hey my broer, he knew what was what. I skiem he just got meid when he saw the rain eksê* –

– *Ja, one time. You're probably right* –

– *[…]*

– *Eksê Silvey, I skiem we should wait until our kitters are dry and then hit the road straight away my broer, even if it is still dark. The onnies and the mapuza will be out looking for us in a few hours eksê, and I don't skiem they gonna look this far but we just can't take that fucking chance. We must also work out a lekker speech to spin the mense that pick us up* –

– Ja, one time my broer, you're right –

Once our stuff was dry we hit the road. Nothing. No cars. The muzzy warmth of the fire quickly seeped out of my jersey and the cold morning breeze started biting its way back through. The air felt wet. The sky began to pale, and thick miserable clouds became visible. I hoped with all my heart that it wouldn't rain again. We walked on nervously.

After crossing a bridge we heard an engine in the distance and headlights suddenly popped into view and came down the hill. We stuck out our thumbs. The car passed us and then— the squeal of brakes. CA registration. Misted back window, unblinking red lights, the engine breathing steamy and hot. We looked at each other shit-scared, committed ourselves and ran for it. It was some big fat travelling salesman who didn't give a flying rat's fart who we were as long as we were company. He took us all the way to Cape Town and dropped us off at the station.

We caught a train directly to Rondebosch and found a tiekiebox. Time to get sorted, but Digre's mother said he wasn't there and he wouldn't be coming home soon either. That was it – we were screwed. Silvey reckoned we could go and look for one or two of his chommies. Eventually he caught up with an ou who quickly got us out of sight before greeting us. His name was Shane or Sean or something. He agreed to meet us at some place he and Silvey both knew about. He said he'd bring some graze and another bra called Budgie.

We walked to Rondebosch Common, went to a well-used spot and dumped our rucksacks. Silvey reckoned that Shane and Budgie would sort us out. Next thing we were joined by three coloured ous – one of them was a nattily dressed, palish-looking ou, and the other two looked like spiritsuipers. Silvey greeted the palish ou as Whitey Whiskers. Apparently they knew each other, and in no time Whiskers had a *stop* out and was maaling on a pipe. Silvey cleaned the bottleneck that one of the spirit-suipers produced and I eagerly rolled the girrick. Whiskers asked what we were doing and Silvey told him we had walloped from reformatory that morning and were now on the outies and trying to make our bene sterk. Silvey bust the pipe. I took a big hit, and to my incredible relief I didn't cough and look like a *pop*. But I did get horribly gerook very quickly. In a stoned haze I remember giving Silvey what marchers I had. Whiskers disappeared and reappeared shortly. Suddenly I was drinking a tin mug of wine.

Everything spinning.

Shean or Sawn or whoever and Budgie. Howzit.

Somebody making a fire. Here eat this.

Someone making a pipe. Some more wine.

Mmmm ... Darkness ...

When I opened my eyes there were thin pink ribbons on a bright blue backdrop and a chilly morning breeze. I could see. Silvey was next to me in a strange sleeping bag. All our stuff was still with us. Whiskers and the other two spiritsuipers were lying on the other side of the fire on a big sheet of plastic and cardboard, each wrapped in a blanket. There was another bundle of blankets that turned out to be another spiritsuiper and his woman. I lay there feeling slightly lame.

After a while Whiskers woke up and started breaking dead Port Jackson branches and packing them onto the pile of hot ash. He kept hacking and spitting into the fire, which hissed back at him angrily. Silvey stirred. He stretched, grinned and asked me what the fuck I thought I was doing passing out at seven o' clock on a Friday night bra?

Whiskers got the fire going proper. The rest of the camp started stirring and he maaled on a pipe. Silvey opened his rucksack and pulled out a bottle of wine which he'd apparently bought with the rest of our kroon. I vaguely remembered drinking cheap white wine from a tin mug. Whiskers bust the pipe. I took a hit, but this time I coughed. *Pop!* Silvey passed me the bottle of wine.

He said we had to meet Budgie at his pozzie. It was the only place we could go because Budgie's old lady didn't know Silvey had been sent to reformatory like Shane's did. We re-packed, strapped on our rucksacks and said goodbye to everybody in the camp. We finished the pipe and wine and I stumbled after Silvey feeling horribly unsteady, my attention narrowing as I followed him step by disoriented step. Two blocks later I puked it all out. It didn't make me feel any better – I was trashed. Silvey was getting really fed up with me. I was putting him in the eyes by the way I was stumbling about.

We came to a fence. There were vines on the other side, with huge tresses of black grapes.

Breakfast!

Silvey went straight over the fence, but I got entangled in the splayed barbed wire at the top. He was taunting me to hurry up while stuffing his mouth with grapes. I could barely move – I was hooked on the wire and I was soooo ... fucked.

Suddenly I heard the arrogant roar of an engine and the screech of angry brakes. A yellow mapuza van had stopped below me. Silvey screamed at me to run, but barbed wire was biting into the crotch of my jeans.

He took off.

The doors of the van burst open and a boer ran up and grabbed my leg. Another one grabbed my rucksack. The one on my leg was a big boer with a boepens and a thick moustache. He ordered me to climb down and locked me in the back of the van. After a short drive and a very aggressive interrogation at Wynberg police station, it was determined that I was a runaway. That was it – busted!

The gattas took me to a place with bars everywhere called Tenterden Place of Safety. Here I was booked in by a big fat Afrikaner tannie. Inside, beyond the bars, were the familiar smells of old vrot bokkos and Guvvie polish, and somewhere beneath that the smell of Jeyes Fluid and pain.

The tannie led me to a cell, where she ordered me to strip and took all my clothes except my undies. I found myself in a very small bare cell with a bed and a covered tin pot in one corner. Nothing else. I climbed into the bed and passed out immediately.

My eyes fluttered open and, as the question of where I was started to utter itself— my whole lousy memory flooded back. That woke me up quickly. I sat up. It was night. The cell was dark. I took a piss in the stinking pot and sat down on the bed.

Oh shit this is bad. They are going to send me straight back. Six shots, F-Group, everything. Fuck. And if they catch Silvey he's gonna think I piemped him to the boere.

Suddenly the light came on in a painful blaze. I squinted blearily at a silent eye gazing through the peephole. The eye moved away and the light crashed out. Bright spots danced in my night eyes and I crawled back into bed, had a nervous wank and went to sleep.

Next morning I was fed by a new tannie but the walls started closing in on me badly. I had not spoken to anyone. I listened for voices but heard nothing except the muted engine of the institution clanking and murmuring its way through the morning. After what seemed like hours I heard loud noises coming up the corridor. There was so much screaming, crying and swearing going on that at first I couldn't make out what was cutting, until I heard a door slam and lock. Then the tinkle of the keys disappeared and everything faded to the muffled sound of pubescent sobbing and moaning next door.

She wouldn't stop.

On and on until I thought I would go mad. Eventually I started banging on the door and screaming at her to shut up. I was scared and feeling shit too and she was just making it worse. Someone else started screaming at us all to shut up.

I had never been locked up in a cell alone before.

Then another laaitie cracked up and started begging them to take him out. *Please!* Yelling it over and over. After some time, heels clacked up the corridor, keys jangled and a muted voice uttered a short directive. Door slamming, click-clack, click-clack ... keys fading— and there was silence again.

Lunchtime was announced by the distant sound of clashing pots. I listened to cell doors opening and banging shut on their way to me. The woman from breakfast was back. I said thank you, but she just slammed the door and locked it. I sat down to chow.

I didn't want to think – yet I couldn't help it. I mean, how long were they going to keep me locked up?

Three days, as it turned out.

Laaities were admitted as runaways, victims of abuse, suddenly orphaned, all sorts of bad reasons – and they locked you up to break your spirit. It simplified discipline for them. After three days you would do anything the beamptes told you, and when they took you out they warned you that if you didn't obey the rules you would go back inside for another three days.

What made it unbearable was the mind-numbing boredom of scrubbing floors and walls unnecessarily all day, every day, for no purpose other than to keep us busy. The beamptes took no shit and you went to solitary for anything. Robert Nienaber had told me stories about these places but I never expected it to be so bad. He said the best thing that ever happened to him there was one time when he managed to fuck a chick he smaaked through the bars one night.

I waited two weeks for a snapshot appearance in juvenile court – blah-be-de-blah, paperwork, paperwork – and got sentenced back to Die Bult for *Dros*.

Nobody gave a damn about why I had walloped.

That afternoon, two Welfare beamptes put me on a train and escorted me back to George.

My school psychologist, Mr Shröeder, was waiting at the station and took me straight to Stronk's office. It was the first time I had ever been inside. Stronk sat behind his huge desk with my file before him and asked me why I had drossed. I stared into those cold empty eyes and told him that it was because I simply could not handle being klapped over and over by Johnny Killian and Rooies every day. He picked up the phone and ordered somebody to call Johnny Killian immediately. Then he informed me that I had already been told by Jaamie that there was a zero-tolerance policy towards dros and I was now sentenced to six cuts and F-Group. I signed the Strafboek acknowledging my crime and punishment. Next to his desk was a beautiful stinkwood riempiesbank. I had to bend over it and grab onto the riempies so he could flap me. It was the hardest I had ever been flapped. I kept jumping up while he was doing it and got eight shots in the end because he said two of them didn't count. Then I sat down, crying from the pain, and waited for Johnny Killian. Stronk ignored me.

Johnny arrived.

Stronk told him I said I had walloped because he and Rooies apparently hit me too much. But, he said, he couldn't see how that could be possible. Johnny would probably know what to do further. Wouldn't he?

– *Ja meneer!* –

Outside Stronk's office Johnny turned on me.

– *You fokken* LITTLE NAAI! *Did you skiem you can piemp me to Stronk? I'm de fokken Headboy of dis whole fokken skool you* DOM KAK! *Stronk made it so. Listen lekker, blougat, you en jou maatjie Riff-Raff is gonna come in front of Studenteraad on Sunday. I'm gonna kick you so deep in your mother's poes that you can chew out her fokken lungs –*

Then he gave me a lekker poeswarm klap and told me that was just a little taste of what was coming my way on Sunday. The snotrag was already wet and it stayed that way all week. I thought it had been bad before, but that was nothing compared to the pain and stark raving terror I felt now. And I still had Sunday to look forward to. I desperately hoped, somehow, that Johnny would have mercy on me, but I knew I was being stupid. Johnny Killian fed on pain. He loved it. He couldn't wait for Sunday night and kept on telling me so.

I managed to see Riff-Raff at school and found out that he hadn't been able to get out of his hostel the night Silvey and I walloped. In fact, he'd been caught making an attempt on his own the very same morning I was escorted back, which made what Johnny had told me— make sense. We were both in F-Group and awaiting our dreaded Sunday appointment with the Studenteraad. The horror was in the waiting.

Sunday came, as it is wont to do. We had Kerk as usual that night. The duty onnie left after a final thunderous rendition of *Oom God van Jakob*, followed by the usual token prayer – Amen. Johnny stood up and ordered two blougatte to keep skei at the doors. Rooies and the other Headboys and Secretaries joined him at the front of the hall, facing the rest of the school.

(Ohmysweetfuck) Ten of them!

– *[Johnny] Riff-Raff, Yster, you know what's gonna happen. Come, stand here in front –*

We shuffled to the front nervously. Johnny grabbed me by the collar—

– *Tell the school what you are –*

– *Ek is 'n poes Johnny –*

– *DON'T FOKKEN TELL ME BLOUGAT! TELL THE FOKKEN SCHOOL AND TELL THEM WHY YOU'SE A POES –*

– *I'm a poes because I walloped and because I broke down the school's spirit –*

– *Mooi. Baie mooi. An' tell them what happens now is you own fokken fault –*

– *WHAT IS GOING TO HAPPEN TO ME NOW IS MY OWN FUCKING FAULT –*

Rooies was the first in and he dropped me to the floor with one bright starry punch. Then Johnny kicked me in the (*!woeba-!woeba*) face and I didn't remember much after that as all their Guvvie shoes thudded into me everywhere. Then there was a very bright painless explosion in my brain right in the middle of it all and (*BA!*) – it all went black into …

Somebody slapping me … to … to …

– *WORD WAKKER BLOUGAT! –*

I was down on the floor, my kerkpak splattered and imprinted with shoe marks. One of my shoes had come off. Blood was dripping from my face and onto the floor, mingling with the dirt and dust from which *Oom God van Jakob* had risen up to the rafters. But the alien thing that rose up in me and (head.spinning.bad) surprised the hell out of me was the (too.sore.pain) bubble deep inside had not burst like it always had before. I was *NOT* crying. Rooies ordered me to clean up my fucking mess and then they started on Riff-Raff.

He screamed a lot at first.

There were so many of them that they had to take turns to get their kicks in. Johnny and Rooies gave way to nobody. Johnny's face was twisted into a spitty grin like he was having a good fuck. He and Rooies were both panting and sweating from the effort that they were putting into it. Eventually they stood back from the sad bleeding mess that was Riff-Raff.

Unlike me, he was still awake when they finished.

Two of my teeth were loose in my mouth, I had several deep cuts in my lips and a bad painful cut in my tongue, and my nose was shattered. The rest of me was one huge horrible hurting mess of shifting gatherings of agony. They hadn't broken anything except my nose – at least that's what it felt like. Riff-Raff cleaned up his mess and we all returned to our hostels.

Meeting Adjourned.

It was time for Blouesaand!

We lost as usual, but only Johnny and Rooies really hit me in the takkie party afterwards. I think the rest of the hostel had just seen ten of them kick me in my poes and figured I had taken more than enough for one night. Nienaber helped me clean up afterwards and taught me a lesson about blood and clothing. Just use clear cold water. Nothing else. It all comes out.

A week later, Uncle Guvvie decided to renovate Hostel 4 and we were all divided up and packed into the other three hostels. Johnny Killian went to Hostel 2 and Rooies went to Hostel 1. To my indescribable relief, I found myself on the Hostel 3 list. The bruises and pain in my face and body were fading. Robert Nienaber was still with me, and my new dormitory leader was an ou named Peter van der Westhuizen. He was from Joburg, a seriously talented artist who was into Roger Dean, the cat who did all the album covers for Uriah Heep, Ossibisa and Yes. He was a mean, surly bastard and dished out klappe left, right and centre. I hated him quickly.

Eventually I passed out of F-Group and got my private kitters back again. I also received a letter from Denise announcing that she had just got remarried. Her new husband was a man named Bill Parker. Apparently she had placed a lonely hearts ad in the sonskynhoekie of some English magazine. The first ou she met through it she didn't smaak. The second ou was Bill. He was a Pom from Northumberland England who had moved to South Africa fifteen years before. They had two dates, he gave her a ring and they got married the next day. I was pleased at the news. Even though she had made me hate her at times because of the horrible sessions with her nails and bashing my head on the floor, I knew somehow that she had only become like that because Wally had thrown her out and left her without money, desperate and half-insane from emotional hurt. She sent a two-rand note with the letter.

I wrote back my congratulations.

The misery of school went on. I passed from E-Group to D-Group. It was nice having Dorp privileges again. Then the first holidays of the year arrived. I had obviously lost my Holiday Permission because of my wallop, so I joined Nienaber, Doom, Baygon-Green, Baygon-Yellow, Koosklutch and the other weeshuislaaities from Hostel 1, plus all the ouens with parents who couldn't go home, at a camp Uncle Guvvie had for us in Hartenbos near Mossel Bay. The rules were relaxed and we basically only had four roll-calls a day. One for each graze and the last one at Opkoms. For the rest of the day we were free to roam across the river and jol on the beach or in the resort. Most of the leaders went home, so there were only temporary leaders from the Matrics and Standard 9s. It was okay though – there wasn't any of the bad shit like at school.

I discovered that Robert Nienaber and the other weeshuislaaities stocked up on private kitters during each holiday. They accomplished this by doing washing-line jobs. Every school holiday Hartenbos was descended upon by thousands of happy campers. They arrived in droves with trucks pulling caravans, trailers and boats, and completely overfilled the resort. Nienaber and them would slip out after Lights Out and go hit wet washing strung up between the tents. They were fussy too, and only went for designer labels in their exact size. Most of them slukked at least a suitcase full. They wore the clothes and also used them as barter goods for zol and spark from the coloured ous who lived in the shacks across the main road. They tried to trade for cash, but the coloured ouens were usually so swak that even if they did want to buy the goeters, they didn't have the marchers. I had no kroon either, so I joined in and went with Nienaber to pull moves.

That holiday me and him became bras.

Then we became company.

It felt good to have a bra again. If you got klapped a lot, the ouens avoided you like maybe it was infectious or something. Nienaber helped me begin to accept that I wasn't going to get out. I was a Guvvie laaitie FOR GOOD. He was hardly ever klapped because he never took it lying down. He had a big bek and he tuned them kak straight back even if he got a second klap. And he made a hell of a raas while he was doing it too. He also *lagged* off all the other kak that we had to go through and tuned me— I just had to realise it was part of the whole jol called Life, and Fuck Uncle Guvvie as much as you can.

Ja, Fuck Uncle Guvvie.

Only one ou got F-Group that holiday. An ou called Poena from Hostel 1. He was a big, fat, sweaty, vuilgat ou with kak boep-chappies all over him.

We were sitting waiting for the onnies after graze one afternoon when we suddenly heard what sounded like a coloured meid yelling from the road leading into the camp.

– *Waar'th Poena!* –

[...]

– *Waaar'th Poena? POOEENAA …! Jou maaa'tha poes!* –

All the ous turned to stare at Poena, astonished, as around the corner came staggering – *very unsteadily* – one of the siffest, miffest, vuil, toothless, old, horribly battered and scarred-looking spiritsuipermeide that any of us had ever seen. She spotted him in the crowd immediately, reared up livid – *swaying dangerously off balance* – and shook her finger at him. Spitting in righteous fury.

– *DAAR'TH JY, JOU MAAA'THA POES! JY'T MY GENAAI EN JY SKULD MY VYF RAND. GEE MY FOKKEN GELD NOU!* –

At this exact point, Jaamie stepped out of his chalet with his clipboard and stopped dead in his tracks – absolutely stunned. He just froze there, struck *dom* by the spectacle. Eventually he kind of shook his head (*not-dreaming*) as she carried on yelling at Poena about pomping her for five rand and not paying. Poena was immobile from shock, so she staggered fearlessly into the crowd of ouens – to grab him and wrest her money from the recalcitrant bastard by force.

At that point the ouens cracked up screaming with laughter and everything turned into an absurd circus with Jaamie as ringmaster.

Eventually Jaamie – *Jaamie!* – had to give her five rand to shut her up and make her go away, which she did, except she didn't shut up once and kept on yelling at Jaamie now:

– *Maa'tha poes fokken witboernaaier! Djy gaan mynie naai nie.* MAAAA'THA POOOOES!! –

On and on, until she was long out of earshot.

Jaamie didn't think there was anything fucking funny about it – so Poena nursed a sore arse and swung a pick on the road to the camp for the rest of the holiday. He had the whole road for a honk.

F-Groep vir meidnaai – MAAAA'THA POES!!

The holiday ended and I went back to Piesang. Piesang was a motor-mac onnie in the shops. He was fair and he was also a good man. I said up my Smoker's Rules at the first Koshuisraad of the new term because I'd turned fifteen in Hartenbos. I didn't have to silent-puff any more. Yeehah!

Robert Nienaber and I remained company.

Denise sent me a pakkie of dried fruit and cookies with a birthday card. I wrote back and thanked her for it. About three weeks later, Stronk summoned me to his office. He informed me that he had a letter, in his hands, from Denise. Denise had written to him to complain about my utter lack of gratitude with regard to the parcel and asked him to deal with me in the strictest possible manner.

Stronk needed no encouragement.

Of course, my telling him that I had written a letter of thanks meant absolutely nothing and I duly received six shots and F-Group. Johnny Killian and his chommies broke my face once again in Studenteraad the following Sunday. I was so pissed off with her that I refused to cry. I wrote and told her exactly what sort of a bitch I thought she was. I also told her that I wished that she and Wally had tried to find the maturity to work out their marriage instead of taking out their sick fucked-up adult frustrations on two innocent little kids like Yvonne and myself. We would have been better off in the orphanage.

Hell went on and I slowly clawed my way back up to D-Group.

There was a blougat in Hostel 3 who taught me something new. If you sniffed benzene— it put you on a buzz. He called it lappie. I waited until my next Dassie-pay and bought a bottle of rectified benzene from a pharmacy in town. I wasn't allowed in the shop but I took a chance anyway and no one seemed to care.

I waited till the afternoon when all the ouens had gone to movies and cut a small lappie from an old Guvvie towel. I took the benzene, locked myself in the toilet, dampened the lappie and began sucking.

VVVrRrRrRrRrRrRrRrRrRrRrRrRrRrRrRrRrRrRrRrRrRrRrRr

After a while the buzz becomes clearer and clearer and suddenly the walls start breathing. Long slow breaths. I'm astounded. I never knew walls could breathe. I put my hand out to touch them but they immediately become shy and stop. Then my hearing clears and I can suddenly hear what the ous are talking about in Hostel 2's bungalow. I know it's the lappie making me hear so well. It's awesome.

The toilet paper next to me starts unrolling onto the floor slowly.

On it, little wet dots and dashes are appearing before my eyes. Somehow I know they are coming from a man locked up in a room somewhere and he's desperately trying to send a message to somebody to come and rescue him – by using telepathic telekinesis. But I don't understand Morse code. I also know that he's using all his power and only in the toilet I'm in— is the message getting through. By the time I get the toilet paper to somebody who can understand Morse, the marks will have dried up and disappeared. I start crying for the man and then I hear Denise's voice. SHE'S DOWN-STAIRS! She's shouting at Piesang!

– *Where's my Alex! I want my Alex! Give him back to me!* –

I unlocked the toilet door and hurtled down the stairs, out and around to the front of the hostel to where I had heard her voice – but no one was there. Then I remembered that I had left the bottle of benzene in the toilet upstairs like a *pop.* I ran back and by some miracle nobody had discovered it. I shakily returned it to its hiding place and sat in the bungalow for the rest of the afternoon trying to figure out what had happened. I couldn't smoke because the lappie made the smoke taste kak. Nobody noticed anything, and by the time Peter van der Westhuizen and them came back I was fine.

The next weekend the blougat who had taught me to lappie joined me. We hid in the tool shed. It was raining hard outside and nobody would look for us – we were safe.

VVVrRrRrRrRrRrRrRrRrRrRrRrRrRrRrRrRrRrRrRrRrRrRrRr

This time when the clearness comes the bricks in the wall start slowly sliding forwards and backwards. Every second brick sliding out as every other one slides back in. It looks so weird. We're lying on a bunch of crates with a pile of sacks and as I look away from the walls and gaze up at the roof the most incredible sight greets my eyes. The entire roof is a swarm of tiny little multicoloured birds all wearing high-heeled shoes like Minnie Mouse and they are marching up and down furiously – making one hell of a racket! I'm still trying to puzzle out where on earth they've come from when the other ou grabs me in terror and points to the floor.

– *Yster help me! How flar's the floor! How flar's the floor!* –

I spoke to Nienaber about it. I wanted to know what it meant when I saw stuff when I was on a lappie pluk. He told me it was called hallucinations. He didn't know what it was but that's what they were called. Robert didn't like me sucking the lappie but the more I did it the more I had to do it. I started living in two worlds. The one of my lappie visions and sounds and the other horrible one where I had to run, get klapped and be scared all the time.

I preferred the lappie world.

The Presbyterian Church had their annual children's camp and us three ous from Die Bult were given permission by Stronk and sponsorship by the Church to go. They took us to a camp called Carmel in Victoria Bay. I packed a bottle of benzene. We had to go to meetings the whole weekend where they discussed Jesus stuff about sin and salvation and man is cut off from God and you must be born again and wharrawharra. I understood (mostly) what they were talking about and a lot of it was familiar ground from the Wearnes but that didn't stop me from going to lappie in the toilets even though it made me feel guilty because I was supposed to walk on Jesus' cross to get to God or he was gonna burn me.

The first day I was there I left straight after the evening meeting and went for a lappie.

VVVrRrRrRrRrRrRrRrRrRrRrRrRrRrRrRrRrRrRrRrRrRrRrRrRrRr

When the clearness comes it brings *everything* with it. I'm not in the toilet any more – I am in a prison cell. The walls are grey concrete and up in the thick wooden door there is a small barred opening. I am scared. What am I doing in a prison? And what have I done wrong? I stand up and go look out the opening. I can see that I am in a row of cells. There is an arm sticking out stiffly from the cell next to mine. The man who it belongs to is dead and the arm itself is gangrenously green and rotting. Then I suddenly know Who it is. The dead man in the cell next to me is Jesus! I sit down again and start crying for Him.

I drop my guard because I am so unhappy and at that point a massive Red Indian with a huge thumb smashes down the door using a lumberjack axe and comes for me. I run out into the night screaming and collide into an American girl who's also at the camp. She takes one look at me and yells:

– *GET AWAY FROM ME YOU WEIRDO!* –

I disappeared.

The next morning I went back to the toilets. I was a little apprehensive because of the Indian but I kept on telling myself that he was only a hallucination and he wouldn't come back. This time when the clearness came I was still in the toilet. Then I saw a cupboard door high up in the wall that I hadn't noticed before. I reached up to open it but at that moment the latch clicked, the door swung open and something rolled out and fell on the floor. It was a clear plastic bag with a greyish-brown mess in it. I took a better look, and to my absolute nauseating horror I saw that in the bag was a dead rotting baby. My mind froze up and I didn't know what to do next. Then I looked at the face of the baby. It was me.

I didn't want to lappie in the toilets again. They made bad hallucinations come.

On the second last day I went to a secluded spot in the bush on the hill leading down to the sea and had a lappie there. When the clearness came I suddenly saw the clouds above me were moving into huge sky-writing against the blue background.

JESUS LOVES YOU

Then I saw it again in the way that the bushes had grown on the hillside.

JESUS LOVES YOU

It made me feel guilty so I didn't lappie any more that weekend even though it was hard not to. Right at the end of the camp we had a big meeting and they played easy songs on guitars and we sang and clapped. It was weird singing church songs to a guitar and clapping but it was lekker and everybody was having a great time. At the end the minister asked who amongst us wanted to give our lives to Jesus. I thought about it and put up my hand. There was a whole bunch of us so the minister said a prayer and we all repeated it sentence by sentence – out loud. I felt really good afterwards. Now I could be like the Wearnes in Worcester.

I arrived back at the school. I could still hear the guitars and the songs in my head. Within five minutes Peter van der Westhuizen had klapped all the songs out of me and told me what a stupid poes I was. It broke everything. I went outside to behind the tool shed, feeling the most horrible that I had ever felt, and yelled at God.

– Is this what it means to be a Christian? That I must stay in Die Bult and get fucked up all the time? Hey? Where the fuck are You now? Fuck You, I want nothing to do with You –

And I didn't. I turned my back and went for a lappie.

I climbed into the cupboard of a little passage near my dormitory and soaked my rag in benzene. I closed the bottle, put it down at my feet, shut the cupboard door and started sucking.

VVVrRrRrRrRrRrRrRrRrRrRrRrRrRrRrRrRrRrRrRrRrRrRr

I got caught.

Piesang turned the case over to Cadbury, Vice-Principal of the school division, who in turn charged me for drug abuse and gave me six flaps and F-Group. They cracked two of my ribs in Studenteraad, but there was less blood that time. I didn't cry. I told Robert that I couldn't stop the lappie. He locked me in the dormitory one weekend some time later after F-Group and took a moerse chance getting me some zol. He made me a fat pipe and forced me smoke most of it until I was almost blind I was so gerook – and it worked. Somehow the zol helped me get spookgerook enough to distance myself from the lappie and hate and fear it sufficiently to vow never to go back to it again.

I NEVER did.

I had reluctantly learnt, over the slow painful course of that brutal year, how to get *gedagtes* and, secondly, how to be *skelm* – as Nienaber put it. Using gedagtes meant putting myself in a mental place where I completely embraced being a blougat and accepted everything within the parameters of my surroundings with the hidden motive to overcome it.

DIE BULT WAS NOT GOING TO GO AWAY.

I had tried to remove myself from the equation entirely, but that only produced worse and more prolonged pain, which I had to realise I had ultimately inflicted upon myself via its boomerang effect. Stuff like Denise's kak letter to Stronk came as a klap out of the blue and I could do nothing about that, and I couldn't blame anybody for reacting to my own bad hallucinations. The answer was not to run away but to hide. Hide right out in the open. For that, all I needed was energy, discipline and to exercise my brain. If I got a klap, it didn't help to go snotragging in a corner – it would probably only buy me a wetter one.

It was okay to hate Johnny Killian – just act as if I didn't. And act well. I also had to ask myself the question – could a honk hurt me? No matter how big it was? No, of course it couldn't – all it would do was waste a little energy.

And that worked.

I treated Johnny and Rooies like deities, jumped on my honk, *lagged* off all the klappe, always looked kwaai in front of the onnies and privately looked after my company. That was step one. That was getting *wys gedagtes*. It freed me up for step two.

How to be *skelm*.

This entailed a lot more than the clumsy methods I had employed in my prior criminal escapades. It meant that I learnt how to engage in any activity that I wanted to – by seemingly being engaged in another, and staging it right under the noses of those individuals who wished to detect my underlying misdemeanour.

Once I had lost the interest of Johnny and Rooies by getting wys gedagtes and using them, the physical pain of being there subsided.

Nienaber and I were mostly broke. We were probably about the third or fourth poorest company in our hostel. However, we still had kitters from Hartenbos, so we decided to make a plan. Robert volunteered to slip out of the hostel one night and mission to the coloured location to try and swop some of the kitters for a parcel of zol. The most dangerous part of the whole move would be coming back. He would need my help to get back into the hostel safely. We pulled it off and so we became dagga merchants. Our clients were VERY, VERY carefully selected ouens who deeply appreciated the risks we were taking.

The leaders among the Dasse were all Rockspiders. Robert's first language was Afrikaans, but he reckoned to me that there were two types of mense that spoke Afrikaans – Dutchmen and ouens like you and me. A lot of our clients spoke Afrikaans but they weren't Dutchmen. The coloured ouens that we bought the zol from *only spoke Afrikaans* but they weren't even considered real mense by the Dutchmen. We never sold to Dutchmen. Dutchmen were like snakes – they would always turn on you some time sooner or later because you weren't one of them. It was pretty easy to spot them. They had a thing about Die Here, Skoolgees, Soutpiele and Kaffirs, which is why Uncle Guvvie made the worst of them leaders no matter what their crimes were.

The end of that first week we suddenly had enough to go to movies for the first time since Hartenbos. We rolled a big three-blader – which was a private dagga Dassie-puff made with three Rizla papers, aka *slow-boat* (from *Slow Boat to China*) – and ducked into an alley on the way to the bughouse. We made that first slow-boat last as long as possible and we savoured it like a couple of larneys enjoying a fine cigar, with a good brandy – after a lekker graze.

Movies was a blast. We giggled our heads off and had such a good jol that I forgot I was in Poesplaas for a bit. By the time we arrived back at school the smell was gone, our eyes were white again and we were still pleasantly goofed. A little skelm gedagtes and nobody noticed a thing.

A habit started. Every Saturday we would duck into the alley on the way to the bughouse. I started living my days to make it to the end of the week and the slow-boat we promised ourselves. After a while it became more than something I loved – it became something I NEEDED MORE THAN ANYTHING ELSE – just to rewire my sanity.

We moved back to Hostel 4 and someone else joined the ranks of those who klapped me all the time. A Standard 9 ou known as Bowie. He was into martial arts. Time and time again I would come waltzing into the dormitory and suddenly find myself on the floor after having stopped a fast karate kick to the chest. Then he would look at me dead-pan and tell me to wake up. One day I decided that I had taken quite enough from him – he was a Das but he wasn't a fucking leader. I was on washing-up duty after graze. I stole a kitchen knife and hid it away under my pillow. That night I lay in bed waiting. The plan was to chill until everybody was dossing and then stab him with it. Eventually everybody seemed to be asleep. I was still waiting. Suddenly Bowie got out of bed and padded over to me silently. I froze. He bent down and whispered softly in my ear:

– *I know what you've got under your pillow bra … But do you know what I've got under mine?* –

Strangely enough, we became very, very close chinas after that. I think I impressed the hell out of him just by having the pluk to want to try. He also became one of our clients. In time we embarked on a spiritual journey together, but I will come to that in a short while.

I had my first fight in Die Bult. Among the ouens, if you were heard threatening somebody— you had to fight. If you didn't, a couple of the big ouens klapped you until you did. Somehow I got into an altercation with an ou called Caveman. Some ouens overheard it and that night Johnny Killian made the two of us fight in the showers – stark naked with the whole hostel watching. I was really the moer-in with Caveman and tore straight into him. He was much stockier than me but I had a fuckload more rage and pretty soon I had him on his knees with my hands twisted into his hair – slamming his head into the washbasin. As the blood started coming out of his face – I had a moment of clarity. I saw what I was doing, above the shouts (*MOERHOM!! MOERHOM!!*) of the ouens, and let him go. I walked out of the bathroom spattered with blood, feeling sick at myself. Johnny and Rooies gave me klappe for not finishing it, but they didn't make us fight again.

I passed Standard 8 and got a surprise Holiday Permission from Denise.

That holiday I met Bill – her new husband. He owned a plot outside Krugersdorp upon which stood a semi-finished nightmare of a self-detached house. It consisted of various rooms tacked together from a bewildering array of used building materials. Rather like a large, very upmarket squatter's shack, which he had spent five years building on and off. Rooms were dirt, patch-carpeted and bare concrete. The walls were even more interesting. Rock, board, brick and old rusty metal plates. Most of it was covered with some sort of a roof.

I quickly picked up on the gist of things.

Bill informed me that unless I worked— I wouldn't eat. He set me to swinging a pick and shovel to dig a long drainage ditch and other skoffel-werk around the plot. I felt angry. It was like F-Group during my holidays! As a fifteen-year-old I didn't have the stamina to work that hard all day, and he took great pleasure in deriding me as useless because of it and continually threatened to cut off my food.

I discovered Denise had changed. She realised Bill would be the last man who would ever take her in. She wasn't any kind of raving beauty and she was still saddled with two kids at the end of the day – so she made her bed, lay down and decided never to question any of it. They sat us all down one night and Denise coldly informed Yvonne and I that we had been disinherited from her will. Eric and Bill's children would now be beneficiaries of everything.

What?

Denise made a great show of telling me that, even though I was the eldest, Eric was the new head of the Nesbitt family by blood. He would be wearing the family signet ring.

Bill hated Afrikaners and Kaffirs. In that order.

His hatred of Afrikaners was so bad that if anybody came into his house and spoke Afrikaans he would throw them out. When Afrikaans TV came on the SABC, it was switched off and nobody was allowed to watch. Bill's joy, and Denise's, came from reinforcing one another's bitterness and savouring the misfortunes of the objects of their scorn. Denise headed off in the opposite political direction, from a fallen Imperialist and a cast-off upper-class (*WhenWe*...) colonialist to a money-grubbing, government-bashing yob. They both hated the National Party government because it was predominantly Afrikaans and they had concluded that P.W. Bloody Botha would never keep the bloody Kaffirs in their place.

Still, they voted for him ...

I had a different journey to go on. One in which I would become the worst of all evils in their eyes – a *kaffirboetie*.

9

SkollieMongrel

Back at school, Nienaber and me immediately started talking politics. He'd been canvassing ouens and had a list of new leaders to nominate for the year. We wanted Bowie as Headboy and Cedric as Secretary. Cedric was a connection in a white street gang from Woodstock called the Mads. We had a list of five other ouens in Matric who were all cool and also clients of ours. See, we wanted to be kingmakers so we could control our hostel in Standard 9 and set it up so that we would be in control of the whole school by Matric.

Right under Uncle Fucking Guvvie's nose!

We hit the campaign trail, polling ouens, making them spliffs and getting their vote. Obviously all our old clients were in the bag.

Light up, schmooze, all inhale … *Boom*-roekers of the world unite!

I had fuckall money but Nienaber had stocked up on washing-line jobs, so we had two suitcases of kitters to put off in the coloured kas. He'd also brought back two arms from Hartenbos, which we had stashed away all nicely waterproofed in the foof. An arm is a newspaper parcel of zol that fits snugly between the heel of your hand and the crook of your elbow. It's a lot …

So you see, we could afford to do a little pre-election voter education.

We were betting that we had more ouens than planks in our hostel, and not because there were slightly more English ous either. There were a few hardcore crunchies who dearly wanted the power to take over where Johnny and Rooies had left off, but we had to stop them – otherwise I would be a blougat all the way through to September.

No fun way to spend Standard 9.

The election began. I nominated and Nienaber seconded me. The Dutchmen punted their ouens, but the rest of the hostel just sat silent. Jaamie peered at me and Nienaber over his bifocals. He didn't like any of it. He closed nominations after adding a couple of names of his own.

We voted.

We *knew* we had a minimum of 60 percent of the vote in our pocket plus the Dutchman swing vote. Jaamie collected the ballots and disappeared. Five minutes later he came back and wrote down the names of the winners on the whiteboard.

The two Rocks he had nominated and all their chommies.

Robert Nienaber had way too much at stake. He stood up and asked Jaamie to please count the ballots in front of us. Jaamie flipped out and asked Robert if he was calling him a Liar. Nienaber politely reiterated his request, to loud rumblings of agreement from all over the hostel.

Jaamie stood glowering at Nienaber, then wheeled abruptly and strode out the graze hall, slamming the door behind him. The glass in the door panes rattled dangerously, and there was a fragile silence. The ouens looked around at each other, stunned, then started whispering furiously.

– *Sssssshhhht!* –

Silence.

Jaamie returned, tossed down new ballots and ordered us to re-vote, before slamming the poor door again. He was very obviously, very seriously, very nicely fucked off.

Lekker.

Nienaber had done what *nobody* had ever had the guts to do in all of our known history, and dear Uncle Guvvie didn't like it. I must admit, I didn't have the pluk to stand up to him like that. Robert had marked himself and me indirectly in the process. So what?

Fuck Uncle Guvvie.

We finished re-voting, collected the ballots and waited quietly for Jaamie. He came in looking like thunder itself. The vote was counted, *in front of us*, and – lo and behold – we were in. By a big, fat, muddy landslide.

Splat …

Bowie gave an acceptance speech and announced that regardless of what the new Headboy Henrico might say – HE and Cedric had the last say over the Hostel 4 blougatte. Afterwards he thanked us, shook my hand and told me I was now a Das. Uncle Guvvie had a fliek for us to watch. When it was over Henrico got up and announced to the school that the Studenteraad had been abolished and that the Blougatboek would be rewritten back to the way it was. Riff-Raff, Silvey, myself and all the other F-Groups from the '78 blougatte were suddenly all officially Dasse.

Things changed in Hostel 4 after that. Being a Das meant I found myself with a freedom that felt foreign. It was lekker. Bowie and I started spending a lot of time together. We talked about everything. Bowie was different. He had his head outside the system. All the way out. He told me that he was a man without a nation because the nation he came from rejected him because he embraced the concept that all men are human and equal. He said that there were two ways of looking at it after that. He could either feel marginalised or he could live on the other side of the margin. Guess which one …

Bowie was insanely intelligent. He told me had a friendly demon called Raqua. He used to tune:

— *Insanity rules the mind of the devil and his kind* —

Robert was my company but I also had two very close bras in the other hostels. First, Dennis Faul from Hostel 3 – who got up in Vocational Guidance and told the seriously sexy onnie (whom we all wanted to fuck silly) that he planned on being a professional criminal after school. In retrospect he was probably the only oke being honest, although I think none of us ended up professional as much as petty, crude and stupid. Dennis and I shared a bond – a mental plane that we operated from which was totally in synch with our mutual insanity and sense of humour. We might have made a very good crew but we never worked together – we were just bras.

The other ou was my biza Eric Jackson.

Eric, *a British ex-pat*, arrived back at school with the dubious distinction of having been on the walloppad for two years. He and Gavin Ferreira were friends from before school, which is how I met him. He had apparently been involved in a stabbing on Wittebome station in Cape Town and ran away to South West Africa to escape from the boere. Eric was in Hostel 2, so it took a while for us to get to know each other.

At that point my friends started to play a very important part in my social development. In a large sense we were forced into being surrogate brothers to each other by a brutally sadistic, religiously insane Step-Uncle in charge of our general welfare. We segregated the world into Uncle Guvvie's and Private – where all the larneys and other *pop* mense lived. We knew that Uncle Guvvie had his power because all the larneys gave it to him. That meant the dividing line cut us off from most of *society*. Inside that line we had onnies, then Dutchmen and local enemies, then ouens, then bras, then company. After that there might be one ou who one could call a biza.

A man, a friend, a brother closer than blood.

After I met Eric Jackson that all changed, and I not only had a biza but I became a kaffirboetie too.

Before I go into what I learnt and saw with Eric Jackson, I want to take a little time to describe my own development and personal revolution in Die Bult.

Physically I changed very quickly in that year. Tannie Mop had to replace my kerkpak twice because I grew so much. I hadn't really noticed it, aside from petty early morning narcissism, but I had put on a hell of a lot of muscle from rugby and F-Group. I got into a lot of fights and won all of them easily, except for one against Little Pixie from Durban in Hostel 3's bungalow. It went on for the whole of big break one day and was watched by most of the school. He claimed to have moered me and I claimed even louder that he was talking kak, but between you and me and these two pages I think he fucked me up a little bit.

I was a Das, and with that came the feeling that I had somehow stepped out of one chamber of life and into another. I found that I could command something I had never had before – Respect. Fear dressed up as respect, no doubt, but at least a facsimile of it that I embraced wholeheartedly. On the other side of the brutal line were all the blougatte, and I would never go back. I finally belonged. I had never had that experience before and it felt amazing.

I smoked dagga every day, all day – at night and ritualistically after Lights Out with Bowie, Nienaber or one of the clients. We never giggled or acted stupid any more. That was too dangerous. We smoked to get fucked so that we could forget about Poesplaas and Uncle Guvvie for a bit. It meant developing an almost abnormal mental discipline and *skelmgeid* so that none of the onnies would ever notice.

Smoking zol was the only thing that made school tolerable.

I klapped Jaamie.

One of the new weeshuislaaities was giving me kak one day so I klapped him. The fucker went to Jaamie and piemped me. Jaamie called me into his office. Inside, I got completely befuck, because the old juice junkie naaier actually wanted to flap me for klapping a blougat. I had walked around with a broken nose and cracked ribs the previous year because of his precious fucking Johnny Killian. We got into a shouting match and I slapped him.

That was it. Off to Stronk, six-flaps and F-Group. I was going to *lag* it off and eat the glory coming to me for actually taking on an onnie, but Stronk had a nasty surprise. He transferred me to Hostel 2 with the sarcastic exhortation to try hitting Mr Potgieter if I thought I was so tough.

Potties, aka The Bear, was the school's 6′3″ 120kg PT teacher, Hostel 2's hostel father and the most thoroughly evil man that I was ever subjected to under the Children's Act. The Bear glowered at me upon arrival and growled.

Meneer Johan Potgieter. Uncle Guvvie kak. Poes.

Eric Jackson was in Hostel 2 with me and was already in the gangs in Cape Town. He was a Mongrel. I began to learn what that was all about. He told me Nienaber was right about the need for me to *raak wys* and get *gedagtes* but there was more – I had to learn *respek* and *disipliene*. These were hallmarks of an *indota* – a blooded ouen. Until I learnt what they meant I would always be a laaitie on this side of the fence. I could have all the pluk and all the gedagte I wanted but if I didn't know how to be *stambula* I would never be a successful *skelm*. If I wanted to get into a gang the ouens would have to know they could rely on me. I would have to do what I had to do, keep my bek shut and be willing to do anything to learn how to do it better.

Wally moved down from Joburg and he and Swallow built a house in Table View in Cape Town. He gave me a Holiday Permission and even paid for my train ticket.

Why? I don't know. It was during the holidays that my new life away from school started.

Eric's girlfriend Tania lived in Buitenkant Street, Gardens, and that was where we hung out. The nearest merchant was a coloured woman called Mams who lived in Canterbury Flats, District Six.

I became very close friends with both her sons.

Mams had married a man of white and coloured blood, and her two sons, though both had features of coloured men, had dark and very light skin respectively. They were Joseph and Whitey. Joseph was a Bun Boy and Whitey was a Mongrel. I hung out with one or the other and they were completely different in other ways too. Joseph only drank and Whitey mostly only smoked.

I mean, Whitey did drink but not a lot. I used to get back from clubbing with Eric, who would fuck off to doss at Tania's pozzie. Then I would go find Whitey at his mochie's spot. His mochie worked for a white woman as her char and her husband was a Captain in the boere. Whitey's mochie had a tiny room just outside the kitchen door. I would knock, Whitey would ask who it was and I would tune him – Yster, or my new nickname among them, Schoolboy shortened to Skollie. He would drag out a mattress with a blanket and a pillow, we'd make a quick pipe and doss. If it was still early enough and I could phone, Mams and Joseph would come fetch me. Him and five or so of his Bun Boy couplings would escort me into The District so I could sleep in my own bed. In the mornings when Whitey and I got up, we would take a stroll down to Milly's in Buitenkant Street. We'd buy two pies and if we had enough money we'd buy a litre of lurk. Lurk is the name for *skoon wit wyn*. Then we'd slip into the alley behind Milly's and down it. If it was still not a good day – we'd go down to Mams.

Mams was incidentally one of the biggest merchants in The District.

One day, about five years before, Joseph had gone down to the station to try and snatch a purse or some move because they were living on the bones of their arses. He spied a white man on the station with a briefcase and snatched it. He got away, and when he opened it— he found fifty grand. The shock was so much that he went straight home to Mams, gave it to her and asked her to give him a little something so that he could go for a dop. He told me he knew that if he touched a single note he would have fucked it up.

When me and Whitey arrived at Mams, she would walk into the room and upon seeing us would start marching around the flat *skelling*. She used to *skel* me too, which was cool because I knew all that yelling, hollering and cursing was just her way of showing love and affection. Making sure we had respect while we stood very meekly, not quite grinning out loud, and two bottles of lurk would appear on the table. Then she went off *skelling* somewhere else. Her husband, also called Whitey, always sat at the table listening to his radio and having a dop of his own. He would wink. And grin. Then she'd come back and suddenly there would be two rand-baalle, *skel, skel, skel*, until finally she'd give us two buttons with a smile – BUT – she'd first make us breakfast, which we *had* to eat, *before* we got goofed, or she'd *really* get befuck.

We smoked on the balcony. That's where my bed was. I used to get completely fucked and pass out on my kooi. As I sank slowly into my float, the sounds of The District would come echoing up all around me. Children shrieking at play, hawkers touting, voices raised in argument over the never-ending dice game in the courtyard. The clatter and ringing of bicycles, women yelling gossip to each other across balconies, a hundred radios blaring out tinny distorted music, the sounds of babies crying. A living kaleidoscope of sounds running around vibrantly in my mind against the backdrop and distant hum of Cape Town's city centre.

Skollie had never felt so at home.

Skollie was home.

Buttons were the pills we smoked in bottlenecks. Their medical name was Mandrax and the active chemical ingredient was methaqualone. According to the ouens, they ̲ ̲een legal up until a few years before. They fell under the sedative ̲ ̲ic category of drugs. I remember smoking my first one as cleari, ̲ first time I had sex with Laura.

It was a hell of a lot better than fucking her, but buttons would eventually break everything in my life – not just my heart and not just once either.

We always used to smoke up on the little soccer field on the District Six side of the bridge across from the Gardens Centre off Buitenkant Street. That little soccer field has many memories. My first white pipe was one night when we were on our way to the Avalon Hotel to go and suip. Eric, his girlfriend Tania, Gavin and me.

There was some serious ritual involved too. The Mandrax tablet is pure white and rounded. The one side is split with a line and has the letters *RL* in cursive script. On the other side is the Mx legend with its tiny underline. It has to be crushed carefully into a fine white powder, using the shiny side of a folded square piece of heavy brown paper. This is very important. Eric told me stories of okes getting stabbed in the face with bottlenecks for fucking up on a button pipe. Once it has been crushed into a completely flat pancake half-moon in the paper, zol that's already been cleaned and mixed is carefully sprinkled onto it. Then it is folded, turned over and more zol is sprinkled on the other side. The powder is carefully worked into the zol until it coats the *boom* completely. Then a very clean pipe with a girrick and a backstop is taken and a little bit of cleaned zol is put into it. The white zol is added and then more cleaned zol is placed on top and tamped down. This is called topstop. The way to smoke a white pipe is to just hit it once as hard as possible and hold it. And hold it. And hold it.

And rush off your tits.

It starts almost immediately. All your senses short-circuit and explode from the middle of your brain, overwhelming everything everywhere. Your body quickly melts away into senseless nothingness as you go hurtling deep into the brilliant pure white sea of rush. Every single fucking time.

There were a lot of gangs in The District. The worst of them in Canterbury and Bloemhof Flats were the Jesters, who were a coloureds-only gang that killed whiteys and darkies whenever possible. They were Hollanders – murderers. So were a lot of the Scorpions. I could only walk home with a gang escort – it was very dangerous if I didn't.

Cape Town was riddled with gangs.

On the other side were the marrobaners, who were the Mongrels and the Born Free Kids. There were also the Bun Boys, Yakkies, Sexy Boys, Funky Junkies, Coral Kids, Americans and Young Americans (all various *nommers*) but they were all smaller in number and had less of a presence in that area. Cape Town's gangs were scattered in pockets all over the city because of politics. Uncle Guvvie moved people all over as it pleased him and this meant that the gangs broke up and rebuilt themselves from smaller cells. Mostly in the coloured and grey areas. The biggest gangs citywide were the Scorpions and the Mongrels. The Mongrels were a mixed gang of blacks, whites, coloureds – both ouens and kinders (who were known as *jostermeide*). There were so many more other gangs but I'm not going to go into all of them now.

I became a Mongrel, that is all that matters. I also entered into a lifelong relationship with the descendants of *emancipated* slaves, cast-offs, wandering white pricks and pure black men – the so-called coloured population of South Africa. For a great many years I spent more time in townships and ghettos than I did inside the white laager of the Group Areas Act, although the only reason I mention this is because of all the kak the gattas gave me for crossing the wire. Their poes. I fucking hate politics. Later on I'll tell you about the kak I had at the hands of coloured boere.

Eric told me the ideology behind the gangs came from prison. It started back at the turn of the last century in a black prison up in the Transvaal. Twenty-eight men banded together and swore an oath to stick together against Uncle Guvvie, the gattas, and everyone else – to the death. They created a place in the world for themselves and called it *nChonalanga*. This place had no borders. It owned no real estate. You belonged there by believing in it and by being able to open your mouth and identify yourself and where you stood inside that world as an indota – a man. As the years went on, rival gangs like the Big Fives started, until eventually it evolved into the modern South African prison gang system.

In prison the nongies (the 28s) are responsible for discipline and most of the smuggling. They are also the largest of the gangs and are separated from the other gangs because they practise sodomy. They rule the prison's nights and their motto is *Sondaf Ag-en-twintig*. They salute by stretching their hand out like a pistol with two barrels across their hearts.

The marrobaners (the 26s) are the thieves. They live for kroon and they steal to get it. They rob, thieve, connive, scale, sluk, skêbeng and schnaai their way into anything not nailed down. The only golden and much broken rule is never to sluk a brother. Their motto is *Son'd op Sesen-twintig* – duime.

The Hollanders (27s) are killers. Theirs is a badge more than a gang and is worn on both sides of the sun. You become a 27 by killing someone.

A Vyf is a piemp.

A Dertig is a grubby, *someone always after food*.

And so on.

On the outside it became blurred. An ou might be a nongie in the mang without being an auntie or a *pop* because he might smokkel for the brothers of *sondaf* to make his bene sterk – but on the outside he would be *sondop* and marrobaan to make a way.

I took to this way of life like a duck to water. The Mongrel$ were one of the oldest gangs in Cape Town. Their full stamp was M$G B.13, from Bungalow 13 in the District where the gang originated.

We mostly hung out at a gang digs in Lester Road, Wynberg. It was here that I began to observe what gang life on the outside was all about. The ouens were fucking hardcore. For instance:

One day Boetie comes staggering down Main Road Wynberg with a six-shooter slung over his shoulder. A six-shooter is also known as a six-man can and is a gallon bottle of cheap wine. Every now and then he stops and takes a lekker sluk. This goes on for a while until the boere obviously spot him. Then the kak starts. The boere first take his wine, which makes him completely befuck, and then they try to lock him in the van. As the one gatta slips the catch to lock the van door Boetie kicks it poes hard, shattering the kêrel's wrist. He immediately jumps back out and decks the other shocked pig lights out. Not finished – he does the same to the other gatta – followed rapidly by taking both their twas and stealing the van. Fucking mental.

Mad Mike goes out one night and buys three *stoppe* from Ali Yakkie – leader of the Yakkie$. He gets back and finds out that Ali slukked him with one dud stop. So he gets one of the gang's twas, goes back to Ali's spot, walks in and just starts shooting in the general direction of Ali, who had been busy – quietly smoking a button. Of course there is an instant and immediate evacuation of everybody concerned – including Ali Yakkie, who everybody else is trying to get away from more importantly than Mike. Apparently Mike only managed to hit Ali in the hand.

As a biscuit boy it was my responsibility to keep my bek shut and maal on pipes or perform chores for the indotas. Questions were discouraged. Eric was my mentor in what they tolerated and he had to do a good job because he had brought me in. They would hold him responsible if I turned out to be a *pop*. If I was good enough as a biscuit boy then I could become a full-force fire boy. After that an indota.

The ouens made a living by stealing. They stole so that they could smoke buttons, dop and jol.

I became a Mongrel after the most terrible fight I have ever been in.

See, I had managed to ingratiate myself into the Lester Street Mongrel$. There was Speedy, Spicey, Budgie, Bennet, Gino, Fuzzy, Mad Mike, Boetie, Honnie, Jimmy, Biker John, Little Alien, Big Alien, Arie, Evil, Bobby Mongrel, Jimmy Mongrel and a span of other kinders and ouens who filled the Lester Road digs every day. I had managed to impress Fuzzy and Gino, which I think had a lot to with my apprenticeship under Uncle Guvvie.

Me, Gino, Fuzzy, two coloured mochies and a white gintu were playing a prison game called dominoes one night at Fuzzy's spot. Speedy and Spicey had been out trying to cause kak in what used to be the Wynberg Hotel. They went into the pub and started a fight. One that was just bad enough for someone to call the boere. When the gattas arrived they got donnered for their trouble.

So there we are playing cards – all hoping for mileys and varkies and trying to make our aces fly – when Speedy and Spicey come running into the digs with their faces all red from fighting. Fuzzy gets up and silently stashes the zol he's merting and they scarper off up the back alley. About five minutes later they klap us. Ten gattas armed with pickaxe handles looking for a barney. They've already arrested Speedy and Spicey, who are now firmly locked up in a van outside. The gattas' problem is there are only the six of us in the pozzie and half are kinders playing cards. So they decide to skut instead, and find a few seeds and couple of dirty girricks, which they pounce upon to fuel their retarded infantile comments about dagga.

Eventually they leave, a whole bunch of other ouens arrive, and we decide to go suip. I'm sitting at a table having a dop when Gino gets up and goes off to the bar. Suddenly there are raised voices. The voices get louder and start moving outside, so I go see what the fuck's cutting. Outside, I find Gino and some other oke both going for quills in their back pockets. Gino has one – an Okapi.

The other ou is bluffing.

He spins around and fucks off up Main Road towards the arcade. Gino and I take off after him. They carry on running towards the arcade entrance but I swing right and sprint down towards Wittebome station and Lester Road. I'm the school 200-metres athletics champion and I give it everything I've got. I turn left into Lester Road and keep going like hell. Suddenly Gino, and the other ou going like the clappers just in front of him, burst out of the arcade and come sprinting up towards me. There're no streetlights, so by the time the other fucker sees me— it's too late. He's trapped between us with nowhere to go. He doesn't have time to think and splits to the right – into a yard.

I tear in after him but it's pitch dark so I can't see a fucking thing. All of a sudden he's looming up in front of me. A huge black square thing rises up, blocking out the starlight behind him, and crashes down towards my head. I hurtle sideways and it hits the side of my face, clipping my shoulder and nearly dislocating it. He's tried to hit me with a huge big fucking dugga-pan! It's so heavy it rips out of his hands. My adrenalin's pumped up to the max and I go for his hair with both hands, ripping his head downwards and kneeing him in the face with everything I've got. I hit dead square and he flies back, hitting the wall behind him with one almighty wet crack. I'm not in the mood to stop, so as his legs buckle and he starts sliding down, I grab his hair again, plant his head on the ground and kick the everliving shit out of him. Literally. I go absolutely mal. The fucking naaier's tried to brain me with something made of wood, corrugated iron and fucking cement.

His fucking poes!

I'm a Das.

Nobody's gonna hit me on the head and split open my fucking skull. NOBODY!

Eventually I've had enough and I'm wondering where the fuck Gino is. I run back out the yard and am greeted by the sight of Gino standing in the street, dead still, hands in the air, saying to someone that it's a private fight.

I know Gino won't be fucking around, so I come out very cautiously and the two of us back off carefully down the road from some ou standing on his stoep with a gun pointed at us ...

Gino told me later that the ou was a gatta who lived there and he had been standing on the stoep graunching his chick when we came tearing up the street. He thought we were after him because of Speedy and Spicey's kak so he ran inside, grabbed his twa, and as me and the other oke disappeared— he pulled it on Gino before he could get in to help me.

We went back to the bar and drank till closing time. Then we staggered back down towards Fuzzy's spot. As we got to the yard I tuned Gino I wanted to take another look. We went in. The ou was still lying there. I bent down and robbed him. I couldn't hear him breathing or fokkol. I turned to Gino and tuned him I skiemed the ou was witbene. Gino just spat on him and told me his poes – Stand and Deliver, Pay or Die.

It was a Mongrel slogan.

I found eighty bucks on the naaier, which was a fuckload of kroon in those days. We immediately went to buy buttons and a parcel from Ali Yakkie, then headed back to Fuzzy's.

Gino took me inside and told the ouens that I had made my bones by protecting him, so now I was a full-blooded Mongrel by his nomination. Only Fuzzy and Honnie voted against me. The next day we went down to Mr Adams from Woodstock and I was stamped with a Fu-Manchu on my left shoulder to symbolise that I had *slatwet*.

I was a Mongrel dog soldier – M$G B.13 – *gazilaam*.

A few days later, I'm hiking when this black Kombi stops and picks me up. Youngish ou driving, tuning me – jump, jump. I jump.

I tune the cat howzit, shot for the lift, wharrawharra, but then I notice something not too lekker. My door handle's gone, so's the window-winder. And the little knob jol to unlock the door is also missing. But what really gets my attention is the fact that the small triangle window is wired closed. And the main window is all the way up.

I skiem, ag fuck it, and we keep driving. But the next thing I know, this fucking ou is talking about massages and I skiem *oh-oh! – Bunny Boy!*

I look round and see there's a bed in the back but no windows.

Oh fuck …

I start looking around for a weapon, all the while talking kak and pretending to play dom. I spot a wood chisel lying inside the spare wheel between the driving cab and the love nest.

I start thinking furiously.

Then the ou pulls into a garage to put in petrol. I'm still skieming about getting the petrol-ous to open my door when he pulls out his wallet and all I see is this thick wad of moela. That's when I get kak gedagte. This ou isn't that much bigger than me, and I could gaan him with the chisel. So I tune him – okay bra, I've never done it before but I'll give you a massage. This gets him all hot and he starts driving. But then the fucker throws me a whammy and heads out towards Langa township. This is bad. I can't do anything because I've already bought into the jol. He stops at a deserted place, pulls off next to the road, whips out the keys and hops through to the back.

The naai is on his jol.

I'm chatting and tuning – I don't know if I'm so good at this, wharra-wharra. He takes off his jeans, plonks down a big bottle of Vaseline and lies down on the bed in nothing but a pair of shiny joggers. I sit next to him. His head is turned away from his jeans. I open the bottle and talk up a storm – this time skêbenging the Shy Virgin.

I take a huge glob of the kak and slap it on his back. Ugh. He rolls over a bit and I can see he has a moerse cockstand. Double ugh. I tell him to lie flat and I start rubbing the shit all over his back with one hand. With the other I manage to get the wallet out of his jeans and deep into my sock. I carry on smearing his back with Vaseline and tell him to lie still and let it heat up and melt – then I'm really going to get going and rub it in. He groans and I say – I'm just going to light up a smoke while we wait, I think I left them up in the front. I get up and as I pass by the spare wheel, I grab the chisel, jump out his door and start running like hell. The road is deserted except for a closed truck about two hundred metres away. I sprint towards it and see three ous standing there – two darkies and a coloured ou. I get to about a hundred metres when I hear the Kombi starting up!

I start yelling at the coloured ou.

I hosh and salute him and tune him I'm a 'six 'formatory boy and the Kombi behind me has a nongalosh in it who has tried to rape me, and if he helps me I'll split the kroon that I marrobaaned from him. This all while I'm doing the sprint of my life with the roar of the Kombi getting louder and louder in my pounding ears. Just as I reach them, this ou pulls to a stop and jumps out with a wheel spanner. I stand next to them and face him, panting, with the chisel in my hand. He starts yelling that I slukked him and I yell back that he is a fucking piece of homo shit who likes to try it on with laaities, so let's call the boere, poeshead. The ou sees there's no future in this and backs off. My mind is still racing and I dive into the back of the truck, pull the wallet out as fast as I can and stuff the notes into my balls, and by the time the coloured ou looks over the back of the truck, I make out like I'm struggling to get the wallet out of my sock. I thank him for his help and we open it up. There is about twelve rand in coins, which in 1979 could buy a bottle of brandy with about five bucks' change. We split the kroon and they drop me off in Rondebosch. I head down to the station, buy a ticket, get on the train and sit where nobody can see me. I count the kroon. There is R375. Now this is a fucking fortune!

Eric and them couldn't believe how I managed to pull it off. Anyway, me and Eric had no money problems for the rest of the holiday.

After I robbed that hol-bunny I started thinking about the shit that happened to me during the holidays back in Standard 7. It confused the fuck out of me but the thing that worried me most was that I couldn't get a hard-on when they were busy. Was there something wrong with me? I could never talk about it without risking getting kicked in my poes, so it was a deep secret that I only took out when I was completely alone, and that was usually late at night when I was hitchhiking.

Anyway, so there I am hiking deep one night when these two seriously hectic-looking Dutchmen with snorre and everything pick me up. I'm telling myself to be careful with these fuckers because I am carrying a couple of rand-baalle on me. The next thing I know the one ou asks me if I suck cock. My mind does a couple of backflips and I think – *what the fuck?*

Then I figure, okaaaay, so what the fuck – I'll go for it and see if I can get a hard-on.

I ask them if they have kroon. No. I ask them if they have spark and they tune – ja, one time, they got a bottle of burns at their pozzie. So I tune cool, I'll do it if they give me the burns and take me back to my spot afterwards. We go to their flat, I make a pipe, down shitloads of brandy, then do them both. Afterwards the one ou takes me home.

I only managed to get a cockstand by thinking about Laura's gang-bang, but the two cocks I sucked and wanked did fuckall for me – even though I tried to get into whatever was turning those two ous on. It kinda proved to me conclusively that I wasn't even half-homo – so I never bothered trying it again.

Some okes are, some okes aren't. That's just the way it is ...

10

A Perfect Das

Matric started with Potties announcing that he was exercising a veto that barred me and two other ous from being voted in as leaders.

Ag, fuck you Potties.

I made an ally in Tannie Potties, though. Tannie Potties was a tiny little woman and very, very pregnant. Many conversations in the bungalow revolved around how she and The Bear had managed to do it. Potties was so huge you'd think he would break her bones just trying to get it in, which led to other conclusions – like he had a tiny cock.

Anyway, she was pregnant and took a phone call one night that I answered for her. The poor woman was absolutely fucking huge. She stood like an obscene waddled-out cowboy trying to talk while holding her back. My insatiable appetite for books had increased my general knowledge on things gynaecological and I knew that she would be having absolute hell with her bladder and more particularly her lower back, so I ran to the graze hall, fetched her a chair and put it behind her bum. She was so surprised and grateful as she plopped down that she nearly kissed me.

However, the reward she gave me was worth more than any kiss. The greatest privilege any boy in the hostel could have was to deck off her and Pottie's table after lunch on Wednesdays and Sundays. These of course were pudding days and all the leftovers on their table, meat and vegetables included, were that particular boy's privilege. And let's not fuck around – it was also hard currency. Their table got exactly the same ration as the others, where everyone else sat ten to a table, and there was usually only Tannie Potties, The Bear and the assistant hostel mother Tannie Botha to eat it. There was always way too much for one ou and his company to chozz – so he sold the rest. Or at least I did, much to the dark envy of the rest of the hostel, because that entire year she called me out every single Wednesday and Sunday. Potties didn't like it, but he couldn't do anything about it because she didn't take shit from him. She was probably the only one who could control him.

Matric was boring. I walloped during the last holidays of the year, came back at the end of it— took my six shots and F-group. Potties broke one cane.

Ho hum.

Now, old Potties considered himself quite the expert on matters pertaining to *boom* – only he called it *bossies*. Us Matrics had block time like most normal Matrics on the outside and studied in our dormitories. One night during study I was sitting at my desk with my feet up, admiring the most amazingly beautiful trophy I had just made from a piece of thin aluminium tube and an empty asthma pump. It was perfect. I had even used the cut-off top of the gas bottle and made it into a filter that fitted snugly on the bottom. I was figuring I'd show Eric Jackson after study and we could test-drive it quickly. I heard a scraping noise behind me, glanced lazily over my shoulder and locked eyes with— The Bear. Oh shit ...

The first punch caught me perfectly and lifted me clean out of the chair, over my bed and crashing into the bed next to mine. I lay there completely dazed, a smoky taste in my mouth and floating little fluffy things drifting down just out of focus. TKO.

Things had just started making sense again when he roared – *Moenie vir my lag nie!* Half-concussed as I was, my face must have twisted up into some sort of rictus making me look like I was laughing, and he rounded on me again. When things started making nasty painful sense again, I was being dragged (literally) down the stairs. He hauled me into his study, threw me down onto a chair, closed the door and locked it. I was still stunned from his fists but it was all coming back very – very quickly.

I was locked in a room with a sadistic animal and he had every reason to soothe his ruffled hypocrisy and unleash the demon to feed. Tannie Potties wasn't around to save me – she was out. My opening gambit was to ask him to appear in front of Stronk. I knew Stronk, he would dish out shots, single portion of F-Group to go, and once the Strafboek had been signed it would all be over.

The Bear let his ugly-piggy eyes boil for a moment and growled – *NEE!* I tossed out the second of my lesser devils and asked for the cops. Take me to the boere.

NEE!

Since then I've been arrested and locked up in five countries. I've spent time in twelve different penitentiaries and shit knows how many police stations in those countries. I've been in five military stockades and lockups, one of which had a regime so harsh that its Provost Marshall and DBIs killed six convicts that I know of, but I have never been as frightened as I was that night.

I didn't know what made Potties tick but he was definitely the scariest screw that I have ever had to face. He was one of those evil men who need *A Cause* because under the skin the urge to hurt runs likes a deep dark river. He had to have us evil so that he could let go with his *righteous* rage. Dagga was the most profane and violent of Potties' reasons to let go. Everything else came second.

I was in deep shit and we both knew it. I had appealed to all the powers higher than him and he'd simply laughed them off. He needed no higher powers. He was God's *personal* instrument. If torture is the prolonged careful application of excruciating pain to procure sick pleasure under the thin veil of seeking recalcitrant information, then what that sick twisted fuck did to me that night fulfils the definition.

He told me to tell him about everybody who smoked in the hostel. He already knew everything (*fat chance*) but I sommer had to tell him again. I told him I knew nothing. He stood up, picked up a piece of paper and pen, and laid it on the desk in front of me.

Don't talk kak – write.

I wrote down my own name and put down the pen.

The bad-piggy eyes boiled with gleeful malice for a moment before he announced that he had no intention of playing games with me. He would give me one shot every five minutes until I completed the list.

And that's exactly what he did.

Somewhere in the middle of all the crying, terror, misery and snot, I lost count of the exact number of cuts he gave me. We went into his office at about 20h20 and I started talking just before midnight. Work it out.

I broke, but not completely. I had to stop him from hurting me somehow and that meant talking. I had to, because my body was going into shock. I told him that I had smoked with Eric Jackson during the holidays. That got his attention. Problem was he couldn't do anything about it. I dragged out Mario Pedroza, Craig Ferguson and Dennis Faul. He knew they were all my best friends, but of course each time it had been during the previous year or during the holidays somewhere, sometime – any time except the present.

He stopped hitting me and I went to bed with the dubious distinction of having the worst-looking arse anybody had ever seen. My backside had turned into a strip of raw, purple, bleeding meat about six inches wide. My right hip was also a mess because the cane had snapped around my body, cutting into the hip. He broke three canes on me that night before

I piemped. The terrible thing was, I could sit properly again after about five days and my arse healed up completely after a month with surprisingly little scarring, but the guilt I felt for mentioning my friends' names I would carry forever.

The piece of shit had a display up in his office. It consisted of a large military-looking camouflage net up on one wall upon which knives, bows, arrows, two crossbows and some traditional African weapons were mounted. Beneath it was a bookcase with the dagga-pipes he had confiscated. Next to the pipes was a large fruit jar three-quarters filled with *boom*. This was Potties' bossies and he was immensely proud of it. It was all the dagga that he had ever bust. I didn't have much to focus my attention on during my long evil hours with Potties that night except for that fruit jar.

It burned into my mind.

A short while later, Potties was away for a weekend. Our assistant hostel father was an ancient old bugger called Dowekoos. He had been at the school since the days when wagon-making was a trade. He was almost completely deaf and twitched a lot. We had no zol that weekend and, worse still, we had no money either. Furious schemes were being made involving kerkpakke and slipping out to the darkie location to swop or sell. This was all terribly dangerous and not very practical.

Yours truly came up with a plan. Let's steal Potties' boom.

Everyone who heard about it thought it utterly insane. Like how, for fucksakes?

Like so:

One ou placed a phone call from the inside tiekiebox to the old outside tiekiebox. Another ou ran and answered it. Then he went to the front door of The Bear's apartment and called Dowekoos. As Dowekoos walked out the front door, we entered from the inside and sharked straight into Potties' study. I took the jar of zol and poured its contents onto a piece of newspaper. The other ou took a sheet of newspaper with a mound of origanum that we'd stolen from the kitchen and filled it to the same level. We heard the oke at the door keeping skei tell us that Koos was coming back.

I had an ou outside watching Dowekoos. Watching him was another ou and another ou watching him and so on so that I had a human chain telling us exactly when the geriatric some-danger was coming back. We put the jar back carefully and exited the flat, closing the door gently behind us.

It was probably the sweetest *boom* I have ever smoked outside of Amsterdam.

Forty Days arrived.

Among us Dasse it was a big thing too. We all enjoyed likening ourselves to the private ouens doing National Service, and apparently they celebrated their impending escape from Uncle Guvvie's warmongering clutches after two years with something akin to mania. Mania we enjoyed. Mania we cultivated.

It was a Das thing.

Uncle Guvvie allowed us certain privileges on and near Forty Days. One was the Changing of the Guard ceremony, which always went off without too many questions concerning injuries. The other was Voorregskaats at the skating rink for the Matrics on the night of Forty Days itself.

I could never figure out how everyone knew that the day had arrived to Change the Guard. It seemed to transpire through some sort of primeval switch that everyone recognised. At any rate, on a certain day, during big break, the okes would shark down to their hostels, gulp down dop and rogue, then shark back up to the big piece of grass opposite the school. Everybody attended. The Matrics would pair off against the Eights and Nines while everybody else watched. The idea was that the Eights and Nines would have to take the right to run the school the following year from the Matrics by force.

Then one hell of a brawl broke out.

Obvious things like punching in the face and kicking in the nuts were not on. Nor were biting, bitch-slapping, poking in the eyes, karate kicks, Jap-slapping or head-butting. But pretty much everything else went. There was always a very generous helping of black eyes and split lips afterwards, in spite of the punching rule (*the elbow loophole*), and at least two broken arms. The snotrags stayed dry.

This was hardcore Das stuff.

I was gated and not allowed Voorregskaats that year because I had been in F-group for my final holiday wallop. And there was no zol in the school. No zol hurt. It made me mad as a snake. I needed zol and Uncle Fucking Guvvie had fucked up my one and only fucking chance of scoring. Pissed off did not even begin to describe how bedonnered I felt. I went down to Hostel 3 and checked out Dennis's butlers. He was skating of course. They had nothing. Down to Hostel 4 to see if my old bras maybe had a knoesie. Nothing. I stalked back up to Hostel 2.

I was livid with rage.

It was while I was walking back that I decided to do it. I did not even hesitate. I went straight up to my dormitory, bummed two matches and a piece of slatch from some ou. Then I sharked back downstairs, slipped out the hostel and went directly to the old outside tiekiebox. Once inside, I looked around. Carefully. Except for Jaamie having a braai down at Hostel 4 there was nothing happening.

Nothing.

I slipped out the phone booth, ran lightly across to the school and went into the English classroom. Still nothing stirred. I quickly opened an untidy classroom cupboard stuffed full of old papers and crap – then I lit a match on the piece of slatch and set fire to the corner of a page. As soon as I was certain it was burning properly I left. Straight back to the tiekiebox. Everything was still dead quiet. I got my shaking ass back to the hostel, went directly to my dormitory, stripped off and went to the showers.

A couple of other ous were with me, including the dickhead who gave me the match and slatch.

We showered for a while until my – ha ha – burning curiosity got the better of me. I quickly dried my feet and ran down to Eric Jackson's dormitory. He had a lekker view of the English classroom. Outside everything was still dead quiet but there was one hell of a big orange glow coming out the windows. I grinned and ran back to the showers. We finished showering and were standing around talking kak drying off. Yster acting like nothing in the world was happening. Inside, of course, the tension was freaking me out completely. It was as we were walking back to the dormitory that Shawn Killian came running up the stairs yelling incoherently that the school was burning. I cracked a joke at him, saying we had all heard that before, until it became obvious by Shawn grabbing fire extinguishers and yelling even louder that something was very wrong. I dropped my act, sprinted to my bed and tore into my clothes. As I ran out the hostel I was greeted by the sight of the roof of the English classroom collapsing into an inferno of flames and sparks that shot high into the night. Fuck. It was raging. The whole night was orange. And spreading.

Yeeeemutherfuckingghaaaa ... ...

Being an electrician I started running around yelling wildly that we had to get the power switched off. The idea was to plant a reason for the blaze. Potties immediately latched onto this and we cut the mains. It worked. The official verdict was an electrical fault. My timing could not have been more perfect because the okes from Voorregskaats arrived back in a breathless rush almost exactly at the same time as the fire brigade.

And then the real fun started.

What I had done was a hot revenge fantasy that lived in the pain, semen, snot and blood-fucked recesses of almost every Das's head. Plenty of ous had spat dark and angry curses into the bungalow's stained floor over the years while uttering bitter bloody threats to the like. Some continuously. Still, I had done what we all so dearly wanted. The ouens were ecstatic. Dennis found me. He grabbed me, looked me in the eye and started pissing himself. I tried to bluff him but Dennis knew me too well. Eric did the same. So did Nienaber. I let nothing out. Even though the mutherfuckers were assuming right – they were STILL JUST ASSUMING. This was serious shit. No TK for me if I got bust. It would be straight to the mang.

It wasn't me.

Of course the ouens cut the fire hoses. Fuck, they didn't want to see this thing put out. And so the school burned. And it turned into a night of a million stories. A bunch of ouens did the right thing. They went from class to class and saved stuff. None of the classrooms were locked but they smashed down the doors anyway. Then they took the desks inside and hurled them straight through the windows – TO SAVE THEM FROM THE FIRE SIR!

We stole all the audiovisual equipment and swopped it for zol immediately with the coloured spectators who arrived en masse (*from fuck knows where*) to watch the fun. And so the long smoky orange night went on. The school's Vice-Principal Cadbury was seen openly crying. His only copy of his memoirs had been in the office.

And nobody got bust for nothing.

To me it seemed as if I was avenging all the misery and agony that Uncle Guvvie had inflicted upon the scores of us over so many long fucking years all the way from the slave whips and The Rope to the boots and broken faces after *Oom God van Jakob* under Stronk.

When the smoke and flames had eventually all died down and gone out we were left with a black burnt-out shell of what was once the school.

O fok nou kom daar kak …

Because the school was a National Monument there was a major stink about the damage. And George being the local constituency of Pieter Willem Botha meant that the Prime Minister Himself had to come and Personally inspect the damage. It was the first and only time I ever saw The Real Uncle Guvvie up close in person. With all his big blond bodyguards trailing a white-faced Stronk. Come to inspect the tiny little klap I gave him for naaing me and my bras.

On my last day in Die Bult I was called to Stronk's office. I was obviously dikgerook. We later established on the train that I was the only one among the Matrics who was afforded this unheard-of privilege.

Stronk sat behind his huge desk, those cold blue eyes bearing suddenly inflicted age. He had ordered the worst beating upon me that I have ever survived and tossed me in F-group fuck knows how many times, and I got him back by setting fire to his dreams.

Maak gebruik van jou kanse, seun.

Beautiful. Poetic. So *Literal*.

And he knew it …

He tried saying some set piece he thought he could use on me as a parting shot, but immediately realised from my perfect Sicilian expression that he was going nowhere. He stopped speaking.

I smiled perfectly benignly and said goodbye – *Sir*. I did not shake his hand. And I never looked back.

A perfect Das.

Fuck you Uncle Guvvie. Jou *maaa'tha* poes – fokken witboernaaier …

PART III

Armies of Gods

11

Lix of Katatura

School was over and I had a choice.

Dennis invited me to come up to Joburg with him and set up a crime crew. Eric asked me to accompany him to Windhoek. I was bitterly torn between the two. I loved these mutherfuckers big time. They were my bizas. I knew Dennis would do a good job of it. Of course he would. He did and was caught with diamonds and guns about three months later and went down for his first stretch.

I chose to go with Eric.

Eric knew Windhoek because he had hurriedly walloped there after the stabbing he was involved in on Wittebome station years before. He'd pitched up in Windhoek in a flat paranoid panic after running from the boere and arrived at Kaiser Corner totally lost and nearly out of money. He spotted a couple of friendly-looking ous and asked them where he could find some zol. They *lagged* and told him he would either have to wait a long time or catch a taxi with them. He caught a taxi and went into Katatura, the Soweto of what was South West Africa. He reckons he went back into town twice in the following year and only worked for three days.

I arrived in Windhoek with him, also lost and very eager to see this place that I had heard so much about. We caught a taxi – an old black Valiant, with six people squashed in the back and four in the front – and cruised down to the legendary black Mecca. We arrived in the middle of this absolutely huge township and it was like nothing I had ever imagined. Katatura was broken into various *lokasies*. There was Nama Lokasie (where we had our spot), Damara Lokasie, Herero Lokasie, Ovambo Lokasie, Polieskamp and the Compounds.

I met Eric's other mochie !Ka, who was a full-blooded Nama. She lived with her sister and brother-in-law Simon, who had been one of Nam's national soccer heroes until he took a klap on the field one day and landed up with stainless steel pins in his left arm and the end of his career. But, as with all my Damara friends, we hit it off immediately. It was a crazy place. Eric was an icon. EVERYFUCKINGBODY KNEW HIM! And of course they wanted to buy him a dop and catch up on the gossip and show him the baby who was born while he was away and have another dop and meet these other ous until everything began dissolving into a long fractious mad alcoholic binge that I desperately hoped I was going to survive.

I was struck by a feeling of coming alive. It's something that has always drawn me back to the townships. There was a vibrancy and kaleidoscope of activity with a human closeness that I experienced but didn't understand. Yet. I simply found myself needing it. Everyone lived in tiny little semi-detached box houses, with maybe one maybe two families per room. It was very crowded and everybody knew everybody's business. Neighbours were simply an extension of living space. There was a lot of laughter and, like I said, scary amounts of drinking.

Force people to live on top of one another like that and you are bound to pick up social stress that expresses itself in violence. What I could never understand is why there wasn't *more*. Anyway, we had our own adjustment problems quite soon after we arrived. !Ka had taken a boyfriend after Eric left to go back to Die Bult. Quite obviously she hadn't expected to see him again. She dumped the ou as soon as we arrived, much to his dark ire.

I never saw the fight because I had passed out. Apparently a brick came through the window of the room I was sprawled out in and landed next to my head. Outside, Eric was showing four okes what a Das could do with a rice flail. The boyfriend and mates disappeared, nursing sore noggins, and that was that.

We went everywhere – and everywhere we went, we drank. The favourite was a sparkling wine called Perlino Perle. Actually it was just poeswyn injected with gas. The other dop was neat cane spirits drunk as a sort of shooter and chased with a little bit of something very sweet like cream soda. Generally we sat in a circle of ouens and there were things like you *never* passed something to someone else behind another man's back. We were accepted by these people because of zol, our tattoos and our gang respek and disipliene.

We found ourselves in a dangerous situation one day when we went to the compounds to see if we could score some zol. Ours was about to run dry. It was a Saturday, and the men's compounds were full of off-duty labourers. Four of us walked into the middle of the quad and stood still. Eric and I very visibly fished out zol, a pipe, girrick and mix, and maaled on. By now the entire compound was dead silent. Hundreds of eyes watched the two of us. We knew we were in mortal danger, but we also knew that walking in as we had was so unprecedented that nobody really knew what to do next. I bust and Eric fired. We passed the pipe to Simon and slowly the hubbub of the compound returned. We found a man who could help us and met some other curious ous who wandered over to greet us. Needless to say, we staggered out late that night having made dozens of friends for life. They didn't like two-syllable names so they called me Lix, and I discovered that the favourite swearword of Namibians is *Kont*. Actually *Kont-se-kind*.

Eric got totally befuck with me one time when I refused to eat offal that our hosts cooked for us. !Ka went out and bought me a piece of boerewors. Eric found me in the backyard passed out on a mat, and kicked me in the ribs. Hard. He was absolutely livid with me. Who the fuck did I think I was? These people were our hosts and were giving us everything they had but that wasn't good enough for me. If I wanted to stay his friend I would have to give up my whitey kak pluk. And fucking quickly. I tiemied what everybody tiemied or I could just fuck off right then and there.

Lix adjusted his attitude. *Kont-se-kind. Witboernaaier.*

I also found out that they lived very close to the spirit world. Eric told me to just listen and learn. It was my first immersion into black culture and I loved it. I had no real anchors or loyalty to anything except my Mongrel boeties and we had no race or sex among us. We were faceless dog soldiers and proud of it. So I was open to staying with them for good, but it meant ducking my National Service call-up. And that meant prison the day I walked back into South Africa. It could also mean arrest and extradition if I stayed in South West, because South Africa was also running that country. And Uncle Guvvie was relentless. He would fucking lock me up. Poes.

Simon was active in SWAPO's political wing. He taught me marching songs and tried to explain the politics (SA vs SWAPO vs DTA) but I didn't really get it. To me politics was just a fucking nuisance to be overcome so that I could live life like I fucking wanted to. Fuck Uncle Guvvie. I had never stopped reading and identified Communism as the new post-Hitler evil. I never discussed this with Eric – he didn't give a fuck. It was just my curiosity but I knew that SWAPO was apparently backed by the Soviets, which is something I balked at. They were just Hitler dressed up in a different colour. I had also been practising mental fighting discipline since Standard 9 – the reason I felt such self-betrayal when I broke down under Potties' torture – and avidly studying everything I could find on terrorism and urban guerrilla warfare because I had some sort of half-formed idea that I wanted to be a mercenary and eventually an assassin of anti-West targets. It made sense to do my National Service for combat experience. This I kept to myself. How could I tell Simon I was going to do what Uncle Guvvie was forcing me into for all my own reasons?

So Lix bid a sad farewell to everybody, and the best, most drunken holiday that I had ever had— finally ended.

12

79321790 BG

The lunatic is in my head – Pink Floyd, *Dark Side of the Moon*

I arrived back in Cape Town from Windhoek the night before I had to present myself at the Castle and went out and had an all-night party with Eric's Cape Town chick Tania. We arrived back at Wally's place to pick up my shit and found him raging out of his mind – pissed on whiskey, and pissed off at me. He even had the audacity to rant at me for being fucked on drugs. Anyway, he dumped us at the Castle. I gave Tania a hug and a peck, and joster-strolled from the street and into a courtyard of dubious-looking idiots, planks, roekers, weirdos, fuckups and other nefarious individuals who were all about to become my comrades-in-arms. We met our first officers and I was immediately struck by the fact that these people never spoke – they yelled. All the time. And they fucking swore. Creatively. You were Piel, Slang, Spinnekop, Troep, Penie, Perd, and they were going to rip off your head and piss down your neck. Laughing at this was a very bad idea. Then they would tear open your chest and shit on your lungs.

We arrived in Kimberley by train and went through kit issue, filling in zillions of forms, seeing the doctors, getting heads shaved, and finally – my own special moment – the issue of rifles. I swung into basics like a duck to water. I'd been living under a military regime for years. It was like kindergarten after primary school. At the end of the second week I was commended in front of our company as the most exemplary soldier in the unit.

Then I found out my regiment was back-line and immediately wanted out. I had choices. Parabats or one of the Special Forces units. I decided on the latter. Special Forces meant I would have to join Permanent Force, so I did a gruelling PT keuring, which I passed, and was sent back to Wally to sign my PF application because I was seventeen. Wally told me I was a stupid fucking idiot and refused to sign.

I arrived back in my camp to discover that I had missed all the other National Service keurings and had in essence lost any chance of seeing active combat. My world crashed in. The only reason I had reported for service was to fight. I needed to prove to myself that I could fight with a weapon and get over my fear like I had done the first time I fought naked against Caveman in the showers. It was a hurdle that I would have to overcome professionally. I knew I could do it and I wanted to prove that to myself – only it was all fucked. I also discovered that the officers liked to fuck you over whenever they could. They found my problem *amusing*. Of course, I had been naive enough to think Uncle Guvvie would go away and leave me alone. Cunt.

I rebelled completely and got into a lot of trouble drinking. The worst being after my first pass:

I arrive back early and only one oke, Charlie, is around. He has his connection's car for the weekend so we go hit town. Kimberley has the only drive-in pub in the country and this is where we go. A few rounds of burns and coke with two beers to go. Then we go cruising, looking for zol. All the darkies who see us are terrified by our short hair and immediately write us off as gattas. Bummer, no *boom*. More doppe at the drive-in.

Back at base, still only a couple of ouens are around. I am not fucked enough. Charlie and I argue. I take the keys. He tunes me to do whatever the fuck I want – he doesn't know fuckall.

I head straight back to the drive-in, order six double brandies and a beer. I down the burns immediately, shuddering from the nauseating taste, and piss off with the beer between my legs.

Soon I'm hanging onto the steering wheel for support. I misjudge and nearly roll at the traffic circle leading to Diskobolos but manage to control the car – yelling wildly at my own fright.

Then I floor it as hard as I can.

I go howling past the base at something over one-seventy and suddenly there's a fork in the road.

I ignorantly hit the brakes as hard as I can.

The car goes into a screeching skid … there is a brief sense of weightlessness … and … suddenly— slamming, screaming metal and crackling, breaking noises, over and over, ending with an almighty—

—BANG!!

It happens so fucking fast that it is over before I even realise it has begun. My head is still thinking: I must slow down for the fork soon …

The bundu has gone completely silent in shock.

The headlights are, miraculously, still on – staring blindly into the slowly settling dust cloud. The only person who could possibly have survived the accident is the driver. The rest of the car is completely crushed into the seats. Wreckage lies strewn all over the veld. The entire windscreen has somehow popped out in one piece.

It's about the only thing not smashed.

The MPs arrive and I get marched off to a doctor, who quickly diagnoses me as drunk, but I am led away and locked up in a civilian police station for Car Theft, Drunken Driving and Driving Without a Licence. At the police station the district surgeon draws some blood and that is me – fucked.

I lay there for thirty days awaiting trial and wished vainly that I could take that night back. I wished it with all my heart but nothing happened. I was in a world of mendacious self-pity but it was to no avail. I had not thought before I did it and now I had to pay the price. I was also completely blind to the fact that I might have died or killed others. I was being confronted with the flaws in my personality and I didn't like them.

I pleaded guilty to a one-armed maggie who had the reputation of being a real evil bugger, told him my story and – lo and behold – he entered a Not Guilty plea for me on the car-theft charge. According to him, Charlie was technically in charge of the car, so when I took it, although it was against his wishes, it was not without his permission. He hammered me on the rest though. Banned from applying for a licence for six months, a fine for both the drunken driving and driving without a licence, and a prison sentence for the drunken driving suspended for three years. I also learnt my first very important legal lesson: Do not ever lie to a judge. Everyone else – especially the mapuza – but never the judge. These ous sit listening to naaiers talking kak to them all day. They are human lie detectors. So, when someone comes into their court and tells the truth, it is so fucking refreshing they smile and sometimes let you walk.

I had more drunken blackouts – one in which I came to and found myself pounding a nail into the shoulder of a fat Jewish ou me and a bra extorted. His screaming brought me out of it. Another in which I attacked a pedestrian stranger in town with an empty tequila bottle. My chinas in the car screaming at me brought me out of it that time. We had a gang fight in the camp with fifteen other ous. Beyond multiple lacerations, I had to have maxilo-facial surgery to drain the bleeding behind my left eye.

I came off with the worst injuries. Three against fifteen and so pissed we could hardly stand – we were lucky to get off that lightly.

I became notorious.

The day I was to ship out to the base at Grootfontein in South West Africa, I received a big shipment of zol. I picked it up and, as I was walking past the HQ with it in my balls— the CO called me. He asked me if I had finished packing. I told him I had. He told his adjutant to watch me and sent his clerk to fetch my balsak.

The entire company fell in, did roll-call and then jumped onto the trucks for the airport. I sat and watched, thinking with every passing moment that I was in deep shit. If only I hadn't scored. Eventually all the trucks left and the CO returned. He ordered me to climb in his staff car with my balsak and – surprise, surprise – we left for the airport too. Upon arrival I saw all the troops being searched by MPs with dogs before boarding the Vlossie. The troops boarded and the MPs left. The clerk carried my balsak to the Air Force ouens loading the plane. I sat in the car waiting until the tail was up. At that exact point, the CO ordered me out of the car and marched me to the Vlossie.

He made sure the ou with the ping-pong paddles outside had been told to check that the door was shut and firmly locked behind me …

*

The secret to having a good time in the Army is not to be noticed.

One of the classic tricks instructors used to get volunteers was to scream – *Jy!!* – at a group of passing troops. Whoever looked around got nailed – and noticed. Why did you look around? Do you have a guilty conscience? I'm gonna have to watch you. What is your fucking number, rank and name, soldier?

And you're Fucked.

So the secret is to try and be invisible. Not proudly out front, not right at the back – in the middle somewhere – not sticking out. Rifleman Fucking Nobody. The ou sleeping three beds down whose name nobody actually remembers. You know … *Dinges.*

We landed in Grootfontein Military Base in northern Namibia not knowing what to expect. Did you notice the *in* in that sentence? That base was so big the Defence Force put down chartered SAA Boeings to ferry in troops during heavy operations. It was like a small military city.

Of course I was noticed immediately. *Jy met die oog! Wat is jou naam troep?* I still had a big dressing on the side of my face from the surgery to my eye.

The kak had already started.

I ended up in 16 Maintenance Unit and absolutely fucking hated it.

They put me in the stores. Dumb idea. Within a few months I had made contacts everywhere and started carting off anything that wasn't nailed down – and made a profit on it. Ten sacks of mielie-meal sold to a farmer contact from a convoy. Fifty cases of Coke to a mate who ran the Signals canteen. Five crates of mini-salamis. Kilos and kilos of fresh meat. Altered inventories to hide losses and so on. Eventually the PFs realised they weren't going to catch me, so they transferred me to the unit's Light Field Workshop and I became an ops-tiffy. I had a few adjustment problems but soon settled in. And drank like a demented fish.

One night I got pissed, drank some more, then got mean and totally bedonnered at the fucking PFs for keeping me out of combat, and broke into our massive weapons store. In and out – past razor wire, guards, dogs and no-nonsense concrete architecture – stealing two Uzis and about 400 rounds of loose ammunition. Just to prove to myself, and fuck them, that— I could do it!

Biggest, most impenetrable camp in the war. Hah!

I carefully hide the SMGs in the oke next door's roof, so they are close to me but not Too Close.

Once I was sober again, Common Sense yelled at me for being so dof, but, hey, fuck it – I'm not one to fret too much. I decided to keep one for bank robberies and give the other to my Mongrel boeties back home in the States.

About a fortnight later I attempted to control my drinking. And all hell broke loose.

See, I was a hardened Das and a Mongrel. I fucking did it till I couldn't do it any more. Fuck Uncle Guvvie. Jou maaa'tha poes fokken witboernaaier. Everything a Das did. Fighting, hoping for a fuck, wanking, drinking, stealing and generally causing as much kak and mayhem as was humanly possible without being dead or bloody close to it.

Oh, and without getting bust …

I tried telling myself – *okay twinkletoes, you may only drink two beers tonight, because: screaming gurgled obscenities and unspeakably shitty Army chow into a great white trumpet, then crawling off blindly to pass out under a softly running cold shower ... is becoming a drag. And, besides, it's creepy that the chow looks the same coming out as it did going in. Not much difference in the taste either.*

That pledge never took because this kind of thinking was utterly foreign to me. But – something just told me, I should try. Really try.

Of course, my two-beer pledge really didn't take *that* night. But I blame it all on the Dankietannies ...

The Dankietannies were like a volunteer organisation that sent us little boxes with lollies, cookies and shit to make it a bit better being away from the States. As far as we were all concerned they should have sent us entjies, beer and *Scope* magazine every Friday – but, ja, they were actually like a Christian jol named Die Suiderkruis-wharra-somebullshit. Us having lustful thoughts while ogling and furiously wanking over girls with gorgeous star-covered tits would definitely have bugged them, especially since we were supposed to be murdering the heathen, Communist, Kaffir bastards up North to ward off *Die Swart Gevaar*. Of course we also all wanted the job of the cunt who pasted on the censorship stars.

Me, my best mate Deon Doyle, Kort-Dik-En-Ongeskik-Vermeulen, Kapie and Hubba are the very first squad to pitch up at the pub looking like hell armed to the teeth.

We never wash after work.

To our utter amazement, we find ourselves confronted by two Benoni-Bellville-type forty-year-old matrons beaming at us brightly and manning a big fucking Curly Wurly ice-cream machine.

They immediately start dishing them out. We are so dazed at the sight of this that we accept. Chomp, chomp and throw the blackened cone away, go for seconds – chomp, chomp – but every single one of the troops pouring into the pub behind us starts thinking the same kind of thing. I mean, none of us wants to think about the States. Some ous did, but it fucked with your head. And these two freakshows have brought Memories into our Hallowed Battalion Pub – Our Sanctuary, Die Vlakvark Watergat – where we come to sometimes fight but generally to puke and piss on each other to forget all that shit.

Deon and I, who both come from the Cape, get absolutely fucked out of our bush hats because we don't want to think about ice-cream and beaches. And all of us go staggering off to our bungalow, crashing regularly into a big heap of rifles, legs, flailing fists and wild unholy yelling that would make the Dankietannies think very hard about bringing another Curly Wurly ice-cream machine. Or ever coming back.

Fucking Army.

I hate the Army. Fucking plank bonehead fucking PFs. I hate PFs. I hate PFs ...

And the rage in me boils over.

I stagger over to the next bungalow, crawl into the roof – fall out – crawl back in and load an Uzi. I fall back out, go staggering off outside and fire the mutherfuckering thing – !.!

– *WHAT THE FUCK IS SHOOTING AT UUUUS!!* –

– *Jesus Christ, where's my fucking rifle!* –

– *Hey poeshead! You not supposed to dive under your fucking bed ou!* –

– *Yay! We must fuck off to the bunkers!* –

– *Move!!* –

I don't just run down the road – I run – and I run – and I break free. The adrenalin has sobered me completely and comes pouring into me like a hot flame exploding into the rage. I run into the bundu, hide the Uzi under a rock and start running back. I'm gonna kick some PF in the Curly Wurlies tonight. They won't let me fight, well fuck'em – I'll give 'em a fight.

I run back to my bungalow to fetch my baseball bat. On the way I'm stopped by a lootie, who asks me one of those dumb-assed Dutchman questions that reveal just how stupid a few hundred years of inbreeding and religious paranoia can make you. I hit him straight off the bike. One klap. Another officer appears at the window and – *bang!* – he scrambles off screaming: *Get him! Get him! For God's sake GET HIM!*

Okay, by now the whole battalion knows a shitstorm has erupted and come running to have a check. I jaag for the door, baseball bat waving, and the bungalow clears out before me like rats before a junkyard dog. They think I am crazy but it's just that I'm not frightened – of anything. And now I want to fight.

The PFs have tried to brainwash us into the shitty politics behind the war and wrap it up in a nice NG Kerk Zionist package but I will never buy into it. I'm a Das. I know it's all kak and all I want to do is fight. I'm too much of a poes to know it's only about diamonds. I want blood. Any blood. I stand on the grass screaming in Zulu and Skollietaal for blood.

Nobody is going to come near me, but a sort of impasse has occurred. Something Has To Be Done.

It arrives briskly in the form a Bedford truck full of MPs. Fifteen of them. They surround me and I ask the highest rank if he is the poeshead running their outfit. He pulls out his nine-mil, points it at me and orders me to drop the bat. I am cruising high and black and decide I want to die right here and now. I have stopped caring. I tell him he has one chance. In the head or the heart, because if he isn't loaded, if he's locked or if he misses— he is coming with me, and without a flicker of hesitation I go at him. He bolts like a cat and they all scatter and scramble back into the Bedford. They fuck off.

A second impasse has occurred. I begin winding down slightly. Kapie my Ouman comes over to me *lagging* and gives me a skollie salute. We go into a huddle and chat quietly while the entire battalion stands at a safe distance, watching in absolute amazement and betting strongly on bad shit happening to Kapie. Fucking idiots – I would never hurt a bra who respects me, smokes *boom* and suips with me, sleeps next to me, and carries a rifle to cover my gat. Kapie reckons I've fucked up too big. I've kinda broken every Military Law in the book. What now bra?

The two of us agree to call the MPs back and go for the Facing The Music option.

The MPs arrive back very subdued.

I stick out my arms to the gatta I just missed with the baseball bat. He slaps on some skates— and immediately rips out his mapuza kak pluk once they are locked.

I realise this stupid plank cunt just doesn't get it. A moment ago he looked death in the face and yet he thinks he can control it with a bit of steel.

The torrent of rage comes pouring straight back.

We get to the DB and march into the charge office.

A parade of these cunts stand arrogantly behind the charge office desk.

Desk sergeant asks me my name – I tell him his mother's siff smelly poes. He asks again and I tell him to go fuck her because the poor fucking dog is sick of doing it.

The rage is there, and they can see it, otherwise they would've klapped me long time ago.

The stupid bonehead bullies have never come across a mallit who knows how to fight in handcuffs and who would actually love to tear their fucking Aryan throats out with his teeth and then howl in pleasure while he chewed.

Nobody prepared them for this – Kaffirs never klap back.

And the stupid fucks have skated me in front.

They ask me (yes, ask me) to stand behind the charge office desk. I comply – more or less meekly.

Then the Big Gun arrives. Colonel of the battalion. Absolute and utter pure hairyback Rockspider to the core:

– *Wat is jou naam troep!* –

– *Fuck you, you stupid cocksucking bonehead piece of shit. Your bitchfaced mother sucks rotten Ovambo cocks and every one of your family is a filthy crunchie plank that fucks sheep and rapes pigs, but you look like the type of freaky poes that likes suiping dog semen. Did you get that clearly you stupid fat fucken hairyback Dutchman sonofabitch –*

[!!!!!]

– *Skryf neer! Skryyff neeeer wat sê hy oor son of a bitzz!!!* –

At this point they reason that Prudence should take precedence and put me in a cell. But Prudence is nowhere near the place – Prudence has fucked off and is hiding under a sandbag deep in a bunker somewhere behind Signals. Prudence is being prudent because I am looking for a way to break out.

I am totally befuck again and want much more than petty verbal bridges to burn before the night is through – and I know exactly where I'm going to get steel matches and gepantserde dynamite to do it.

That's why I need to break out.

The door? Uh uh. Steel-plated. Window? No. Ceiling? Maybe. IF I can get up and break a hole in the ceiling then Yours Fucking Truly is out of here and into the Sappers' TPT heavy vehicle park across the road. A hop, skip and a jump into a gepantserde heavy bulldozer – followed rapidly by a short drive straight though the fucking charge office like a sledgehammer. KablamMMM! That will really tear out their Curly Wurlies! They'd need a rocket to stop me.

Maybe the noise might satisfy me enough. Thing is – I want blood.

But I'm still inside the cell – got to get up. No holds except the sharp diamond mesh above the window and a sliver of a foothold on the light switch, which is quite high up. I vasbyt hard, curse to myself quietly, reach up into the sharp steel and climb. The pain tears into my rage like jetfuel gatecrashing the party, and the warm, sticky, red sweetness that comes running down my arms is like sucking the prettiest chick at the party's pussy.

Oh yes – at long last – Blood!

Suddenly I have a four-point hold and the pain in my hands settles down to a 747's warming-up howl. I rock to it inwardly like Beethoven on speed, waiting for a heavy vehicle to rumble past.

A small convoy passes, and flinching against the tidal wave of white-hot pain, I hold on and kick up as hard as I can. The roof plate and underlying diamond mesh break out immediately. The stupid cunts have strapped it on with thin steel wire! My legs scrabble down and I find my footholds quickly. I can take the fucking pain – but I am going to damage my fingers too much and then I can't drive that mutherfucking bulldozer through the charge office. I tense my legs as hard as I can, reach up, get a good grip and pull myself into the roof. I sit rocking on my heels nursing my poor fingers, trying to ascertain what damage I have done to them. In the dim light it only seems to be deeply torn skin, but both arms and hands are soaked in blood so I can't really tell.

They are bleeding way too much.

I crawl on my fists towards the narrow passage behind the toilets. I find it and jump to the ground at the bottom. I give the slatted aluminium cover-screen a hefty kick and it pops straight out! Right, now for the fun! I step out into freedom and two pistols slam into my temples.

A guttural and very bad Hollywood voice says – *Freeze!!*

FUUUUUCK!!!

They march me back into the charge office with the pipes against my head and heart high in my back. They make me spread facing the wall – presumably so that a bullet passing through my head doesn't hit one of them. Fuckers are starting to wake up. They make horrified comments about my hands and all the blood that I am smearing on the wall – but the twas stay …

One of them comes charging up with a length of chain, two padlocks and a pair of handcuffs. He chains my ankles together on a short tether, then loops the remaining chain through the skates and cuffs me, locking the rest of the chain to my ankle in a triangle. Yes, the cunts are definitely learning. I am not playing games. All the Aryan cockiness is gone now – people could die. Fuck up and people will. Tonight's a good night to die.

They allow me to turn, and stand looking at me in outraged, confused and angry aversion – trying to decide what the fuck to do next.

The pistols are still there but from the front now. Clever, because I can't do jackshit.

Eventually some bright spark phones the Colonel again. A long conversation ensues, sprinkled generously with grave *bloei baies* and *Ja Kolonels!* Eventually it is decided that I must go to the base hospital.

We arrive as an entourage. Me in the middle, with one of them on each side gripping my elbows, and backups in front and behind. All of them have their twas out. The nurses take one look and swear a blue streak (PF Army nurses are way more hardcore than the Diensplig tampon tiffies they work with). A tampon tiffy is summoned. Tampon arrives – fresh-faced scab. We shackle-shuffle off to an emergency room. Now the trouble starts. The MPs refuse to unlock the restraints. I'm grinning like it's Christmas. Nobody else thinks it's fucking funny. A plan is made. Someone fetches a steel chair and they chain me to it. The tampon goes about his grisly business, which turns out to be washing off a lot of blood and popping in quite a few stitches. Duty nurse comes back and slaps a tetanus shot and some pain crap into my arm. She is not gentle.

I smack her a fat kiss.

Back at the DB I'm back against the wall and somebody has a pistol against my spine pointed directly at the throbby valentine bit. They unlock the chains.

These fucking Romans are crazy.

Suddenly there's been a change of plan. I am to be taken to Grootfontein civvy boere station and held overnight.

Two of them lock me in an Army boerevan and start driving. There are two roads into Grootfontein – tar and dirt. They take the dirt. This can only mean one thing – they've finally grown ballfluff and want to give me a lekker opwarm. Befuck! I start howling and screaming at them to stop and do it.

They come to a standstill in the deserted road and I yell:

– *Yes, you stupid fucking naaiers, finally decided to grow balls! Come open the fucking door!*

You forgot to handcuff me!

Yes! You dumb fucks forgot to handcuff me!

My hands are full of novocaine and I'm on lekker pain drugs. I'm gonna kick both of you in your mother's poes!

Come on, fight me! Naaiers!

I learnt to fight stark naked in a reformatory. Mommy's little poes-lickers. C'mon let's see what you meidgatte can do! –

These *poppe* don't know it yet, but I'm going to pull a Boetie Mongrel on them. Break the gatta's wrist as he unlatches the door, take out the other vark, go back to bust-wrist and finish him, then finish it all off. Maybe put them in the back if my hands can handle it and fuck off with their van. They walk off behind the van about twenty metres away and I start howling at them for being meidgat.

They get back in and we continue to the boere station. I laugh and call them yellow naaiers when they take me out. They ignore me and book me.

Inside the cell I am feeling the aftershock of all the adrenalin and reality starts setting in. I'm in deep kak. I sit down by the bars and after a while an old black Konstabel comes around. He asks me kindly if I am alright. We chat quietly for a while and he brings me some water and a cigarette.

I sleep.

The next day, bright and early, my company commander arrived. He was an ancient old WWII vet who had constant tremors. What the hell he was still doing in the Army was anybody's guess. However, he really, really liked me, told me he had taken control of everything, then booked me out under the escort of four big ous in our company and took me to the base hospital. After a short interview with a doctor it was declared that I was a psychiatric casevac and would leave for 1 Mil forthwith. Some hours later Kapie and I jumped onto a Vlossie to the States. He was supposed to be my armed escort. What a *lag*! What wasn't funny was my hands hurt like a merry bitch.

*

We landed at Waterkloof Air Force Base and were met by some 1 Mil tampon. I said ciao to Kapie and got my ass booked into 1 Mil.

Ward 22 was down at the bottom of the old hospital and consisted of two very long wooden buildings. The one facing the new hospital was the patient's ward and the one at the back was for the kop-tiffies. They stripped me of all my clothes and I was issued with PJs and a gown. The patients' ward had about thirty beds in the main section and three in isolation. It had a nice stoep. The patients looked like a weird mixed bunch. I didn't want to know. I managed to slip my guards quickly and went for a bit of a wander. I didn't go far. I just needed to sit and think a bit. I had to figure out how to play the shrinks and not be RTUed to face a major court martial.

Still thinking furiously, I look up and see another gown come wandering over. He plonks himself down and introduces himself as Joe. So what is it that I did? I tune him. I got shitfaced dronk, lost my temper and caused some mild mayhem. We laugh, smoke some zol he's got on him and become instant friends. It turns out he is a number-one Bren-gunner who lost it during a very bad firefight and they decided that he needed to take a break but in an environment where they could observe him.

He showed me the ropes.

The ward was divided up into four categories. The ous trying to jippo, ous like the two of us, real mallits and the gays. The Army did not accept gays, which was a perfect way to get a G5 and obviously lots of ous thought they could act their way out of National Service. The Army was not stupid, so they sent them to Ward 22 and slap bang into a group of chicks whose job it was to find out if *Darling* really was. They were truly entertaining and they loved it. They did their hair and makeup, had tea parties, dressed up outrageously in hospital attire with over-the-top non-military accessories, and played with their marks. They told their marks that it was Army policy to keep them there for their entire National Service, which was soooo much *fun* because all that *Everyone* ever did was fuck, suck, stroke, tease and have a *Grrreeeaaat* time. The real gays giggled, *Kiss-Kiss Lovey*, and jumped right in – the play-play faggers begged to go to DB or Angola. Nice scam and clever of the Army. The real queens were apparently rotated out with their G5s in hand as competent new ladies came in. Probably the only time I've ever seen perks to being gay.

In Ward 22 the referrals did not come from other kop-tiffies, they came from normal Army doctors facing something they thought needed observation but might be bullshit. Whenever the tampons, sisters and shrinks were not watching, ward politics changed subtly. Real mallits just carried on normally in whatever derangement they were enjoying or enduring, while the jippogatte tried harder. They tried playing the other patients furiously to establish the insane persona they working on for outside verification in group sessions, but their mistake lay in this – they avoided all the real mallits too. One of these jippogatte was some laaitie who apparently threatened his corporal with a knife. Ja, of course. He wanted to hang out with me and Joe but my Das sense told me he was a poes so we told him to fuck off.

Joe and I slipped my guards often. It was so much fun coming back to find them milling around in a blind flat panic with bitter thoughts of dereliction, dishonour and courts martial scrabbling around frantically in their heads. And I would rub it in by looking outraged and asking them where the fuck they had gotten to – I'd been searching for them everywhere!

We roamed the whole hospital. Joe introduced me to the 32 Battalion ous. We smoked and drank with them regularly and scored all our zol off them. These ous had their own segregated ward right at the bottom of the old hospital – because they were all fucking crazy – and to a man were very black Portuguese-speakers. It was a mad place where the nursing staff struggled vainly to practise medicine. For instance: one ou casevaced straight from the border, to the roof, by helicopter, comes in from theatre with both legs in plaster. One minute he's in a firefight in Angola, the next he wakes up in 1 Mil. After lying there a couple of days he hops it on crutches – still wearing hospital kit – and disappears. He arrives back a couple of days later, with two mammas in tow who are carrying his zol and beer. They are there to see to his non-medical needs! Fuck Visiting Time. You simply gotta admire a man like that. Thing was, they were all mostly like that. I think the nursing staff would have gladly liked to strap the whole bloody lot down and pump them full of Thorazine till they healed up. About the only thing missing in that ward was a bunch of chickens and goats roaming around under the beds. Maybe I didn't look hard enough.

Meanwhile, back at the squirrel farm, the shrinks were trying to figure me out. I had decided not to play them and told them I had black rages when I got dronk. They put my head in machines and made me do tests till I started getting sick of it and maybe a bit worried too, because ... hadn't their stupid fucking machines and tests told them there was nothing wrong with me?

Then Drug arrived.

Joe and I parking off doing nothing one afternoon when we saw them bring this oke in who was so fucked that all he could do was shuffle slowly into one of the isolation wards. We asked the tampons what the score was and they tuned us the ou was in for chronic drug addiction.

Our favourite smoking place was behind the shrink building.

Joe and I are sitting smoking a couple of days later when we hear this same ou skoffeling up around the corner.

Librium drip-pole in tow *nogal*.

We look at him in astonishment, followed by disbelief, as he begs us for a drag. The oke looked absolutely fucking terrible, but still, a roeker is a roeker, so, after discussing whether it would kill him, we cautiously gave him a drag. This became a habit as he didn't detox.

Next to the shrink building was this rusty old Signals van. One day Joe and I decided to explore it and inside we found something that really freaked us out. Somebody had dumped a shitload of medical supplies in the back. Drugs, operating theatre shit, scalpels, needles, syringes, suture – everything. We scratched around looking for stuff to take but we couldn't find anything except Valium. So we called Drug. Talk about a kid in a candy store – he went totally befuck. This scared us silly because there is enthusiasm and there is slavering mania. He found morphine that we had missed and some other stuff that we rapidly confiscated from him and told him we would keep and ration out to all three of us. We got him back into isolation fast.

Fuck, the oke was crazy.

Drug taught me how to spike. And I fucking loved it. Joe and I would sit stoned and high on morphine or Valium or Sosegon syrettes watching the gays have another hilarious tea party. It was cool. Then trouble started.

Drug was taking a hell of a long time to detox baby, and the medical staff knew there was something wrong. One night I was coming back from the 32 Battalion ward when my Das sense went off. I had zol on me, which I stashed safely and went inside looking for Joe. Five minutes later the ward was suddenly surrounded by armed troops and the sister walked in. She was a Captain and also, without any shadow of doubt, the worst piece of shit officer I've ever had to answer to. An absolute eighty-proof bitch. She assaulted patients, swore worse than any soldier I had ever heard and fell into that very, very rare category of dangerous woman whom you fight hard, fast and like a man or else she'd take *you* out, poeshead. Captain Bitch ordered us all to sit on our beds while they brought in drug dogs to sniff out the place.

They found nothing, but the trouble had started. About five days later Drug got hold of something we had missed. And overdosed. Joe and I discovered this and flipped. He had puked all over himself, pissed and shat his bed and PJs, and was completely incoherent. First we cleaned him up and dressed him in new PJs. Then we stripped his bed and put on a clean set of everything. We managed to get some coffee into him and he seemed to stabilise. It freaked us both out hectically. Something touched and then passed my attention while we were working on Drug. I happened to glance around and noticed the poes who had threatened his corporal watching. I ignored him and carried on working on Drug.

Big mistake.

Afterwards I went to the toilets and fished out a 30 ml bottle of morphine, a syringe and alcohol swabs we had stashed in the roof. I needed a spike. I was busy when Joe came into the toilets and announced that Captain Bitch had arrived in the ward. Not thinking, I put the works in my pocket and went to take a look.

Second big mistake.

As I strolled into the corridor, I saw two okes standing there.

One of them said:

– *Gaan haal die honde* –

Shit! Gattas! Dogs!

It was too late, because Captain Bitch immediately ordered us all into the middle of the room.

I couldn't get rid of the goeters!

I also had a *stop* in my pocket, which I managed to slip into my mouth and swallow. They made us sit in a row in the middle of the ward. The SANAB gattas brought in the dogs to sniff us and everywhere in the ward. Then Captain Bitch started body-searching each one of us. When she reached me, she obviously found the works, and by turning my robe pocket inside out— she found a single dagga pip.

I told them the works was Drug's and that I had confiscated it from him to stop him from ODing. Fuck him, he brought this onto us. I went and showed them the Signals van and picked up two boxes of stuff from the floor to show them. It was some Valeron and Sodium Gardenol.

They kept the boxes.

Drug and I were loaded up and taken to Pretoria Central Boere Station. On the way I started to fake a massive overdose type of thing. They almost fell for it and chained me up and took me to Hendrik Verwoerd Hospital. I could not bullshit the doctors though. I made out as if I was semi-comatose and unresponsive, but I couldn't fake blood pressure or pupil response. I kept it up and they stomach-pumped me, bringing up the half-digested *stop* in a mess of green and newspaper. Thank goodness they identified it as gastroenteritis. Anyway, they weren't completely convinced, so they booked me in for observation. I was chained to a bed for the night. The next day I couldn't fake anything any longer and I was dragged off and booked. The fucking SANAB cunts had charged me for everything I showed them, together with the pip. A quick court appearance where bail was denied and I was remanded into the custody of Pretoria Central Prison.

The nightmare had begun.

13

Shooting Skollie

I knew all about the mang. We used to sit in the bungalow and get told stories that came down from ouens' fathers, brothers, uncles, mothers – you get the picture – and of course all the other roekers that we were connected to.

Anyway, I wasn't in the mang yet – I was awaiting trial. It was known as being a stokkie.

It was shit.

I stokkied over Christmas and Denise dropped off a roast chicken and some goodies. Bless her heart. I know Bill would have had Things To Say.

At the trial I was taken to one side by the prosecutor and told that if I pleaded guilty, I would get a suspended sentence and get court-ordered to rehab. Sweet.

I was sent to Phoenix House in Auckland Park and found Mark Tressy from Hostel 4 was there! It was quite a cool pozzie to stay out of shit in.

Of course, I didn't.

Me, Mark and two lesbian chicks stole the centre's Kombi and went to Hillbrow for a jol. The dykes piemped me the next day and I was expelled and taken to court.

The judge invoked my sentence.

The absolute terror and hopelessness I felt in the van on the way up to Pretoria Central Prison was like the first morning I was driven to Die Bult multiplied by a hundred. There was no way out. I was going to bandiet at the age of eighteen. I couldn't get out of it for being a juvie any more. Oh, fuck. Horror and self-pity raged and hit me like a tidal wave.

We arrived, went through the huge steel doors into the front office and were lined up, stripped and searched. Then all our shit was put in bags and we were given bandiet clothes together with our card. It was pink and verified your name, number, thumbprint, crime and Earliest Release Date. Once we had signed for our sentences and personal goeters, we were marched out and I walked through the steel doors into the main hall. The sound of them slamming behind me— rang long, lonely, metallic echoes in my soul. The three wings of the prison led off from it. We went to

B-Section. First to the storeroom for a full issue of prison kit, toiletries and bedding, and then for a meal that coincided with our arrival. It was four thin slices of brown bread with half a spoon of unidentifiable pink jam and white margarine, and a watery substance with a few cabbage leaves floating in it that I took to be soup. There was also some dirty, foul-tasting water that I took to be coffee. I refused it. Some other bandiete begged me and I gave it to them. It would be the very last time I ever refused food. Ever.

To this day.

Pretoria Central Prison accepted convicts from the local regional courts, but its primary purpose was that of a hub. If you received a sentence over two years from a bench anywhere in South Africa, you were transferred there for Observation. After Observation you were transferred out, usually back to where you came from. Among the bandiete this caused a divide. A sentence under two years made you a short-timer. A nuisance. Dirtying dixies while other bandiete did real time. The Department of Prisons ran on the old British Borstal system. There were four groups. D-Groups were the psychopaths. They had their own special high-security segregation wing in another prison named Zonderwater. C-Groups were anybody who had escaped or had been sentenced to more than ten years. B-Groups like me were entry level. The A-Groups were the kings. They had more privileges and thus more power.

I was placed in C2-Right Cell 24. My prison number was 66982. My sentence was four months for the zol pip, 150 days or R150.00 fine for the other stuff. My earliest release date would be in three months if my fine was paid.

Nine months if it wasn't.

*

I wake to the sound of the prison. It never sleeps. Groans, coughs. Bootsteps echoing slowly down the section, metallic rumblings deep in the bowels of regret and hate, dark cries of pain ringing like hollow bells in the night. But now it must arise. Somehow I always manage to wake into the lonely wintry sounds and smells of my cage before the gattas come. I lie quietly, shifting miserably from bad ethereal dreams into the real nightmare. Then I hear the boere unmastering the cells. I reluctantly take my thumb out of my mouth.

ClackChack!!

My cell. *Môre meneer!* – to the peephole.

Right, half-hour till inspection. Swing out of bed, feet on taxis. Get dressed. Brush teeth. Shave. Make bed. Okay, carefully now – dust above the bars, cupboard, under the bed, the rest of the floor. Any fucking dust when they rub my pillow on the floor and it's Drie Maaltye. Maaltye are one of two types of *Dieetstraf* – dietary punishment. If the boere are feeling mean they will give the whole section maaltye because of me – then I am dead. There. Okay, wait for the bell. Right, put on shoes – stand to attention as they unlock and open the outside door. Nod to the two ous opposite. Don't speak. If you speak – it's Twee Maaltye. Here comes the Officer. *Klagtes en versoeke? Nee, Luitenant.* Okay, inside gate open, time for kakpotte. Oh God, how can anybody take this smell? Alright, down the stairs to *tand.* No talking – no smoking – Twee Maaltye. Breakfast. Runny pap, an exact ration of sugar, anorexic coffee water, and a dash of weak milk. Put some pap and the whole sugar ration into the boepbeker of coffee, eat the dixie of tasteless pap first – with a teaspoon – to make it go longer. See if anybody around leaves a bit. Some ou does. Oh God, thank you! Grab the dixie. Mingy bit. Ignore the looks of disgust. So what if I'm a grubby? I can't help it I'm so hungry. Always so fucking hungry. I'm eighteen and my body is still growing. I need food, in spite of my shame or what anyone thinks. Now I know how bergies and gintus feel.

You need something bad, so you pass through a portal of shame to get it. Afterwards you feel sick and disgusted with yourself but reason it was only a momentary thing brought on by desperation. Try to ignore it. But the need comes back, so you do it again, and again. And every time you confront the shame, you become deader to the part of you that was intact until there is nothing left but the shame. You accept it as yourself.

I am a grubby. A Three-O.

I have been here for two and a half months. Maybe today The Letter will come!

I've been to the bomb for three weeks for being caught with sarmies that a Welfare worker threw away in a bin. Not my Official Ration – hence I was obviously smuggling. I've worked out a way to steal rogue when we get *tand* at night and I've succeeded in doing it twice. Then there was that time us grubbies attacked the food trolley with our dixies. Three other ous got bust and went to the bomb but I got away with a half-dixie of butternut!

They've been filming a movie in the prison. Called *Vyfster*. They did the chowing shots in my section, and the actors won't eat prison *tand*. Double thank God. Fuck, ou, that was some time. Us cleaners went to town! I hope they still have to shoot more eating scenes before they finish the fliek.

I thought being locked up is the worst of it but the Department of Prisons is here to Punish. They keep us in a constant state of semi-starvation and punish us with clinically controlled starvation in solitary confinement. The only ones who get by are the A-Groups because they are allowed to order *tand* in their monthly pakkie. The rest of us smokkel whichever way how. If I had money I could buy a B-Group pak and smokkel entjies and twak for *tand* but I've got fuckall money on my name In Front. The only other way is if I work in the shops. Uncle Guvvie will pay me. But that's only for long-timers. Except for the gintus, my only other source of income is as a wash-meid for a couple of other bandiete but the goeters they pay me with doesn't buy much. Two slices of rogue for two ous' clothes.

My deepest secret shame is I collect all the discarded *Huisgenoots* I can find and cut out the recipes. I've got a whole file of them. At night I force myself to keep my rogue and sit listening to boep radio, gently nibbling whatever I have managed to keep – reading the recipes and pretending I'm cooking and eating them.

Sarge the Bingo King from Hostel 1 back in Die Bult is here with me. He used to work in the kitchen and helped me out a bit when he could, but he was bust for carrying six matchboxes of zol for some other main ous. Eight shots on The Mary and two stretches in the bomb. Forty days. And twenty days that were suspended from a previous case.

I'll tell you about it quickly. First, The Mary...

They do it in front at Reception. The Mary looks like a painter's easel. At the bottom of each leg of the A is a footrest. You strip to your underwear, step up into these and get tied there with thick leather straps. Then the easel is opened wide until you are almost horizontal and your hands are strapped above you. A blanket is placed over your kidneys because a Miss will burst them and kill you. The same for your thighs. A Miss on a skraal ou like Sarge breaks bones. A Miss also doesn't count. Then they read out and execute your sentence.

The Mary is corporal punishment by means of a heavy cane. The canes lie in a tub of salt water to give them more weight and to introduce further attrition to the wound. The gatta administering the sentence selects one, whips it lekker to get the feel, positions himself, measures the shot, and waits for the doctor. The doctor nods and the boer rears back and moers the cane across your gat as hard as he is physically able. Doctor has his hand on your pulse. And you scream. The whole fucking prison hears you scream. You cannot help it. The other bandiete make book on how many times you will scream before you lose consciousness. The current record is six, held by a murder and armed robbery lifer in C-Max. The doctor reads off the count. Afterwards they take you to the prison hospital.

They have to.

Then, for an ou like Sarge the Bingo King, as soon as you've healed up a bit you go back to the doctor to see if you are fit enough to do your forty days. There are two types of Dieetstraf: Maaltye up to nine meals and Spare Diet. Maaltye are meals you are forced to skip in communal cells in the bomb. Spares you do on your own. On spares you start out on Day One with a full ration weighed out exactly to the gram. On Days Two and Three you get exactly half. Days Four, Five and Six you go spare. Spare breakfast is a carefully measured cup of krummelpap cooked without salt, lunch a dixie of clear soup with a few cabbage or spinach leaves, and supper a repeat of breakfast. And you repeat this cycle until your sentence ends. Then back into main population for two weeks, followed not so rapidly by the next twenty days if the doctor permits. I've heard some ouens saying that Uncle Guvvie's shrinks are doing studies on it and they reckon it drives ous mal if they get klapped with spares more than three times in any stretch.

The only pleasure you can eke out up there is if you take a bomb kit. They skut you thoroughly before you go in but there is a way. Usually they don't fingerfuck you, so you bottle the biggest poke of snout and newspaper you can. Then you get a lighter flint, a small piece of razor blade and some tinder. Make tinder by burning a piece of cloth. You also need a small flat stone, a piece of cloth and a length of strong thread, long enough to reach down three storeys. You can get thread for a bomb kit from Jenny in the tailor shop. She'll charge you five entjies. Hide it all on yourself. If they catch you it's another case in Kangaroo court. Use the soles of your shoes for the blade and the linings of your duckie or straights for the tinder, folded very flat in the cloth. Put the thread in there too. When they skut you, you will strip and give them all your clothes. You will also have to grab your cock and balls and lift them, and open your mouth wide, tilting your head back. Keep the flint high up in your cheek. Put the stone up in the other one. Okay, once you've passed through the skut and you are in your bomb cell, unbottle the poke. Unwrap it. Hide the plastic in toilet paper and get rid of it during the following day's kakpotte. Put the poke inside the toilet roll next to the kakpot. Use the blade to cut a hole in the bomb mat or look for an old hole. Put the stone and flint in there. Search the rest of the cell for a geluk. It's traditional to leave something for the next occupant in case he didn't bring a bomb kit. The bandiete call it a halfway. You stash one full Dassie-puff and whatever is left of your bomb kit when you leave. If the next bandiet hasn't got a kit he will wait until exactly halfway through his bomb stretch to smoke it. To smoke, simply roll a number. Take a triple piece of toilet paper and fold it into a square. Place the toilet paper over the hole in the roll and push it in slightly. Now take some tinder and put it in the cup. Take the razor blade and strike the flint into the tinder. When it starts to smoulder, light the entjie. When your snout is finished, pick up your fish.

If you have one.

You take the piece of cloth, wrap the stone in it and tie it to the end of the thread. This has to be coordinated with a bra. On that day just before lunch you wait for the whistle to tell you the block is cool. Then you toss the stone out the bars down into the Yard below and your china ties on a new poke. Reel in.

Ja, Sarge the Bingo King. Poor bastard.

I am still hungry after the leftover pap I grubbied, so I savour the good stuff in my boepbeker. I stir the pap, sugar ration and supermodel coffee into a thin sweet gruel. I eat it spoon by joyous, illicit teaspoon.

Okay, now to the Yard.

See if I can scrounge a drag or two somewhere.

There are a lot of boere in the Yard. The film crew are setting up. There's a line of masking tape about one third of the way down, making a border. Apparently if we cross it we come into focus of the cameras. The ou with no hair, and the actors – Marius Weyers and George Ballot, who plays my namesake Skollie – are chatting. The actors are quite cool ouens. Me and one of the other cleaners spoke to them when they did the eating shots. They reckon the Department of Prisons is keeping a very close eye on the script and the way they are portraying conditions inside. We all know they did up a cell in A-section like a hotel room to shoot in. Anyway, try holhang a drag. No geluk, but kwaai, there's a section of tappie in the gutter. Bell goes for graft. Time to go back to my section and do my honk. It's weird, I've got the exact same type of honk as in Dassie Bult. I do the bathrooms, the married quarters behind them, and the long black corridor polished up to a dark mirror finish all the way down the section. They did a shot of a bandiet with dik chappies on his back kapping it on his knees like we do. The bandiet across from me only does the landing and the corridor on the other side, because he is senior. On my knees. Work. Lovely mindlessness. Makes the time go. I think about Frodo Baggins. I discovered this moerse big book in the library. It's called *The Lord of the Rings* and is an amazing story about hobbits and ents and orcs and all sorts of other mal goeters. I'm reading it now. But I ration myself. It's the most amazingly beautiful adventure story that I have ever read. I'm not having an adventure and at this moment it's the only thing that gets me beyond these walls. That and the hope that maybe The Letter will come today. I disappear. Go with Frodo. Visit Tom Bombadil and his beautiful wife Lady Goldberry.

I'm still busy when Blommetjie interrupts me. She wants to know if I can organise her a cell. She's got a jol. Okay, I put her in the one third from the bathrooms. Costs her five entjies. The jol arrives. Know him. Older ou doing a baadjie for Armed Robbery. A-Group. Obviously can afford her. I go to the cleaner on the other side of our section to warn him to suss out for the boere. I don't understand this ou. He's a Conscientious Objector. Reckons he won't do National Service. Look, I know the Army allows ous who won't carry a weapon to work as clerks and shit. But he won't even do that. Now he's doing four years and apparently they gonna give him another four when he comes out if he persists in refusing. Madness. I asked him if he is *bang*. Because he should be more *bang* in here than up there. I know. He reckons nooit, it goes against his principles. His choice, I suppose. There's another ou here for the same thing but he is like a Christian ou who keeps to himself.

I go back to see if Blommetjie is done. Animal grunting and squeaks of delight inside the cell. Obviously not. Cruise back up to the top to see if Objection is still keeping skei. It's okay, though our section boer usually doesn't come up to inspect until after the boere's teatime anyway. The section head-bandiet pitches. Very cool Afrikaans ou in for fraud. He doesn't take a cut of my rent. We make tea using a bomb.

A bomb is a broken light bulb with a shielded wire tied to each of the electrodes that used to light the filament. The other end is attached to two safety razor blades strapped with thread on either side of a peeled wooden matchbox. This contraption is then plugged into a live light socket and simply placed into water until it boils.

He gives me some tea. There's even sugar in it! It's okay though. He's not a hawk. The hawks will come to you and offer a cigarette, a cup of tea, a biscuit – maybe even a joint! Everything you accept from a hawk is a transaction. You are selling something you are completely unaware of. Do I need to paint a picture? You have to be wakker. I'm eighteen – I look like a chick to some of these naaiers – I have to be Very Wakker.

We drink our dop and discuss the Falklands War. It seems insane that England – *England!* – is at war. Fuck, no First World countries go to war any more. Bets have been made on how long it will take for them to win. The Argentinians are obviously going to lose. They're up against a NATO member nation. This conversation takes us to the upcoming fight. The film crew are shooting a prison boxing match. Marius Weyers is playing a character named Tiger and he is going to be the winner. We actually know quite a lot about the script. The Major has said we can have a real tournament. Entries have been made and bets are on. The boxers are training and wannabe trainers are popping up all over the mang. Old grudges are going to be settled. A real bloodbath on the make. We discuss our favourites for a while. I leave and check up on Blommetjie. She and her jol are gone.

Then Jenny pitches up. Oh fuck. She also wants a cell. Fuck. Third from the bottom. Five entjies. The jol pitches. Some ou I don't know. This is dangerous for me. Jenny stays in A-Section 2 married quarters with her steady boyfriend who also happens to be the biggest mutherfucker in the entire mang. All he does is pump iron in the Yard all day. If he finds out she's turning tricks and I am giving her a place to do it— I am more than stone dead. I don't mind the kroon. Ten entjies, or two slices of bread, or one piece and five entjies. Blommetjie and the other gintus are good money because they are gintus. Fuck, the gintus are rich but Jenny's Spoken For. She does it because she likes it and makes kroon in the process. I nervously wait for them to finish up. I just want to get the fuck out of here.

I am so tired of being scared and hating myself for being caught. I am trying to keep my promise to myself not to smoke any more. I've had offers from okes who aren't hawks but I've refused. I am so sick of being a shadow of a man surrounded by monsters. I am here because of a seed. A single seed. In the cell across from me is a skinny little wimpy cunt I have to look at every morning. One klap and he's out of it. Can you believe that this evil little poes has beaten The Rope twice. It's Rodney Ax – The Hillbrow Jawbreaker. Serial rapist. Eight victims, from a teenager to an octogenarian. His signature is breaking the jaw of each victim after he is done. Fucking cowardly sick animal. They were going to hang him in Beverly Hills behind us. That's where they keep Tsafendas – the ou who poked Verwoerd witbene.

There's an old bandiet I know who used to work there. It was his job to take the bodies to the hospital on a gurney after they were done. He reckons all them stories about you can get off if you survive the drop are kak. They drop you over this pool-type jol (for all your kak, piss and guts to donner into), then the doctor walks up and klaps a moerse fat needle into your heart. He waits a minute or two, smokes a lekker slow entjie and then checks your heartbeat. By then you and your kakked-out guts are fucked even if you aren't dead yet. Prison doctors aren't here to heal. They are here to keep you alive ... or not, depending on the case, so that the Department of Prisons can punish you.

Ah fuck, at last. Jenny and jol are done. Pick up *Lord of the Rings* and let's hit the Yard.

Go downstairs, wait for the gate boer. This gatta is an absolute poes. You never want him to call you or speak to you. You will go to the bomb. You will. He is the naai who had me put in the bomb for three weeks for a sarmie I got out a dustbin back when I was a cleaner In Front.

In the Yard I see the film crew are going to do a shoot. The actors are all done up in their brand new green bandietklere and Regardt van den Bergh, the ou with no hair, is tuning the crew what to do. The other bandiete reckon he's got some majorly rare disease that makes him bald. They are shooting a smokkeling scene. With real zol! There's a big jam bottle of it. The bandiete are all watching the zol like a bunch of hungry vultures waiting for the lions to vreet fokken klaar and fokkof. What a *lag*.

I cruise the Yard to see who's around. Spiderman is here. He's this ou with a spider tattooed on the top of his completely bald head. I've never seen him speak to anybody. Ever. The Jesus Coke Freak is here too. He's this big blond ou who's doing eight to ten for cocaine. The only thing I know about cocaine is when they soaked thin strips of bandage in it and shoved it up my nose before they did surgery on it in Standard 9. He's taken a shine to me. I hate it because he always starts going on about how Jesus Saved Him from Cocaine and Jesus Can Save ME Too! But he's also always good for an entjie – if I'm willing to put up with it. He's seen me. I stand meekly and come away with singed ears, some tracts and two entjies. Seems Everybody is in a festive mood because of the shooting. The bodybuilders are working out in the corner. I try not to look at Jenny's boyfriend. Down near the taped border I find my bridge instructor. He's an old man doing life for doing his wife. He allows me to sit behind him and watch. They play for matches and they play fucking fast. High stakes. Each match is a packet of entjies. I'm learning the bidding slowly but the scoring is still a mystery.

They start shooting and the boere tell us we must walk up and down trying to look natural. Hey look! It's the real Skollie and I'm in *Vyfster*! This is so fucking dof. I smoke one of Coke Jesus' entjies. Savour it. I've got one more and ten to buy two pieces of rogue tonight to console myself – if The Letter doesn't come. But c'mon ou – I can be out in two weeks' time! Think of that. Two weeks … and today is Thursday and it's peanut butter tonight. I've learnt to not live by days. I live from peanut butter to peanut butter. It's a better way to measure time. I wait for lunch and allow myself a ration of ten pages with Frodo Baggins and Friends. The ous come in from the shop's skut. I see Honnie, my Mongrel boetie from Cape Town. He helps me out whenever he can. He doesn't understand why I don't want zol from him, because he's offered. I can't explain that I am trying to run away from what brought me here. Tuning him that would be dangerous. Meidgat. I also see the Baygon Boetie's older brother. He's also a classic baygon. What a *lag*. Eventually the lunch bell rings. Announcements. Graze. I walk into the great black hall and my stomach cramps. Please dear God let the cooks have a bit of mercy. It's the usual merciless fare of soyas, goeboes and dehydrates but they included some grated carrot. Befuck! That means lots of leftovers because the other bandiete aren't mad about raw carrot. Grubby paradise. Fill up that never-ending hole.

After lunch, off to our cells. Not allowed to sit on your bed. Twee Maaltye. Half an hour and it's afternoon graft. For me that's the whole afternoon in the Yard. I'm so tense. I smoke Coke Jesus' other entjie. They do Letters about a half-hour before the shops come in. They bring out a table and the Letters Boer goes to a blackboard on the wall and starts klapping down prison numbers. These are the ous with letters. I'm waiting for a letter from Wally. I have a bank account but I cannot sign on it. Wally opened it when I was a laaitie and the signing rights were never transferred to me on my eighteenth birthday. I eventually got the social workers to convince Denise to come and speak to me. She says she will not help me. It's up to Wally. I wrote him a letter telling him I need a postal order for R150.00 from my Army money to get out. I've got over two thousand in danger pay. I'm just waiting for it. If it comes today I can go to sleep tonight in peace. I can measure how many pages are left in *The Lord of the Rings*, divide by fourteen, and have a big ration to read each day! Maybe he'll send a bit more and I can order a pakkie. Pakkies are on Monday.

The tension is killing me.

The long afternoon wears on. I crack under the stress and I smoke one of my gintu entjies. That means I can only buy one piece of rogue tonight. I'm feeling reckless. Today is the day. I can feel it! Eventually the Letters Boer arrives. Starts writing down the numbers from the oldest to the newest. I'm gonna be far down the list if I'm on it.

I'M ON IT!!

I'm fucking on it! Befuck. Thank fuck, thank fuck, thank fuck.

I get my letter but I'm immediately puzzled. There's no money receipt stapled to it. I open it and begin reading. Oh dear sweet God no. Wally says I'm a filthy human parasite and that as far as he is concerned I can rot in jail for good. Jesus no. What kind of man will not give another man his own money to get out of jail? Why does Wally hate me so much? He's tried to kill me. He steals from his work. He's an alcoholic. He should be in here with me. What makes us so fucking different? *WHAT??*

I am shattered. I can't do this any more, I can't …

*

I pretty much lost my mind after that. I started smoking zol and taking the risk of carrying it.

I got bust.

I was transferred to Zonderwater Prison, where I defended myself from two rape attempts and survived an attack by a serial killer who tried to blind me by hurling boiling coffee in my face. At least in Zonnies there was a lot more food. The other bandiete told me that Central was the hardest white male mang in the country. Eventually Wally relented and gave me the money to pay the remainder of my fine a month before my release date, so I effectively did eight months instead of the full nine. I was released into the custody of the Military Boere and taken to Poesplaas DB awaiting transfer back to the border. There I was beaten up in a cell by six bandiete because one of them recognised me as a Mongrel. He reckoned his sister had been raped by a Mongrel. Head X-rays again. I put out a hit on him later.

The ouens caught up with him eventually.

Something happened to me after that. I became hard. Very hard. Merciless. I didn't give a fuck about anything except going out and doing back to the world what it had done to me.

14

Angolsh

I arrived back on the border to the wild delight of my buddies.
I still hadn't abandoned my intention of becoming a professional soldier,
so with some half-formed plan in my head I started collecting current
intelligence. I needed to know how to get into Angola without crossing the
river via some heavily defended post. I needed to slip through. The new
Oumanne had loads of ops experience, and after a hundred conversations
and cases of beer I thought I had a good route.

Under Military Law I had extra days for the next two intakes and slowly
went crazy from boredom. Me and my Damara chommies AWOLed into
the local townships for jols and generally caused kak. I met some other new
chinas: Alex Pereira de Coita, Little Italy, another ou named Mark and my
scab Shane. Little Italy was actually a Portuguese ou who got stuck with
his handle in basics. We got smashed every day and I soon knew exactly
who had zol in the camp.

And where.

I managed to make myself assistant barman in the Battalion pub, which
meant that I sat behind it and extorted the scabs into keeping our gratitude
dustbin full of beers.

My Sergeant wisely sent me on more long convoys.

One night I had one of my rare fits of temperance again, and in the
aftermath— a buddy and I broke into the hospital dispensary and stole
a balsak full of drugs. He was an ou with a foot injury whom I met in
hospital when I had malaria. We were seen pulling the move by a roeker
tampon we both knew and subsequently warned to keep his bek shut.

I went mal spiking with my scab Shane.

A couple of days later we were arrested. The gattas had gaaned the
roeker tampon's bra, so he piemped us. I understood. But I was not going
to mang.

Ever.

In DB I decided to stage a suicide attempt to get myself into hospital
and escape. I couldn't trust any of the other bandiete to help me because
I'd seen that kak fail too many times. Ous scratching themselves lightly

with razor blades with a chommie handy and very nearby to raise the alarm.

It had to look real.

Okay, it's after graze. Gattas aren't going to come into the cellblock till lockdown – so now's the time. I must break the blade out of this Bic razor. Cool. Done. Okay, the ous are all playing cards. Now, my timing must be just right. They mustn't walk in too early or too late. Fuck. This is it. Sit down. Cut the right wrist. At an angle, otherwise it looks *fake*. Alright, here goes. Owwww! Shit, I hate when it goes all white and open like that before the blood comes out. Shitfuck, there's not enough blood. I fucked up. All I did was scratch myself. Oh, Fuck No! Fake! I must cut again. Oh mamma this is going to hurt. Just do it. AaaaaaHHH!! Shit Fuck, Jesus look at that blood. Fuck it's a fountain – fuck, Fuck, FUCK! Pressure point. Okay it's slowing a little. Release. Shit I'm bleeding. Okay that's enough, now where are those fucking ouens? Come, mutherfuckers. Come. I'm bleeding badly here.

Oh fuck what if nobody comes? I'm not going to break, I won't shout for help. Jesus, I'm starting to get dizzy. LOOK AT ALL THE FUCKING BLOOD!! I've lost too much. I'm so dizzy – fuck they better come, they better come. I'm fucked if they don't. Oh my God, what will happen if I die tonight? All I can see is black. The Black is coming for me. Please ouens, come help me, The Black is coming for me. I can't shout for help. I'm not going back to prison. Please come …

I was saved in the nick of time by some ou who came to take a piss. The floor was one huge pool of blood. The tampons did their thing and I was booked into a private ward with an armed guard. Ha ha! I didn't need to escape, because once again the doctors shipped me down to 1 Mil as a psychiatric casevac. I was a bit too weak from blood loss to make a break anyway. Ward 22 had become Ward 24 but Captain Bitch was still firmly in charge. She took one look at me and said that she didn't care whatever the fuck it was that I had done— I was bullshitting and was to be RTUed straight back to my base to await trial for – let's see, what's it for this time? – Possession of Drugs and Housebreak and Theft. A week later I was processed back through Waterkloof Movements and flown to the border.

Without any escorts.

Ooopths …!

I never officially cleared Grootfontein Movements because my roeker bras exercised zol-diplomacy and walked me straight through. I disappeared underground into the base – a free agent.

First priority a weapon.

I wanted a captured AK, mags, rounds and grenades, but I couldn't bribe the ouens who guarded them and I refused to carry SADF weapons. Eventually, I had to make do with a very good bush knife and a panga. I packed a mountaineering pack with mostly water, food, an Army sleeping bag, cammo cream, mozzie repellent and packs of malaria pills. Then I scored a big stash of zol from my mates in Movements, bribed Little Italy to hide me on his truck and began waiting for the next Rundu convoy.

The night before, we had a farewell party and all got so badly slaughtered on tequila, Little Italy and me nearly missed our 05h00 departure. I managed to sneak under a tarpaulin on Little Ite's truck while they were having roll-out inspection.

Out on the open road I clamber down into the cab. We're on a routine non-stop run to Rundu. Me and Little Ite talk kak and smoke zol.

Rundu.

We show our military IDs at the gate and I'm in the base without anyone the wiser. Little Ite disappears with the truck. I find the canteen, dump my kit and wait. He arrives some time later and tunes me he's been talking to some ous he did ops with and one of them has agreed to give me a lift in exchange for some zol. The bonus is that they are a special black ops unit called Hoof Staf Intelligensie who only operate at night. Oh ja, the ou is a Portuguese dude who doesn't speak a word of English or Ovambo.

Night arrives. It's been my longest day. Only Little Ite and his mate are aware of me and my bizarre lone military mission. I have not spoken to anybody. I must fade into the background. I certainly cannot sleep, I'm too tense. Okay, Little Ite reckons it's time and disappears. Returns with big, very black oke and interprets my destination. My last zol exchanges hands. Ciao Little Ite. Let's waai …

Okay my broer, this is the Big One. You can never back out from this. This oke is going to stop once between here and Buffalo – to drop you off. Buffalo is not Rundu – you will get arrested. Now or never. Are you ready? Ja, fuck – I must do what I must do.

We drive out the camp, no official military checks because we don't exist, and head towards the Caprivi Strip – Cheto, Buffalo, Katima, M'pacha. But I will be getting out long before then. I cammo up in the dark – nose, ears, fingers.

We keep driving deep into the night until the intersection at the entrance to the Strip with a right turn to the Botswana border post. There should be a short, tarred landing strip doubling up as the road. Watch carefully. Got it.

A thousand metres further to the left is a small dirt road. Drop-off point. The driver cannot believe this is my drop. I convince him I know what I'm doing and grab my kit. See you.

The familiar Magirus engine grinds and farts away, slowly fading to nothing. My night eyes and ears begin adjusting to the bundu around me. I savour the moment. After all these years I have finally broken free of Uncle Guvvie. Yeefuckinghaaah! About thirty or forty clicks down this road I will find my first UNITA base. I strap on my rucksack. It is fucking heavy but designed so that I carry the weight on my hips. There is a thin high cover of cloud cutting out the starlight and making it very difficult to see the road. It will burn off just after sunrise, but for now it makes the bundu around me loom and lurk ominously with darkly moving shapes. I know from training that it's only my eyes playing tricks on me, but the mysterious night sounds put substance to the slithering shadows, giving them tangible hostile menace.

Suddenly I realise what I've done.

I have contrived to place myself alone and mostly unarmed, in virgin bundu, in an active operational area – inhabited by African wild animals. And the fear hits me like a pole, almost buckling my knees. Oh my sweet fuck, what have I done? This is absolute fucking madness. There are cats out here, buffalo, hyenas, wild dogs. Oh shit. And what about the soldiers? SADF, Koevoet, SWA Gebiedsmag, UNITA, SWAPO, FAPLA, MPLA, FNLA – all fighting each other. This is Angola. The most active theatre of bush warfare in the world.

I have maybe come all of one click. My cock-eyed plan was to walk at night to avoid the heat, but that plan has run off in terror and is in deep hiding. I am so scared I can barely walk. Okay, stop and sleep. I've slept out in the open loads of times, but not in any place where I can be eaten or shot because I snore. I reason with myself. I have not planned for this. Kwaai, I cannot move at night unarmed, because I can't read the bundu, so I must wait till klaarstaan and then start moving fast before it gets too hot. I estimate it's about one in the morning. It's freezing cold, so I get into the sleeping bag with my knives, risk the pungent smell of mozzie repellent and zip myself in with just my nostrils sticking out. It's weird. I can hear the muffled sounds of the bundu around me, but with the added warm seeping smell of the sleeping bag, the cold steel in my hands and the absence of the threatening bundu darting into my frightened vision— I am comforted like a child wrapped in blankies and hiding from the nasty beastie thing in the cupboard. The last forty-eight hours catch up with me as I snuggle into my pack and fall asleep.

It sniffs …

And catches a whiff. Its terrible dark attention swivels and locks onto the source. It sniffs hungrily, trying to locate the prey, and begins moving into the whispery tendril. It is an entity that has no substance or shape. It is black. Not black in the sense of the absence of white but black in the sense of the absence of light. It sucks the night, radiates pure darkest hatred and feeds on fear. The fear it smells. The fear it hunts.

It is ancient and it is African. Cast down from the Ancestors to roam the wild ancient earth at night looking for the fearful and unprotected. Evil and hungry for the blood of men. It has many, many names among the men of Africa – but tonight it hunts Me.

I awake. I am in the sleeping bag but I can see the bundu around me. The dark shapes in the surrounding bushes and trees move quickly, hunkering down into firing positions. Tension rises. Then they fire. An unholy reverberating racket erupts, shattering the night – flashing fire into my eyes and hammering tinnitus deep into my eardrums. I watch in cold dread as lines of colourful tracer whip over me from the spitting, buzzing, chattering crossfire. I am paralysed with fear. If I could scream and beg for mercy I would.

The firefight goes on.

Then I see it. A huge black thing blocking out the night, leering black hatred and advancing on me with horrible intent. I cannot move with the hot steel zipping overhead, and with a silent roar of black rage, it reaches down, picks me up in my sleeping bag like a featherweight doll and hurls me to the ground. Pain explodes into my ribs, crushing out my wind with a puff of agony.

I awake. I am hurting. My ribs feel as though somebody has kicked me.

Hard. The night sounds are back. I am still in the bundu. Ohmyfuck. What was that? That Black Thing – what the fuck was that? Now I am truly frightened. I am more frightened than I have ever been. My shit muscles are shuddering uncontrollably. I sit up, clutching at the knives, and light a cigarette. Fuck who or what smells it. I'm trying desperately not to piss. Nothing could be worse than that Thing. It isn't hatred that it radiates – it's the hungry saliva of that hatred dripping from a deep dark demonic maw that bites, rips and devours. If I sleep it will eat me.

It knows where I am.

I spend the last two hours before klaarstaan in a silent state of gibbering shitfuckedlessness. I know that if I survive this night and the route march ahead, I will survive anything. I force myself to ignore the skittering shapes and sounds teasing my trepidation. Time stretches endlessly.

Weird barks, jittering clicks and mutated grunts continue to stab and punctuate the surrounding darkness. Shadows, endless and black, relentlessly rustling, darting and ducking – pointing and creeping up on me with malicious intent.

Oh God, it feels like it will never end.

I don't want to think about what I am doing. All I want is to survive the night. Eventually the darkness recedes and the world becomes diffused with a high deep purple and the sound of a million birds awakening to greet each other on the morning of a new day. Strangely, the bundu looks even more dangerous, but I am ready for it now because the sound of the birds is the most welcome thing. They will warn me of real danger around and ahead. I am spurred on knowing that dawn comes quickly in Africa. In a silent yellow effort to forget the previous night and my uncontrolled cowardice, I pack my kit and eat quickly in the gloom. I drink deeply, strap on my knives, buckle into the backpack and begin walking slowly … carefully listening to the birds. The purple is replaced by a low deep blue that quickly feathers up into pink. By the time a deep red dawn erupts I am walking well. The birds are flying normally and looking for food. I must not disturb them. If they flap away in panic or suddenly go silent— I'm in shit.

I must hurry.

If my intelligence is wrong I could find myself in the bundu for another night. Something I don't wanna think about. I settle into my quiet, steady marching pace. This is what I want. I want to fight Communism and make money in the process. Am I capable? I can fight. Yes, but can I kill? I can kill. Ja, you're a Das and a Mongrel and you can fight in the dark with your hands but can you kill a woman and a child? This is a dirty bush war china. You not gonna just sommer walk in and out. I stop walking.

What if you had to kill a woman and a child because you were ordered to?

I close my eyes and imagine it …

It is a small kraal. Just a few ugly mud huts with faded ratty grass canopies. Several scrawny chickens scratch and peck stupidly in the dirt. Nearby, a filthy goat stares out of filmy yellow slit-eyes at nothing. In the thin shadows of one of the huts a mangy dog lies asleep, twitching – all skeleton and gaunt wet sores. Flies buzz in the suppurating pus and the line of thick greenish snot on the lip of the child. They crawl undisturbed to its dusty eyes, which are swivelling wide and uncomprehending between its mother and me. The mother is very dark and looks at me inscrutably through dull, smoky eyes. She may be aware of their fate but I cannot tell. I must not think – I must just do it.

I stand. Do it – I can't!

This is something I cannot do. Then you must turn around and go back – or else why are you here with these people?

I look away to distract them and slip off my safety. I cannot walk one step forward until I fire. If I do this, there is no turning back. Bearing down to the left I fire a sweeping burst up through the child and into its mother. The bullets smash into the kid, hurtling it back like a wet spattering ragdoll, while the mother staggers back drunkenly and falls down hard, her eyes bulging in shock as she slumps over and convulses silently into death. Black red blood slithers into the dirt from under her corpse, mingled with the sharp smell of urine as her bladder lets go. The flies attack hungrily while the bundu goes silent and listens in astonishment.

Nausea rips through me, almost making me vomit. I am shaking hard. I stand for a long time. I still cannot go forward. I must do it again.

This time my burst takes off the top of the child's head but hits the mother in the legs. I have to fire a round into her head to make her stop screaming. The stuff in their heads looks horrible. It is worse than the first one. The third one I do better. A short burst into her chest and the same for the child – as its face crumples up to begin screaming. Clean. Fast. That is they way to do it. Do it again. And again. Until I feel nothing and only the flies get excited.

I drink, strap on my pack again, listen carefully to the birds and start walking.

I have a long way to go …

The heat was like a soft pounding hammer sucking moisture from me with each blow. I walked mindlessly, silent and fast. And dehydrating. Shooting through my water ration fast. I had about fifteen kilos but by 12h00 I was pissing sweat and had already drunk about five. A litre more than the SADF's daily ration.

Strangely enough, the only animals I saw were snakes. I moved like they were after me. Eventually, about three in the afternoon, I reached my target – an outpost manned by a group of, *hopefully*, UNITA soldiers.

Of course, I hadn't really thought things through …

My first problem, once the group had gotten over the shock of me strolling in from fucking nowhere, was their language. I couldn't speak a word of Portuguese. Their disbelief increased as I explained via sign language that I had arrived to help them win the war against Communism.

They promptly did the only sensible thing and arrested me. This was not as bad as it sounds. It was more sort of that they didn't want me wandering off before an interpreter had been found to straighten things out.

A sergeant named João was appointed as my liaison officer and we were transferred to another base to the north. João, like any good Porra, was a dedicated soccer freak. It was my first exposure to a revolutionary culture and we became good friends.

We lived on a plate of rice a day cooked in muddy river water. My shit turned green. But, weirdly enough, I didn't get sick. We smoked acrid bundu tobacco. Talked soccer. Cleaned our AKs. Went on ops loaded up in battered little green captured Russian trucks through towns absolutely and utterly shot to shit and back. All the walls scrawled with graffiti.

VIVA JONAS SAVIMBI!

VIVA FALA!

VIVA UNITA!!

VIVA LA REVOLUÇION!!

The camps were complicated camouflaged affairs but everybody had a position and a task. I saw nine-year-old kids dressed in monkey skins, proudly wearing SADF boots. Something considered gold. They usually carried the RPG rocket launchers, because they couldn't handle the upward kick of an AK and could fire them sitting cross-legged without risking burns from the backfire.

All the troops liked friendly contact with the SADF because they could bum Bibles and ratpacks. We smoked the Bibles. See, there was no paper. Signals were written on pieces of paper, then bordered off and sent. On the other side they were received and crossed out until there wasn't a scrap of space left. Then they were released to be used as communal rolling paper.

That's the thing I remember most – the feeling of utter camaraderie. After saluting an officer you would give each other the thumbs-up salute of victory. Outside our hut we had a baboon tied to a tree. I would sit nearby and it would spend hours trying to find nits in my hair. Our camp was near a river so we had a good water supply and washed fairly regularly.

One night João came into our hut looking unhappy and evasive. He told me we were being transferred to another camp. I looked at him, puzzled, because we had received orders two days previously that I was to be transferred to a unit of mercenaries north of Jamba, but grabbed my kit anyway. We left with a truck full of troops. Suddenly the truck pulled up in front of a white bakkie and stopped. I saw the troops around me stiffen, watched as two white SADF officers climbed out and realised I was fucked. I tried to jump off, but João grabbed my shoulder and shook his head, telling me quietly it was no use. He took my weapon. I climbed down and faced them.

They asked me some questions in Portuguese and I answered, but the Porra I could speak was nowhere near fluent enough to convince them I was native. Then one of them switched to English and told me to give up pretending, they knew exactly who I was. Ironically they were HSI officers. They told me my name and where I came from. I said nothing. Fuck! Then they handcuffed and blindfolded me. Panic— Oh God, they gonna shoot me! Instead they led me to the bakkie and we drove off with me in between them for what seemed like the entire nightmarish night.

We finally drew to a stop. I heard Afrikaans voices outside and knew I had arrived back at one of our bases. Someone led me somewhere and I heard a door slam. I stepped back slowly until I touched a wall and shuffled along it until my foot hit a sponge mattress. I slid down in relieved gratitude. The blindfold wouldn't come off – they'd tied it on too tightly.

I slept.

Next morning the door opened, and someone came in. I heard something metallic drop down and sat up. The person ordered me not to touch the blindfold, undid the skates and moved my hand down to a varkpan where I found things that felt like sandwiches. They were. I ate them ravenously. Tasted like Army eggs. I asked for water and a firebucket was pressed into my hand. I drank greedily. The skates were locked back on and the door slammed.

A little while later I was led somewhere. We stopped and the blindfold was removed. I stood blinking before a Jakkalskop Captain. Intelligence. King shit among the dick-yo-nuts in the electric-firebucket brigade. I stopped blinking and stared directly into his eyes, thinking idly how nice it would be to bite him. He asked me who I was. I ignored him. He probably couldn't take what he could give. None of these cunts could. They were paid to be bullies, cowards and so absolutely fucking necessary to war, but that didn't mean you had to like them. I hated bullies. He picked up a file, opened it and looked back up, nodding:

– *Ja … takes this piece of gemors back to his cell –*

I discovered I was back in Rundu.

My quarters for the night had been a squat concrete bunker. Second discovery, I was locked up with a terr, blindfolded and cuffed like I had been.

Some time later an infantry escort delivered me to Grootfontein DB. Fuck. I stripped in the charge office without being asked and some tall blond fuckwit DB Instructor with lovely blue Aryan genes went through my shit. Stereotype plank gatta. He apparently waited specially to book me— *personally*. He pulls out my knives, sneers to his mates and asks me if I think I'm Grensvegter.

Grensvegter was a fotoverhaal, or what we used to call poesboekies because of another one called *Tessa*, who was sort of a secret agent who worked in a bikini courtesy of the South African Censorship Board. There were loads of other titles, like – *Ruiter in Swart* (cool), *Die Arend* (very cool), *Die Hart van Dr Conrad Brand* (dof lonely-chick shit). Anyway, Grensvegter always used to single-handedly penetrate enemy camps to save some distressed woman, killing (*between the montage*) Russians, Cubans and other nasty individuals there to spawn *Die Swart Gevaar*. At the end, the archvillain would receive his comeuppance by means of Grensvegter's throwing axe. Then Grensvegter would graunch the chick, and fly off in a plane with large windscreen wipers and an instrument panel that looked suspiciously like a Toyota Landcruiser's with fake stuff pasted on the dashboard. That was another thing – his gun always looked kinda like a wooden jol with an old bike baffle nailed to one end and painted black. Anyway ...

This gatta asks me if I skiem I'm Grensvegter and, dropping into contemptible baby talk – *Where's* your little tomahawk? I say fuckall but I look at this ou and I realise it's coming ... Oh fuck, he's picked me for a fight and it's going to be a fucking bad one. Angola is far away but I am right back on a battlefield ... I had better gear up mentally.

The Staff Sergeant who bust me for the hospital case sits behind his desk chuckling happily to himself and says he bet I never thought I would see him again. He is overjoyed, it seems, that he can now add a capital charge to the docket. Fuck you gatta. Back in the block I'm surprised to see Mark and find out how I got bust ...

Apparently the MPs hit Little Ite and company and caught them with some *boom*. The obvious question was, whose zol was it? Mine, they told them. The gattas freaked and wanted to know where the fuck I was because I was supposed to be awaiting trial for Possession of Drugs and Housebreak and Theft.

Angola, they told them.

Done deal ...

Obviously the SADF has been in contact with UNITA and they agreed to hand me over. That's why we went to that camp for no reason. If UNITA wanted to get rid of me they could simply have handed me over to HSI on one of their nightly runs. And it wouldn't make sense for me to have been with them for so long either. So my own bras have fucked it up for me. Cunts. I am not happy and go to sleep not happy.

I awake unhappy because my Aryan friend, Hitlerhead, is kicking me in the ribs and telling me to— *Staan op Draak Addik!* I get up without complaint. I'm gonna play it by the rules until he breaks them. Then Hitlerhead is fucked.

He makes me and another bandiet fetch chow. See – this is a mang rule. Any two bandiete must fetch the chow but it's a kak job. It's far, freezing cold and all you wear is a DB overall. But, like I said – mang rules, so I do it, impassively, with no complaints. He makes me eat breakfast locked in the dark with my hands. Fuck ou, I just came off a diet of one plate of rice à la mud, this is nothing. But I am thinking hard ...

Hitlerhead obviously skiems this is harassment.

But, I know full well the childish kak stunts are going to escalate until I react. He is a Detention Barracks Instructor with Physical Training Instructor (crossed swords) status under the rank of Sergeant. He is, in fact, one of the very few people in our Army legally allowed to kill one of his own by working, drilling or running them to death. This DB boasts a record of six kills already and he wants to hit me with Military Law and have a piece of me. He's drooling for a piece of me. The old snake in my gut awakes.

It's coming ...

The Provost Marshall does block inspection every morning with all the duty DBIs. At my cell he faces the bastards and gives them strict orders:

Order No. 1 – They are to leave me alone. Completely alone.

Order No. 2 – I am not to take part in DB drills, strafwerk or PT. I may only participate in normal cell block activities.

Order No. 3 – I am under NO circumstances to be placed in solitary confinement.

Finally the Sammy tells them I am a dangerous bandiet who is only being held awaiting trial in a civilian case. They must not, absolutely NOT, confront me. Understood?

The Sammy and me know each other. I'm the troep who attacked his MPs and escaped for the sole purpose of putting a fucking armoured bulldozer right through the middle of his charge office.

However, I'm scoping Hitlerhead. He's not fucking happy. I can actually see him skieming – *What makes dis donnerse Draak Addik so fokken special? Huh? Fokken rooinek. I will krack him before his eyes can blink.*

That morning I'm on light work detail, cleaning out the cell block storeroom. But hang on, here's a fucking thing. High up on one of the shelves— I find two rusty pangas. They must have been left by the bandiete who were sent out to chop bush. At the first opportunity I grab one and hide it under a pile of overalls right next to the door. The storeroom is never locked, but I know as sure as shit, Hitlerhead is still coming for me and I had better be fucking as prepared as any soldier going into battle. They might be my only weapons if I survive ...

Lunchtime arrives. I chozz quickly and put down my spoon. Hitlerhead yells at me and asks me if I have finished eating. The bandiete all go silent and check me out. Ja Sersant. He orders me back to my cell. I comply silently, but as I walk past their table and I'm slightly out of earshot of the rest of the ous, he jumps up, grabs me, and shouts – *Oh, you say Fuck*

You, hey? Whatever he is, this naai is not stupid. He has accomplished two things – one, he has humiliated me in front of the whole DB, and two, he now has legal recourse to take action. But I have already flipped my spoon so the eating-end is in my fist, facing my elbow, and I'm skieming – which eye should I put the holding-end into? Two hands like hammers hit me in the back and grab me. It's this short enormous MP who's actually a quiet amiable ou but who is obviously responding to what he rightly perceives as a colleague in trouble. They drag me to my cell, toss me against the back wall and lock the door.

My old friend Rage walks in right through the door. Nods his head. Leaps into Draak Addik.

I fucking lose it and go into The Blackness.

And wait there …

Lunch ends and the other ous pour into the block. Mark comes to the peephole and asks me what the fuck? I tune him to go call the Sammy. He ordered this poeshead to leave me alone and the fucking naai has tried to frame me. Mark ducks.

Hitlerhead blocks him on his way out and comes to my door with some skinny, rankless MP in tow. He asks me what I want. I tune him I want to see the Sammy because he has locked me up for no fucking reason.

And the skinny gatta laughs.

I burst out of The Black into pure white hate—

Scream— and from the back wall I hurl myself into the door. And bounce off painfully. It's solid wood with steel plates riveted together on each side. Fuck! Poes! My shoulder!! Electrical sparks of pain buzz in it. I don't give a fuck. I get up and hit it even harder.

CRACK! Einaaa!

Crack?? Crack is GOOOOD!!

I hit it the third time with everything I've got, and the entire door, still firmly locked into the frame, rips out of the concrete and goes smashing down deafeningly into the middle of the block – moerse fat hole in the wall. I do not even hesitate – straight to the storeroom, reach in, grab the panga, and belt for the charge office. It is Wednesday and all the MPs stationed on the base have Parade right after lunch. I burst through the entry to the block and into a forest of red hats gaping in amazement. They've heard an almighty crash followed by Hitlerhead and Pissgat sprinting in from B-block – the devil on their heels. I see Hitlerhead in the doorway to the charge office and with an unholy tearing scream— I go at him. The hats all drop to the floor as if I had just sprayed them with an LMG. Panga-high there are no hats. As I get to the door I hear my case Staff Sergeant baying – *SKIET HOM*!! *SKIET HOM*!!

But I am out and follow Hitlerhead, who goes flying into the HQ long before anyone can get off a shot.

Inside the HQ a door unlatches behind me and I swing backwards almost to within a snor of decapitating some poor innocent lootie— and hear a pistol being cocked.

Behind me an MP Sergeant is bringing his weapon up from the Safe Loading and Locking Position to Fire. I flick the panga away and drop to my knees with my hands clasped behind my head. He can't shoot – not with the lootie a witness to my surrender. Boots thunder up and suddenly I'm surrounded by yelling gattas with guns. I keep Very Still. They are shaky as hell – fucked on shock and adrenalin.

I'm not. I'm cold as ice, panting lightly from the exertion.

I convince them to let me walk back slowly, with my hands firmly clasped behind my head. I go straight through the white-faced crowd of red hats to my block, walk over the ruined door into my cell and sit down. A very short while later my case Staff Sergeant strolls in over the door and sits down too. Ever the amiable old Dutch uncle. Informs me I am going to be transferred to the local prison in the interests of everybody involved.

Ja, fuck off mapuza naaier.

In prison, I caused a riot. I was one of maybe four white men in a fruit-salad representation of Namibian nations totalling about a hundred and fifty bandiete. It was run by two white men and about twenty poizas. I pretended to go mad from drugs/bullshit/bullshit, and the Army doctors obligingly injected me with soothing lekker to help keep my madness at bay, but it didn't last long. Fake suicide. All the usual shit in an attempt to get out from behind bars into low security and escape. Nothing worked.

I began to get desperate.

I was up on a capital charge and the housebreak had extenuating circumstances. Somebody may have died if they had desperately needed the drugs I had stolen. The possession charge ran into pages. Then there was my record. I was only nineteen and definitely going down for my second stretch or maybe the fucking Rope.

I panicked and did something I had never done before.

I made a pact with God.

I told God that if He got me out I would become a Christian.

And thought about it.

What kind of fucking *pop* and hypocrite would that make me? I hadn't asked God to help me do what I had done. Why the fuck should He suddenly jump up and open the front door of the mang? Toss a rope from heaven? Besides, God must hate me and be more than fucking bedonnered with me. I've screamed at Him – His Poes. No bra, there's no ways in hell God was gonna get me out the mang.

So I thought – What the fuck?

I told the devil that if he helped me escape to the camp, steal weapons, ammo and a vehicle that I could flee with to the States – I would rob banks and shit and when I was twenty-five he could have my soul. I don't know where it came from, but in my head some vague piece of the Bible popped up that said that if I called the Holy Spirit a Mutherfucker – I would surely go to hell because that's the Unforgivable Sin. Then I would belong to the devil.

I flipped—

Crazy!

God and the devil were both crazy! I decided I wanted nothing to do with either one. I would take whatever was coming my way …

15

Between the Devil
and Colonel Coke Bottle

Walking out of the courtroom felt almost unreal. I had prepared myself for what seemed utterly inevitable. I had known – or least *hoped* – they wouldn't give me the death sentence for the desertion charge. That would make the UN even more pissed off with South Africa. The HSI ous who arrested me in Angola had done so illegally, and hanging a South African National Serviceman in South West Africa – whom they had kidnapped illegally from a foreign country – would have been a Lekker Diplomatic Incident. Still, I had expected to do some major fucking time, with the joy of being deported back to Zimbabwe the day I finished my sentence. The MP Staff Sergeant on my case had tried to arrange that nasty little addendum because he couldn't charge me for the attempted murder. The Provost Marshall wouldn't let him. Then there was the other thing …

My mind was careening between ecstasy and disbelief over the verdict but I made a sober decision right then and there. I would make good use of the opportunity afforded me by the magistrate. And, come what may, I would work the rehabilitation programme to the best of my abilities. Just thank God I was free and clean. I was going to Get Off Drugs for good this time!

Nothing else mattered.

Apparently my Vlossie to Waterkloof would only be taking off at 06h30 the following day. I was to report to Battalion HQ for my Route Form and Ritmagtiging to the States. After that I would be completely free to do as I wanted – only try and stay out of trouble for the next forty-odd hours!

Not exactly.

I had one other person to see.

And I really thought the old man had been bluffing me …

I'm sitting in the court cells on the day of the trial. The boere come. They lead me to a courtroom and leave. Inside I am confronted by a Major and a Colonel – both NLK. The Colonel has glasses like Little Dutch in Basics. They look like the bottoms of Coke bottles that have been chopped off. I wonder if he sleeps with his eyes open too. He gets right to the point. He tells me he isn't going to elaborate, but if I want what it seems I want – I have to do exactly what he tells me. I am to plead guilty in court. Fuck, I have already decided to do that. And that is all. I must not discuss this with my fellow accused or anybody else. After the case I am to come directly and see him in the NLK compound.

At the time I thought I was being set up but it didn't make sense. I was fucked already anyway. The Army couldn't make it worse for me (*I didn't know about the deportation order at the time*). But then there was the trial and a whole lot of mysterious things happened. First, my entire record of imprisonment in Central and Zonnies disappeared. Then, equally mysteriously, the MP Staff Sergeant couldn't make it to the case. That gatta wanted to see me dangle on the end of a rope so badly I'm sure he fucking skommelled over it. And, weirdest of all, nothing was said in court. We both entered guilty pleas, signed papers and that was that. I can't remember the other ou's sentence but mine was heavy suspended sentences on all charges and four months' rehab.

Go figure.

I got fucked with my chinas that night and woke up with a horrible hangover. I did a little vasbyt, washed and fed myself, and double-timed it up the NLK compound. I had never been inside the mysterious main HQ before and found it filled with Jakkalskoppe and the khaki berets of the NLK. The major who had been in court with Colonel Chopped Coke Bottle glasses found me and took me to his boss. He was seated behind his desk. Squat, bullfrog ugly and obviously visually impaired. I came to attention and saluted.

The Colonel ordered me to stand at rest and remarked in stentorian Afrikaans that he was very glad to see that everything had gone as it should have done. Hadn't he told me so?

Yes Colonel!

He wasn't going to beat around the bush – he had work for me.

Very serious work.

But first I had to go to Pretoria and complete my rehabilitation programme. After that we would talk about special training for me and so on. He needed people like me urgently. We were stuck with Russian and Cuban Communists north of our borders and other insurgents mingling among the local black population, but then of course the UN would *only* accuse *us* of destabilising a foreign country! Absolute bollocks. But that's the way of the world – *isn't it, troep?*

Yes Colonel!

I had to finish my programme and return directly to him. He had a small elite team who did specialist work for him. He wanted to fit me into it.

But, there were two things I had to be aware of:

Number one, no more bullshit with drugs.

Two – never speak about being one of his people.

Did I understand?

Yes Colonel. Perfectly understood Colonel!

I strolled back down to the bungalows, very chuffed with myself. We all knew Northern Logistic Command was running the war. They were the ones who sat on the sidelines and said nothing when the Jakkalskoppe did the intelligence feedbacks every week. They were the real power behind the whole move.

Enough to swing a capital court case too.

Obviously.

I mean, they were bullshitting two countries and the UN. In the feedbacks they would tell us that we had x number of incidents with y casualties, but every single Vlossie I boarded had $x+a$ number of ous in stretchers hung in tiers – with frantic tampons running up and down squirting fucking needles of shit into them – and $y+b$ number of coffins strapped to the tail. The lies the PFs tried telling us were weak and pathetic.

I thought about his offer.

I knew I couldn't do a keuring to get into Reconnaissance again. Not with my military record. He evidently wasn't sending me to Buffalo because he had told me it was a small unit I was going to and 32 Battalion was a couple of companies of okes. Maybe I was going to do specialised wet work against SWAPO or the ANC in some black-ops unit like HSI. I hoped so. I still wanted to be a mercenary. Absolutely. The way I was inside, there was no possibility of going back into civvy life and getting a normal job and all that kak. He was right though. I couldn't fuck around with drugs and stay alive doing what I wanted to do. I had to become completely focused and professional. And let the South African Government think I was their pet Doberman for a while. I would suck all the training and experience I could out of them and then fuck off and make the really big bucks overseas. There were so many options: take out Basque terrorists for the Spanish,

IRA for the English, Brigate Rosse for the Italians, Shi'ites and Syrians for the Americans in Lebanon, Shining Path in South America or Japan – so long as it was anti-Soviet and anti-Terrorism, I would be doing the world a big favour and making good money in the process. Then I could move onto private work and retire early. I was intelligent, insanely fit and I could still throw three bullets through a cigarette. All I needed was practice, experience and to Get Off Drugs.

Maybe the devil had come through for me after all ...

Well, that was *tog* why I would be flying to Pretoria in the morning. Sort of.

The rest of that day was quiet, except for one incident just after I fetched my Ritmagtiging. Corporal Van found me. I don't know how he did but he found me. He went off about how pleased he was that God had *kept His hand on me.* Then he gave me a little green Bible and a bunch of Christian comics that were actually gospel tracts. I stuffed them in my balsak and tried to get rid of him. He was not to be put off very easily and went on about God loving me and all that shit again. I managed to get away before he could do his praying thing. Fucking Jesus freak. He scared the crap out of me.

I'm standing outside the bungalows, back in the time when Deon Doyle and the boys were still with me. Me and two other roekers are about to make a pipe when we see Corporal Van approaching. The other two ous panic but I tune them to chill – the ou is a Jesus freak. He won't bust us. They aren't about to take any chances and duck. Leaving me with Corporal Van. He tells me he's been waiting for an opportunity to talk to me about God's Love. I shudder. He starts going on into some longwinded thing about Jesus and what-what. I'm looking around frantically to see if anybody is watching this shit because I've got my rep to protect. Fuck, I want to get away but the mutherfucker is persistent. Finally he stops speaking – I think he's realised he's not getting through. He asks if he can pray for me. Fuck, how do you tune an ou – No, you can't pray for me? I sort of shrug noncommittally, hoping he's gonna take the skimp. Ja, right. This ou has all the sensitivity of a runaway Putco bus. He puts his hand on my shoulder, bows his head and goes for it. Now I am desperate to get away, Fuck, people will see this. And then I start listening to him and get really scared. Van is speaking to Somebody as if Somebody is listening. Not talking with his eyes closed or yapping away at no one in particular. Speaking to Somebody, asking them to show me something

I know nothing about. Now it's scary. And I'm not looking around any more. I'm listening. Either he's befuck in his head, or – and this really freaks me out – Someone is listening? And Who?

Back in the present, I got away from Van once again and spent that night with the ouens trying to find rat's arses, convincing myself I could take it easy until I got into the rehab itself.

The next morning I was up at 05h00 and had presented myself at Movements by 05h30. Lo and behold, my two old kanonnies in Movements were there to process me out, and thus it transpired that I boarded the Vlossie nicely dikgerook with a lekker knoesie in my balls.

I wasn't in rehab. Chill bra …

Denise and Bill were waiting at Waterkloof. She was none too happy about any of it. I didn't give a fuck. I was goofed and I still wasn't in rehab yet. Fuck'em – chill china!! Denise moaned the entire way about how they didn't like being saddled with my shit again, and so on and so forth. I hadn't realised that the rehab centre was on the same land as Zonderwater Prison, and it was a bit of a shock driving past the Wagonwheel and the Old Jail that Wally had left me in. I hated him all over again. The twisted fucking bastard should have been in there himself for the attempted murder of a kid! We arrived at the centre and I discovered that Magaliesoord was actually three separate camps. There was Erica for the women and Protem and Elandia for the men. Denise dropped me – still moaning – and disappeared. Good riddance. I was taken straight to the small hospital and booked in. I tuned them I was alright but the nurses on duty told me that everybody got booked in for observation upon arrival. No exceptions.

I went through the procedure and rattled off the litany of drugs I had used or was still using. Okay, let's see now: alcohol, dagga, Mandrax, Obex, glue, thinners and benzene. Followed rapidly by: Peracon, Phensedyl, Valium, Morphine, Valeron (*Tilidine hydrochloride*), Phenobarbital, Vesprax, Tunil, Seconal, Largactil, Sosegon and the odd bit of Codeine. I threw in pinks (*Wellconal*) for good measure, even though I had only popped them. I didn't like the idea of spiked-out arms all siff with tracks and chalk lumps everywhere like a junkie laaitie or some teenage blow-job gintu from the Bronx or La Rochelle in Joburg. I only wanted clean manufactured shit in my veins. I reckoned that was enough for the record. Of course I wanted the list to be as long and as excessive as possible. Exaggerating to doctors came as second nature. I described the severity of my addiction. If I said it was really, really bad, maybe they would give me shit like they did at Phoenix House under Dr de Miranda.

Oh Doctor I'm craving – No shit?

Okay here's a nice fat spike in your bum.

My first big shock was that the ward was mostly full of old toppies. I had thought a drug rehab was only for young ous like myself. Sort of like it had been in Phoenix House. The toppies were mostly only alkies but some of them were actually fucking spiritsuipers who slept in bushes and pipes! I found out that everybody had been sentenced there like me. If you walloped and got caught you went straight to Zonnies Old Jail B-Camp for the rest of your stretch. The steamers called the whole pozzie *Papplaas*.

I had to Get Off Drugs because I knew I had a problem. I knew when I stole the Uzis. I really, really knew when I went mal with one of them the following week. I couldn't blame Phoenix House for not working. I always took everything way past any fixable point. It was my speciality. My calling card whenever I fucked everything up – Way Beyond Acceptable Limits. But this time I was gonna make it work. For sure! I had no fucking choice but to make it work. It was either jail or Colonel CCB.

No other options.

The next day I was discharged from the hospital and released into Protem camp. Protem had initially been for drug addicts and Elandia for alcoholics, but it had changed and both camps were mixed at that point. High fences with razor wire surrounded us but there were no guards with guns and dogs like the two mangs up the road.

My second shock was when they issued me Guvvie clothes. I couldn't believe it! Guvvie shoes, pants, shirts – the whole fucking works. Just like Dassie Bult. With it all came a list of Rules/Reëls – and as true as fuck they wanted me to wear their Guvvie shit all day. Even if I had my own privates! Privates could only be worn in off times (*Rule 5b / Reël 5b*).

It was the rules. And you guessed it – Rules is Reëls meneer.

The Department of Welfare paid all the ou toppies in charge of us and predictably they were known as Beamptes. I could not believe it. I should have expected it though. I mean, it was a Guvvie rehab and all – so who else would run it? It's just that rehabs (*to my mind*) were kind of like co-ed Phoenix House–type jols with pretty pictures and gently sage homilies on the walls. Art therapy, chicks to chaff and stupid doctors that could be conned into giving you a shot of something lekker for dear old— *Craving*. Something these naaiers evidently weren't gonna do.

Come back Dr D – all is forgiven …

I found out that everything ran by the Rules/Reëls. In fact, the measure of the progression of my cure would be gauged by how well I kept to the Rules/Reëls. In my room was a piece of paper and marks were awarded or subtracted to this end every day. I wasn't very pleased about this. I also found that the only therapy there was work therapy. There were shrinks and social workers, but they sat up in the offices and we saw them once a week for an hour. We'd also watch the occasional educational fliek devoted to tired old outdated subjects relating to alcohol and mild dagga abuse. The rest of the programme was— do your work (I was placed in the kitchen), wear your Guvvie clothes, stick to the Rules/Reëls and soft-pedal till you got out. I could also attend Alcoholics Anonymous or Christelike Alkoholiese Diens meetings on evenings during the week if I wanted to. Fat fucking chance. I wasn't a shuffling old juice junkie. I had already decided to *los* the hard tack. I only drank beer.

I was placed in a dormitory with a bunch of steamers, a couple of laaities and a thick list of Rules/Reëls. This was a long way from the soft comfort of Phoenix House. I sat on my bed and wondered what the fucking use was. While I was sitting there, I caught the familiar whiff of zol drifting in through the window.

What the fuck?

I looked outside and there were a couple of ouens smoking a boat. My jaw dropped onto my chest and I went back to my bed, sitting down for all of twenty seconds before running outside and begging for a last hit.

That's how it started.

Within a week I was smoking every day. All day. I had been placed on veg prep and found out that the key position in the whole camp was running the kitchen. The current ou in that job was leaving, so I bribed him with some of my Army money to nominate me for his post. In week two I took over. The steamers were no competition and the laaities were all *poppe* except for a Born Free Kid named Lionel who had been in TK and who immediately became my company. By the third week Lionel and I were running all the drugs into the camp. I picked three of the biggest ous there, took them into the kitchen one night and made them fat mixed grills of steak, eggs and chips. Then I told them they would be paid that way on a regular basis, and they could get all their zol from me at cost – but they had to work for it as my muscle.

That was it. Nobody could, or would, fuck with me.

A part of me was pleased. I had achieved it all so quickly. I knew how to keep to the Rules/Reëls and still do my own skelm goeters …

BUT …

The BUT was something I was having real trouble dealing with.

I had very selective memory as far as my circumstances were concerned. Colonel CCB was not my problem. I doubted that he was keeping more than distant tabs on me, and I had been clever. Nobody except Lionel and my immediate crew knew I was responsible for all the drugs in the camp. That wasn't the problem. The problem was the secret promise I had made when I was in Grootfontein Prison.

I had promised God that if I got out of jail …

I would become a Christian.

Now I was out of jail …

So I owed God *first*, regardless of my deal with the devil or Colonel CCB.

It cast a pall over everything I had achieved. I could not enjoy my drugs, my position or my power because it nagged away at me all day. And on top of it all I began to worry about my life expectancy. I knew the path I had chosen for myself was a quick and deadly one. Without Colonel CCB, the violent black rage in me would get me into lethal trouble sooner rather than later. I would definitely wind up dead, facing a baadjie or The Rope again. And what lay beyond that? The Blackness I saw approaching when I slit my wrist open in DB? The Black Thing that attacked me in the bundu that night in Angola? Fuck, I didn't want that. Nobody, no matter how much pluk he had, could ever consciously want *that*. Not unless he was totally befuck in his kop. I was crazy, yes, and very, very angry, but I wasn't totally befuck. Not by a long shot. Deep down I did not consider death, real death, that casually, and trying to overpower that fear inside had tired me out. On the other hand I would be a cowardly fool for taking one step backwards from the path I had embarked on. I would look like a major nwata. I didn't want to die but I sure as fuck didn't want to be the kind of weak *pop* that would back away from my chosen course either.

And then there was Corporal Van …

Who was listening that night he prayed for me?

Somebody was …

I had heard hundreds of mense pray. From JWs and the Wearnes to the Army chaplains, but the only person who freaked me out was Van. Somebody *listened* when Van prayed. Somebody paid attention. I knew it. I could hear it. He spoke to Somebody he *knew* was listening, And that Somebody *listened*. It was right there in his voice – clearly.

I started wondering what being a Christian was all about.

My ideas of God were limited to my experiences of prison, industrial school, military camps, Denise's weird shit and my own strange excursions. Those beliefs were vaguely motivated on my part by necessity. I had to weasel my way out of the hell I figured *had* to be coming my way.

Van was a disturbing phenomenon of his own because he wasn't passively rude, and he never came across smugly like he was better than me just because he had a thing about God. He even left notes for me under my pillow. I would come into the camp at three in the morning from AWOL into the local townships and find Van outside the bungalows with some ou praying.

I got a completely different vibe from the other Christians.

They had a coffeeshop-type jol in the base where they usually hung out. But mostly they stuck to themselves or got into condescending arguments with other ous. I knew there was something in me that needed answers and I knew I didn't have them. But I didn't think they did either if their Big Old Man made them act like snobbish cunts. The way I'd grown up convinced me that if God was anything like Wally or Uncle Guvvie, then it was *nag* for me. It had been *nag* for me for a long, long time. In my imagination God was like some vague old toppie with a long white beard and cold eyes who had very nasty ouens working for him and who would toss you in hell if you made him befuck.

It baffled me.

Secretly I began reading the comics Van had given me. They all seemed to say the same thing. Man was separated from God. If I died separated from God, I would go to hell and the devil would get me. Jesus had died and made a sort of bridge to God. In the comics the bridge was a cross. Jesus would get me to God.

That part I didn't understand.

Jesus wouldn't want fuckall to do with me, china. I had been tossed out of my family and sent to reformatory. I had been in prison for drugs. I stole, lied, swore, fought and took drugs every day. I was a Mongrel back in Cape Town. I had been gripped by moffies and I wanked. I wanted to be a professional assassin and Colonel CCB wanted me to kill special darkies for him. Jesus wouldn't even spit at me.

But still – I had made a promise and I wasn't the type of ou who went back on a promise, or a dare. Ever.

Okay, so how would I become a Christian?

I figured if I made two lists and stuck to them I would be cool. Maybe Jesus would stop being pissed off with me. But I had better not fuck around. The one thing I didn't want was to look like some Jesus freak to the ouens. I would end up without chommies and there was no way in hell that I wanted to go through that. Maybe I could do it secretly. Set up a list and not tell anybody. Then I could please Jesus and still keep my chommies. Okay, so set up a list:

<u>The Do's and the Don'ts of being a Christian</u>:

Pray	* Stop swearing
Go to Church	* Don't be a gangster/mercenary
Read my Bible	* Stop wanking/taking drugs
Hang out with Christians	* Don't fight
… Etc/	

I had a list and now I needed a plan. By the time I reached this decision a month had passed. I had been promoted to a new set of bungalows and now had a private room because of my exemplary behaviour in keeping to the Rules/Reëls. The only black mark against me was for wearing my takkies in the kitchen but that was kind of minor until I challenged some poeshead to a knife fight for piemping me but I managed to weasel my way out of that shit unscathed.

At night, just before going to bed, I started secretly reading the little green Bible that Corporal Van had given me.

I had a quiet laugh about it too. Here I was, kamstig the main makwera, yet I was reading my Bible like a Jesus freak and planning to become a Christian. What a *lag*! But I was serious, so I didn't laugh too much. The Bible puzzled me hectically. Nothing I read stuck in my head and a lot of it frightened me. There were Bible words I had never heard of, let alone understood. And I obviously read it from the perspective of How, When and Where God was going to fuck me up. The *Why* was obvious. In Van's little comics He was like the ultimate Wally screaming at me to go and wait in my room until He came to moer me. I stayed away from the Book of Revelations – that's where the angels row like galley slaves to toss the mense into fire. I knew that from the JWs – they were big on it. The tracts all ended saying that the only way for me to stay out of the hot-pot was to accept Jesus as my personal saviour. Why would Jesus want to save me when He was the one angry with me? The ultimate end to being in the Big Headmaster's Office. It sucked. It was just another court case that I was already losing. I had gone crazy a couple of times while pissed and asked the ouens what they thought it was all about. Really truly all about? I was willing to treat the whole idea of life as a what-the-fuck-type jol but, if there was some proper way of understanding the real meaning to finding myself in a crazy place where hurting, hurting and hurting some more was all that I wanted to do – then I wanted to hear about it.

I wanted to be like the ous that Jesus made better in the stories because I knew I was sick inside with hate and very efficient at hurting. I knew I had done too much sin. I could imagine His face going hard with anger if I even dared to speak to Him. He had never sinned and my sin was terrible. I had killed.

No china, He definitely wouldn't want me as one of His ouens.

One night I decided to see if the Bible had any practical advice for me to get out of my predicament. My little green Bible had a list of references in the front, so I looked up: Sin. I figured my most obvious problem was sin. The reference was 1 Cor 10:13.

1 Cor turned out to be Paul's First Letter to the Corinthians. I didn't know who the fuck Paul or the Corinthians were, but the passage I found said:

There hath no temptation taken you but such as is common to man: but God is faithful, who will not suffer you to be tempted above that ye are able; but will with the temptation also make a way to escape, that ye may be able to bear it.

The old English made it difficult to read but I figured it out okay. If I trusted God then I could get out of temptation and then I wouldn't sin and if I didn't sin then Jesus would stop being angry with me and I could be a Christian.

Easy peasy just like that.

I slept.

When I woke up the next morning at 04h30, I had a shower as usual, but afterwards, instead of hitting the asgat pipe I'd stashed outside, I did something I had never done alone for real before. I got down on my knees and prayed. I told the God who listened to Corporal Van that I meant business and that I wanted to be a Christian like I had promised and that I was going to try and stop sinning. All I needed was for Him to come through and help me out with the temptation.

Amen.

It was a nightmare. I had a running battle with myself all day, punctuated by what seemed to be a voice in my mind telling me how to stay out of trouble. By the end of supper I was going crazy. Lionel had some *boom*, the only zol in the camp in fact, which the voice told me he would smoke alone with a new guy who had been in reformatory with him.

I was almost too late. Disregarding the voice, I broke into a run and sprinted down to where I knew they would be. I arrived just as they were about to bust the pipe. Lionel looked mightily guilt-stricken but I ignored him and smoked. After my hit I went into skollie mode and asked his bra who the fuck he was and how he thought he was going to fit into my picture of the way things were run around here. I could see the ou was like me and didn't take kak from anybody but he was obviously not dof either and recognised that I wouldn't set myself up as an indota and not deliver the goods. He told me he was a TK old boy and that he would fit in well as long as nobody took him for a nwata. Feeling magnanimous, I gave him a thumbnail sketch of how Lionel and I ran the camp and told him I could see he was an Ou like us, which was a rarity, so he would be welcome to join in on equal terms as long as he did his bit for the company.

The negotiation with the new ou was mundane in the bigger scheme of things. I really did need another oke to help with the smuggling because we had expanded our operation and were making night-time forays over the fence to make deliveries to our connections in Elandia. It was risky but profitable and I needed somebody with gedagte to handle it for me. Problem was the risk – he would have to be one of the inner circle.

The voice had gone silent as I babbled away, and all I heard echoing around inside— was the sound of me.

Me asking myself some very heavy questions:

– *Who do you think you are fucking with, china?* –

– *Do you really think you can make promises and deals with God and then rip Him off?* –

– Is God like your own personal blougat, my broer? Your pop, your butler? A skievvie? Skiem maybe you're going to get away with making promises and playing games and what-what? –

– Huh? Speak up china, I can't hear you eksê! –

A very bad horrible feeling had settled in my stomach. I didn't want to play games with God. I really didn't. I didn't know who God was, but Van seemed to. I hated myself for what I was doing. I had meant what I said that morning. With all my heart I had meant it. It's just that I'd been like I was for so long that I had no idea how to stop. At that point I stepped out of all the fear and rage in my mind and I put myself into the deep cold place where I always fought from.

The place where I had no emotion and saw nothing save what I had to do next to survive.

Okay, let's take stock.

You have smoked, used bad language, acted like a skollie and generally done everything on your list that you shouldn't do except wank.

That's the bad stuff …

There is no good stuff except that you did try and listen to the voice and the Rapture hasn't happened yet because you would have heard about it on the radio.

The Rapture was something I got out of Van's little comics. Apparently, any day now, the Christians were all suddenly going to vanish into thin air. Aeroplanes would fall out of the sky, cars would smash into each other on freeways, scalpels would drop to the floor in operating theatres, food would burn and general chaos would ensue. All that would be left would be a bunch of hardened Misbelieving Buddhists, Infidel Moslems and Heathen Hindus – terribly confused, one and all. Then the atheistic, filthy, godless Russians and New Age Movement would combine to take over the world in defiance of God Himself, with the newly self-appointed Antichrist as head of the New World Order. The Satanic Pope and Heretic Catholic Church would be right there in the thick of it too. Anybody who became a Christian after that would have his or her head cut off because they would refuse to have the Mark of the Beast made on them so that they could buy or sell things. If they did get the Mark, God would reject them and that would be that. Jesus was coming and, fuck ou, was He pissed off. Scary, scary stuff.

Okay so the Rapture hasn't happened yet. At least you might still have until tomorrow.

So what you wanna do bra?

I meant everything I said this morning, and I still mean it, even if I didn't get it right.

The only thing I can do now is forget about today and go to bed. I'll sleep it off and then tomorrow I will try again, TWICE AS HARD.

Okay go …

Back in the real world, Lionel and his china were asking if I wanted to come with them and watch TV. I politely declined. I'd decided that I really was just going to go to bed and try again in the morning. Lionel looked puzzled, but I shook my head adamantly and told him I would see him in the morning.

– *See you china* –

16

Madness and Miracles

I reach my room and open the door.
Step in and look up—
Someone is there looking at me ...

Scientists say the human brain is wired deep down in our limbic system with something like a master panic switch. It's one of the very good reasons why we are here at all. Upon coming across a sabre-tooth tiger, your alert early man would either have to fight it (*early man was a delicacy from the early sabre-tooth tiger's point of view, and sooo easy to prepare*) or more likely run like hell straight up the nearest early tree.

When this switch is, as it were— *thrown*, the brain immediately emits adrenalin, endorphins and other chemicals into the bloodstream to deal with the emergency. This part of the brain has a boss, called the Higher Brain – which sends a short urgent signal, saying, in essence:

– *omysweetfuckHITTHESWITCHGOGOGO!!!!!!!!!!!!* –

The most important aid to the Higher Brain is found in something called the neo-cortex. There are many things in the neo-cortex that aid the Higher Brain, but the most important is the sight stream, which the Higher Brain processes and streams up constantly into the Mind – right side up, de-cone-cell pixillated into millions of colours and in 120-degree surround 3D. This stream is processed into a triage of factors, breaking it up according to the importance of the images, but the first background process is always fight or flight.

There is a huge built-in subconscious section of the brain that is as aware as the Mind and has control over the Higher Brain – called Instincts. Inside Instincts is a record of every bad thing that can go wrong. Every single one. Instincts is *very* paranoid. Instincts' job is to protect the body and to decide when to hit the panic button. Kinda like walking into your office and finding Instincts furiously at work behind your desk grimly clenching a .44 Ruger. Instincts' work consists mostly of yelling wildly about nasty things about to pay an antisocial visit and hitting the panic button. (*It's my brain, I can think of it like I want. I've also got little men with pointy green hats in my tummy who have like a factory thing going – to process my food.*)

Open the door,
Step in and look up.
Someone's there looking at me …

If I had looked up at the person, scanned down (*Instincts looking for sharp teeth, claws, spears, crossbows, Heckler & Koch MP9-SP urban assault weapons, rocket launchers – in that order*) and scanned back up to the eyes, it would have been normal reaction. *Assess the situation. Do I know this person? Possible friend or foe? Fight, flight or— or*

… embrace?

Brief twenty-thousand-point threat assessment sent to the Mind, and the Mind, getting a negative danger signal from a jittery Instincts, passes control back to Higher Brain and awaits further instructions a few nanoseconds later.

This did not happen.

Look up. Someone's—
Looking at me …

I look up into the Eyes of a stranger, and something unlocks deep inside. I became aware of *knowing* those Eyes, really knowing … like the intimate *knowing* of a lover or a very close friend, and this knowing is inside me but I had never realised it. With it is another veiled memory of knowing that these Eyes have always been watching over me. From the far blood-filled darkness of before I can remember inside my mum and beyond. And these Eyes have always looked at me with a purpose. Watching over me with a love so profound, so deep, and so completely immutable in the knowledge that I, together with every other human being, was born to live forever in that gaze.

Deeper inside me something else opens up and I can see *with* them. And what I see is me.

All of me.

I begin as a tiny splash of special light. A precious little pebble dropping into an infinite pond of emptiness. A lightless void waiting to be filled.

Thin colours ripple out in dim meaningless hues, rapidly becoming vibrant ... alive – cohering into early images – flashing, blurring, as I see myself as a child. Images, images, faster, faster as I grow older. Bad and terrible things stick in my head. The worst I don't want to remember and have banished to dark caves in my heart. There are so many of them. I am not a very nice person on my secret inside. I am aware that this is what it is like to feel me – *from the outside*. But while I am still so aware of what I am seeing and feeling, I realise the person letting me *see* myself— must have felt all these terrible things too.

Something tears loose inside me. I can't face myself – so I break my gaze, turn—

and run.

I run down to the bottom of the camp and start crying uncontrollably on a rock. I've worked so desperately hard to build a shell around me. A shell that's harder than most. But nothing in the world could ever be worse than seeing and feeling myself. I cry for what seems like hours. I cry like I've never cried before. I don't care who sees me, although nobody does. And all the time those Eyes are still with me. Eventually the ripples subside and it seems I've reached the very deep bedrock, far down in the murky darkness – on the ocean floor of my soul.

And all I can say, silently, is ...... *I'm sorry.*

I feel a physical weight move from me and once again I *see.*

I look down a long rocky road stretching before me to something far, far away and so vast I cannot not call it a city – what kind of city seems millions of miles long? There's a light coming from it that makes the setting sun seem tiny and dim. This illuminates the road ahead. Then, with the Eyes, as I watch the city – I hear a voice say to me:

∞ *YOU ARE COMING HERE* ∞

*

I was convinced that I was 'Born Again', as the bumper sticker says. I was tossed out of the Army almost immediately because I announced brightly to Colonel CCB that I now wanted to *help* people – black people included, especially children – not kill them any more.

Go figure.

The local Christians on the base had always been terrified of me, but now they dragged me off to *meetings*. To me church was a Sunday jol but after my experience I reckoned buildings and Sundays didn't matter. *Every day mattered. And every place mattered.* But still, I didn't know what the *Rules* were, so I looked to them for guidance.

They asked me if I had ever been baptised in the Holy Spirit. I said no. So they sat me in a chair, put hands on my head and started praying loudly in English – and something *else* – that something would happen. Nothing did. I started feeling very stupid.

As much as I willed it, nothing happened ... except I got real sweaty and embarrassed. I eventually asked them to stop – saying I was pretty sure God was not deaf. They informed me I had too little faith. Oh, and I hadn't been baptised.

Now that disturbed me very deeply.

I was supposed to have broken out into this *Speaking in Tongues* thing. I think that was the first time I started deeply questioning myself and my own private little experience in the face of everything I saw around me.

These were squeaky-clean kids from upper-middle-class backgrounds. They came from big important churches. They were like private Christians and I was like a Guvvie laaitie Christian. They also told me they loved me with *the Love of the Lord*, although I felt irritated that they couldn't love me with their *own*. It reinforced it for me. There were better Christians than others and I wasn't one of them.

However, the truly disturbing thing was— I didn't *need* more than I had experienced. I didn't need *meetings* or weird stunts. It was dead simple:

YOU ARE COMING HERE

No *Ifs*, no *Buts*, no *Conditions*. Applicable to everybody – starting with bitch-born-bastards and working upwards from there.

A simple statement of fact.

An open, unconditional promise to everybody, if you wish.

It wasn't: YOU ARE COMING HERE *if you go to the right meetings, talk in tongues and get baptised. And you have to do it in the right order. And you must have faith or else God won't give it to you. Here, see, it says so in Scripture.*

The person in my room that night wasn't like that.

My razor-sharp Das sense could see it clearly.

So, how could *they* be wrong?

I walked out deep into the bush that night and sat down alone in an old deactivated minefield and thought deeply about that night and what I saw and heard on that rock. A long while later I came away with something private that has sustained and protected me to this day, although admittedly it took a very long time and a lot of heartache for me to discover that.

Then I caught a Vlossie back to the States.

I began devouring the Bible. I read it like I have never read any book before or since. But alone, because I had no one to teach me what it all meant. See, I was working as an appie motor-mac with Yvonne's husband and staying with them at the time. No transport and no church anywhere near their plot. So I read and I read.

With interesting results.

One night a Thing like in Angola attacked me again. The first three times it hit me it terrified me with its hate. But that's when I realised something – the Black Thing's only weapon is hate. The sixth time I told it to go away because I could never belong to it again. The reaction was terrible but it left and I have never been bothered since. I hate Bullies. Just stand up to them. However, I began to feel the old echoes of something that had dogged me since childhood. Chronic loneliness.

And I had questions.

I couldn't handle the isolation and the absence of answers, so I moved back to the Wearnes in Worcester. I got a job in Fire and Rescue and became a fireman. I got engaged to Diane, one of the daughters. The Wearnes had left the Congregational Church and were now in the Salvation Army. This was not nice. Somehow, being a Christian meant dressing up in nineteenth-century uniforms and standing on street corners banging drums and blowing bugles, begging for money – or going door to door, also begging for money. I felt it alienated people and made us look like prats. I refused to wear the uniform, saying I didn't believe one needed a uniform to be a Christian. Once again, I was on the outside of what seemed to be the norm. Now the real self-doubt set in.

My long internal war had started. They had to be right. They *had* to. I was the fuckup – not them. Had been all my life. In spite of Diane, loneliness and ideological isolation were still my constant enemy.

I remedied it by sleeping with Diane and thereby in some pathological way confirmed what I knew to be true – God had made a mistake. I was filth and He had made a Big Mistake. I left the Wearnes and started hanging out with my bunkmate at the Fire Brigade, an ou named Brandon. Up until then he had been taunting me by coming into our room with a bag full of buttons – asking me if I missed them. I walked in one afternoon just after I broke off my engagement, with a cardboard box and a heart full of shit, and packed away all my Christian books, music, posters and my Bible – telling him that if he ever mentioned it or tried to take me for a poes because of it— I would fuck him up worse than he could imagine. He wisely kept his bek shut. And silently chopped me a nut. I accepted I was going to hell and that was that.

It's not as easy as it sounds.

Then I met up with a cat name Dean who became my best mate and confidant. The only thing that irritated him a lot was that I started having a scene with his sister in Matric. This went on for a while until I was fired for being goofed the whole time. I was trying to kill the pain of being rejected by God by smoking buttons.

Told you I was creatively stupid.

At some point I spent a weekend in Stellenbosch at the invitation of a friend. Here I was taken to a new type of church that had started because the pastor had been thrown out of the local Anglican church for practising Pentecostal rituals. What satisfied me deeply was that it was multiracial – at least in that *decent* coloured and a tiny smattering of black folk attended. However, they gathered exclusively in the white part of town, but at least it had no permanent building. And you could come dressed any old how.

I moved to Stellenbosch, crawled back to God and started a pattern that after years I eventually had the courage to break. I begged for mercy, forgiveness – all those good groovy things that I *thought* I needed – and joined my first charismatic church. In the beginning I needed the emotional experience and fix every week.

However, it wasn't long before trouble reared its head, because I always had things to say ...

Take something *really* contentious like the money thing. Even back at the Guvvie rehab in Magaliesoord, my Das sense started clanging loudly.

The only Christian literature available to me had been an apparently free magazine by this American evangelist named Kenneth Copeland. But ... when I read it, I was struck by the fact that although the articles touched on fundamental Christian themes, they were very short and every single one of them was actually an introduction to a set of tapes or a video that could be bought for a *price*. My new Das sense went off, surprising me for the first time. It made me begin questioning this ou. It couldn't be a free magazine – I mean, all it did was sell stuff. It was a sales brochure! If

I was some majorly rich ou and I could afford all the goeters he had on sale inside its pages, it would have a shelf value worth a few thousand dollars. The oke was a skelm. A marrobaner. And a dik slim one too, because mense let him sluk them like that. I saw another one by this other supposed healing pastor named Oral Roberts. He had this vision from God or something of an angel called Wharrawharra and you could buy a plastic reproduction of Wharrawharra, which was actually a lamp!

For a price too …

Look, new Das sense, old Das sense – I could still spot a dik skêbeng when I saw one. And what did it mean when so many people calling themselves Christians bought into it?

I read in the Bible how Christ confronted priests who lied.

Called them snakes.

Because of those magazines I became suspicious of okes who asked mense for money in the name of God, and by thoroughly studying Scripture I found out that every cent being collected in Christian churches in Christ's name is being done so fraudulently under Biblical Law. The way this fraud is committed is through enforcing a twisted adaptation of an ancient Jewish spiritual discipline called *tithing*, using the Mosaic laws of *sacrifice* and *offerings*.

See, in the Old Testament, the Levite tribe of priests were not allocated farmland in the Promised Land like the other eleven tribes of Israel. As an ordinary oke, you were commanded to take a portion of your annual crop, called a tithe (*meaning tenth*) – to the priest. The priest was then supposed to kill, braai, ferment or bake the sacrifice, and then *you and the priest* gave thanks to God and shared this meal together with all your family and servants. Physical sustenance and spiritual sustenance being *exchanged* at two levels in a ritual holy feast. There was only one provision made for money coming into this ritual. If you lived far away from the Temple, you were allowed to sell your tithe at home and travel to the Temple. When you arrived in the city you were then obliged to buy a new tithe of animals, wine, wheat – whatever – locally and then go for your sacrificial feast and blessing with the priest.

It's this exact law that was perverted and made Christ so bedonnerd that He moered the priests in the Temple for doing it as a blatantly fraudulent business. Like I said – lekker, dik, vet skêbeng.

The modern Pharisee up in the pulpit with the microphone and TV cameras lives in what 95 percent of the country considers a mansion more than fit for any world leader and gets around in a late-model German or Italian supercar, while the poor stupid working stiff renting a flat and driving jap-scrap sitting in pew number three gladly helps to pay a bit of it off. The modern pastors don't even bother with reselling the same phony goats and shit any more, now it's all hard cash or credit card. The really hysterical thing is that the cleverly brainwashed *pop* in pew number three has come to firmly believe that God *wants* him to do that with his money and will kick his miserable sinning arse if he doesn't.

Another big shock came when I discovered that the mense in the pews themselves conspired to keep it like that in order to buy an easy cop-out of their own responsibilities towards those in need in their communities.

I also found out that the fastest way to get kicked out of any Christian church is to tell the faithful that the Bible says they are *all* Christ's priests. And, as priests, they are equally responsible to each other in everything that they have materially. And not just cash either. Talents, skills, everything. By giving cash to the pastor they sell their Christian priesthood. The only thing that they are supposed to formally exchange regularly in Christ's name is food and drink. Exactly like the Old Testament, except now both parties in the exchange have been made priests by Christ's sacrifice. People hated being told that. They hated even more being told that you cannot give money to God because He doesn't want it and He won't give it to you because if you expect that of Him then money is your god. And you cannot give money to the church because you are the church. All you can do is share.

Christ had such disdain for money that he let Judas Iscariot keep it all. Once, He makes a lekker joke with Peter and sends him to catch a snoek with some kroon in its mouth to give to the dominees who demanded a *temple tax* from Him. The Pharisees get dik slim one day and try and kap Him vas about Roman tax but He points them right back at the minter of the money – Caesar.

I felt the key to Christianity was measured in the way churches paid attention to the needs of children. All children.

I conspired to become a youth leader in that church in Stellenbosch before the real trouble started, and I found that the worst spiritual abuse took place right inside Christian families. One of my schoolgirls tried to sleep with me. I was horribly shocked and blamed her for it until I realised from gently counselling her that she was half insane from loneliness and kinda despised God. Her dad was a senior Elder and everybody in the church looked up to him. Up on his pedestal, he was so *On Fire for Jesus* and had so much time, money and energy for Jesus and evangelising all the Jews in Israel, that his daughter was convinced he did not love her and she despised Jesus for stealing all of her father's affection. I met hundreds of kids like her in my time, ridden with guilt, fear and pain.

Her father lost his Eldership when she eventually mislaid her virginity and fell pregnant to the first oke who came along. He left in a fury and started up a rival crunchie outfit with some other rich Dutchmen. This time he was a Pastor.

How the hell do you tell the parents of a confused adolescent that their shitty, self-absorbed theology has brought the child almost to the point of suicide because she did something as unspeakably evil as touch her own body privately in an exciting way? I wanted to slap the parents and tell them to stop waving at the sky and look down for once and listen to their children.

All around me, from my kids in the church to the Stellenbosch street-laaities, I saw human *neglect* and outright spiritual abuse. People had huge starry-eyed visions for other exotic countries (*especially some quasi-romantic idea of Israel*), and ultimately themselves materially, but they didn't give a flying fuck about the hundreds of wretched black squatters and their children suffering without water or basic sanitation and near starving in squalor a minute down the road. It was all bless me Lord, bless me, and Lord bless those who can bless my idea of me ...

I cracked up again and ended up in bed with a chick when the anger and isolation became too much. Sinner! But I reckoned it couldn't be like that everywhere, so I did the next best thing – to my eyes, anyway – I became a theology student and missionary for a few years, with Youth With A Mission, or YWAM. This was spectacularly stupid of me. I thought that because the curriculum came from PACU (*The Pacific and Asian University*) it would not be tainted by the usual fare of extended Protestant Imperialism in a bad marriage with Protestant Afrikaner Zionism playing subliminal wife-swopping with American big-bucks fundamentalists. Braaaa!! Hello ... Al? *Wrooo-ong*. The South African bases were *all* run by white South Africans and *only* by white South Africans. I'll give you a couple of brief examples of my ongoing conflict, then we can go smuggle some zol and have what seems like fun for a while. I want to get this downer part of the story over with.

It leaves a bad taste in my mouth.

You see, I always had a diametrically opposing idea. One that didn't fit in with The Program and usually conflicted with the leadership. Example …

We arrive in Worcester to do an SOS (Summer of Service). The leader of the base – a guy named Brian Kinghorn – tells us we'll be working on eleven farms in the area. All the farmers are Christian friends open to the idea. Tonight we will be going to one of them to minister to the plaaswerkers just before they have their dop. All the farms in the area run on the dop system. I dunno if you know how that works, so I'll tell you. The workers are given a choice of a cash wage or a ration of wine. The volume of dop the farmer gives them is way more than they can possibly buy at a liquor store, and therein lies the hook. It costs him a pittance to produce and effectively buys him narcotic slaves.

Brian tells us that we must prepare three songs, a testimony and a drama. I suggest to him that, maybe, because we are here for three months, why don't we just go and meet them tonight? Each of us befriends a couple of people, gets to know their names, and we chat with them the whole time – so we can pray for their personal needs more effectively. He turns to me, furious that I've contradicted him, and tells me that he was the YWAM director of the entire Philippines operation and he is NOT about to be told how to run his base. We will do The Program …

It was horrible.

I stood in front of a bunch of obsequious, miserably poor coloured folk seated on benches in rows under the roof of a dusty shed – and did The Program as ordered. They sat in mild trepidation, the men with their heads bowed in respect to us, nervously gripping their hats in their hands, and the women with their colourful doeke, staring carefully, hands folded meekly in their laps. Their kids were not allowed. Too noisy and inattentive, which freaked me out because my study speciality was children's ministry.

I also got one hell of a shock when we arrived. Brian and his wife spoke down at them, ordering them around as if they were stupid, obstinate, wayward children. Almost not even people. And the rage started to rise again.

It was, is and always has been like this for me. After Brian finished preaching a little Frankenstein evangelism, he asked them to raise their hands if they wanted to accept Jesus – or sommer die and go to hell.

Everyone's hand went up for Pastor Baas Brian. These were counted and diligently added to the statistics of drunken heathen snatched from the Lake of Fire.

Later that night I try dealing with my rebellious spirit. My leaders tell me this is my deep sin. Out in a big wheatfield, I begin praying. I know exactly where these poor people are coming from. They live in tiny crowded hovels, do backbreaking work for a pittance, and live from generation to generation in alcoholism. Here in deep apartheid, that is how things work – but I cannot believe this is how the Person I believe to be God wants it. I cannot.

And that's where my spiritual schizophrenia is coming from. We destroyed these people's spirits but maybe we can change it for their children by changing it for them.

I pray and pray.

I pray almost the whole night and nearly collide with a big snake, which I hear hissing menacingly near me. The old pap-driven meaning-making machine on top of my shoulders tells me that I'm on the right track because A Serpent has tried to shut me up. Yes, yes – I know I'm nuts ... but ... I get my answer with a warning that I don't heed because I think it could never be part of it.

Following the strict chain of command, I go to my flock group leader – a really gentle, red-head giant named William, who loves playing a droning alto sax – and tell him what I think we must do.

First we must get rid of our beautiful leather-bound Bibles and dress in our oldest, strongest jeans, a plain shirt and jersey or jacket, but nothing with designer labels. Leave everything else behind. Boomboxes, CD players, all our gospel music, books, money, and other appliances and cosmetics. Put a toothbrush in one pocket. Then we are to split up into able girl–guy pairs and go to the different farms. But we must walk – we cannot take the Hi-Ace, because it is brand new. Upon arriving at the farms, each pair goes down to the dop shed and waits. When the workers come in we must sit with them. Those of us who want to can drink a dop. When the folk ask what we are there for – we tell them that we have come to visit them for an entire month and make friends. And very, very important, we must NOT, absolutely NOT, speak about Jesus.

Not once.

William looks at me as if I have gone completely and utterly stark raving mad. I try explaining from what I believe I heard or felt after praying the night before – and back it up with Scripture ...

When Christ sent out His disciples to perform His miracles and preach

His message, He sent them out in pairs in all directions and told them to take nothing with them except the clothes on their backs. I told William that I had prayed very hard about it and felt it was because we needed to give power to these broken and completely powerless people.

My Das sense told me exactly why they lived in delinquency, but I couldn't judge them for it. I had been the same all my life until That Night. I knew exactly what it felt like to be one of them.

I loved them because of it.

I explain to William that what they need is to feel empowered, and the only way to do that will be to strip ourselves of everything that makes us appear superior in any way, and then make ourselves dependent on them – yes, *them* – for food, water and shelter. We can't do anything about our white skins, but if we are really sincere and – most important – friendly, without ANY fokkenhotnotkaffir attitudes inside, they will accept us and look after the two of us from their own poverty until the farmer pays us for our work.

I know this from District Six.

It might mean sleeping out under the stars for the first night or two. But we can just make a fire. And we might go hungry but we can fast. Water is plentiful. I know these people – they will not chase us away. They have big hearts, even if they are broken. We can drink a dop with them too, because Jesus did so with lots of people like them. The Pharisees hated him for it, so it has to be okay for us too – because we're NOT here to put them on a guilt trip and tell them how they must live their lives or what they must believe. We want them to know Love by *showing* it to them. The reason why we absolutely must NOT speak about Jesus is because He is the God of the white people who treat them like dogs. We have to make real friends by living and working side by side with them every day, because none of them have ever had a white friend, and having a white friend will help them understand that some people aren't white or black or coloured or whatever – they are just people. Once they realise that we are truly people who want to make friends – it will make them curious. They will ask but we mustn't tell them until almost at the end when we are truly friends and our friendship has built that mustard grain of self-esteem. Then we can explain that there is a White Jesus, and a Money Jesus, a TV Jesus and a Political Jesus, sometimes all mixed-up Jesuses too – but there is also a Real Jesus, and we tell them about the Real Jesus and how much the Real Jesus loves them. How we believe He set the whole world free without us even asking. How simply knowing that changed everything we thought important in life. I know they will listen to what we have to say then, because we will have showed them how the Real Jesus feels inside. The Real Jesus will do the rest.

William looked at me and started crying. Really crying. He freaked me out a bit because he sounded so genuinely heartbroken. He told me that he was so, so sorry that the leadership didn't like me, that they always got angry at what I said and refused to listen. He promised to speak to Brian but also warned me that I had to accept realistically that he might not want to hear.

He didn't. And that's the painful irony. I felt I had been warned in my answer the night before:

– *Do not go to your leaders with what I have told you. They will not listen to you* –

Understand please, I am not arrogant or insane enough to think I can personally and singularly hear The Voice Of God, but I am also not so stupid that I won't diligently try to *listen* – and follow up practically with what my gut instincts and empathic choices tell me Scripture is trying to *really* mean. Always and only from the point of:

What does what I believe in make me pray for, and then do, on behalf of others – who have nothing and no one to believe in?

Brian Kinghorn had a speciality in ministering something called the Father Heart of God. I think he wrote a book. Famous for it. How could he be wrong? Why would I feel I had been told he was *my* leader? Wasn't he supposed to be God's leader? See what I mean? Deep down in me – in my sinful, rebellious and kaffirboetie heart – he was just another mad religious Dutchman I had already begun to dislike.

Brian's wife told me I was cursed because of my tattoos.

These were speaking-in-tongues, hands-waving-wildly-in-the-air, Charismatic Christians. Better than anyone else. God's *anointed*. White Christian parents sent their kids to them from all over the country to teach them how to be like them. The anger I felt at these self-centred fools tore me apart. They were supposed to be our role models, like Christ was to his disciples, yet all they could practise was a Program ... of self-adulation, petty emotional manipulation and racism.

As a missionary I saw it so often. Everywhere. So much blindness to the basic needs and pain of others. So much unbridled arrogance and disrespect. The poison in the roots of the entire tree. Making men who could be good— bad. In my heart of hearts I could not believe one of them had *ever* met the Person I had, because if they had they would realise – THAT PERSON IS NOT LIKE THAT. To anybody. Ever.

The very worst I will ever see is after I fall from grace. At the urging of some friends who don't like watching me drink myself into an early grave, I go to the mountains to spend time with a couple who are apparently going to counsel me back into the arms of Jesus. They live in a massive house on an apple farm and are well known in local charismatic Christian circles, operating as counsellors and a praise and worship team. During the time I'm with them I attend meetings and tea parties all over the Western Cape and watch them in action with lovely white people and a smattering of decent coloured folk they enjoy fellowship with. Lighthouse this, Bayview that, Rhema on top, Vineyard the next thing. Later I find out that they operate together with another couple and are a registered Christian charity organisation. To this end they go to all the mega-supermarkets with their registered ministry credentials to obtain shop-soiled goods for a small administrative fee. This is a lot of stuff – cars and trailers full. It all goes into a big storeroom at the back of the house. I am very naive in some ways, so it takes me a while to twig to the fact that they are not doling it out to the starving – they are actually selling the stuff. When I enquire how it works, they tell me they sell it all to the local squatters and poor farmworkers for ten percent less than the store value, and by doing this they finance their *ministry*, give poor black people cheaper food and pay a *tithe* to God – all in one fell swoop.

We don't eat any of this food because the smugly righteous little lady of the house subscribes to a very expensive ultra-health diet invented by a certain Reverend Malkemus of California. She says tinned food is bad for our health. It impairs our immuno-systems and could cause cancer. Our bodies are apparently God's temples and the dear Reverend Malkemus says that we should eat like Adam and Eve did in the Garden of Eden – together with his special, very expensive, patented ultra-food made with seaweed and other weird shit. At that time, a big prayer party for Cape Town takes place at Newlands. They are part of the organising team and enthusiastically sell tickets in their area. Back home we put on our prayer bangles to pray for our region. The little holy cow starts:

– Dear God, we pray for our town and we pray for all Our People. And we want to beg you Lord Jesus, please make these dirty squatter people who bring violence and crime into our town go away. Make them go away back to where they came from … –

Doesn't make financial sense – she wants God to *chase away* her primary source of financial income – but there we go. She complains bitterly when they sell the charity stuff on Saturdays because the squatters smoke and they all smell bad.

Then they hear that they might be able to obtain overseas financing targeted for the upliftment of poor children in southern Africa and immediately start hunting for a farm to buy for their *ministry*. Apparently they want to get addicts and abused people in to work the farm for them – probably at a profit too – while they *minister* to their needs. They unanimously vote it will have to be multiracial – else no money would come through.

I leave in fury, shaking the dust from my heels, and write them a letter in which I tell them they are possibly the worst, sickest snakes and hypocrites I have ever had the displeasure to meet, and people like them are the reason why Christ became so furious in Herod's Temple.

Back when I had finished studying, I was on the management team that organised an international YWAM Expo in Durban. Kids at the conference were supposed to witness for Jesus after the big-name Super-Christians had finished prancing around on the massive sound stage. The leaders armed the laaities with invigorating zeal and verbose evangelistic tracts and sent them off smartly to *convert* the heathen. Black and Indian heathen of course. The stupid, dumb pricks who sent the kids out simply could not understand that a hungry, homeless black man on the streets of Durban would answer – *Yes Baas* – to *anything* a white man said, and he would be way too ashamed even to admit his hunger (unless he were truly desperate) and there was no way he could read English (*his third language*) tracts, because he'd been denied a basic education by the Government that the same leadership had voted in.

The international candidates (*all predominantly white*) refused to eat the catered food. To avoid the strangling red tape, me and a dinkum punk from Holland, with kaleidoscopic hair and a million piercings, stole it all, with a Kombi, in the middle of the night, and went driving all over Durban dishing out the cater packs to bergies sleeping in the streets. We fed hundreds like this every night until I was kicked out. It wasn't worth our trouble asking – the bergies would have gone hungry.

I had another sort of nervous breakdown during the Expo because of this continual raging conflict in me. My madness kicking in after years of it. I walked out of a meeting where people were furiously waving their arms – *singing in the Spirit* – went to Point Road, bought a button outfit, and got fucking gerook.

I was kicked out immediately.

Told me that they all still loved me with *the Love of the Lord* but He had told them that He had opened another door now and had a Very Great Blessing for me in Stellenbosch. Their way of telling me to fuck off in nice clean Christian jargon because once again I had rocked the boat and proved I was an emotionally unstable troublemaker. Bothered by demons and my sin.

*

I borrowed mountaineering gear, went to the Drakensberg, solo-climbed to 2800 metres, made camp just over the border in Lesotho and sat on the cold, lonely, whispering peak, crying in the snow. Up there I realised how small, insignificant and meaningless I was. What the fuck could a socially inadequate skollie like me do to change desperate people's lives? I lit a spliff and was reminded that I had become a backslider too. Apostate. Maybe even lost my Promise.

Hah!

Should not shepherds take care of the flock? You eat the curds, clothe your-selves with the wool and slaughter the choice animals, but you do not take care of the flock. You have not strengthened the weak or healed the sick or bound up the injured. You have not brought back the strays or searched for the lost. You have ruled them harshly and brutally. So they were scattered because there was no shepherd, and when they were scattered they became food for all the wild animals. My sheep wandered over all the mountains and on every high hill. They were scattered over the whole earth, and no one searched or looked for them – Ezekiel 34, Verses 2–6.

Okay, okay, that was a bit of a sermon but it was not meant for you – I needed to make a point to myself, get over all that ugly shit, get on with my life and carefully climb down a bloody high mountain because I had run out of zol and was going to hell again.

PART IV

Schmangled

Here in the old water
where we trudge,
Wandering the muddy aftermath
That drowned The Tree of Life,
And as we go about our New Planting
We hear a curse.
Old Sailor has tried to grow a memory
Of The Forbidden Tree again
But he could not.
It never survived The Flood ...

I die from a plant I ate,
Somewhere in New Eden
and drift back to water memories,
the blood-filled darkness of my birth.
I find the way up to HEAVEN,
And You are there!!
I lie down in HELL,
AND You are here!!
This means: You have always been Here
And somehow You know the way out ...

17

The Double-Dip Rooibaard Test

gibt dem opi opium
den opium bringt
dem opi um
(Swiss German pün)

＊

I think I should have started this tale by saying— I was born to smuggle. I learnt the nuts and bolts at school by selling *stoppe* to the other ouens and polished my skills during the holidays. I think the first proper zol operation I ran was with my then best friend Martin and an ou called Kees. I might be wrong. Some parts of the last twenty years have been absolute raving chaos, much of which I don't remember in any reliable sort of chronology. At this juncture it's probably good to mention that by now my life experiences had developed into clearly detached parallels. By this I mean that I lived in worlds separated from each other by work, drugs, twisted religion, our beautifully fucked-up politics and my own emotional shit. So, in true African style, this part of my story will reflect incident-driven sketches rather than a singular unwinding chronicle. This way I can separate the major events and issues and avoid being confusing about exactly what happened when.

It's not that important anyway.

I climbed down that high cold mountain, replete with my lonely rejection by God – as conveyed to me by His special servants – then briefly enjoyed the incredible hospitality of the rural Zulus, something which helped to heal my spirit a little. They scored me some very good zol and I prepared to get my arse back to Angola and fight. I bought knives in Joburg, packed a kit for the bundu and started hitchhiking.

What else was I good for?

In Kimberley I met up with two teenage fuckups walloping from reformatory to go work in an escort agency in Cape Town. They were about to be gang-raped by a bunch of truckers, so I did the right thing and escorted them. In a township where we stopped to score zol, they created absolute bedlam by dressing up in the cammo uniforms I took with me to cross the Angolan border. We were chased all over the place by anti-terrorist gattas in a Casspir armed to the teeth.

I have never been so glad to see the backs of anyone.

I ended up back in Stellenbosch, because I had wasted my meagre funds on the two little fools. I found a job in a restaurant, but the Christian family I was living with kicked me out of their house when they discovered I was quietly suiping and smoking zol. That was it. I was out of the church and back on the streets. I wandered around in a painful parallel world that we will still get to, made a new best friend named Martin and fucked up a marriage to a multimillionaire's daughter who I don't want to speak about – for her sake. The only good thing in our marriage was hunting marlin with her dad off Durban. I drifted from that mess, met women and bedded them, and was recruited by an American supercomputer manufacturer and trained to program. I'm apparently stupidly good at it, even though it bores me to tears. Something or other in my right brain seems to work in hex and occasionally in binary. Then I had a brief hot relationship with a girl so energetic that after a wild drunken party I awake to find myself in darkness. As I try to puzzle this out I realise I'm stark naked, lying face down on the floor in my bedroom, and my sex-kitten – Ratbag – is sprawled on top of me snoring gently in my ear. And we can't move. The entire double bed is lying on top of us. On top of the bed is my wardrobe. And I have absolutely no idea what happened except that I have a torn muscle in my midriff. I broke up with her by choice because of my addiction to buttons, and met and started shacking up with one of the most gorgeous women in Stellenbosch. A stunning chick with a perfect body and tinkling musical voice named Norma.

Anyway, we were living in a state of low-grade anarchy in a semi-commune with murals of Judge Dredd and insane graffiti scribbled in eleven languages everywhere. Housekeeping was treated minimalistically and the kitchen was utterly overrun with about five hundred empty Tassenberg bottles lining every inch of free space. I had one room with Norma. Martin had the other. Incidentally, he and Norma have two lovely children now, which is the reason why he is my ex-best friend (*beating the everliving shit out of him fucked on acid and jealousy may have helped*). Various strange people wandered in and out and got fucked with us on pipes in the Band

Room or pissed on beer we sold out of a huge yellow fridge with Evol painted on it raggedly in crimson – a backhanded tribute to Sonic Youth.

Some completely mal writer ou lived in our kitchen. His name was André. Real funny fucker too. Woke up one morning and announced brightly that he needed to piss off to the nearest Wimpy, bum LOTS of coffee and start writing furiously, because he needed to pull off a cultural revolution – but only after he had shaved his head and changed his cultural name to Koos Kombuis. He wrote a song about the drummer in our band – Johnny. Says in his song Johnny isn't dead. If I know Johnny at all, wherever he is, they are wearing earmuffs and everybody else is cranking up their amps because no one can hear jackshit.

Oh, our band's name was 18 BC.

Reason for this was quite simple. But let's first introduce the band:

There's Johnny, maniacal fan of Lars Ulrich from Metallica and drummer from hell – although they wouldn't tolerate the noise down there either. Martin, best ex-mate and purloiner of girlfriend, on rhythm guitar. Freddy, currently eminent paediatrician in USA and stridently intense German lead guitarist. Then Maya, bassist with attitude. Maya freaked out everybody in Stellenbosch in those days because she never wore shoes. And to top off this disturbing behaviour she wore rings and bells on her toes too. Probably the most intelligent member of the band because she cum lauded her Electrical Engineering degree and then went and kicked the shit out of a Fine Arts one. Then there's yours insincerely, running around with freaky wild hair, tattoos, a million bangles, piercings and even freakier wild clothing. On vocals. Scaring the crap out of the audience. All indulging in cacophonous mayhem for entertainment and a creative means to avoid studying or, in my case, de-stressing from my high-pressure IT career.

We shared equipment with a very good bra of ours named Pierre who formed a band at the same time called Valiant Swart with an old school mate named Vikkers and a seriously talented guitarist who was one of my neighbours called Little Anton L'amour. In our band, me and Freddy did all the song-writing except for one called 'Dog Mind' which Martin and I wrote, but the problem for us was we didn't have a band name yet.

Jesus Jumps, The Humping Grannies and Soilent Shit Brown are a few I remember being tossed out by the band members – but nobody could agree. We were trying to be a democratic band while furiously attempting to resolve artistic differences and get Johnny to fucking play softer – *please bra.* Still, nobody could agree. As we were packing up one night after practice, Maya pointed to a box in which we kept leads, pedals and other communal band shit. On it was printed— *Simonsberg / 18 Baby Cheese.* We loved this, and decided that because the band name issue was now resolved we could finally book a gig. Though we shortened it and postered ourselves as 18 BC.

This created something of a stir among the local happy clappies, as I'll explain ...

There was this bra of ours named Konrad. A slightly depressed ou who dressed in black, painted his room completely black and only listened to The Cure. He had hand-painted pictures of Robert Smith painted in – you guessed it – black. We got him to design a nice goth poster for us, so he painted a picture of a character called The Horned God from the Judge Dredd comics. He stands in a sea of skulls, branded with barcodes and riddled with bullets, swinging a good likeness of a Fender Strat over his bust horn. Venue, time and cover charge appear elsewhere. Emblazoned boldly above a huge meteor-pocked planet rising behind the deific buck-meister is our name – 18 BC.

Bloody nice job.

Okay, so we go to the gig. The usual crowd is there, although only Mal-jan is out of hand. He's fucked on magic mushrooms and has a box of firecrackers I stupidly left in his care, and keeps throwing lighted big-bangs at the Rastas, who are playing later, yelling – *Waarth's Jah? Waarth's Jah?* What a *lag.* Anyway, we always go on stage in pitch darkness, because I made this huge anarchy symbol out of thick steel wire. We took an old sheet, tore it into strips, wound it around the frame, and dipped it into molten wax. We wound sparklers around everything and put it on stage. As we started playing our warm-up song, I lit one of the legs on the A.

In retrospect, Stellenbosch was not ready for us. Traditionally, Stellen-bosch bands were greeted by their audiences all sitting down talking kak loudly, lighting surreptitious spliffs and downing copious quantities of Tassenberg and Black Label. Not ours. Our audiences used to back away from the stage as far as possible and mill around wild-eyed and uncertain. Nobody could hear a fucking thing – mostly because of Johnny. I expected panties, but all I got were terrified looks on flickering faces from the blaze behind me.

That particular gig was a total riot. We finished playing, downed some tequila and decided to piss off for a lekker pipe. Outside there was a huge crowd of people armed with tracts, trying to stop mense coming in. Martin and I staggered up to one well-dressed young man who seemed to be in charge and asked him what the score was. He gave Martin a tract. On it was a small reproduction of our poster and some convoluted warning about Satanism. Inside, amidst a jungle of fiery scriptures and the usual stupid ranting, was a breakdown of the band's name. Apparently 18 BC was 6+6+6 Before Christ and we were trying to trap people subliminally into a life of devil worship. Martin lurched towards the obviously misguided young fellow and asked him if he had seen us play. No, they didn't need to – The Lord had shown them in a vision and led them into spiritual warfare. Even scarier was the fact that the boere Anti-Satanist Squad were parked outside too – glaring balefully in our general direction.

Mal-jan, in the meantime, had made a wise theological about-turn and was throwing firecrackers at the Christians instead of the Rastas, which in itself was causing a sub-riot as pious cheeks not only turned meekly but ran like hell to get away from him.

Anyway, back from the digression – Martin and I could not afford our budding alternative rock careers, so we decided to make a plan for money. We agreed one night that we were sick to death of people knocking at all hours to buy beer and that the only sensible thing to do would be to close our shebeen. I have no clue where Koos and our chicks were, but we had a crate full of pints and a few loose ones left in Evol. We also had a fat bankie of Durban Poison courtesy of Norma's sister who lived there and sent us some from time to time.

I put on Pink Floyd and cranked it all the way up. We couldn't sit in the Band Room because the noise from the PA would shatter the bottles. Undeterred, we simply dumped them on the kitchen floor, sat down and tried to drink the whole bloody lot. I screamed to Martin that we should score a big stash from the Kei and sell it off to the ouens. Problem was, neither of us could go, because of responsibilities. I had a car and Martin would finance buying the zol from his student loan, but we needed a driver. Our buddies were all confirmed lunatics, which narrowed down our recruitment drive, and although some of them were stark raving crazy, not all of them would necessarily jump at the idea of embarking on an organised crime venture. For fucksake, try whatshisname – the mutherfucker who had a live boomslang running around in his room. Ja, James.

Never. And Makatot the mallit who cracked my occipital orbit with a pistol I stole from him. Er ... no. Kees, we decided. Kees would do nicely, and we knew he would do anything criminal if he thought we could get away with it. Tiefchild.

He leapt at the idea, so Martin wrote a cheque, I gave him my car keys and Kees fucked off in the general direction of Port St Johns. A few days later we are sitting in the Band Room, bored, stoned and playing a variation of dominoes we invented called double-double. Kees walks in. His expression is badly inscrutable. Did he score the zol?

Ja bra. But, there is a small problem.

The small problem turned out to be a HUGE FUCKING DISASTER for me.

He had managed to kill a sheep on his way back, because the Transkei locals had no concept of what the fuck fences were. The car's nose was smashed in. On the bright side, though, the whole boot was full of good *boom*.

I locked the boot, pocketed my keys and the three of us went up to the Band Room for a protracted screaming match.

I was adamant that nobody was getting nothing until my car was fixed and klaar, bra. Fuck me, Martin wanted his money back. Kees was freaking because he had done the job and risked years in jail. I won. The car was fixed, Martin was paid back and the rest of the profit was enough to buy a bottle of Tassies for us to share morosely in De Akker. It seemed Crime was a Fucking Bad Debtor. You make out? One of those naaiers who never pay.

I think the next mission I pulled off with my girlfriend. We went down to Port St Johns, crossed the river in a fifty-cent ferry and walked all the way to Agate Terrace. There we hired a hut for two rand a day. The place to score was further north and called Poenskop. I used to go deep. I would find children who had never seen a white man before. They would run up to me and touch my skin in amazement. Here we swopped old clothes, blankets and shoes for an enormous amount of Rooibaard. This was then promptly stuffed into a rucksack, and we headed for the filthy, cold Grahamstown Festival. We sold it and smoked it surreptitiously with celebrities who were all terrified *Huisgenoot* would find out and fuck up their careers. All except ous like Koos, who chowed too many space cakes we made one day and was so completely fucked that he couldn't sing. He just sat grinning wildly at the audience. It was the – *I haven't taken my Thorazin, arsehole* – expression in his eyes that freaked a few of the more faint-hearted Afrikaner bokkies who came to watch him play. That was quite a hectic gig, if I remember correctly …

Koos was doubled up with Pierre, and after Valiant Swart had played, the kak started. These ous are some of my very best friends and I have an enormous amount of respect for them. They managed to give South Africa's white Afrikaans Generation X an alternative identity that has bloomed and prospered beautifully. Obviously some of their more boneheaded contemporaries didn't dig this. Three of them started in on the members of the band. I was sprawled at the back of the place absolutely smashed from space cakes and a bottle of whiskey. With me were Bradley The Good Sprog and Norma. Bradley The Good Sprog was my stuffed toy gorilla and my favourite *2000 AD* character next to Judge Dredd. He went everywhere with us and was the most amazing babe magnet imaginable. Chicks digged him. Anyway … The small yappy one was giving Little Anton L'amour kak. The ordinary crunchie was backing him and Baksteen-met-'n-boepens was keeping everyone else at bay. They were taking the band to task for not being right, loyal Dutchmen. I clambered to my feet and lurched over badly. One of them, I think it was the ordinary one, was waving some Beemer keys around to prove how much better he was than anybody else there, so I told him – *I suppose that makes your dick a foot long*. Then somebody punched me. I think it might have been Baksteen-met-'n-boepens, because he looked like he might be dumb enough to think he could take me on. I turned around, staggered off to my table, picked up the empty whiskey bottle and came back. Maltese poodle tells me they are not afraid of my whiskey bottle. So I skiem what the fuck, toss it away, grab a mike stand and beat the shit out of them, starting with Baksteen-met-'n-boepens. Him, I eventually grab and hurl face forward into a corner. I'm gonna kill the mutherfucker. Break his fucking bonehead neck. Norma jumps onto my back like a wild cat screaming at me not to.

I didn't – and so a couple of well-beaten-up fuckwits ran like hell from a cultural revolution.

Smuggling a bit of zol every winter became our habit over the years, and not only financed the festival for us but also allowed us to carry on up to Durban and watch the ouens surf the Gunston 500.

Luckily we never got caught.

Then I did my first acid trip.

Fuck china, what a ride.

Martin scores the shit, and we all drop. The entire band plus girlfriends and onlookers. They are double-dip smileys and knock the everliving shit out of us. An hour later we are rolling around on the ground screaming with laughter. Somewhere deep inside the roller-coaster hilarity I realise something is getting out of hand. I'm losing it. I put myself into Das mode and order Norma to get up and come buy beer with me – *now*. This is so absurd we all crack up again. Eventually I manage to get the poor woman on her feet and we stagger off in a very warped flightpath towards the nearest bottle store. On the way I decide to freak Norma out and point towards the sky and ask her to tell me how blue it is. This is in the middle of the Pick 'n Pay parking lot and we're very nearly pissing ourselves, rolling around on the tarmac, which is causing traffic problems and very definitely attracting attention. I get her back on her feet again and we fragily point ourselves towards the NBS. I buy a bunch of quarts, down half of one outside the bottle store and pass it to Norma. Then I stand waiting for it to help. The fucking thing doesn't, and the journey back to the Priory is an absolute circus being butt-fucked by a nightmare.

Later we are supposed to go for band practice. This is difficult. We all pile into Johnny's car but he can't drive. It has started raining and the windscreen wipers are freaking him out too much. So I drive, because I seem to be the most intact of all of us – fucking carefully.

We are sharing a practice room with a jazz band called the Kreefgat Swingsters, Valiant Swart and a Dal Rasta band. The Kreefgatte are busy and Slaptjip on Sax tells us to come back at nine.

I insist on going to De Akker.

A small argument later and we are on our way, everybody trying to chill Johnny out because of the windscreen wipers. So we arrive, go in, say hi to Aubrey and Jose, and order a round from them. I down mine immediately and decide to roll a spliff. I am, by the way, carrying a parcel of zol in my pocket. I suppose I should mention that the pocket in question is attached to a Dutch Army bush jacket, with Russian flags sewn to the shoulders and a big badge on the back declaring Led Zeppelin to be the Hammer of the Gods. I am not wearing a shirt and I have absolutely terrible jeans on and no shoes. I march out of De Akker boldly and walk over to the garage. Not the new one, the old one. I plonk down my beer, open the pak on the grass, tear off a piece of check to roll the spliff in and start maaling. Martin and Norma come back out, giggling to each other, and pass me on the way to the old Porra café up the road. I finish rolling the spliff and step back into the street to see where Martin and Norma are. Nowhere to be seen. So I step back towards the pak and hear brakes behind me. I look over my shoulder and see a boerevan. Fuck!

I step towards the pak and in one fluid movement I pick it up and begin tossing it into the long grass. I drop the newspaper and start tearing up the joint. This done, I pick up my beer and move back towards the pub. That's when the gattas react. They jump out. Two coloured boere. The one grabs me and the other starts hunting in the grass with a torch. I skutted the pak well because they don't find any of it, but they do find a half-inch of the joint that I never tore properly. They arrest me and take me to the van. At this juncture Makatot comes staggering out the pub, sees this, and is about to tell the boere they cannot arrest me because I'm tripping on candy. Somehow he realises this is a kak idea and lets them put me in.

I am always getting harassed by the gattas. Especially the coloured ones. They don't like me because I'm always crossing the fucking Group Areas Act and going into Stellenbosch's townships to my bras. I lose every single giggle and get befuck like I always do with these cunts. We arrive at the boere station and I get taken inside. They start on me with their infantile shit. I start yelling and swearing at them, telling them how we are going to kill them all with pangas and necklaces when the revolution comes.

This definitely does not help matters.

They take me to the cells, still trying to get my name out of me, so I scream that my name is James Marshall Hendrix. Jimi Fucking Hendrix! They lock me up in a cell and I start baying my head off, kicking the bars and making one hell of a racket. About ten minutes later, seven of them arrive. They unlock the cell, grab me, hold me down and empty a can of CS teargas into my face.

The first few hours, I almost cannot breath because of the pain. I am just crawling around in circles trying to whimper. Eventually it becomes more bearable, but the acid is amplifying everything.

I trip on pure pain – micro-second by micro-second.

Next morning I hear them coming for me. I will not give them the satisfaction of a free smirk. When I walk into the charge office, all the bastards are waiting to see the fun – but so am I. I give them all the biggest shit-eating grin I can and tell them loudly I love their sense of humour, it was lots of fun – now who is gonna book me and take me to court? I am formally booked and charged as Jimi Hendrix, although their tiny brains are clever enough to recover and taunt me by calling me James Arsehole Hendrix.

In court, Martin lends me shoes and Kees lends me a shirt. We rip the badges off the arms of the jacket – the magistrate can't see the Led Zeppelin badge on the back.

The magistrate is still not pleased to see me in his court – yet again – and doles out a fat fine that everybody whips around to pay off.

I come down – but I burn for three days.

In spite of all the kak with the gattas, I really, really enjoyed that acid. I was tuned in and turned on! It also became the beginning of how I managed to eventually escape buttons in my ugly parallel world after Johnny died. But ja, come – let's go get that all over with …

18

Puff the Magic Dragon

I am probably one of the reasons why Johnny died. See, at the beginning Johnny never smoked zol. But the rest of us all did. I was probably also his closest friend, although being a lot older, I think I was more of a mentor to him.

Pause for a bit of history ...

We were booted out of our original semi-commune by the irate owner of the pozzie for simply not paying the rent for months. Then, to rub salt into it, we got our chicks to sign a new lease, moved straight back in and still refused to pay up. After our final and very firm eviction we ended up moving into the old nunnery next to the Catholic church.

It was called the Priory and we turned it into a den of narcotic iniquity. Especially acid.

When we smoked zol, we almost always did so in Martin's room, because he had a good hi-fi and a computer with games. Now, as I've told you before, the politics of bottleneck smoking is that you always get fired from the left and the fireman automatically scores the second hit. I cannot remember the number of times Johnny fired me, because he always sat next to me, and without thinking I would pass him the pipe. And immediately have to apologise as he passed it on. It became a bit of a joke after a while.

On his birthday I stupidly did it again, and to the amazement of everybody he said nothing and hit it. Impressed the hell out of me because he hit hard and straight like an ou-roeker without coughing.

So that was it – Johnny was now a *boom*-roeker. And three months later he was a buttonkop.

Before I carry on, let's jump back. Right back, to when I first came to Stellenbosch from Worcester and joined that charismatic church which kicked me out a few years later. A pattern had started from the time I had my very first spiritual breakdown in Worcester. I would come tumbling out of the doors of the church riding a pious boot and end up face down in the mud of the mean streets. Dark mud. Smelly mud. Interesting mud.

Let's go have a look at that mud.

But not in Worcester, let's start later on in Stellenbosch, the very night I broke up with my Miss Matie girlfriend. I decided that I was the world's biggest polecat, on God's enemy list number 1, and the best thing to do under the circumstances was to get as fucked as humanly possible and wait for hell.

That meant I had to score.

In the South Africa that I grew up in during apartheid the only place to score was in a kas. A location.

Stellenbosch has three. Two coloured ones – Cloetesville, better known as the Dal, and Idas Valley, known as the Vlei – and Kayamandi, the black one. That night I grabbed my panga, shoved it up my sleeve and walked to the nearest one – Cloetesville. I felt safer with the panga and wanted it because it was going to facilitate me scoring what I needed.

Let's not fuck around. Townships are dangerous places late at night.

At any rate, I found the nearest dice game, asked the okes where I could score and got sorted out easily.

This is how I met my friend Gertjie Schoeman, better know as Oudste. In the measure of things, he is my oldest china. His teenage son Alex is my godson but back then me and Oudste were buttonkoppe. He also had a small crew of ouens called the Bad Boy$. They were: Bernard, Kevin, Ma-oes, Arthur, Innocent, Peikel, Skollie, Pietertjie, known as Mr Kuiken and who later became Pikes – and of course Oudste. They welcomed me as an immediate honorary member. Because there was another Skollie in the crew, our *gamas* were lengthened. Ronald became Skollie Gangster and I became Skollie Papillon.

It was an uncanny feeling walking from my place in the white part of town to go visit Oudste in the Dal. It was like walking straight from one world into another. Like I was travelling from a false world to a real one. From a narcissistic white Jesus who always wanted more empty buildings and money to a colourless Jesus who cried in the garden for the many children living in shacks without drinking water. From white Afrikaner to coloured Afrikaner. From social rejection to blanket acceptance. From wealth to abject poverty. From *kaffirboetie* to my *ma se-kind*.

And for years and years I was the only white man who walked there.

The truth was, I really and truly loved my coloured friends, and going there felt like going home. The spiritual conflict was terrible. In terms of drug addiction they were just as fucked as me, but I didn't see any grounds to judge them for it. I only judged myself. I could never explain to my white friends that I *needed* to go to the townships regularly because it made me feel real and alive. Skollie was a much more real person than the socially misfitted Buttonkop Alex everybody knew in the white Bos. And somehow in the township there was always a plate of food and a bed to sleep in somewhere. In the Dal I could go jolling anywhere with Oudste. And we did. In the white Bos we had to pretend that he was my garden boy so we could be seen on the streets together. I gave him drugs that whiteys liked, including his first two trips.

What a *lag*.

I give the bugger one and he drops it. Damned good candy too. Half an hour later the ou starts demanding another one from me. Tunes me it's a dud, it's not working. I tune him to chill, just wait. Nooit, he wants another one. I tell him no. He comes back at me and asks what would happen if *he* had all the candy and I asked *him* for a second trip. Okay, he wants to haul out the big guns so I give the fucker another one. Then he insists on going home. This entails walking from the Priory back to his ma's pozzie in the Dal. Only now he's starting to feel it.

Apparently the boere picked him up for *Dronk op Straat* and he told me later that he wasn't even aware he was in a cell he was tripping so hectically.

By the time I met Johnny, Oudste had been my closest bra in the Dal for years.

My other very close china was Evil. Joey Leith. He came from a desperately poor part of Idas Valley called the Kreefgat.

Of course I met all these ous scoring buttons and *boom*. But I eventually knew all the merchants in Stellenbosch, and with a few exceptions they certainly didn't become my close friends. The reason I mention it is because the boere used to skut me constantly and tell me repeatedly that the only reason why I was there was because of drugs. Especially the coloured gattas.

Evil used to work for another china of mine named Ash, who merted wine, beer, buttons and zol. I worked for him too. I had a car, and me, Evil and a couple of guards like Tande and Boetamanki would take guns and a bag of money and go buy buttons all over Crossroads, Guguletu and Khayelitsha. I was the driver and tester. At each merchant we would test a pill and match the kick to the price, trying to get the best bang for bucks.

I was damned good at it.

At the time, the second biggest industry in Stellenbosch was Corobrick. One of the results of Bishop Tutu's disinvestment programme was that it closed down. This did absolutely fuckall to the white mense in the Bos, but it fucked things up for everybody in the Vlei, the Dal and the Kaya. Some of those mense had two families subsisting on a single salary. There was no other work, so the okes sat around bored and frustrated, smoking button pipes and suiping. This in turn led to an upswing in street and domestic violence and higher demands on the local drug trade.

And a war started in the Vlei and eventually split over into the Dal.

There were two major merchants in the Vlei. The Yard and the Kreefgat. Ash started off the Yard behind the house his father owned. At some point he went down for a stretch and his brother Red took over. By the time Ash came out the mang, Red and their little brother Joe'a had well taken over and expanded the business. Being the eldest, Ash reckoned it was time to take back control, but Red offered him a job on the floor instead, working for commission. Ash told Red to go fuck himself and started his own business in the Kreefgat. That's how the war started, because Ash soon took over more than half the market.

Now, the okes who were working and buying from Ash formed a loose crew. There was nothing to do except kap nuts and watch videos, which the ouens did avidly. Their favourites were B-grade war flieks. Especially Vietnam. To this end they named themselves the Vietnam Rotte. Once again, I was an honorary Vietnam Rot, but I drew the line at peroxiding my hair.

The Rotte and the Yard started fighting. I was caught in the middle because I was very good bras with Joe'a. It ended in tragedy when Joe'a stabbed Ash to death one afternoon. But the brothers and fathers all killed each other during power struggles in that family.

Understand that for me to find acceptance among these people and to list them among my closest friends meant that I had to be a skollie. Survival is one of my skills. I've lost count of the number of times I've been shot at, threatened with sharp goeters, wharrawharra, but, like I said, it held a strange attraction for me.

Maybe you can understand why I used the term parallel worlds. I was living out of two completely different personas. Different language, name, cultural identity – the works. Like a bizarre cultural chameleon.

Having always been a bit of an idealist, I decided to start bringing my white chinas to the townships with me. Martin, Norma, all of them. However, I could see that my crude attempts at social engineering were an anarchism to both sides. My coloured chommies went into *baas* mode and the whiteys felt nervous, uncomfortable and sometimes downright nauseated. That said, a hell of a lot of people really appreciated the experience. Like a trip to the moon or something. And it did change for them all a bit eventually.

Johnny was one of those.

When I met Johnny, Skollie Papillon was already a township institution. It was known that an oke had tried to steal my car radio and got chased through the Dal with an axe. I'd survived being caught in the crossfire between gangsters and gattas and a host of things I'm not gonna go into now. Let's just establish that Johnny saw me in my Skollie persona and wanted in. I so wish he were still alive and could read what happened to me at school and why I stopped being a white man and became a skollie, because I struggled to explain this to him. It only *seemed* like fascinating fun. It was dangerous, depressing and fucked everything up. The problem was, people in glass houses and all that. I'd been living in racial duality for years, so how could I deny Johnny? He was the kind of ou who would try and imitate me without understanding the underlying cultural tensions and get himself into trouble. My reasoning was that it would be better if I took him under my wing.

There were quite a few whitey buttonkoppe in Stellenbosch at the time. And we obviously knew each other and schnaaied, fought and chopped nuts together. It was a loose fraternity of birds of ragged feather, most of the time arguing over creams and second hits. Very much the lost generation. Addicts are usually only narcotic acquaintances, but Johnny was not only an artistic partner of mine, he was also an oke I loved.

He wanted me to teach him how to be a skollie. Lots of reasons why too. For instance:

One night we're at a big gig just outside the Bos but we don't have zol. Me and Johnny decide to take his car to the Kaya and score.

I knew where.

On the way to his cabbie we pass the kitchen and look in to see crates of beer stacked on a table with nobody around. We nip in, grab a crate each and run. We dump them in the boot of Johnny's car and hit the road.

To me it's like, what the fuck, Al? You're fucking stealing again and you know it always gets you into kak – but Johnny's just done the most insane, naughtiest thing in his life. I mean, it is kak funny, and I forgot to mention that we were both tripping at the time. That's why we wanted zol so badly. To come down a bit.

So we get to the Kaya, stop the cabbie and go into one of the compound bungalows to a black bra of mine. He scores a pak to us and we leave. We get back to the cabbie and find some ou inside trying to steal the radio. Johnny reverts to whitey fury and starts yelling. The next thing the oke is facing us with a knife. I slap Johnny in the chest to shut him up, go straight into Das mode and tell the darkie it's cool. Just go. I can see the ou is terrified and if anybody gets stuck it will be because he feels trapped. He's able to read my gedagte and my pluk so he turns and runs away. We go back to the party.

It was a big jol to Johnny. Almost a mystical mystery. For me it was so ingrained and instinctive that I don't know how I did it myself sometimes.

Another night I decide I've had enough of whitey pseudo-liberal-intellectual bullshit washed down with Tassies in De Akker and decide to get down with the real mense. That means Kayamandi, because I feel like having a jol with my black bras. Get on a pluk and find a pool game. Okay so I walk in. Cruise off to one of my chinas and score. Quarts and *boom*. What saved my life was the fact that I wasn't in a hurry. I already had a pipe maaled on and *stopped*. All I needed was a fireman. I'm standing outside the bungalow when I notice a big crew of youngish tsotsis coming my way. None of them are smiling, and in the townships I know people always smile on their way to the shebeen. Okay, so I figure they have to be after me.

So how do I deal with this situation? I can't run like hell because that would mean losing my Black Labels and I didn't just walk one hell of a long way only to leave them behind. Their leader gets to me and I realise I'm in shit. The okes are APLA. PAC military wing.

Human nature is totally weird. The simplest of acts can derail an entire chain of carefully planned events. As the dude gets to me I give him a box of matches and ask him for a light. Now, on a list of dumb things to do when being confronted by an oke who wants to put a tyre around your neck, shove a rock in your mouth, pour petrol all over your kop and set you on fire – actually giving the crazy bastard a box of matches has to rank at number one. But this very act completely disarms the oke, because he's waiting for me to say something but all I'm doing is waiting for a light. African nature is so predictable in some ways, even though it can infuriate whiteys. See, this oke was intent on performing pyromanic mayhem to my person, but being the good picannin his ma raised, his African politeness kicks in and he fires my pipe instead. The moment it is lit, I pass it to him, reach down and pop the cap off a beer. Now, in township drug politics you share everything. It's the ubuntu thing whiteys don't understand. I had initiated an African ritual by giving the pipe to him. And you can never stay befuck with an oke you smoke nchangu with. That includes all his buddies too. Drinking in townships is usually done in a small glass which is passed from man to man, exactly like that dop I had with those coloured ouens as a laaitie. I had a glass, which I'd borrowed from the ou I scored from, and I immediately pour myself a shot of beer, down it, and by the time the oke finishes taking a hit on the pipe, I have his shot poured. That sets me up as what is known as the driver. It means that I will determine who drinks with me. Smoking I've already taken care of. Now I say to him, howzit bra, what's the story?

Fuck, ten minutes later these okes are whipping around for more beer and zol. We've exchanged phone numbers, they've told me at length that I am without any doubt the coolest white man they have ever met, and they all want to come visit me in town asap. What a *lag*.

See, Johnny would never understand that words like *kaffir* and *hotnot* did not exist in the way I saw the world unless I was being facetious. I had spent all my life making it my business to cross boundaries. Make no mistake, the coloureds and blacks loathed each other far worse than ordinary white racism. Too many black okes also remembered the sting when Botha gave the coloureds a token government and they snubbed them. And coloureds didn't give a shit. In the coloured community a kaffir was still a kaffir.

See, so I actually had dual racial identity between the black township and the coloured ones too. Very few people crossed the township borders. And when they trudged all the way into town to serve the whiteys, they ignored each other. Living a life of crossing those boundaries only made me a kaffirboetie to certain whites and the boere, but strangely enough the black and coloured ous didn't care that I had friends everywhere, even though they didn't.

Johnny wanted me to teach him how to survive in the townships and

I wanted to, but how would I make a Das out of him? Because that's what it would take for him to walk where I walked and have the friends that I had. And of course, most of all, he would have to try to survive being a fucked-up buttonkop. Just like me.

Some time after Norma, Martin and myself broke up badly, I started going out with a girl named Helena. We arrived at a chick named Tania's for a house-warming party, which had turned into a wake. Johnny, his girlfriend Michelle and another oke called Stewart managed to get hit by a train coming back from Kayamandi. I found out from a black connection of mine named Haastig that it was the third time they went in to score buttons that day. And, because every cent they had went on pills, the Beetle could barely run. You had to climb into the car through the one window, because both doors were fucked. So was the starter. Haastig told me Michelle was driving because Johnny was almost too fucked to stand. He was the only one who knew how to keep the cabbie going.

And then they stalled on the train tracks in afternoon rush hour, with the five o' clock Metro to Cape Town approaching.

*

Johnny, I'm sorry I never taught you how to be a Das, boetie, because that would have kept you alive. I'm also sorry that you smoked your first pipe with me. It's cheap, but I chopped a nut on your grave the day we buried you. After your ma and pa and your sissie and all your chommies had gone – I came back and I smoked a button on your grave. I cried for you, my friend, and tried to make it my last one. It wasn't immediately. But they never got hold of me as badly again, and when I finally stopped crying for you and all my other dead friends – I found I had also stopped smoking Mandrax and all the other shit. And my real friends still remained.

You should have waited, boetie. There was so much on the way. New music, drugs, parties, ideas – love – and Uncle Guvvie let Nelson Mandela out the mang. It all helped to make it a little bit better.

I miss you Johnny.

19

Informal Apothecaries
and Toxic Priests

A mate of mine named Paulie put word on the street that he was look-ing for me. I found him and he offered me a bed in his kitchen and chow from the restaurant where he was an executive chef. We came up with the bright idea of going to the *land* and scoring zol. We had two connections. One in Crossroads and the other in Gugs. We started buying from them, making up bankies and flogging them to our mates. The demand for acid was critical. People would pay almost anything for it. At this point we decided to expand the business a little and score some from Cape Town, only we didn't know where to score except a club called The Playground. We went there and Paulie bumped into an old mate of his named Raymond. They used to run all the goeters into The Doors in Joburg when Paulie was still at school. We were connected! Seriously.

We dropped the whole zol thing except for our own rookstop and got serious. We moved acid, coke and some pills I had never tried before called Ecstasy. I had to learn all about coke. I was taken under the wing of one of the owners of The Playground. The mildly infamous Mr Freebody Esq. – half-insane Chinese, half-lunatic Pom, and totally psychotic don't-give-a-flying-fuck mad cunt. The dear man taught me how it all works. He showed me how to put baby's teething powder into very good coke and make it average. And how to measure a gram on a diamond scale to point nine of a gram so that on every nine grams you get an extra one. I learnt some new vocabulary and found that snorting it up your nose is called schnaaaaaafing. Makes sense. Paul showed me how to wrap Ecstasy and acid (wearing surgical gloves) in tin foil and then stick it to a very long strip of black insulation tape on a reel – with Prestik stuffed into the hole. The whole reel was then rewound and stuck to a wall or under a bar counter in whatever club we were servicing. Customers would come up and we'd simply unroll whatever they wanted, tear off the strip and then stick it back where it was. In the event of a raid, we could simply walk away. No possession – no bust ...

And I met my first crackhead.

I didn't even know what crack was. I knew it had something to do with coke and rocks or something.

We arrive at this ou's house and the first thing I notice is that it's inside a heavy security building. He has tom. The second thing is this idiot is waving a Taurus around. Now I don't like guns unless they are going to be used – so this oke is freaking me out big time. Then he gets a phone call and swears to some other ou that— he's not touching charlie any more, bra. What a naai. If you want to do something, just fucking do it. Anyway, so this fuckwit tells us he wants to look at a gram. We give him one and then I discover he is insane. He takes the mutherfucking thing and throws it into a little herb bottle half-filled with water. Paul looks at me with a bit of a grin in his eyes because he actually knows the score. I don't give a fuck, I'm gonna disarm this poes and he is gonna give me my tom for that gram. Ray sees what I'm thinking and tunes me to chill and watch. Crackhead takes a packet of bicarb out and puts a half-teaspoon in with the coke. Then he proceeds to twirl the bottle slowly over a candle. To my fucking amazement I see something like a larva lamp jol starting to happen in the bottle. Ray tells me this is called turning the coke. It's a chemical process called freebasing. Eventually Krakkop takes it and dumps into a glass with a silk scarf stretched over the top. The oily ball dries instantly and Ray explains that this is a rock. I'm amazed. Krackbrain decides that my fascination needs fulfilment and makes me a pipe. He takes out a small, thin, beautiful lathed brass baseball bat and starts burning a tiny ball of steel wool with a lighter. This he inserts into the mouth of the pipe and cracks the rock. He takes a piece and melts it carefully into the steel wool. Ray tells me this is called batting. Duh. Then he tells me to take two lighters that he has bound with a hair band, make a big flame and heat the coke. I immediately understand what's cutting. I make a flame and, at Paul's urging, do it ultra-slowly and make sure that the flame never touches the coke. And I fuck off somewhere into our solar system. The rush hits me so hard – because I did it right – that I start convulsing and slide off the couch stretched between Sea Point and Star Wars. About a minute later I realise that this is exactly the same kak as buttons with the exception that buttons are diving off the edge of the world but with this it is like being shot straight up in one of those cartoon cannons. Welcome to the universe of fuckedupness. I immediately hated the crap. Still do.

Fast way to get off the planet for a tiny while only to come hurtling back down the rabbit hole to find it's a teeny bit more fucked than when you left – and the cookie that Alice is nibbling while you blowjob the devil— is your life. And it gets nibbled and nibbled and nibbled away. I put smack in there too, except I will tell you about me and heroin later.

According to a certain strain of thought, junkies are the victims of drugs. Corollary – drug dealers create junkies.

And junkies therefore need help.

Bullshit.

I am of the opinion that drugs do not make junkies. I have a number of reasons for saying this. When speaking of the human condition, I obviously cannot make any hard and fast rules, but, yeah, drugs don't make junkies any more than tom makes a gambling addict or wops make a nympho.

Junkies debase themselves with drugs to make the external picture fit the internal.

See, the world of drugs and dealing is a filthy one.

It starts with the punter. The punter can be anyone from a laaitie with shitty dreads and bad acne – dressed in greasy gothed clothes, pants carefully slung under his butt to show his equally greasy shorts – clutching a grubby wad of money from a CD player he slukked at school (and put off at Cash Crusaders) – all the way up to the high-priced hooking fashion dilettante deftly fishing crisp two-hundreds from a small Gucci crocodile with gold trimming and set off subtly by a diminutive jade clasp.

The laaitie is trying to beat the pain of living with his mother in a tiny single bedsitter while she stares stupidly into a snowy portable TV and cries into the bottom of a vodka bottle for an evil bastard of a husband whom she finally managed to be rid of but whom she cannot do without. The eye candy's gig is different. All her life she has been the centre of male attention from the time when daddy showed his little princess exactly what a man's cock wants. The only things in life that have never made her feel like a meathole are: beautiful clothes, her current girlfriend, and lots of coke.

In rehabs, when junkies go through that tough time – the row, row, rowing your boat up de river de-Nile moments – they speak fondly of their dealers. Irritations develop during informal group sessions as their man's generosity, patience and overwhelming superiority of product is lorded one over the other. Such disdain leads to even greater embellishments, till eventually the trip down memory lane becomes jammed solid in the frenzied trafficking of benign and oversized demi-gods jockeying for position.

The reality, of course, is different.

Dealers are the first step up from the slime in the food chain and they almost always work for somebody.

It is simple – they are issued x amount of stock and need to cash in y amount of money. Cash-ups depend on the territory where the business is being done. On a street corner it would be done hourly and is closed by the end of the day or night. In a club it would be as the stock runs out or at the end of the night. In a fixed residence like a crackhouse you can run a book. It is here where the demi-gods prowl, lurk and sometimes sell credit.

It is the laaitie's temple.

The laaitie is in kak with the priest of the demi-gods because he has been borrowing from Peter to pay Paul. The Skinny-White-Hipped-Out-Pseudo-Chemist-Guru-Ou / Nigerian / Heavily-Golded-Up-Cape-Coloured-Gangsta / Rude-Boy-Rasta … currently serving narcotic sacrament in the house is— Da Man. It is to him that the supplicant delivers his frantic supplication. This went wrong, that too and—

At this point he is chided gently and the promised land is revealed …

The priest explains that all the laaitie has to do is knock off say … twenty quarters a week and all will be forgiven. The book wiped out. Salvation and absolution in one package.

Really?

The laaitie gets to work and finds paradise comfortable. He has enough for himself and enough to supply the school. But of course little things happen, like his own school buddies who took on credit and then got lame when it came time to pay. He's also always so fucked that it's like too much of a *luss* to go find them and get the dealer's money off the cunts. Know what I'm saying dude?

After a few weeks of this the priest gets pissed off and confronts him one afternoon in the street. The laaitie has been furiously avoiding the crackhouse. He and his sleepy little girlfriend with the black eyes are invited into the priest's glittering dopemobile. At the crackhouse they are both taken to a back room. The dealer's muscle hold guns on him while he rapes the laaitie's girlfriend. That, he is told – is just a warning. Pay up. Next time everybody is going to have a turn and when they are done with her – your turn will be next.

The laaitie pulls off a burglary on a bra's house a week later. Him and his mense are away for the weekend. He sells some of the goeters. Pays off most of what he owes. The next day his girlfriend is discovered by her hysterical mother – all ODed out in the bath, her skin scrubbed raw. He feels so depressed that he does too much without selling any and gets into kak with the priest again. This time he is frantic. He isn't going to get hurt like his dead chick, so he plans to piemp the dealer. The dealer is as old as the hills in this regard. He confronts the laaitie once more, yells and makes a little noise – then gets real nice and gives him a half on the house with the firm admonition to settle the debt asap. The laaitie scoots off to his bra's house intent on selling him a very small quarter, buying another full one and slowly chipping the rest for himself. Then he will turk and call the boere to get the priest … off his fucking back.

At the bra's house he does the deal and watches his chommie cook and slamdunk a hot spike. It's not anything as stupid as poison. Forensic evidence of poison would make the boere go after the dealer and his masters like animals. No, it's just pure heroin. Pure, pure heroin. The laaitie's bra just shot up about four times his tolerance.

With two dead chinas, the laaitie now figures he has a drug problem and seeks help. Pity is, he has got at least sixteen others at school hooked. Not that the priest has any problems with that. So he ends up in rehab behind a rough turk arguing over cigarettes just how wonderful the Skinny-White-Hipped-Out-Pseudo-Chemist-Guru-Ou / Nigerian / Heavily-Golded-Up-Cape-Coloured-Gangsta / Rude-Boy-Rasta heroin priest had made his otherwise miserable, cheap fucking life.

On the other hand there is the fashion dummy gintu's jol, but let's leave her alone – she's got more than enough kak to deal with as it is. Soon she's going to lose her pretties from the odd bad trick and her poes will get too *slap* from all the piele – so she will be trawling the main drag with the other washed-out ugly street girls doing the whole greek and cocks for rocks jol. If she ever gets into rehab she'll wear too much makeup and tell everybody she was a mafia boss's girlfriend.

Nobody must ever talk about her – she can have you killed.

The chick takes her anti-retrovirals whenever she remembers …

But you get the picture. Priests, temple guards and errant, recalcitrant penitents.

Dealers are generally under the dominion of runners. Runners are the middle-management of the narcotics industry. It is their job to pick up cash and drop off stock. Efficiently. It is also their job to report what is happening down on the street to their masters. They are usually trusted and are expected to call in muscle at the slightest hint of problems with troublesome dealers or clients. They need to be clever too. They provide the buffer between the boere and the bosses. If a dealer goes down and piemps – all the gattas can do is try and trap the runner. A good runner has the pulse on his dealers. He is also usually well protected by his bosses – as long as he is not stupid and keeps his fucking mouth shut. A good syndicate needs a lawyer on the payroll to deal with these types of irritations. A really good one has boere on the inside who can make dockets go away. Typically a stupid runner is left out to dry.

Stupid runners present a threat, which is why you always do business with your runners away from home. If they don't know where you live or where the drugs are, and they don't know where the money is – the gattas, vigilantes and other gangsters can't do a thing except gather intelligence. And you take care of that by sowing wild counter-intelligence that sets them barking up all sorts of wrong trees. Being a runner is a privileged role because you make quick, easy money and enjoy protection.

The bosses need to insulate themselves from the street to concentrate on money laundering, smuggling and procuring or manufacturing product. For them, it is usually wiser to import and export directly from the point of manufacture to gain maximum capital return on investment – with astronomical profits, of course.

Then of course there are the turf wars. They are always waged over market share – or more likely bullet-scarred street-corner share. And that's the point. Nobody wants to fucking share. Only so many people are going to buy trips in a night. That's the market. Whoever is most successful in selling them is most despised. Two good mates of mine were standing outside a very successful club called The Boiler Room one morning. Both were involved in the club itself and security in general in the Cape Town club scene. Suddenly a minibus taxi pulls up, doors open and gangsters jump out shooting. One of my bras was hit four times, the other twice. That hit went down because there was more stock being sold inside the club than the street dealer's bosses liked or were willing to tolerate. That's just one example.

Paulie and I learnt to be very paranoid. We were driving into Stellenbosch one morning on the way home from all-night business in Cape Town. In the car is about twenty grams of coke, a couple hundred trips, Ecstasy pills, zol, a Browning 9mm HP, a black book with all our business details and about twenty grand. We pass a bunch of cops who hit brakes as soon as they see us and make a U-turn. Luckily we were at the main thoroughfare robots, so I screamed at Paul to go left and take off towards Paarl. He did. The only way they could trap us was if they had someone ahead. Paul put foot and we lost them. He turned into a deserted farm road and we hid everything in some bushes. I lay down on the back seat and he drove me to my chick's place. Later we retrieved the goeters using another car. But the writing was on the wall.

The other thing was, we were taking so much of our own stock that we weren't getting rich like we originally intended. We blew everything on expensive restaurants, hotels and partying non-stop. Eventually I had had enough. Enough of the paranoia. Enough of the hangovers that were so bad at times it felt like I was fucked on mescaline. Enough of the guilt. And the violence.

I booked myself into a rehab – a Christian rehab. Did I mention that I was creatively stupid?

Rehabs range from proper medical clinics practising psychiatric medicine to the state-sponsored Magaliesoord-type jol, to Christian rehabs and mom-and-pop operations. They are a very big bucks business. The ones that claim to be Christian are fucked because they start from the presumption that intoxication is a sin. And of course, man, especially a junkie, is separated from God. Add little or no medical expertise and you have presumptuous disaster applying for a license to happen somewhere. The worst are the okes whom Jesus got off drugs because now they have a handle on it. Absolute truth always seems to bring out the worst in people.

Like the bizarre outfit in Noupoort run by a religiously insane obese ex-ducktail. Some adolescent smack addict is found dead there, chained up in a cell. The mal giemba who runs the place isn't even a medical doctor. Just some religious freak trying to practise amateur psychiatric medicine for Jesus, fun and profit.

Check it out. If I tried to transplant a baboon's heart into a living person and that poor fucker immediately pegged, I would be dealing with the business side of the Department of Corrections toot sweet. Why? Because I'm not a fucking heart surgeon, china, and that makes it homicide or some kinda freaky man-and-monkeyslaughter. Hell, if I chained a kid up in my garage because he owed me money for gear and he died of his turk I would go straight to the mang for murder. But somehow nothing happened about this kid's death because dear Liewe Jesus told someone to do it to him to cure him of smack addiction. At the very least, the kids get fucked up because when they crash and burn back into drugs they have to deal with the kamstige promise of hell for letting Jesus down.

Anyway, during my own stint in rehab, they dragged out the whole condemnation thing, which I had the sense to laugh at. I ignored all their anal crap, planted a big veggie garden and tended it until my dry-out was finished. Then I returned to Cape Town, stretched my CV and went back into IT.

20

Da Love Drug

I worked and lived in Sea Point for a while, but moved back to Stellenbosch eventually. I missed another best mate I nicknamed Bobby Boy too much. We partied pretty often and spent an inordinate amount of time philosophising and smoking cannabis – meaning we smoked a lot of dagga and talked even more kak. I was buying my trips and what have you from dealers like everybody else, and although I was horribly competent at my IT job, I pissed them off by being key technical personnel and taking too much sick leave. Weekends started turning into a ritual. I usually bought my drugs from bras in Town. Then I arrived back in the Bos, got dressed and went to hit it with Bobby and them. We would go all night without sleep, through Friday and Saturday night, and wind down with a braai on Sunday. Then I would crash out cold at about two in the afternoon and make sure I was on my feet for work Monday morning. After a while, word started getting round among friends that I was able to score good shit. So they began pestering me to help out. I thought, what the fuck, borrowed Bobby Boy's GoldCard and scored a shipment from my chinas – at bulk price, plus discount – as an incentive to future business. I remember when I did it I was thinking – what if I can't sell this? I'm fucked because I have to put the money back into Rob's account. But of course I knocked it all off. With a little profit and enough for my own free score. I called it My Party Fund, and it kept my salary intact.

This went on until one morning when I was doing a cash-up at Bobby's place and his brother wandered in. He looked at the piles of cash in disbelief and asked me just exactly how much it was. Just under nine thousand, I told him. And we still had enough drugs to keep us all fucked for the rest of the weekend. At this point I came to the shocking realisation that My Party Fund was just a lame euphemism for— Al, You Are A Fucking Drug Dealer – Again. Not that I stopped. But I burnt through the tom fast.

Now you might not believe me, but this was the mid-nineties and I had never taken a pill up until then. I thought disco-biscuits were a bullshit trip for sweaty rave bunnies. I took sheets of acid, which in turn got me the nickname Acid Alex. I cultivated it, though.

Acid Alex was a very generous psychedelic reptile.

I would arrive at after-parties and find fifteen or twenty people sitting around, smoking spliff and talking kak. To liven things up I would cut trips in halves and quarters. Halves for experienced jellyheads and quarters for those about to become so enlightened. I never forced anybody, but a combination of intelligent persuasion and enthusiastic peer pressure usually did the trick. They dropped. In this fashion I gave literally thousands of people their first trip. And they came back the following week and bought three.

Of course.

This went on for a while until one New Year's party at the River Club in Cape Town. I'm standing in the queue and all I have is cover charge, having blown everything over Christmas. Suddenly I hear some ous calling my name. Turns out to be a couple of club bosses I know very well. They escort me in for nothing. Inside, I start moving through the colourful, flashing hammer of good house thinking I should buy a trip with the bucks I have on me. Then I hear some other ous yelling at me. Also mates. They want to score candy but don't know where. So I tune them I'll help them out. How many? The bra tells me, gives me a wad of cash and tunes me to bring him the goeters and twenty bucks change. I go up to Mikey. He's one of the bosses and DJs as Screaming Lord Slate. I ask Mikey to be kind. He gives me a very good price and some tiny paper drawings of Bart Simpson, and some of the larger, more artful Reserve Bank kind changes hands. Downstairs I find these ous and give them what they want. They disappear. I decide to see what I made and found out I had been overpaid by something like three hundred bucks. Kwaai. I don't care. Fuck, I gave the oke what he asked for and sure as hell I'm not going to spend half the night trawling through twenty thousand insanely fucked people looking for him. So I wander around. I'm not in a hurry to get goofed. I've got enough for a gram of charlie and whatever else takes my fancy.

Cape Town has always had a tiny chip on its shoulder when it comes to identity. It is very wannabe. And in our small underworld of shady characters it was ridiculous how much info you could garner from other roekers by being in the know and dropping morsels of intel about everyone and everything, because nobody could keep their bekke shut in a frantic race to belong and Be Somebody. Paul taught me to play that game and reciprocate with disinformation just to fuck everyone around. It was fun and gave you a picture of who was who in the zoo. I knew who all the big

Ecstasy suppliers were. I knew who smuggled and I knew who bought pills, who chopped them and who re-pressed them after being cut. I've always reckoned – well not always, but most of the time – if you gonna spend money on drugs, buy good shit. So I went to this one cat at the party who I knew. He was part of a syndicate. They had standards – they only moved pure MDMA. I was moderately sober, so I figured I wanted to try it on its own, instead of deep inside the fruit salad of narcotics usually sloshing around in my head. The ou gave me a big grin. They all knew I moved the shit but didn't take it. He told me he was going to give me something special. He explained that a couple of UCT Chem Engineering students cooked up a small batch of capsules that went to very, very select and special friends to sort them out over weekends. It was a colourless capsule with a white powder inside. He told me it was a one-fifty mil hit. The max. He winked and said it was on the house. The bastard was playing me at my own game – he knew I would be back. And he told me something I didn't know about some other cooks. See what I'm talking about?

I pop it under my tongue to make it metabolise faster, harder and longer. I always play it like this. I wander back into the party to have a look around. Sjoe, it's almost as bitter as malaria pills. I cruise to the bar for a dop. Wash away the taste. I get through the crowd and buy a double Absolut and Red Bull.

I wonder if I'm starting to come on yet.

Outside.

The main dance arena is a high sound stage loaded up with decks, a rig and killer lighting under a huge cavelike dome. Screaming lasers slash writhing calculus spiders – instantly burning rain into frozen coloured jewels – bright kaleidoscopic beauty trapped in slices of time and space.

Cape Town is having a lekker, wet, very noisy PARTY! Kwaai.

Out beyond the crowd, a circle of tall wigwams flicker orange heat somewhere below. I move nearer. Conflicting bass lines swim into each other, sea serpents biting slicing twisted beat. The stonking, banging, panting fades into backdrop – and hammers, spiralling lightly into trance. Huge blazes burn in an open laager. Licking warm flames snapshoot damp happy faces. Psychedelic beauty drifting high above and dancing everywhere. The music jerks the crowd and pirouettes them, dreaming love's eternal freedom – deep in tribal seas.

I move back into the strobing festival's front.

Upstairs, Lord Slate has the Revolting Cocks gang-banging on an overloaded industrial waste-disposal unit. Dark-leathered goths fake-fuck, moshing hair – yeah baby – having nasty fun. Cool. I used to love this shit till I got turned on by house. I wander back into warmer sexy music and find myself in the chillout lounge. I see the cat I bought the candy for and they yell at me to join the sprawled-out instant family. I wander over and plonk myself down. I talk kak to my bra, slightly irritated at white and neon colours leaping into my eyes from the ultraviolet dark. I decide to roll a spliff, even though I have none. When I tune him for a knoesie, he asks me what I dropped. I tell him the score and he pisses himself laughing. Fuck my broer, you gonna have some real fun – then he tells the group what I have done. He tunes I must drink water and not down Black Jack or Bells like I always do because that will fuck me up. Yeah, alright, I know all the lore. And when it kicks in and the rush starts I must get off my arse and skank it on the floor.

All of a sudden I notice the colours are changing.

Tendrils of an unknown softness drift in, touching me and kissing gentle foreplay all around my eyes. The chillout music draws me into its arms. I feel love awaken sleepily and want to float into its embrace. My mate tells me just to feel it and be patient until the rush. Inside me things start unlocking. Good, bad, unknown and everything else. I have them all held badly in tension but they tumble into no importance. The world is all around me if I stop looking at myself. I open my eyes groggily. Warm female hands lightly embrace my arms from behind. A woman's voice tinkles close to my ear and asks me to relax and let her do something. The feathery fingers reach down and remove my T-shirt. I relax. Breathe. Hot handclaps and rustling behind me invoke the smell of Tiger Balm's prayers. Six hands plunge slowly into my back. Swimming deep delicious backstroke, breaststroke, butterfly into a pool of steaming fragrant muscles rippling all the way down the twin median shores of my spine. The music lets go its embrace and becomes transparent in and all through me. Meandering. Ethereal. Living …

My mate drags me back into the melting light. On your feet, he orders – but I don't wanna, I whine. Over against the wall from me a beautiful lone girl masturbates her downy moist vulva in wide open innocence and, as her fingers reach deep within her pretty vagina, I know exactly how she feels. My mate is having none of it and drags me to my feet. I'm having difficulty walking. It's more like wading in the general direction of the sound. I want the main arena. I need aggression to wake me up. The air and rain clear my head, and somehow the DJ is managing to play the best hard house I've ever heard. Music like this is too good to waste and I plunge into the strobe robotic crowd. Somewhere deep in the middle I turn and face into the beat. I start moving, trying to find the dance. It's in me, I can feel it. Coming. I find something in the fusion between my nerves and the thump. Yes, vibrating, prickling, shooting – hot sparks. And then the rush hits me all the way up my back. I rad-surf a thundering pipe up my spine, into my brain and wipe out into the song. I know this is only the beginning, so I decide to take a ride.

I always wear bandannas bound around my wrists to wipe sweat from my face when I boogie in clubs. I take a black one and blindfold myself. Then I take out my black aviator Ray Bans and put them on. Nobody can see I'm blind at a glance.

I climb back into the jumping music and start jumping right along. Soon I've danced into the core – my muscles and the rhythm have finally become one. I let them go where they want to and dive out onto the shore of a multiverse – to explore a quantum grain of sand. Around me universes explode, expand and contract. Time is banished and space fades away ... Someone nearby clasps my arm. I'd forgotten I have one and instantly I am back on Planet Earth. A plastic bottle is put in my hand and a voice yells that I must drink. This goes on for what seems like hours. People come up to me and massage me while I am dancing. Sugary lollipops find their way into my mouth. Water and smart drinks are pressed into my hands and people lead me around. Eventually gentle hands urge me to a place through canvas flaps and voices tell me to sit down. A girl kneels down next to me and tells me she is going to remove the blindfold but I mustn't open my eyes just yet. I sit quietly and slowly let the dim distorted light painfully creep back in. I'm in a darkened wigwam. I'm surrounded by people swimming in my tender vision like whispering tendrils of sea bamboo. A girl suggests to me that it was my first time and asks me if I enjoyed it. I tell her yes. She hugs me and everyone else claps hands.

I loved it back.

Ecstasy did something for me that no drug I had taken up until then had managed to effect. I changed emotionally for the better. I started looking at my identity, and my spiritual values – trying carefully to assess their meaning, influences and validity. I heard a lot of stuff and was struck by the fact that clubs, the new Generation X and the music and drugs were emerging as new virtual church venues and an alternative spiritual opiate to bring cerebral ecstasia to the masses. The new priesthood spoke little and spun vinyl for their momentary flocks.

God was now apparently a DJ. And God was telling his children to accept each other's belief systems, genetic paint jobs and individual sexualities and get their naughty little butts skanking on the dance floor – *pronto!*

But it took me a long while to realise that love supposedly divine, love as spinning vinyl or love very definitely chemical were all still superficial. My unformed idea of real love could never sustain itself as a passing chemical, emotional or social event. For me, real continuous love was elusive. Everybody mattered but I didn't know how.

However, in the midst of this chemical and aural New Age Love Revolution, a very real, beautiful and precious type of love was rapidly on its way to me. Like E, it had a depressing downer coming in its wake, but because of the ensuing tragedy I eventually had to face, I would never see the beauty of love or the eternal nature and value of a single person I love— differently again. But that came with wisdom.

And pure wisdom is always distilled in a vast steel cauldron of pain.

*

Valentine's Day that year finds me alone in a pool bar when an absolute babe of note comes up and starts flirting with me. We know each other vaguely and it's the first time where I'm doggedly staying single for good reason.

The good reason being that when I start getting desperate for sex, mental stimulation, sex, companionship, sex with a joint afterwards, sex with joints before and after – you get the picture – I usually fuck up and end up with the wrong person. Twice, I've doggedly remained single to wait for the right girl, and that night was the first time I met her.

She stops flirting, grabs me and kisses me. Awesome.

That's it.

We were inseparable after that.

Christine was petite, very petite … although actually the term jailbait comes to mind because that is what I felt when we started going out and I got sharp looks from strangers. Okay, okay, she looked thirteen at a glance.

There.

But, oh my God, she was so beautiful. Inside first and then out. Twenty-two. She was also a virgin. To this day she is still the most amazing woman I have ever met. Besides looking very young and insanely pretty, there were weird idiosyncrasies about her. She only had one pair of shoes. How many chicks do you know who only have one pair of shoes? And we are speaking about an urban woman here, remember. It took me six months to convince her to let me buy her another pair. But, brothers and sisters – her underwear – the stunning lingerie she avidly collected … she was a girlfriend all the way from heaven. Did I mention that Christine was a wild flaming red-head and a virgin? Yes, a virgin. And, against all odds and possibilities— she remained that way too.

No bullshit.

I nearly went insane from horniness but I loved her too much. Losing my own had been so shitty that I wanted hers to be on her own terms and in her own time.

At the time, she was completing her Honours in Marketing Management and I was working in a major software house as a Technical Systems Analyst (party animal fundraising aside), so I was at least presentable to her very conservative Afrikaans parents.

Christine and I had what felt like the perfect relationship and I loved her with every ounce of my being. She was my best friend and soul mate. Someone who will never leave me.

Not even through death.

The funny thing was I was the one who was supposed to die.

I nearly did.

With Christine holding my hand.

My drinking was hurting me. My choice of dop was gin and tonic. I was introduced to it in a club by a good chommie named Conrad. He came up to me on the dance floor with this weirdly blue fluorescing drink and told me to have a taste. I loved it and asked him what it was. G&T. Okay, so I started drinking almost a bottle a day. This went on for months until I got sick.

I blame it on the G&T.

One night we were sleeping in Christine's boet's flat, looking after the place for him, when I got up to take a pee. On the way I shuffled into the kitchen, opened the fridge and pulled out a litre of apple juice. Strangely enough, all I'd had to drink that night were a couple of Scotches and a cider. We also had a stuffed roast chicken and veggies that I cooked for us for supper. And that was it. A joint or two in front of the TV and bed.

I downed the juice and headed for the toilet. Switched on the light, stepped inside, pulled out my dick, and that's when something ripped a shark hook into my guts. It was such agony that I lost my breath. My knees buckled and I slid to the floor, grasping my guts, almost blind from the pain. What the hell was wrong – I had no idea. I just knew that I had to wake Christine up, so I tried to scream. No sound came out. I couldn't scream. I could barely breathe. Something told me I was having a heart attack because I was suddenly sweating like a pig. I crawled out of the bathroom and, some awful long minutes later, managed to inch into our bedroom, get my arm onto the bed and shake her awake. She screamed when she turned on the light and saw me. That's how bad it was. At the time I probably weighed in at around 90 kg and she was barely over 60, so getting me downstairs and into her car was a serious mission, with me still trying to scream and Christine crying her eyes out, begging me to hold on and please not die.

I couldn't sit, so I knelt on the flattened car seat and gasped at her to drive from Town to my doctors at Medi-Clinic in Stellenbosch, but because the pain was so bad, we pulled in at N1 City. That's what saved me. The duty Emergency doctors looked at me, freaked, called in a specialist surgeon and then shot as much Pethidine into me as possible without killing me already. It brought the pain level down to a point where I could begin screaming. And that's what I did.

I had contracted pancreatitis. My surgeon was one of South Africa's best, which is why I am alive. He quietly went to Christine, who was alternately sleeping and crying on a couch in the hall, and told her he was fighting it tooth and nail, but it didn't look good. Not many people are able to survive the disease. What happens in essence is your pancreas starts eating itself. Alive. That's why it's one of the most painful ways to die. We managed to phone Wally and Denise to tell them the doctors didn't expect me to survive. Wally wasn't interested and Denise said she wasn't going to waste the petrol money coming in from Pringle Bay.

For nearly four days I lay screaming in that ICU with a weeping Christine holding my hand whenever the nursing staff would allow her. They were on strict orders to give me as much Pethidine as I wanted – a sure sign that they wanted to make my death as comfortable as possible.

On the fourth day it suddenly stopped. My surgeon was beside himself with professional pride, because he had managed to stop the organ from consuming itself. He had a good look with a sonar scanner and showed me something like a three-inch scar all along it. I gave him a huge hug and ordered my very good medical aid to cough up.

Our beautiful love relationship changed after that. It brought us much closer together at an unspoken level, but it brought with it an uncertainty of permanence that made Christine terribly worried about the future.

The greatest tragedy of my life up to this point— is that she was so right.

But now let me tell you a bit about Christine's family.

Her boetie was gay.

Now, I'd gotten over my hang-ups with gay men, because I realised at some point that not all homosexuals are baby-raping pederasts. I've had gay friends so close that I've shared a bed for the night – just for a doss. My negative experiences as a laaitie made me explore my own non-existent homosexuality a short while after those ugly incidents, and since then I've been very comfortable with both myself and gay men. Christine didn't care about her boet's sexuality at all. She felt it was his own very private business. I felt the same, and at any rate he seemed like one hell of a nice guy. His boyfriend was shy and a bit petulant-campy, but her boetie was a totally cool oke in my opinion.

This did come as a bit of a shock to her parents though, but they were able to deal with it more or less within the parameters of being his loving parents, counterbalanced against the traditional norms of the NG Kerk. Christine's mother had told her that even when he was a baby she already knew some-how that he was a little bit different. A mother is probably able to see and count chromosomes. But Christine reckoned her parents did have deep, unspoken reservations about his lifestyle in light of their religious convictions.

But it was a major problem with Christine's sister.

The poor girl was a first-year in Stellenbosch and very firmly in the religious-psychological stranglehold of some self-declared coloured prophet who had titled himself Senior Pastor Fred May and who'd started a quasi-cultist charismatic outfit called Shophar Christian Church on Stellenbosch campus.

This ou was so far outfield and freaky that to get this Shophar jol going, he had these poor laaities running around in the forests surrounding Stellenbosch – *IN THE DEAD OF NIGHT* – looking for Satanists. The terrible irony being that they were the only ones there hunting demons in the dark.

This ou told the students that God had sent him to Stellenbosch to chase out the devil. And to this end he carefully corralled them psychologically into a siege mentality. An embattled minority fighting the forces of darkness under the guidance of their prophet. Of course, those evil forces were narrowly defined by the prophet himself and were usually disguised as other white students in the NG Studentekerk, suspiciously New Age-looking hippy-attired roekers on campus, the tiny handful of Roman Catholics, all goths on sight, *anybody* whom he could not control or manipulate, and of course the bedevilled gay community. Like any good cultist, he denied high, low and furiously that he was a psycho-logical hijacker.

It works for him too. Ask any one of the kids for an opinion of what I've written here and they will tell you it comes directly from the *devil.*

And, man, does this ou love incessantly talking about what a Great Man of God he is to keep the laaities under his spell – but never honestly. Never, ever honestly. This oke will tell you he has raised the dead. Yes, boys and girls – he's made a stone-dead, heart-not-pomping, brain-not-grafting, breathless, dead-dick, wormbait mutherfucker come back to life.

That's what he says, cousin. Check it out. Find him and ask him.

He's one of these ous you know is lying continuously because his lips move when he speaks. You make out?

Let me digress from how easily the love in my girlfriend's family got torn apart by this infiltration of utter religious crap and tell you a slightly connected story about a very good friend that explains a lot of things that I struggle to say.

Like me, my good friend Henry had a terrible childhood and a type of spiritual epiphany as a young man. As a youngster he was forced to shoot and kill his father because the sick fucker was busy beating his mother so bad once again that he thought she wouldn't survive. The homicide cops thought so too and told him he had done nothing wrong. His one sister walked into the kitchen and, upon seeing the body, spat on it. The bastard had raped all his daughters.

Unlike me, the rage within Henry took him into secret AWB camps.

But, as I said, at some point his way of seeing himself was opened to inward vestiges that he had been blind to and he changed deeply as a person.

Anyway, I was alone in a flat with a girl who had gone through pretty similar sicko shit with her grandfather when we got hit by SANAB. They found nothing on us, but they did find a little bit of zol in a bankie. So they charged us both and released us on bail awaiting trial. I was already sitting with a three-year suspended sentence for zol and I knew the chick would never have the goeters to face up and take the rap, with her background. She was terrified, and I was definitely going to do time. I told Henry about it during a phone call, and he came back down from visiting the west coast and did something I have never ever seen. Before or since.

It is the Day of Judgment:

To the utter astonishment of the entire court, all three of us climb into the dock.

I am shitting myself ...

Our joint lawyer has informed us he will instruct the court. The court consists of: court police, the SANAB officers who arrested us, the prosecutor (a very grim red-head straining under the scales of the Law that rest heavily on her seriously pretty shoulders as she glares at me), the girl, Henry and—

All rise!

—The Judge.

The prosecutor calls the case as Possession of Dagga to His Worship but instructs him that there is an unheard-of addendum to the docket, which she sincerely hopes the defence will care to enlighten the court about forthwith – since it seems that, astonishingly enough, without any further investigations carried out by the dedicated members of SANAB— a third accused has miraculously appeared to answer to the charges in the case before the court.

His Worship dismisses the pinkly tinged sarcasm and looks over at our lawyer expectantly.

Our lawyer nods gravely, then informs His Worship that he represents all three accused, waives explanation and would like to immediately move to plea.

His Worship takes a mild look at us and nods, then writes Henry into the charges and utters the renewed charges tonelessly for the record. Turning back to our lawyer, he demands that he plead for each of us. The lawyer pleads me and the girl not guilty and Henry is given the rap.

His Worship nods balefully and instructs me and the girl to step down from the Prisoner's Dock.

We are free to go.

We have not spoken a word. Later our lawyer will tell us that we did not even have to appear, as long as Henry was there to satisfy the court with a guilty plea, the prosecution could not say a word about it. Prosecution trials are apparently only about a denial of guilt. Guilty pleas always move directly to judgment.

We step down, walk back to the public gallery, and watch Henry get sentenced. I'm thinking that I have never quite understood the real legal implications of what the Bible said Christ did for the world when he was executed. I mean, isn't this a perfect enactment of the Divine Drama?

Up in front on the judgment seat there is God the Father – His Worship. There's all the angels too – the court boere. There's the devil – the seriously sexy natural red-head still glaring at me ogling her perfect boobs through her robe, and painting Henry as black as humanly possible in her pre-sentencing statement. All the stupid gloating devil's demons – SANAB. Some Forbidden Fruit from the Tree of Knowledge of Good and Evil – the tiny bit of zol in the bankie (Exhibit A). Adam – Meeester El Lovejoy himself. Dear Eve – the scared silly, molested-by-her-dirty-old-*grandy*father chick. The Holy Spirit – our lawyer. And of course Jesus Christ – my good friend Henry.

Hell, it is only two of us being set free, but it could have been ten of us in that flat – or twenty – up for every crime in the book! And we are guilty of it too. She provided the money and I bought the zol. We both smoked it. Henry had nothing to do with it, but he has volunteered to come in from far away and take the penalty because he is our good friend.

The Judge finds Henry guilty as charged and klaps him with the maximum punishment allowable under the Law …

The irony of this story is that Henry was a member of this same Shophar Christian Church jol, and although he'd acted in a Christlike way, although he'd made a mighty sacrifice based on love, he was tossed out of the church for his troubles, and now, like me, he was apparently in imminent danger of permanent banishment from heaven. He was ordered to break our friendship, because I was a sinner who smoked zol and schnacked Es, but he told the very good and very freaky Senior Pastor that he refused to stop being my china. How can you order somebody to stop being some other oke's chommie, cousin? What the fuck kind of sicko, manipulative, steek-taragoppie, cultist horsecrap is that? Could you begin to imagine God pulling those kinda bullshit stunts on mense? Even on a really shitty day in heaven? Jesus told us to love each other no matter what.

So this was the kind of crap Christine's sister had in her head. She believed her mother's son was going to hell for making love to a man. And her parents for disobeying God and not being baptised or praying in tongues. And her sister for being in love with someone cursed by God – like me. To her, we were all going to burn. The poor chick was surrounded by overdone braaivleis-walking.

See, as I drew closer to Christine, I felt the burdens of her cares for her family more and more. She loved her ouboet so very much and was in a terrible conflict with the same love she felt for her religiously paranoid little sissie, and of course on top of all this was the hurt she felt for her folks because they felt they had gone wrong as Christian parents somewhere.

Her sissie was convinced by her rancid Oreo-cookie pastor that her poor boet was utterly lost, possessed by *A Demon of Homosexuality* and on his way to hell. Christine was obviously subjected to the same bullshit too, just on a milder scale. If Christine dumped me, joined Shophar Christian Church and turned to Jesus in the only way that Jesus and the Senior Pastor would be satisfied with – *and of course made absolutely sure she got baptised, prayed in tongues and paid him the full 10 percent of her monthly cash (in that order)* – she would be *saved* and her sister could finally stop crying her eyes out to God to please not eternally burn at least one of her siblings.

It was the usual stupid ranting shit that I had fought against for so long, except now it was close and wouldn't go away. And it was horrible to see that unnecessary fear at work in such a beautiful, gentle and truly sweet girl.

Christine used to get seriously pissed off with the crazy stuff her sister was being told by her pastor because it changed the way she spoke and acted towards her radically. She simply couldn't get past the fear and cultist doctrinal barriers and make her little sister understand that she felt *everybody*, starting with ouboet, had been given a heavenly right to respond to God's love in their own way. It irritated Christine very, very deeply that her sister made wild assumptions about her own spirituality simply because she refused to go to Shophar meetings, give them her money, perform silly public rituals with the Senior Pastor personality as ringmaster and talk incessantly in some kind of stilted Christianspeak. It made her even more furious that her sister sat and allowed this oke to gay-bash their boetie from the pulpit.

Love is so beautiful but dear God sometimes it hurts so much.

I have a china called Blommie. He's proudly gay and he reckons that he wants to go to Shophar and demand that the good Senior Pastor cast *The Demon of Gayness* out of him. Sommer that demon's close chommies – The Imp of Wildly Camp and The Black Sprite of Occasional Dragbitch – too, but if the *prophet* can't and Blommie reckons he still digs the shit out of boys – then he wants to sue his discriminative black ass for religious fraud. How's that for a serious *lag*.

We must fucking videotape it. We've gotta.

Anyway, so you can probably understand that the real, deep and intensely beautiful love Christine and I shared in the fast, fractured aural and chemical kaleidescope of Generation X while hurtling through the wild, paranoid, sleepless nineties was almost perfect, it suffered the burdens of love being poisoned around us. In her family, bonds had been hurt by an overdose of bad religious opiate, with her sister unable to recognise the simple validity of ordinary unconditional love for someone as precious as her ouboet. Instead her loved ones had to pay the price of her sibling love being tainted by that bad religious fix.

I will always love my babe with every single ounce of my being, but in retrospect we both made the same mistake. We had an idyllic, eternal relationship, but neither one of us was able to foresee that an unseen clock was ticking among all these warped esoteric diffractions of love and we would not be allowed the luxury of unlimited time to explore, deepen and bear the living fruit of our love together in this world.

PART V

World-Class Naughty Boy

21

DIY Syndication

Okay, so there I was, this seriously converted, hardcore, disco-biscuit-chomping nineties child. A rave bunny of note, wonderfully in love with a totally gorgeous chick, and who now could not get enough Ecstasy. I started trying to find out as much as I could, and discovered all sorts of conflicting shit. It seemed the topic had been flogged, beaten and schmangled to death. But I was going to learn. And learn good …

One night, about a year later, I am hanging in a local pool bar when a very old friend of mine walks in. Her name will be Sister E. We are piss-pleased to see each other and start catching up on news. This one, that one – where is he, she, it and them now? At any rate, I get round to asking her what she's doing and she tells me that she's moved back to the Bos with her boyfriend. Of course I ask who he is and she points me to a roeker sitting in the corner at the end of the bar. I take a look at this ou. He has a large strong face in which classical aquiline beauty and ugliness seem at war. Brown eyes, wide sexy mouth and long straight supermodel hair. And like me he just simply looks dangerous. Sister E is a truly beautiful woman so I can see her attraction to him. His name will be Brother E, and he is about to become my soul mate, a very good partner in certain types of outlawed activities and a man who I would carefully plan to execute.

They had come to Stellenbosch with the intention of tapping the student zol market. They had good *boom* as it turned out, so I bought from them regularly and actively courted Brother E's friendship. He was a TK old boy. Weirdly enough, he had been under Potties too. Apparently The Bear had never changed. One night we were dronk and talking kak when we decided to go fuck him up – we both knew where he lived. Eventually I said no. If we did that, we would screw up Tannie Potties and her baby's lives, and I wouldn't pay her back like that for being kind to me in Die Bult.

Our friendship slowly deepened.

Brother E had just come back from Amsterdam. He'd been working for a crew of smugglers over there. He started filling my head with stories.

He and Sister E were planning a mission. I wanted to be in on it, but

Brother E kept it close to his chest. So I played the loyal card and waited to find out if they managed to pull it off. They did. We had a mutual friend who was a butcher. Brother E had the zol compressed and they took it to this ou to vacuum-seal. Then they simply took the blocks of zol and put them in Sister E's baggage. She flew over to Europe, met some of Brother E's friends in Amsterdam and swopped the zol for pills. These she sewed into a hand-tailored leather jacket she had made with thick piping running up the back and front. She nearly missed her plane because she didn't realise it was going to take so long to finish. Anyway, she made it back safely, and we were in business.

I impressed the hell out of Brother E because I always paid cash up front for everything. And I moved a lot of his stock. I had the same policy with all my clients and runners. Cash only. Up front. My mission statement was: *If I give you something – it's free. If you ask for it – you pay.* There were basically three venues that I controlled: a club called Upstairs, which later became Lemon Fubar, a pool hall called Mash, and the Chinese Restaurant, which later became The Drunken Springbok. Bummer was, the new management of Springbok had a zero-tolerance policy towards narcotics.

It was in Mash that I'd met Brother E. And Christine, I might add.

We very quickly sold all the pills Sister E brought back and started planning the next mission. This time I was in on it. Brother E would do the run. He and Sister E bought five kilos of weed and I bought a plane ticket. I managed to do this because I had taken on a company-sanctioned moonlighting job that had been very profitable. I designed and implemented a networked laundry management system from the ground up – hardware and software. We took the zol to the butcher and packaged it. Then we put the blocks in large cornflakes boxes and packed it all in a huge scuba-diving kitbag with rollerblades, CDs, tins of hoerpoep, boots, clothes – all sorts of shit – and put him on the plane. I spent that night with Sister E trying not to worry. She insisted on smoking a button and fell asleep, much to my relief. Then I crashed too. The next morning we got a phone call. It was Brother E. He had made it through, with a small hitch that I'll tell you about in a sec – but he had also left his traveller's cheques behind. For some unknown reason he seemed to be fucking upset with Sister E about this …

Ja, so let's talk about Brother E, women and temper tantrums.

He had a certain charisma that got to women. Like this small hitch with Customs in Belgium. He was late and going through for his connecting flight when he came running up to them *sweating* ... so the first official who saw him put her hand up and beckoned him over. He helped her open the kitbag and held it while she poked around inside. All the time he was calmer than a war criminal on trial and started chaffing her. She actually had her hands on the cornflakes boxes when she suddenly grinned and told him to piss off. Nerves of absolute fucking steel. But on the flip side there was the petulant screaming child who would erupt every time he couldn't get his own way. He tried it on me once or twice but I refused to react. In the beginning I think he interpreted it as fear, but as time went by, he saw the dire effects of what happened to other people when I lost it. And he also began to realise that I didn't make a noise when I did so either – I just unleashed.

I was aware that he and Sister E had terrible fights, but I didn't know that he hit her. I didn't know that he beat up all the women he had been with. I didn't know he was a violent rapist. I only found this out much later. Much later, when it was too late and I was way too fucking angry.

At any rate, I was in. We began planning another mission. I was adamant that, as an equal member of the syndicate, I would need to take the same chances as Brother and Sister E. In the beginning they balked, saying that we had enough cash from our pills to hire mules to do the dangerous work, but I retorted that I could not and would not live with that, for two reasons: One, I would always feel as if I had only been a sideline member of the business – and two, why did we need to waste hard-earned money on paying somebody when I would do it for nothing except my share? Brother E eventually decided that I could do it, and he would put a thousand pills in my back pocket for my trouble – no bearing on my share. I agreed, and although Sister E was at first reluctant, she later had a dream and told me it would be okay.

I stopped shaving and began planning my mission. It took quite a while because there were a lot of ducks to get in a row and we had to make all the fuckers quack.

We decided unanimously that we wanted to take ten kilos with us this time – the most ambitious consignment yet. Up until then we had been penetrating Europe through Belgium – reason being that they were the most lenient of the EU members when it came to sentencing offenders for carrying narcotics. Later I would find out that they had no mercy on syndicate bosses who sent mules through – but we will still get there …

Amsterdam zol offices wanted, or rather demanded, blocks in a twenty-five by twenty-five centimetre format – weighing a full or half-kilo at a time. We had presses tailor-made to do exactly that. Cost us a small fortune getting them designed too. We used them with car wheel-jacks for hydraulics and pressed the blocks to eight tons. Then we bought an industrial vacuum-packer and packaged them to a ninety-eight percent vacuum seal – just like meat. And for shits, giggles and a touch of professionalism, we marked each block with its exact weight and kamstige strain of zol on a piece of paper inside the plastic bag. Swazi-Red 1028g, Durban Poison 1120g, Jamaican 1054g, Rooibaard 1014g, etc…. Of course we donned rubber gloves and washed each one very carefully, packed them in a box and then put them to one side.

Ten kilos was a hell of a challenge. It was way too much to hide in a suitcase easily. I used my graft's free access to the Internet and began doing furious research. My initial findings confirmed what we already knew. Belgium was probably the best country through which to penetrate the EU, because of its soft legal system – but with this came the fact that Brussels had one of the most technically secure airports in Europe, it being the headquarters of NATO and all that shite. I began researching X-ray and scanner technology to see how we could beat them. Along the way I found out via reading Congressional fund appropriation reports that America had an international airport in Washington which only had black and white scanners and NO dogs. Apparently they had no money for either. The airport in question was Washington-Dulles, the same one bin Laden penetrated years later for the 9/11 bombing. I told Brother E about it but he said no fucking way. The DEA would chase us across the world, extradite our arses that side and then toss us in a Federal pen – IF we landed so much as a key on their soil and got gaaned. Fuck the Yanks – major money but way too much trouble and stupidity. I didn't like the idea really. I could imagine myself in Yankland walking down the street and fucking up strangers simply for being American and doing bugger all about it.

So I studied. Eventually I picked up on something. All the scanner technology in the world worked on the same principle – material density. I managed to figure out how to beat them, thanks to one of my old sergeants in the army. That poor old bugger was one huge mess of scar tissue from a glass mine he stood on during the Korean War. (What the fuck a South African was doing in the Korean War is anybody's guess.) He was an expert in camouflage and taught me everything I know. During a training exercise one day he cammo'ed me up and, while doing so, explained in detail what he was achieving. He reckoned that in the bush or jungle the eye is attracted by the abnormal, and the secret is to break those abnormal lines and trick it. It works. Then I realised something fucking profound. Maybe some geek will pick up on this. ALL the images being processed were elevational. Jaamie, that old Guvvie juice-junkie taught me this in Technical Drawing back in Die Bult. Elevational. Front, Back, Top, Bottom, Left, Right. Cute – it meant that if my suitcase was a dice cube, all the mutherfuckers would ever see was a number. A single number. And if I could metaphorically hide the zol behind that number, *They* would never see it. I had to think in three-dimensional terms. I would have to, as it were, float the *boom* inside a coating of things *materially* denser than it, using them as camouflage material. And that is exactly how I did it.

I had beaten the dogs. I knew I had beaten the scanners. Now I had to beat me. Brother E coached me on the airport. He described in detail, over and over, exactly what I was up against. The real issue was not in being familiar with the layout, but dealing with my body language. Brother E had drilled Sister E before her run and knew from experience what he was up against, but I still had to learn because I hadn't been part of that mission. Brother E explained that the biggest obstacle to overcome was going to be the human surveillance. I didn't have to worry about the cameras – by then it would be too late, and at any rate the big obvious ones I could see would all be dummies. The real ones were hidden in ventilation shafts or little black bubbles on the ceiling. He told me these cameras were connected to such sophisticated computer systems that up in a massive control room they could place a cross hair on your image, click on it with a mouse, and the cameras would then synchronise on you. As you moved out of range of one, another would pick you up, automatically tracking your movements on the same monitor wherever you went in the airport. They could even trace every camera shot with you in it – *backwards*. Fucking scary. He also explained that almost everybody working in the airport, from floor sweepers upwards, were all on BOB's payroll (*Border Guards – Illegal Trafficking, Human Slavery and Anti-Terrorism Task Force*).

All of them had been trained in reading body language and their arrest success rate was 98 percent. These mense were what I would be going up against.

Rule No. 1: Do Not Sweat. Thereafter – be – *whooosssaaaafffaaa* ... BE ... somebody they take no notice of. Mr Nobody. Exactly the same as the Army. I was going to get into it. Real good.

I also learnt that getting out of the country is a piece of piss if you know how. It starts with a passport.

Getting one usually takes around three to six months, but if you have a valid reason you can obtain an emergency one. I shaved my beard into a moustache and bought spectacles with clear lenses to break the hard lines in my face. As you can see from Big Dog's cover, I look like a bit of a mean cunt. (*Thank you Sarge, your cammo works!*) And then I had passport photos taken. I applied by making a statement to the effect that Denise needed emergency surgery and Eric had phoned me from London saying I should fly over immediately because it was very serious. It was my first major acting role. The curtain opened on me – bewildered, stricken, mildly apologetic – and came down to wild applause, twenty minutes after I'd spoken to the first official – *with* a six-month passport in my hand and a second, more permanent one in the post. Thank you, my director, my producer – ladies and gentlemen!

Step two is having enough money to leave the country. We had spent a hell of a lot of money from the first two operations. Brother E bought an old Landcruiser and refurbished it. He reinforced the chassis, installed an Australian Old-Man Emu shock system, fitted the biggest BF Goodrich off-road AT tires that they made, and completely redid the engine. That was over fifty jimmys. As I mentioned, we'd also bought an industrial vacuum-packer and got an engineering firm to build our presses. Just over seventeen jimmys. All this, together with the cost of buying the zol at just under Cape Town's lowest wholesale price (about eight jimmys) and our air tickets (just over twenty jimmys), meant that we did not have the jimmy a day we would need for the Dutch to allow us a three-week entry into the country. So we made a plan. We bought the air tickets, because we couldn't get forex without them. Then we took all the tom we had and got it stamped into one of the passports in guilders and immediately exchanged it back into rands somewhere else. And got it stamped back into Deutschmarks, American dollars – and so on, until each of us had enough stamped in to apply for visas. Bloody expensive exercise, but we wrote it off as another overhead we needed to suffer through.

Penetrating the EU was a piece of cake. All we needed was an EU country to give us a visa and we could travel freely anywhere within the eleven member nations. We had to specify an itinerary on our applications but wouldn't have to adhere to it once the visa had been issued. Brother E had the address of a mate in Amsterdam, and The Netherlands issued us each with a three-week Benelux visa. Welcome to the European Union!

*

I'm in bed. It's October 1997. My chick is asleep next to me and it is the night before the rest of us fly. I've burnt all my bridges. I've resigned from work. I never want to work in IT again. I am going to give everything to our little syndicate – become a professional smuggler.

By now I have permission from Cape Town through Big J to control the entire white part of the Bos. Jackie's boys from the American$ handle the coloured areas. Cape Town thinks that is all I am doing, which is cool because they accept me as a player but they don't know that I am now syndicated with Brother and Sister E. Town is changing fast. I remember back when me and Paulie were running around in The Playground – we had a sit-down. All the local players. For a chat. We all knew Jackie, Pinocchio, the Staggie Boeties and the Moroccans. We did profitable business with them and some of the other makweras, but they played in a league above us. We, being the usual ou skelms – and all knowing each other for years – from school, jail and the streets – were mostly friendly and cooperative with each other, but we knew that would change. Soon everything would be Controlled. And foreigners were arriving by the day to try and force their *wors* in. Which is why the Big Boys were going to get tough.

And that is exactly where our little jol finds itself tonight.

We are walking a thin edge in our syndicate. They must not notice us.

Stellenbosch is not a problem. I've got it running like clockwork. An asset I've brought to the table. I have two brothers who handle everything for us there. Boetie J and Boetie D. Boetie J has a slight brown sugar problem, so we make D handle the stock and cash. J is a big oke, so he does all the muscle work in their partnership. It's a nice operation. They have a stable of runners who work the clubs and student pubs without too many mistakes. They are cashing in about fifteen to twenty jimmys a week. We only let them work with pills. I have a thing on the side with them flogging acid for me (old habits die hard), but it's for throwaway money. Brother and Sister E aren't interested. The boys are allowed to buy coke but not sell. Management policy. The same applies to smack, as long as Boetie J keeps his shit wired tight. They've seen what me and Brother E do to people who fuck up. In Town it's a different story. I still have a good hold on the Turtle because Freebody is so nuts nobody knows what to do with him and he gives me a free run of the place. I also pick my runners very carefully. We've got the Vortex parties sewn up tight, but the others are fucking dodgy. All the clubs are a no-no. Gone are the sit-downs Paulie and I had with owners and managers working out rent and security issues to supply their jols. I have to walk into a spot and buy a pill off a floor dealer to keep myself out the eyes. The problem is deeper. We have a couple of runners who sell in bulk to floor dealers under the noses of their bosses. Floor dealers are the rats of the trade – they'll suck cock with anyone if they can make an extra buck to put into their heads. But, if one of them gets caught and they trace our runner, they'll kill him – after he's told them Who and Where we are. I leave that side of things to Brother E: he reckons he knows what he's doing – a lot of these ouens went to school with him.

I have my own scams. The best I've ever done was forty-seven jimmys in an hour and a half one night. Three runners all boarding planes to Joburg with the goeters stashed inside fake videotapes. I remember my flatmate seeing me do the cash up the next morning. Nearly had a heart attack. Never seen so much money. Blew my cover a little too. My other gig is my girls. I've got a nice stable of barmaids who only sell to chicks. The whole club scene is so totally fucking macho that they never notice the kinders sorting themselves out in the bogs. Most chicks hate the hassle and the violence that goes with getting ouens to score from other ouens. And I have one very good runner in the gay community. Nice doing business with them too – they similarly despise violence and shite and are far more professional.

It is a turning point in my life. I suppose everything that I've gone through in life up until now has prepared me for this. I will not feel guilty. Uncle Guvvie put me into the worst white male mang in the country at eighteen for one pip. Fuck him – I'll smuggle tons if I can …

And tomorrow is step one. I must fly ...

I have to master myself.

The idea is to BE who my appearance says I am. Ja, Skollie.

We packed tonight.

According to my plan.

I took brand new luggage for the clean smell. It has never been around open zol and we washed our hands before buying it. The dogs would smell the slightest trace of pollem on the bag. Then we bought plastic hangers, which I layered on the bottom of the suitcase, making lots of hard, disruptive, triangular patterns. My assumption being that the largest surface of the bag will be the one surveyed first. On top of the hangers, clothes folded roughly in the same squares as the blocks to similarly shimmer their lines. Small bottles, cans of hoerpoep, shoes and other hard shit we bought – placed all around the sides. On top, another layer of clothes laid out wide and tucked in tight. Then, on top of that, electronic shit with carefully scattered CDs covered with a towel and also packed in tight.

Brother E has a poster on the wall at his place – it is a picture of a suitcase stuffed with zol blocks and the caption – Are You Packed?! He laughs like hell at it regularly.

Our route out is safe. We've discovered a flaw in air travel that works perfectly. Cape Town only has black and white scanners at the airport. We know because they were bitching about it loudly in the papers. By taking a flight from Cape Town International to Joburg and connecting for Brussels from there – we never have to personally check our luggage out of International Departures. If it is the same carrier, it's loaded onto the connecting flight automatically. And Domestic Departures only check for explosives anyway. The dogs can't smell bombs *and* drugs – they're only trained for bombs. So the outward-bound flight is sorted. It is the airport of entry that is the bitch. I know exactly what to expect. I will disembark and walk out into the gate. Once through and inside the terminus, I will find myself in a corridor about a kilometre long. Apparently our flight always hooks to one of the last gates in the terminus. Flat conveyor belts will run down the entire length of the corridor to a set of tollbooths. Here my passport will be inspected by a hard-eyed person and stamped. On the other side is Sovereign Belgian Territory and the baggage carousels. I will grab a trolley, wait ... pick up my luggage, proceed to a line of office dividers, and go through a gap only big enough for one person at a time.

On the other side of the gap— a line of tables and a big gang of stern Customs officials, who study every person coming through, will confront me. If they call me over, the first thing they will probably do is ask for my passport and instruct me to write my name, address and other details on a form. They'll be studying my handwriting for signs of nerves. If they're not satisfied, they will then ask me to open my luggage. I shake at the thought of this, but the maxim is: It will never happen. I will so be Mister Nobody on holiday in Europe for the first time. Tired, jet-lagged but a little happy – me being a middle manager in a bank or a schoolteacher or something like that. We carefully bought a full costume for me to wear for the occasion. After we packed I did a little fashion parade and the resultant yells of approval by all and sundry mean we are satisfied. I look like an absolute doos.

Doos Nobody.

But now I must relax and sleep.

*

Next day I awake late. Brother and Sister E arrive and pick me up. I say goodbye to my baby and we leave. I don't want her at the airport with me. I need to focus and concentrate. One small problem at the airport. I've got a chunk of hash on me. Part of a kilo I bought for fun some time ago. We haven't got time to smoke it, so I eat it. We board our flight and hop up to Joburg uneventfully except— Brother E keeps freaking the other passengers out by yelling – *Hey! Hey! Hey!* – loudly.

It's his 'I'm gonna fuck over the world' mantra.

He's irritating me mildly, even though we're not sitting together. We land and proceed to International Departures. Customs stamps us out the country and we go hit the bar. I am starting to feel the hash in my stomach. We buy a dop and I nip off to a duty-free shop for a litre of whiskey. Our flight is called. We board. I'm thrilled and freaking slightly at the same time. The hash is not helping either. It's cranking up my paranoia level no end and really fucking hitting me hard. I fasten my seatbelt, sink back into my seat and fall asleep. I did this once before just as an acid trip started kicking in. I dropped it at the office as I walked out the door to go home, but was so tired that when I arrived at my pozzie I crashed out immediately. I woke up two hours later and it took me a further half-hour to figure out what fucking planet I was on. Hectic. Back in reality I wake up strapped into a howling Airbus on take-off into the night. I'm gonna play the meek and slightly air-freaked geek. No real acting talent needed. Thing was, I knew that some airlines had civilian observers on board and you never knew who the fuck your fellow passengers might be. That's why I don't want to sit with my partners. The aircrew obviously compartmentalised you too. Geeky teacher, H1, window seat left. Polite and quiet, nervous flyer, reading thick book. (And quietly knocking off the litre of whiskey Das style …)

It's amazing, down there is Africa. I can see on the cabin screen exactly where we are. I'm finally starting to really break free. I feel morally justified in what I am doing. The zol I am [NOT] carrying all comes from Swaziland. There it is traditional and sanctioned by the King. He makes a lot of money out of it. Buys him a lot of wives. It doesn't matter, because the most terrible drug ever to come to Africa has always been white man's alcohol – and the psychotic hypocrisy in that industry is ludicrous. We really have to have the weirdest liquor laws in the entire world. I cannot buy a bottle of wine for Sunday lunch from a supermarket in the white part of the country, but I can buy a bottle of vodka or whatever I want, *legally*, from any tavern in a black township. And apartheid is supposed to be over! Apparently Jesus will get fucked off if the whiteys buy dop on a Sunday or something. These Romans and their gods are crazy. And until recently that was the worst. Then, of course, there was the evil shit like Mandrax in the late seventies, sponsored by the dark side of the previous white government, and more recently heroin and coke, brought in by overseas mobsters, triads and cartels when we wisely tossed our borders open to the shit of the world. But I am a dealer in cannabis and MDMA (ja, ja, Acid Alex). Oh yes, I have learnt all about Ecstasy. N-3,4-methylenedioxymethamphetamine. Da Love Drug. Unlike zol it's only been illegal for about ten years, but already it has the guns coming out. Our syndicate refuses to sell chopped-down shit. Pills with a bit of E and a fruit salad of other cheap chemical crap. Down on the street the punters are clueless and run after a colour and a stamp. Green Apples, Red Ferraris, White Nikes, whatever. They are too dumb to know the difference or just don't give a fuck. But then again, we always hammer the hell out of the market with what we put out because those same dumb punters can also spot the difference when they taste the real thing. I know I can.

I won't sell drugs I can't take myself for fun.
I won't sell pussy and I won't be a hired gun.
I will also never carry another man's tom—
If I do so – I will stop being a free outlaw.
A world-class naughty boy …

22

Amsterdammed

I never slept that night. It seems I will always struggle to do so on international flights. The next morning I was bleary-eyed and hung-over. Perfect. Just after breakfast we found ourselves descending into Belgian airspace. The time had come! I was actually very calm, although the real thrill of being Overseas for the first time was palpable. My rigorous mental exercises had taken hold. Deep down inside somewhere, paranoia was hopping up and down wildly, desperate to leap out the box – but I was having none of it. I breathed, placed myself in a state of mental limbo, and acted. Like I had never done before. Each deep, calm breath helped me prepare and focus on the next set of actions. I arrived at the carousel, grabbed my luggage and walked straight through. Nobody even noticed me. I was so good that the Customs officials chatting with each other didn't even glance my way.

On the other side I went to a quiet part of the airport, bought a phonecard and went to a kiosk to phone my girl and Brother E's mom. They were waiting for the calls. Brother and Sister E came up laughing and yelling wildly and we all tumbled down the escalators to the train. Our air tickets went all the way to Schiphol, but we knew we would never get through there, so we skipped our connecting flight and boarded the railway shuttle to Brussels. The moment it pulled out of the station, I ducked into the toilets, shaved and changed. We arrived in Brussels. I was still shell-schlocked. I had made it! I walked, talked and made all the fucking ducks quaaack!

In a bright exhausted daze I followed Brother and Sister E and we boarded a TGV directly to Amsterdam. Now there's a fine way to travel. Those trains fuck off at unimaginable speeds, but inside everything is dead quiet and done up in gentle good taste. A waitron sells beer. My kind of train! Smooth – well, not exactly – more like a steady hum as the country literally flashes by. I wondered what Sandy would have thought of driving one if he was still around. We stopped in Antwerp – Den Haag – Haarlem – Amsterdam. The other places' names I forget. I was going through over-sensory input as the foreign land flashed past. All the postcards, travel brochures and books I had read were threading themselves together into the amazing reality I was hurtling towards.

We disembarked, found pay lockers and stashed the zol. Then Brother E walked us out of Grand Central Station. Before me lay Amsterdam city centre. Straight ahead was the Damrak – a long wide road thronged with hordes of pedestrians, bicycles, cars and trams – wildly festooning what was clearly a very old city in a kaleidoscopic frenzy of bustling activity. From the entrance all the way to Dam Square – it was all one crowd. Trying to cross the road was a disorientating nightmare because everybody drove on the wrong side and there were six lanes of completely different traffic to get through. We managed to nip across unscathed and ducked into a pedestrian walkway leading into an even more crowded and bewildering maze of shops and shopfronts to arrive at our first destination – The Blues Brothers Coffeeshop. This was going to prove to be our base of operations. Of course, Brother E knew the owner and all the staff.

Befuck, now what am I gonna smoke?

Hash. Good hash. That means Moroccan Zero-Zero. This I learnt from the staff, who enthusiastically welcomed me as Brother and Sister E's South African partner. I was presented with a yellow block in a small Ziploc baggie with a bright green zol leaf printed on it – and rolled a spliff. Brother E disappeared.

There's a lot of kak spoken – urban myths, wharrawharra – about how coffeeshops graft. I'll explain. It works exactly like an alcohol bar. First you need to apply for a cannabis licence from the government. You cannot apply if you have a criminal record. You are only allowed to operate between the hours of 08h00 and 01h00. You may not serve anyone under the age of eighteen. You may only sell cannabis products and refreshments – you may not sell alcohol. For the rest – get creative! A lot of them run an upstairs cannabis shop with a downstairs wet bar. See. In central Amsterdam there are in the region of six hundred coffeeshops. The best one and the one with the largest menu is also the oldest, The Bluebird, currently run by the third generation of family that has owned it since the fight in the seventies to get it re-legalised.

The hash spliff was fucking me up. No, *really* fucking me up. I felt exactly like I had once – *and only once before* – in the Transkei.

We arrive at Agate Terrace and I immediately set out for Poenskop with the laaitie from the camp. It's a very long trek to my old man, so I always take a tent and some dry food and water. I also take about four quarts of Black Label. Fucking extra weight on top of my trade goods but well worth it. I estimate it to be about a fifteen- to twenty-click hike into the hills, and I mean The Hills. It gets remote there fucking fast. And arduous. Anyway, I always see his plantations first. He has them enclosed in bomas between his maize and other husbandry. He puts zol plants in between his own food crops because they keep the insects off. I know, I asked him all about it. Speaking with him is very tricky, because my Xhosa doesn't even bear a passing glance at rudimentary. That's why I've got the laaitie. He can speak a little English and comes with me as my interpreter. We usually hire our huts from his mother. His baba is always away up in Joburg working on the mines.

The laaitie picks up a couple of bras along the way who come running down the hills yelling – Numba 1! Numba 1! I ignore them, because even though they sometimes do have fairly good first grade, my old man and I have been doing satisfactory business for years. I arrive at his small cluster of huts looking like a pale-faced Pied Piper with at least one or two stunned nippers who have just seen their first white man. The laaities always drop to their haunches and I go a few paces ahead and do the same. After a while the old man comes shuffling out. I greet him in his language and he greets me back. When I reach the limit of my linguistics, I beckon the laaitie and ask him how his livestock is doing. Then I enquire after his crops and ask if his family are all well. I know I must be patient. This old fellow hasn't been hopping up and down in his hut waiting for me – I'm in his world – his space. Piss him off and he won't do business. Eventually we get around to the potency and abundance of his last nchangu crop. He beckons me and I take a place beside one of the huts. He disappears into another and returns with a sack. It's a number two. He always does this – it's a bit of a ritual. I tell him that the zol looks very good but it's not what I'm looking for – the farmer three hills from here, in that direction, has zaanies twice as good and he's begged me to buy from him. He disappears and comes back – this time it's the real deal. Rooibaard. Big fat green heads, bristling with dark red hairs and glittering with crystal. You don't even need a loupe to look at it properly. At this point I always ask if I can test a spliff. I don't really need to – a baboon would know that nchangu was poison – it's just that at this point the beers come into play. I crack open one and give it to the old bugger. And slowly roll a perfect joint. Then smoke it. I drink a bit of the beer too, but I know my capacity is enormous. So, by the time I am done, the toothless and greedy old rogue is nicely sloshed. Then

I do business. To my benefit. Only this time, after I have my sacks stowed with the laaities, he grins at me and disappears – into his living hut, I notice – and returns with a small raffia sugar sack. He shows me. Inside is red zol. Deep rusty red. Not one bit of green. He has taken all the points off big red heads and filled a small sack. Resting in the middle of it is a large lump of hash that I would later learn is called charis. It is made by collecting all the resin that sticks to your hands when you harvest zol and reap the heads. He takes a matchbox and stuffs it with the red zol. Mahala. I thank him and push my luck by asking for a piece of hash. He just laughs, making me pay for the beer trick no doubt, and dodders off to stash the sack. I greet him well and piss off back to camp. I sleep at my usual overnight spot, but I don't smoke the red stuff. I wait till base camp. Being a pig and strong contender for the World's Worst Bogart, I smoke alone. Bottleneck. I mean, hello? ... I'm the goonk who just walked two days to fetch thirty kilos of poison, okay? I manage to take three hits and then the boom hits me. As hard as good acid. And I sit for three hours on a rock unable to move or speak. Just trippin' ...

Back in, *what city?* Ah yes, Amsterdam! – something similar was happening. I was fucked out of my skull. Brother E returned expansively *Hey! Hey! Heying!* – with a gram of charles. Into the toilets himself *gou-gou* and then slipping it to me. He tuned me zol was legal – everything else was not. Keep it *under cover*. Especially the Peruvian flake. I disappeared into the bogs. Within the high rituals practised by the opiates of the senses, the universal confessional is the obsequious toilet. The pilgrim enters to divest his waste and ingest his sins. I took a piss and looked at the coke. It was mildly pink and reflected the bog-light like mother of pearl. Wow. Me Greedy. Me Boss. Me – Chop-chop. You Schaaaafed ...

Ja, one time. Snuif, snuif.

Back at the bar I passed the dented gram back to Brother E. He gave me his snake look and grinned lasciviously. Then it fucking hit me – wiping out into the hash and the potent Belgian beer I had been drinking and all I could do was cling to the bar and hope I didn't die. White noise ... ...

AMSTERDAMMED!!!

I had been in the city twenty minutes.

I eventually managed to get my shit together and we disappeared into this huge fucking spot where I had absolutely no notion of where I was for a minute. Next to Planet Hollywood was a small coffeeshop. I wandered up and down, stoned silly, measuring my hands against the stars'. Arnie and Rambo must have tiny dicks but, my fuck, Clint has to be hung like a fucking proverbial donkey. Great shades of old Dysel back at school.

Our host was in the coffeeshop. Came from Surinam. Country I had never heard of. Apparently it was still a Dutch colony. Wow. He lived in Osdorp a little ways out of the city centre. We collected our goeters from the station, caught a tram and found our way to his pozzie. Outside of the centre of the city, away from the canals, houseboats and beautiful old buildings, was the usual grim urban ghetto. Huge dirty grey high-rise apartment blocks in regimented rows, housing thousands in low-income units. We dropped the move, grabbed a block of zaanies and gooied back into the town centre. I lussed all my life to get out of South Africa and I had come to the best pozzie in the world to do it. Lekker.

We cruised around to a number of coffeeshops, dropping the entire key at one spot for just over eight jimmys. Brother E was on a fact-finding mission.

That night we went to an Indonesian restaurant and ate some of the best food it has ever been my pleasure to pay for. Then we went partying at the Mazzo. I was mostly in a total dwaal from too much excitement, drugs, culture shock, et cetera, and when we arrived back at our apartment later, I crashed out stone dead to the world.

The next morning found me waking up, pinching myself to make sure that I really was in Amsterdam – in the province of Holland – slap bang in the middle of the Kingdom of The Netherlands – with just under a hundred jimmys of zol to flog!

Bite yourself just to make sure. Eina, poes, ja ja … seems that way.

We sold the zaanies. The whole pak to a zol office at just over eight jimmys per key some time later.

Brother E took out something for each of us by mutual agreement and we went shopping. I bought clothes and started getting to know the city a little.

A major part of the attraction of the Dam is the sex industry. It's in your face everywhere. Sex shows, sex shops and of course the famous Red Light District. Very easy to find too.

Walk out of Grand Central Station up the Damrak, past the YMCA building emblazoned with *Jesus Loves You*, and turn left across one of the small bridges towards a club called The Grasshopper. The street behind it is called Warmoesstraat. Walk down it and turn into any alley.

You are now in Pay-for-Pussyland.

Young pussy, Old pussy, Black pussy, Gook pussy, Fat pussy, Pale pussy, Red pussy, Thin pussy, Skanky pussy, Pretty pussy, Boy pussy, Shaved pussy, Hairy pussy, Not sure pussy – you get the picture …

We had been there a couple of days, and had still not tracked down the pills we wanted, at the price we wanted – so we spent most of our time partying in clubs. Melkweg, Escape, Time, Mazzo, Paradiso, etc.

One night we were in Club Time. The owner decided to play old skool that night and it was some of the worst shite I've ever heard. The punters were yelling at him, pulling zap signs and what-what, but he just kept on spinning crap. All three of us had dropped sample pills and we were completely schmangled, so going to another club was out of the question for at least a few hours.

I disappeared upstairs and plonked myself down behind a bar, bought a dop and started chatting up the Dutch barmaid. I was missing my chick terribly. We were there strictly on business, but it would still have been nice for her to have experienced it all with me. My chick, not the barmaid. She and I were getting on famously when suddenly the music stopped and all the lights went on. I got a big skrik because in clubs back home it meant that the boere were about to run in with blazing video cameras and a squad of uniformed gattas to bust the place. The honey serving me explained that the mayor of Amsterdam had decreed: All clubs close at exactly five. Music off, lights on – fuck off and go home. I tipped her, regretting deeply that I should have picked her up (*she made it very clear*) – but I wasn't going to fuck around behind my baby's back – no matter where I was. I'd learnt the hard way.

Downstairs I found Brother and Sister E with a very, very fat woman and some skinny, chinless ou with a wispy moustache. Brother E introduced me. Linda and Johaan. We were apparently going to their spot for a bit of an afterparty. Cool. Cruise and head directly for the Red Light District. Eventually we arrived at a building with a bunch of booths.

Prostitution is very well managed in Amsterdam. The workers need a passport, medical certificate and deposit for a booth. The streets of the District are lined with them. Security is very tight – very large fuckers in leather jackets stand around watching the punters. The booth has a front and a back divided by a curtain. In the back is a chair, a bed and a table. The girls bring what they need with them. Usually a boom box, CDs, lotions, creams, condoms, toys and drugs. They sit on a stool up front dressed in bikinis or erotic underwear watching the men – and some women – who come by under their red lights. When a punter knocks on the door, she'll either ignore it or open and negotiate a price. Keep on knocking and one of the big fuckers in leather jackets will have a chat with you. You go in, she closes the curtain and turns a trick. The owner of the booth gets a percentage for each trick. It's safe and well managed. The girls make a lot of money and get to keep it without the interference of violence from pimps and johns. Part of the percentage goes to pay the big fuckers in leather jackets ...

Linda owned a string of these booths. Upstairs was her boudoir. Everything was done in crushed red velvet and gold plate. She was obviously a very wealthy woman. She fell back onto an enormous bed, blubber heaving alarmingly, and ordered Johaan to bring a bottle of Armagnac. Then she pulled out a bankie of pills and gobbled a couple. Johaan returned with the Armagnac. She patted the bed next to her and told me to make myself comfortable. I did so, much to the crude amusement of Brother and Sister E. She told us she was the fattest whore in Amsterdam. Johaan poured us all drinks and I rolled a hash spliff.

I reckoned we were her guests, so I asked her when she got into it. Thirteen. She had apparently been very beautiful and much in demand, so she made a lot of money but knew how to keep it. When she'd made enough, she opened her own brothel with herself as the Madame. And that is what she was still doing. The girls in her booths were all working for her. She explained that she handled the weird tricks – but not S&M shit. She laughed at this and stated emphatically that no man would be able to push her around anyway. *No shit?* She only handled the seriously weird. The usual golden showers and the odd crapping on some poor sick cunt's chest, but weirdest of all was a Jap businessman who flew out a couple of times a year and arrived bearing a bottle of roaches. Live roaches of the scurrying-under-the-sink kind. She would have to dress up in frilly underwear – *the mere mental image of Linda in frilly undies made my eyeballs ache* – lie down on the floor with the bottle of taragoppies, take off her shoe, fish one out, say a very specific ditty that he had composed for the occasion and kill the mutherfucking thing. Each gogga she klapped was rewarded with a thousand-guilder note. And there was an entire bloody bottle full. No wonder she could afford to gold-plate everything. And the john never even undressed. Got off just like that. She explained that the happily grinning Johaan had been one of her jols too. He apparently pitched up and asked for her. She took pity on him and turned the trick. Next day he was there again. She did him again. Later that night he returned, gave her a big wad of cash and explained that it was all the kroon he had in the world. She took him in. As she had explained, she didn't need a pimp – he was just her pet and he could fuck her whenever he wanted, provided he was a good boy and asked nicely. More power to you, Johaan …

We were still in negotiations to buy pills when one evening Brother and Sister E decided to go and watch a sex show. I had just over a gram of coke, more test pills, hash and very good zaanies. I also had about eight hundred guilders, so I cruised down into the Red Light District like Brother and Sister E kept teasing me to do. I started window-shopping. A trick usually costs fifty guilders. There were some truly gorgeous dead-eyed women on display. I wandered around, but the more I did so, the more disgusted I became – at the men. The alleyways thronged with lewd, ugly, red-faced yobs of every shape and description. The more I saw, the more I knew I couldn't do it. I have slept with so many, many women. I suppose it was a little detail I forgot to mention concerning my break-up with Norma. I'd screwed all her best friends behind her back. Like I said, I learnt the hard way about fucking around. I could not imagine how shit* it must be for most of these kinders to make a living like that with these fucks. No wonder they looked dead-eyed. But I felt stupid for that kind of thinking – I mean, hey ou, it's a big wide world out there and isn't it sort of time you kinda grew up? I mean, I lived on the other side of the hard line professionally – so what was my problem? It's just that I was a predator. I went after single unattached females. I've never fucked another man's wife, although I had a lover for eight years once and we screwed each other through three of her boyfriends and two of my girlfriends. We never thought anything of it – we just really enjoyed casual, energetic sex together. Maybe it had something to do with Laura and how she fucked up my impression of women. I could not pay to fuck a whore because I knew women find sexual expression through their emotions. I believed I needed talent, tenderness, patience and understanding to satisfy a woman – not money. I fucked women to satisfy them – that's how I got *my* rocks off and patched up my fractured self-image in the process. Quite simply, I knew full well I couldn't buy a real female orgasm and I wouldn't fuck up my relationship, so I wimped out and went to satisfy a bar owner.

The next night I found myself in the weirdest club I've ever been to. Club IT. The head of security – some very serious-looking ou, who knew Brother E – invited us in. I found out that it had a very strict dress code and you only got in if you were *Somebody*. IT was a celebrity gay club. Well, not so much gay as gender non-specific. A Madonna, Prince, Marilyn Manson–type jol— … It.

The lighting, the sound system and the interior décor must have cost millions. Glisteningly oiled steroid boys posed on the dance floor, muscles writhing like pythons in amongst drag queens dressed like royalty in five-jimmy frocks from the latest catwalks in Milan and Paris. The rest was just plain wild. I had never seen or dreamt of anything like it. And, my fuck, did they know how to party! The lid was coming off my narrow mind – big time – although before Amsterdam I would have sworn high and low that I was a liberal anarchist. A laissez-faire outlaw determined to live and let live. Yeah, right. But, hell, it's only a fault if I let it stay that way. Yeah, live and let live – the worst is that I'll learn more about life and how little I know about it.

We eventually bought pills from a brother whose identity I will keep to myself. He was an international DJ. Very talented and rated top in The Netherlands at the time. We met Green Velvet through him – a totally crazy and brilliant DJ from Detroit who had started out way back with Frankie Knuckles, the Grandfather of House. So we scored from the big man and took it all back to the flat.

We were going to get them back into SA in small parcel packages. They needed to be packed. The quantity of pills we bought came in four shopping bags. We were only paying seventy-five South African per tablet. First we swaaied them into rolls of twenty using large Rizlas. Looked like rolls of sweets. Eventually we had hundreds of these. These sweetie rolls were bound five at a time on either side of a piece of exact-sized cardboard – effectively making packs of two hundred. They actually smelt like sweeties too. A sickly sweet liquorishy smell that really got up your nose. We always wore gloves and face masks when packing, to ward off forensics and not overdose on the dust and fumes. Then we went and hit all the toy stores we could find. We bought little zip-open pencil purses. Each one contained pencils, some koki pens, a small stencil, ruler, rubber, sharpener, small stamp pad and some play stamps. We bought all the stock we could find. These we took to the flat with plain bubble and colourful birthday envelopes big enough to fit the purses into. The packs of pills were then carefully wrapped in carbon paper – *scanners can't see through it* – and wiped clean. Then all the packs were dowsed in *parfum* and sealed in Saran Wrap. We packed them into the purses two at a time and sealed them in the envelopes with children's birthday greetings in bright koki and finally into the bubble envelopes addressed to temporary postboxes we had opened all over the Western Cape. Four hundred per drop. Expensive but safe, and split up so we wouldn't lose the entire pak in the event of a bust.

The next step was to start scattering them carefully into the Dutch postal system all over Amsterdam. Everything from outlying post offices went to the central depot and from there was transported to Schiphol for airfreight to Joburg. We had to make sure that we timed and distributed it so that we did not have too many parcels on the same flight. We knew that parcels under 500g would not be subjected to a scanner inspection. They were packed into large sacks, and dogs merely smelt each sack. We also took care when addressing them, using different pens and handwriting – then held thumbs and waited to get home. In the years that we used this method we never lost a single package. Not one, although Brother and Sister E insisted on each carrying 200 pills for the return flight that first time we were all over there together.

They bottled them in her koek and up his hol.

That flight home was a riot. The next morning, just over Zambia, we all dropped candy for fun. Trippin' while flying is truly trippin' cuzeeen.

Picking up the parcels was not a problem. This was expedited easily enough by finding a crackhead fuckup, promising it a nice big rock and carefully setting it about picking up the parcels – making very sure that it didn't run away with a package. Like I said, not a problem – Cape Town is riddled with crackheads.

We quickly activated everybody on our payroll and started moving the shipment.

Until I made a mistake.

23

The Great Homecoming
Fuck Fantasy

I was in The Loft – a club run by a bra but controlled from outside as regards drugs. I never did business in the place but I usually had a good couple of pills and enough money for personal fun. At least until that ran out and I needed more cash – then I'd maybe knock off a pill or two quietly for dop marchers. Red Bull and double Absoluts are expensive. So is charlie. Nothing happened at The Loft and I left with two very good chinas. An Angolan and a Pom. We arrived at another very seriously controlled club. I should have ditched everything in the car but I didn't. Inside the jol I bought a dop and sat down somewhere. A good friend of Bobby Boy's came over and perched on my lap. I had a bit of the hots for her but would never do anything about it, my baby and all, but all the same – I carefully extracted a pill and slipped it to her. Unbeknown to me I had been followed from The Loft. They were all watching me like hawks – and grabbed me. I was taken downstairs, into a circle of about six to eight Moroccans, and searched. Three jimmys, fifteen pills, bankie of zol, keys, Zippo, entjies, Rizlas.

Pain Time – they say.

I prepared myself for it, very thankful that all the E I had taken would pull some of its bite. Abdul was the first one in with a solid punch to my bek – it hurt like fucking hell but I refused to rock to it and similarly refused to react. I stepped forward and dropped my centre of gravity – ready. I had to fight my way to the street. Their jol would be to get me into a car for a quick ride to Chapman's Peak and a very fast drop off a cliff. Gangsta bungee sans rope. It was going to bloody hurt alright, but if I couldn't pull it off I would simply be dead.

Suddenly we all heard somebody say quietly … *Stop.*

They all stood back, glaring at me. I turned towards the voice and was confronted by The Man himself, and I'm not talking about any of the steroid monkeys now. The Man. He tells me to come with him. I follow him out into the street, and he strolls down to the corner.

– *Do you know who I am?* –

– *Yes* –

– Good, then you know I'm only going to tell you this once. I can see you are a big man and you know how to look after yourself. I've asked about you, so I know about you. Don't ever come to one of my clubs again. If you do, I won't stop them the next time and I'll make sure they take it all the way. My way. Do you understand? –

– Yes –

I knew where it came from. They had tried to recruit me some time back but I had refused. Very carefully. And obviously dissed them in the process. They had wanted to recruit me to work as a runner, which, if I was clever, I could use as a front for my own goeters, but I wasn't going to take the risk.

I had blown my cover a little. A lot, as it turned out. Now they knew I was operating in Town. This was confirmed to me by Aziz, one of the Moroccans. He said that Abdul was worried that I was going to take it personal and sent a message that he apologised. This of course was their way of being sweet – to soften me up. Never in a million years would one of them back down and ask forgiveness for giving me a klap. Admittedly the only forgiveness I would accept was if I dressed up as a vuil old bergie one night, sprayed them all with an AK and disappeared. I knew they wanted to find the pills, take them and put a bullet through my head. I took it as confirmation when one of their hit men started following me everywhere.

That's when I panicked.

Opposition is eliminated in a number of ways. Piemp the problem to tame gattas – for a docket in their pocket – and everybody is smiling. Or shoot it. But before shooting it, rob it. If you can't rob it, tip off the vigilantes. They'll shoot it for you. Either way, everybody is more than smiling.

Except me.

I was aware that Cape Town's drug politics changed by the hour, so I elected to take a mule on a zol and pill run – send the mule back and take a winter holiday safely in Europe. By the time I got back, everything would have changed. A lot of the dangerous ouens would either be dead or in the mang. Guaranteed. That's what that type of *want-to-be-the-main-ouen* lived and died for.

I needed a mule first. Zol was no problem. We had a bunch of chommies from the old days, and by chance we ran into another dude who had good enough zol at the right price. He had half of what I wanted. I also needed money to look after myself in the Dam and I wasn't going to do that from our business, so we decided that I should take fifteen kilos. Nineteen point something kilos, as it turned out.

Crime is a fucking bad debtor. Fucks off with your – or maybe others' – money, and almost always leaves you in a cage. The way you get bust is simple – you make a mistake – or – you get piemped. This comes to you by karma. Trust me on this – I know, because I learnt the fucking hard way.

Brother and Sister E wanted me to take an ou whom I klapped six months previously for ripping off the Boeties in Stellenbosch.

Let's call him Fuckhead.

He came to my boys and spun a yarn about working for the Russian out in Somerset West. The Russian was some heavy ou who had been booted out of Cape Town's inner clique for being too violent and ran a club there. I could not believe that my boys were stupid enough to consider a monkey mobster hiring somebody like Fuckhead. And they put us in danger by dropping the pills into a club we didn't control.

There was no fucking way on earth I wanted to start a war.

Behind it was the fact that Fuckhead had a sincerity gland he could switch on at will. Almost everybody fell for it. Including my runners. Ten jimmys worth of pills. Two shipments of five grand. One to pay for the other. I was livid with the boys. So was Brother E.

I drove through to the Bos, picked up one of them, and went to Fuckhead's mommy's house. I told him to bring Fuckhead out while I hid in my bakkie. I wanted to bliksem the arsehole, toss him into the bakkie, then drive off somewhere that would certainly not stay lekker quiet for long – for a chat. He came out and I grabbed him. By the third punch he was screaming so loudly that he woke up the entire neighbourhood, which is why I needed somewhere fucking quiet in the first place. His brother came running out to help him. In trying to handle them both, I lost Fuckhead, who ran tearing off up the road yowling hysterically and alternatively moaning in dread. Brother E pitched up later, pissed off with me that I hadn't waited for him. He immediately jumped on the wagon though, and terrified Fuckhead's mother by threatening to plant coke in her house and piemp her to the boere. Eventually his dad paid off the debt. The fucking morons actually thought that we'd be stupid enough to give them a receipt for the tom.

Medical reports presented in evidence at my trial as a mafia boss later in Belgium told me the medics had put in twenty-one stitches to repair the damage I did to Fuckhead's face.

What else was I supposed to do? Phone my fucking accountant?

I told Brother and Sister E I didn't want him. They argued. I argued back. Eventually they turned democratic on me and I had to take him. And in a big bloody hurry too. The Moroccan on my back had taken to following me everywhere. I quietly moved from Gardens back to Stellenbosch, where I disappeared and cooled off from the Cape Town scene. Quite by amazing coincidence the spot I found was downstairs from Christine and her little sister's pozzie.

Brother E and I managed to source the rest of the zol from some other roeker I knew who was connected to the boere mafia. It seemed that syndicates were crawling out the woodwork from everywhere. Apparently the zol we bought came from a shipment of a half-ton stashed down in the basement of an NG Kerk somewhere up north. The dominee was one of the bosses and it was grown quietly on some farms somewhere else. It was very good zol too and came up in forensic testing later as having a 12.9 percent THC content – well worth about nine jimmys a key in the Dam.

I sat down with Brother and Sister E and we started discussing the future of our business. I felt we needed to move out of Cape Town completely. The place was becoming chaotic. The gangs of my youth had broken free of the Group Areas Act and had mostly settled their territorial disputes, consolidating themselves into a cartel called The Firm. The two biggest gangs in Cape Town controlled it – the Hard Living$ and the American$. With all our friends from North Africa, a couple of bent SANAB boere and the local white mobsters as supporting cast. On top of this, the vigilante group PAGAD was becoming increasingly insane and violent. Of course we knew the boere had open files on us. Later we found out *exactly* how detailed. It was terrifying. Anyway, it was no sane place to run a business, so after long discussions we decided to take our operation up the east coast with the intention of setting up a runner in each town all the way from the Bos to PE ...

It was the thing with Fuckhead ...

He was waxing hot and cold. I still didn't trust him either, which brings me back to my point concerning karma. I don't subscribe to you die and get reincarnated with all your bad *or* good karma in your pocket or what-ever the hell it is you have to lug it around in. I strongly believe that the shit you cause comes back to you very quickly, and I think that when you finally die you have completed your perfect purpose and all the celestial books are in a state of balance. I learnt it from being a thief. Whenever you steal— you make yourself poorer. Proved it to myself time and time again until I learnt. I reckon it applies to pretty much everything else too. I decided to use him – but fuck him if he got bust …

See, that's where the bad karma lies. I could have changed that attitude but I didn't. I had become a hard-nosed professional the tough way – by learning not to be taken for a poes. And Fuckhead had taken me for a big one. So fuck him, if he got bust. His problem, although we bullshitted him and told him we would bail him out with lawyers, etc. I made him get an emergency passport, something he dragged his feet over until Brother E and I started growing horns.

Then we went to buy tickets. My plan was to buy two tickets in different places and in different seats, but as fate would have it there were only two seats left on the flight, so I took a huge chance and bought them.

Big mistake.

We went through the usual, booking money into our passports, none of which Fuckhead would ever carry, and went to apply for visas. The Dutch refused. Fuck! – but luckily there was some coloured dude who was booking visas for a travel agency he worked for who took me to one side. He told me to leave it up to him and went to the Belgian Consulate there to sweet-talk them into issuing us Benelux visas. They did. Sjoe! I tipped him big time for his help. It never crossed my mind that I was being too windgat. My Das sense could have gone into a raving tantrum and at that point I would still have played deaf.

We packed Fuckhead's bags the day before we left. Here I made my second windgat mistake. One of the blocks had broken its seal. Brother E asked me what I wanted to do. Leave it in, I replied callously. I spent my last precious night with Christine, kissed her goodbye and left for the airport.

*

I'm back, descending into grey Belgian airspace. I take another big pull on my bottle of whiskey. Screw Das style – I don't have anything to be bang of. Fuckhead looks like the weather outside. He keeps on wigging out, groaning and shit. Fuck him, he can't back out now. I tell him as much in no uncertain terms. We land and I leave the aircraft ahead of him – alone and impatient. I get to the carousel, grab my suitcase and go through unchallenged to wait. A short while later he comes through white-faced and walks right up to me. I try to ignore him – but he's lost it and yammers at me frantically that they asked him questions. The stupid fuckwit isn't supposed to come near me, so I make as if to give him directions and stride off towards the station. Eight of them come for me, with guns out, and have me down on the floor, screaming at me in French not to fucking move, while I'm still only a slightly pissed-off heartbeat away from contemplating I could be bust already. Not that I understand French, mind you, it's simply the tone and volume of the warning delivered behind hardened steel tubes stuffed with nasty explosive things like hydra-shok hollowpoints (no doubt) and pressed painfully into the back of my immobile head – which very clearly leaves me in no doubt. They are fucking paranoid. Way too much so in my experience. The bullets are designed to enter my body and fragment without waxing innocent bystanders.

Déjà déjà wa-wa vu – the old nightmare has started once again.

They skate me painfully to a terrified Fuckhead – me of course ad libbin' the outraged innocent passenger to the max. Doesn't help. On the way they cheerfully announce that we have a lot of cannabis in our luggage. I immediately deny it hotly. They retort in happy, bad-accented sneers that this will be investigated thoroughly. Obviously speaking broken English and being an international plank is a job requirement.

We get taken up to their offices and re-skated to different benches – away from each other. SOP. Two serious gattas with folded automatic bang-bangs watch me stone-faced. Soon Fuckhead is taken somewhere. He returns and they grab me. As we pass by – I tune him in Skollietaal to keep his bek shut. The flics round on me snarling, telling me to shut the fuck up. I ignore them and get taken for a strip search. Been there, done that, frog fuck. I stand loud and proud while they search all my clothing with a fine-tooth comb. Nothing on me except smokes, money, ticket, passport and some tattoos. I refuse to give them the satisfaction of being embarrassed standing naked. I'm still a sexy cunt. They finish the strip search and take me for a urine test. My blood comes back positive for a fruit salad of narcotics, some of which I don't remember taking – although I'm not going to pit my misty short-term memory in a dark club's dimly lit toilets against cutting edge forensic science.

I get cuffed back to my bench, sans money, ticket and passport. The dog handlers come in and I see the dog that bust Fuckhead. It's a beautiful, really friendly little cocker spaniel. My last one was a border collie. Beautiful animals doing a shitty job for shitty people. The same crunchie flics still stand guard. In the next room I listen in astonishment as Fuckhead piemps me. Nice going, Fuckhead.

Eventually I get taken for an interrogation. I'm cool, the ultimate pro. The officer conducting the interview asks me for a statement and I tell him I have no statement to make – I want a lawyer. He smiles ever amiably and informs me that that is my right, but he wants me to know that he is charging me with:

1. Drug Smuggling, with the alternative charge of attempting to commit Chemical Poisoning upon the Sovereign Subjects of the Kingdom of Belgium, and
2. Conspiracy to commit International Organised Crime.

The maximum sentence on each charge: Life Imprisonment.

Secondly, under the Profiting from the Proceeds of Organised Crime Act, he is confiscating all my money and will be in communication with Interpol and the South African and Dutch governments to freeze my assets and bank accounts – and simultaneously check internationally for outstanding warrants for my arrest.

Thirdly, he is also confiscating my passport and air ticket.

Did I still have nothing to say?

Ja.

Well that was going to be a problem because they could link us through the air tickets – Bought at the same time and place …

I knew I was fucked, even then. Really and truly completely fucked. I clearly heard everything Fuckhead said about us through the open door – at least what he thought he knew about us. It turned out that Fuckhead was so eager to please and weasel his way out of the sentence – *they gave him anyway* – that SANAB coughed up two air tickets and sent out a team to personally interrogate him about us and whomever else he tried to screw for freedom.

I was looking at Life – *With or Without Parole?* – in a country that I was only supposed to spend two and a half hours in.

24

Vorst

The Bandiet awakes. The cell is bare. Nothing in it except a raised block of concrete in the centre. He is lying on the floor in a corner, tightly wrapped up in his coat. Tied firmly around his head is his vest, an effective blindfold. He learnt to do this many years ago in other prisons. It cuts out the light and muffles the constant clamour of the concrete bowel he finds himself in. Here human evil is consumed in hard crashing bites of steel and slowly digested until deemed rotted enough to regurgitate back to the street from whence it came. But the Bandiet does not have that luxury. He will leave from the back entrance where the real poison goes. Alone. And into a nameless different hole – this one in the ground. The Crown will rake its paws to cover the waste with sweet ancient earth and it will be forgotten. Oh yes, that lay ahead, but here in one of the seven lumens of Hades— he will never hear the whisper of heaven's doors scraping back open. Not above the din of the slamming sphincters that are going to keep him in.

Life.

He judges it must be early morning. He knows why he has woken up. His blood sugar is screaming for a fix. The last drink he had was back in the aircraft on approach into Brussels. DTs are not only in the post, the mail oke is about to hurl them through the slot. The Bandiet's hands tremble, his skin prickles and deep in his gut— cramps writhe, screaming in protest – as something smashes and breaks glass viciously within.

Life.

Oh dear God, why? Fuck, why? He doesn't want to think about it.

Oh yeah – it giggles nastily – *and exactly how do you intend doing that?*

He tries to ready himself for the mental fight ahead, but his will has collapsed and he needs a drink. *He needs to pass out—*

The Bandiet's fantasy is not freedom as much as being able to switch off his mind. Just stop the noise for a minute. One blessed minute. Drown out the cries of Self-Pity, False Remorse, Hatred and Revenge. Kill the thin brittle wails of Fear and Self-Loathing. Crucify the agonising groans of Loneliness.

Kill them for a minute, for an hour – just for one more day. But he cannot shut them up. They will most certainly refuse to die. He knows this. He has been here before in another place that wasn't a dream. Only this time, this time … … time is up—

Life …

He sits up and piles himself into a heap of misery against one corner and vaguely wonders what mang he is in.

The narrow arched entrance to the cell is a rivet-studded steel door with a sleeping metal Cyclops and a one-way lock. The lock chatters hollowly, schlocks, then rumbles open quietly, and a French screw appears. He will find out that in *their* penal system they are called *chefs*. The chef beckons him to come. The Bandiet emerges into an old red-brick prison section. Cells rise up on each side in three grey steel tiers. The smells of His Royal Guvviness are different. Soap, shit, foreign rancid food, and strange disinfectants, although the subtle stale odour of mortal agonies below them all are exactly the same as the other holes he's been in.

The mang sleeps badly.

He follows the screw to a room. Two chefs sit behind a table, his suit-case and carry-on luggage before them. A clock on the wall indicates that it is 02h30 and tapping slowly. He feels Time and the mammoth burden of its slow crawl settle on him – a smothering blanket of black despair.

Life.

The gattas are hard-faced and French. They indicate to the Bandiet that he must strip. He gets down to skin art and cock. He stands naked while they take inventory – his dick glaring balefully under the desk. They've stolen the Bandiet's utility knife, cigarettes and whiskey, and the bastards gleefully throw all his biltong away. He protests all this and evokes amusement – he cannot understand a word of what they are saying.

They finish and indicate he must sign for his stuff. He refuses. This creates a hell of a fuss. The main screw presses a button on the wall behind him. A little while later an officer who speaks bent, spindled and arrogantly mutilated English appears and asks what is the problem. The Bandiet tells him he refuses to sign for his things until the stolen goods are returned. The officer informs him very coldly that all complaints are to be addressed to the Direkteur by means of a *Rapport*. The Bandiet realises what he is up against. It is utterly foreign, but there is nothing alien about it. Gattas, boere – naaiers. He signs, gets issued a prison kit, dresses and is taken to another cell.

To his surprise it has a small pine cupboard, bed, table and chair. In the corner is a flushing toilet. It's the same size as the mang where he first did time as a laaitie for a pip. The toilet is a luxury, though. The lock grates its metal teeth and the door bites tightly shut behind him. He is alone once again.

The following morning a chef wakes him and he is taken to a doctor. The DTs have arrived, are unpacked and are making themselves rudely un-at-home. He tells the doctor he is a drug addict and an alcoholic. With this the tampon agrees. He is injected heavily with diazepam and taken to the prison hospital's psychiatric wing. Here the Bandiet is placed in a cell with his first cellmate, a fat, badly balding middle-aged Belgian with thick glasses. His first and only delight is that he can actually speak a little English. He is very hungry, but the giemba says he will have to wait for lunch. They only serve *mange* twice a day. Mange turns out to be fucking good food, but it doesn't make him feel much better. He does not speak to the giemba. He is not stupid. The flics could have put him in under cover. Later that day he is called to speak to his Crown-appointed lawyer. He bears shocking news.

The Bandiet has been charged under French Napoleonic Law. He has been declared bound over for trial in which he will be given the opportunity to defend himself against the charges. At this point he has *already* been found guilty. The lawyer explains that the onus is on him to prove his innocence, because the burden is NOT on the Crown to prove his guilt – that has already been accomplished via computer forensics and the statement made by his accomplice. Realistically he can expect anything from five to eight years on the drug smuggling and thirty years on the organised crime charges. The charges will probably not run concurrently. The court might be more lenient if he helps the police with their investigation and reveals who his other foreign accomplices are. No. Fuck no. They would definitely screw him over anyway.

The Bandiet goes back to his cell, broken at last. He should never have built his tower of cards on the table with the wobbly base. They are keeping him heavily sedated to counteract the drug and alcohol withdrawal. He didn't realise that he would have to go through drug withdrawal. The alcohol he expected, but the coke turk is a hell of a surprise. Just under a week later he is taken for his first court appearance, but only after a row. The chefs have stolen his boots. A lot of angry screws, and his boots mysteriously reappear. He joins Fuckhead outside the courtroom in Le Palais de Justice, a huge filthy building with beautiful old architecture. Both are skated and signed into the custody of boere. A snapshot appearance and they are bound over for further investigation. Apparently they made it into the Belgian daily newspapers. The Bandiet becomes quietly frightened at a country that gets so excited about a suitcase full of weed.

Back in psycho-section he slowly gives up and lets the terrible blackness envelop him. His cellmate has tried to tell him that he killed two cops, but his Das sense knows he is a paedophile. He has already trapped the sick fuck in a conversation about relative immorality and marriage age in the Middle Ages. They always fall for it as the fantasy kicks in – except the bastards who make little boys' arses bleed. The fat baby-fucker makes him ill. But—

If the Bandiet did anything to him it might be – *Life Without* ...

The Bandiet has no money, no tobacco – except what he can bum off a sympathetic chef. He has written several *rapports* to the Direkteur for his entjies – all have been ignored. Eventually Christmas rolls around. He has been locked up for about ten days. He hates Christmas. It always reminds him how fucking lonely he is without a real family. Being in prison is ten times worse. He thinks back ... There were so many other cages. The first one was in Pretoria Central. No, actually it was Worcester, but that wasn't prison, that was boere lockups. Then there was Die Bult, followed by Kimberley (military and boere), Grootfontein (military and boere), Pretoria Central, Zonderwater, Voortrekkerhoogte DB, Rundu DB, Grootfontein (military, boere and local mang), Stellenbosch (boere and local mang), Pollsmoor, Victor Verster, Hofstraat in Paarl, and now Vorst.

He looks at his prospects. Thirty-eight years. He can't do thirty-eight years.

He can't.

He would never see his girlfriend again. He would grow old and very possibly die in there. And, after so many years, who would he go back to? Who would be there to welcome him back?

He is as good as dead already.

The lawyer told him that under their law it is possible that he will only have to do one-third, because it is his first offence. But nothing is certain, because of the seriousness of the organised crime charges. Yes, nothing is certain. They are giving him pills three times a day, so he starts hoarding them carefully. Just after Christmas he reckons he has almost enough.

He needs to build up the courage to do it. He is not going to die in a prison their way.

Two days later he does it.

That evening, quite late, he climbs into his bunk. He sleeps on the top. He takes all the pills and breaks a disposable razor blade from its plastic stick. Then he blindfolds himself, settles back and waits for the pills to hit him.

They do.

The Bandiet's last action is to take the razor, place it diagonally across the artery in the crook of his elbow and press hard. The razor cuts into his skin like butter and slices the artery wide open. Blood sprays out in a hot sticky pumping jet, soaking him, his bedding, his mattress, and eventually starts dripping through it onto the paedophile beneath. As it all fades to black, the Bandiet hears the giemba ...

Scream—

*

Somewhere in the blackness, far, far away in Africa, the sun has come up on the new year. On the freeway to Stellenbosch five people are in a car driving home, dog-tired after the New Year's party at the River Club in Cape Town. For reasons later unknown to the police, the car suddenly leaves the road and smashes malevolently into the concrete pillar of a freeway bridge. Two of the occupants die instantly upon impact, but poor Christine and her best friend Alzaan take twenty minutes to go. Alzaan's boyfriend Fabian is one of those who die on impact, but his sister survives. She is the only one. She does not remember the accident. Like the Bandiet, she is unconscious ...

25

San Michelline et St Gilles

I awoke and found myself in another cell. I was so weak I could not lift my head. Above me I managed to make out a pole bedecked with plasma bottles and a very yellow drip bag. My arm hurt and my ankles and wrists cried out from the handcuffs biting into my flesh. I was firmly skated hand and foot to a steel bed. Eventually a gatta and what I took to be a doctor came in. The tampon took my blood pressure and remarked in a thick accent that he was glad to see I was awake.

I had apparently lost a hell of a lot of blood and needed two plasma transfusions. The reason I was so weak was because my blood count was low. But with vitamins and other shit being injected into me, I would probably be okay to get up in about a week. I lay there in abject misery. I suppose it was a good thing I didn't know Christine was dead, because I would definitely have joined her at the first opportunity. Let's not fool around. I was chained in hell because I felt sorry for myself and didn't want to face a lifetime in prison without her. I was also going mad from not having alcohol and spliff. And I could not face thinking about God. I think maybe the real reason deep down was that I could not face God. At least *my adopted idea* of God. I was sober after years of hiding, and my guilt and fear were driving me crazy. That's why I'd been pouring drugs into myself all that time. That's why I became a big drug dealer. Because I was told I had turned my back on Jesus and lost my salvation. Because I thought I was going to an imaginary Hell worse than this one and I could not face the idea. In twelve-step programmes this is called rock bottom. In other empirical and decidedly more Hippocratical quarters— it's known as being insane.

They came back later with food. I refused to eat it. The chef on duty told me that it was futile trying a hunger fast – they would simply put a tube down my throat and feed me from a bag. So I ate.

For two days I lay in that cold, dark place – hating every breath I took. Hating myself and my stupidity. Hating the fact that it hadn't worked. Hating the fact that I'd got caught. Hating the emotional and mental pain.

On the third day my cell door opened and a cheerful little old lady appeared. At first I thought it must be some mistake. That she was looking

339

for some other bandiet. She came to the side of the bed and asked me if she might talk with me. She spoke English, slightly accented but fluent nonetheless. I nodded.

– *What is your name?* –

– *Alex* –

– *My name is Michelline. What country are you from?* –

– *South Africa* –

– *Do you miss home?* –

– *Yes* –

– *I'm sure you do. I'm sorry you are far away and lying here. I come here a few times a week just to visit the people in hospital. You don't mind if I visit with you for a little while, do you Alex?* –

– *No, I don't. Are you with a church?* –

– *Yes Alex, I am a nun. I think it is bad to be in prison, but it is even worse being in hospital in a prison, and that is why I am here. Maybe if you speak to somebody who is not part of the prison it will make you feel a little better. Do you mind if I ask you a personal question?* –

– *Ask me* –

– *Do you know that God loves you?* –

– *Sister … I knew God once … A long time ago … but I got angry with Him because of what He let people in my country do in His name and I sinned because I hated the people that kept on doing it. I left the church, turned my back and became a professional criminal. I am a hard and terrible man. I am here because of that. Now I am going to be in prison for a long time and when I die I will go to hell* –

– *Ha ha ha! Excuse me please, I apologise, I am not laughing at you, I am laughing at what you are saying. Alex, who on earth told you that? You cannot do anything either good or bad to make God feel differently about you. You cannot change His feelings. He loves you because He wants to love you. You cannot change that, no matter what you do or what anybody else says. And He sees everything, including the bad things done in His name* –

– *But Sister, I was a missionary once* –

– *Alex, do you think that you can offend God with your rejection? Do you think maybe He will get hurt feelings and go and sulk in a corner of heaven? Do you think He does not see you here and it does not affect Him?* –

– *I don't know* –

– *Do you mind if I ask why you hurt yourself?* –

— I will never see my girlfriend again, I will never see my friends, I might never see Africa again, and when I die it's over —

— Alex, we cannot say what tomorrow might bring. But I understand you are lonely and afraid. I cannot change that now, but I would like to visit you regularly if you don't mind ... maybe we can become friends —

— Okay —

— Tell me a little about yourself until I must go ... —

I lay there after she had gone and thought about her words.

Who was the God I was running away from? Was I running? I mean, running as in actually getting away. There were three layers to my self-hate, at least the ones that I knew of—

There was my impotent rage at the crude and sophisticated hypocrisies that I had seen so blatantly all around me and could not change. I believed utterly that church leaders are responsible for poverty and social injustice. It is the only response that validates the Christian experience in my opinion. And I mean responsible as in curing it – fixing it, correcting the imbalance. And spreading that effect. Yet everything I had seen in South Africa screamed that *they* were responsible for *creating* it – both directly and by sheer callous indifference. I did not ever see myself as some kind of lone prophet. I certainly didn't want to stand up in front. It's just that I had tired of trying to stand up to them and could not keep myself from questioning everything. Besides, I was way too fucking impatient and refused to play church politics. I only had two stratas of life that I had occupied emotionally. The mean streets and church. And I had wanted to take the church to the mean streets but failed miserably. So I buried everything and fucked off back there. My advice to anybody on the mean streets would be to stay the hell away from any organised religion.

And what kind of mental illness is it when somebody believes they are right and an entire set of religious organisations is wrong?

Then there was my dark well of loneliness, which, before Christine came along, I cured with my even deeper shame – sex. I gave women pleasure the way they wanted it to cure my own emptiness. It was only wrong because I thought so. Because I needed to feel appreciated and went about it the wrong way.

And there was my own cowardice and lust for power and attention. I was a deeply fractured human being and I knew it. I was also intelligent enough to know I was being confronted with myself and didn't like it. My shit, their shit and nobody's shit. I was eating a dish of my own karma and it tasted kak.

And you didn't care that Fuckhead might have to go through this? So howzit working for you so far, china?

I lay there until I was able to walk a few days later. I was absolutely determined to, because I hated the bedpan. It's funny how I was willing to slice my veins open but could not bear the thought of being alive and have someone clean my arse. It also put me in a place where I lay with nothing except silence. I was living this recurring horror that I kept finding myself in. Was I destined to die like a caged animal? Was this my fate, my karma, my kismet? Was this cage what I wanted from life? Because I seemed to gravitate back to it in cycles. Was there some subconscious drive in me to push myself into a corner I somehow believed was my destiny?

*

I eventually found out that I was not in Vorst any more. I was in another mang called St Gilles. I'd been rushed there unconscious from Vorst because they had a hospital with a trauma unit. I saw Michelline once more before I transferred into the main prison. It helped me a lot.

As it was intended to.

St Gilles was the second filthiest prison I've ever been in. Only Pollsmoor beat it. I have no idea what possesses a person to make as their career the task of walking into a building that stinks to high heaven of raw shit and caged humanity and endeavour diligently to keep it that way. I used to get physically nauseous walking in from the yard as the stench hit me.

Screws are sick.

My first cellmate was an Iranian. To my surprise, he spoke Nederlands and Persian. Persian was the surprise. I thought Persia was some anti-quated place only spoken of in ancient texts. He explained that indeed it was, except that now what was left of it was called Iran. I found out from him exactly how bad it was in an Iranian jail. My second cellmate was a Russian who became quite a good mate. Russian jails were even worse. Then they put me in with some truly filthy fat Spanish ou who cowered away in the cell. He never showered or took exercise, because the oke in the case with him wanted to shut him up. I appealed to Michelline and she pulled some strings.

I was put in a cell on my own.

That jail never slept. Each night someone somewhere would start screaming. Mostly Moslem youngsters. They would drive themselves into hysterical frothing madness, issuing ear-piercing maniacal shrieks and wailing incoherently in Arabic while banging and slamming their heads on their cell doors. In response to this the whole section would kick and slam their mugs against *their* doors. That would wake the bandiete in the next section, who would join in until the entire jail was going mal—

… And would carry on until the nightshift boere brought in the master keys so the medics could drag the fucker off to the hospital section. I'd seen these laaities come into the hospital section – where, like me, they would get patched up, administered a knockout shot and chained to a bed. If they had damaged any prison property during the tantrum it was added to the list of charges.

I stuffed my ears, blindfolded myself and slept very badly.

Two horribly lonely months passed as I waited for the trial to get under way. And the joy of nothing to take up my time except a tiny bit of tobacco I managed to scrounge.

I met up with some Chinese ouens. All in a triad. The poor fuckers had had a terrible break. They were a crew of seven on their way back to Singapore with 50 000 tabs and 100 000 dollars US. They were booked in quietly at a Holiday Inn on their way through Belgium from Amsterdam to Italy. It was their shitty luck that a Federal hostage rescue team was on a kidnapping case and hit the room next door to theirs. Belgian gattas are hectically paranoid – so they decided to hit the rooms on either side just to make sure. And the ouens got bust. Inside the mang they turned me on to something. The way to get books was to go to church on Fridays. This, I discovered, was an informal book club, of which I became an avid member.

Reading was the only thing that kept me sane. Howzit working for you, cousin?

Belgium's legal system allows an offender in a criminal case full access to the case file. You are allowed to travel to court two days before the case and review the file. This is so that you can brief your counsel. I decided to make use of this privilege and requested to see my file before my next court appearance. To my utter fucking amazement, Fuckhead had made three conflicting statements – one in which he claimed that I had made death threats since we'd been locked up! He fucked up because I wasn't even in the same mang. The kikkervreters knew it.

We were transferred to another mang. This one in a small university town named Leeuwen about sixty clicks from Brussels. Famous for tourism, student pubs and beer. Sounded very familiar. It was also completely different to the other two mangs. For one thing it was quiet. That came as a hell of a shock. I didn't realise how much noise I'd been battered with. It had five wings, and the awaiting trial section was above the solitary section. High security – long-term prison. This scared the crap out of me again. I still had no money. It seemed my dear partners had elected to leave me with my arse hanging in the wind. Fuckhead and I were in the stokkie section together. I realised from reading his statements that I needed to Sicilian the mutherfucker, else he was going to sink me in the trial.

Through my triad connections, a man from Hong Kong – whose name I didn't know and of course whose face I've never seen – paid for my TV and tobacco. The prison authorities allowed us the opportunity to do piecework. I did this to make some pocket money for stamps and other little luxuries. I made some friends. An ou from Romania who had lost most of his family in that country's mangs under Ceausescu. He was a really good oke with a kiff sense of humour. My other bra was a Nigerian.

Then I found out about Christine's shattering death in a scrawled letter from Brother E.

'*It's a pity about Christine and them dying in that car accident ...*'

The world as I knew it ended, and I began a terrible, dark, bitter and lonely crash course in grief.

*

The court case came and went as a blur. Enough of me was operating in save-my-numbed-arse mode for me to get documents to prove my recent and – more important – *legitimate* IT career from home. My story was going to be that I planned and financed the whole thing as an idea I got from some okes I met in Amsterdam the previous year. A wild stupid once-off chance I took for quick money. Luckily for me, Fuckhead had contradicted himself so much that the court refused to believe him – dismissing everything as fantasy. I was found guilty as charged on the smuggling but acquitted on the organised crime charges, based on documentary evidence I presented the court. The assizes gave me six and a half years. The time I had done awaiting trial counted in my favour, so all I had was *possibly* about two years before I could get out.

One nasty part during sentencing was Fuckhead's medical report, which his dear family had sent over. In the middle of the tribunal, the judge asked him if I was a violent man. I had taken the opportunity before the trial to drop a caveat in Fuckhead's lap. I wasn't going to be in prison as *long* as he thought – and he had possibly *forgotten* I had *partners*. He told the judge that I had just been very angry with him that night. It wasn't the best, but considering they gave Fuckhead half my sentence, I didn't think they took it into account.

Back in Leeuwen Sentraal I was working as a cleaner. A privileged position that earned me a bit of tom and other things. I made another friend in the stokkie section. This one Moslem ou had sussed me out and called me over one Sport period. He asked me if I wanted to smoke a hash spliff. Fuck, yeah. He let me smoke most of it, laughing at my craven delight, then made me another and gave me a lekker piece to keep. It was the first I had had in four months and it fucked me up six-love. It was the only thing that took some of the sting from Christine's death. The denial had eventually succumbed to dark, black grief – something I was powerless against. Then came the shock.

Fuckhead was transferred to a medium-security mang somewhere else and I was transferred to D-Section – General Population. It's what used to be Death Row in what I later found out is the toughest jail in the Kingdom of Belgium. Apparently Fuckhead's medical records had come into play. I was sectioned as violent and placed with the murderers, other capital offenders and dangerous inmates.

Since I had given up on suicide, there was only one recourse. Make it through my stretch.

Survive.

I arrived in D-Section, not knowing what to expect, but preparing for the worst …

In the stokkie section we were only allowed to shower twice a week and had an hour exercise each day, which severely hampered contact between prisoners. For the rest it was lockdown 24/7, except for cleaners, who got out a bit more. I only saw one fight, between some Eastern Europeans and the Nigerians, but it was like— so fucking wussy, sweetheart. More aggravated shoving around than anything else. Still, it got us all lockdown for several weeks. Everything I knew about prisons was dangerous. Gladiator schools like Zonderwater, evil gang universities like Pollsmoor, where the ultimate way to *slatwet* is for several men to kill a man, then eat his heart raw – in utter disdain of punishment because they are doing life anyway, and if the gattas tried to do anything they would simply kill one of them in retaliation.

In D-Section I was placed on Tier 3 Left – Cell 26. I had no idea what to expect. It was more open though, because lockdown was only for meals and at night.

Initially I scared the crap out of the other bandiete because I took a shiv with me to the shower every night. They all thought I was some kind of homicidal maniac. I was just being careful. I stuck to myself, watched everything, and waited. The beginning of my stretch was terrible. It seemed I had to resign myself to the fact that my *partners* were not about to make it any easier. Brother E had fifty jimmys of my personal tom that I'd given him for safekeeping, but he was obviously not going to send any of it to me.

Christine was dead and would stay dead.

I was extremely suspicious of the first bandiet who tried to befriend me. He offered me shit, but I refused. You never accept anything in the mang from another bandiet unless that convict is company. The rest is extortion that you've bought into but don't realise. I didn't need anything from anyone, although the ou seemed to be legit. Or at least legit in the sense that he wanted nothing from me except companionship. Until I found out he was an ex-gatta and the pariah of the entire jail. I found this out in the most unlikely quarter too.

I decided to trust this convict, and ordered a piece of hash from him with a phonecard. A little while later another bandiet came to my cell and dropped it off. He was tallish, swarthy-skinned and had a big droopy bandido moustache hanging below a narrow set of coal black eyes. It turned out he was Jimmy the August Strangler – a serial killer doing life behind a death penalty moratorium in a cell on the tier below us. I was actually going to get to know Jimmy quite well, and maybe I shouldn't talk about him, because he was an ou I looked into and saw the Black Thing again – and I don't wanna freak you out. Difference was that the Black Thing was inside him but it couldn't get out except to hurt things like unsuspecting women – Jimmy admitted that to me and embraced his sentence. He knew he couldn't stop it and accepted he was in the best place in the world. He reckoned he had about another thirteen kills in him that the Black Thing wanted and They needed to keep him inside until he died.

A very sick and very brave man.

He told me the other bandiet was a corrupt senior gatta officer who had been bust big and that everybody in the joint ignored him – screws included. It would be a bad idea becoming bras with him. There were convicts in other wings whom he had locked up. He went mal eventually and was transferred to a hospital mang.

Almost at the same time, I made my first real friend.

We all slept in single cells and used pots to shit in at night. These were emptied and washed in a special low basin located in the toilets on each tier in the section. I was busy emptying mine one day when another bandiet asked me if I wanted to smoke a hash pipe with him. I told him I was fresh out of phonecards and couldn't afford it. He assured me it was completely cool – he just wanted to smoke, drink coffee and chat with me. I figured okay and went to take a look.

He was a Moslem oke, the only one on our tier – by the name of Abedislam X. Sam for short. A full-blooded Moroccan and the main drug makwera of Antwerp. As good as his word, he welcomed me to his cell, made us strong Arab coffee and initiated me into some new drug culture. Hash was smoked in thin aluminium foil tubes fashioned into a hollow spoon at the sealed end, then perforated with tiny holes on one side. A hot snowflake of hash was placed in the hollow above the holes and smoked through the pipe. After about three pipes, I was flying. He asked me the usual. Where I came from, what I was in for, wharrawharra. I told him. He explained that he had invited me to speak with him because there was something he wanted to inform me of and warn me about.

I had bought a Moslem prayer mat from the canteen and used it on my cell floor so my feet wouldn't get cold. Sam explained that this was a sacrilege in his religion and if *any* of the other Moslems in our section saw it— it would be very bad. I asked him what would be done in such a circumstance. He told me that the mat would have to be ritually scrubbed with salt under running water. I said nothing, but I did hide it away under my bed.

On my next order from the canteen I bought a bag of coarse salt. Then I scrubbed the mat with ordinary detergent till it was spotless. Afterwards I washed myself head to toe and then scrubbed the mat with my hands using the salt – under running water. Then I very carefully dried it, rolled it up and put it in Sam's cell on his bed while he was fetching chow one day. He was absolutely delighted and we became firm friends.

I started to get to know who was who. The layout of the cell block running up from Sam to me was: Sam, Kareem, Alain, Yo, Me, Bible Sailor, Gatta, Jean, The Mad Old Man and Ludwig. Ludwig had the cell on the end of the tier. It was the best cell in the section and, considering he was a top boss in the Belgian mafia, it was probably his right. Opposite us on the other tier was a soccer hooligan who had kicked a girl half to death, raped her, then shoved a two-by-four in her fanny for fun. Next to him were a couple of successful *familiemoodenaars*, followed by all the violent rapists and paedophiles. Oh, and Skinny too.

Skinny was the mang's painter. There's one or two in every chookie. He walked into a crowded bar one night and opened up with an AK47 because one of the women working behind the counter had stolen two million francs off him. He spoke good English and was friendly to me.

On the tier below us were the white supremacists with their skinheads, swastikas and altars to Hitler in their cribs. Nestled in next to them were Arab terrorists and criminals. Considering they both hated Israel and Jews in general – it was a pretty shrewd move by Prison Administration. For the rest it was all mostly murder. The most senior bandiete being the ones right at the bottom. The original death row inmates. The ones who survived because of the moratorium. One oke, Ronnie, was my hash merchant for a while. He was Ludwig's company.

That sort of made up D-Section. Here, release dates came and went by very slowly, and for quite a few – like Jimmy – not at all.

At the time, Kareem was considered one of the most dangerous men in Belgium, and contrary to his Arab-sounding name he was a huge redheaded giant. Fucking intelligent too. Managed to escape twice. If you meet me in a pub one day, buy me a beer and I'll tell you the whole story.

Alain was a nondescript French murderer.

Yo was one of my good mates. He was also doing life for murder. He had a very similar background to me as a kid – and at age eighteen he got into a bad fight. The other oke pegged, and it was left up to a jury to decide whether it was premeditated or not. They decided it was.

Bible Sailor was in for murdering two prostitutes. He apparently fell into deep remorse over his crime. He did nothing except sit in his cell and read his Bible. The only time he ever came out was to work, wash and eat.

The Gatta I've spoken about. Then there was Jean.

Jean-Claude actually, my very good friend and the most notorious bank robber in Belgium. We became company. He had got himself nailed for the third time. This heist he got caught inside the bank and ended up in a five-hour siege shootout with Belgian SWAT. He told me that they eventually drove him back and had him trapped in the sewerage pipes under the bank, with a shotgun and an M-16 on his chest, completely blind from tear gas, choking on the stink of shit. He lay there thinking about it for a while, then reckoned enough is enough, and came out meekly.

Thirty years.

After Jean was The Mad Old Man. He was a *familiemoord* that went horribly wrong. He killed his wife and kids, turned the gun on himself and survived. He wouldn't wash, work, exercise or anything else. Like Bible Sailor he just sat in his cell and only came out for food. A mad old man with filthy silver hair down to his arse.

D-Section was not dangerous as I had expected. In fact, it was the least dangerous institution I've ever been in. Normal public boarding school in South Africa was scarier. I ascribe this utterly weird phenomenon to the effectiveness of the Belgian penal system. Maybe you don't know it, but the efficiency of any legal system that subscribes to rehabilitating the offenders it incarcerates is measured by the recidivism rate. Recidivism is when a bandiet comes in for something like burglary, does his stretch and then goes out and does it again. The driving force behind this is the Belgian penal code. It stipulates that it is possible that a convicted felon may only do one-third of the sentence handed down by the assizes.

It is possible.

See, it isn't a guarantee. And therein lies the hook. Fuck up during your stretch and you will do most of it. On a second offence you automatically do two-thirds, with the history of your first stretch taken into account. But three strikes and you're out. The third time you get out only when His Majesty decides to let you out. And His Royal Majesty simply does not worry about your freedom and happiness when he awakes to take a royal shit and start ruling The Kingdom each day.

Jean was one of these ous.

The Department of Prisons also focused heavily on rehabilitation through a work ethic. Something I personally thought our government might need to think about very seriously.

The Crown provided you with clothing, housing, food and medical attention by law. Anything else you paid for with money made by working for NGO factories on the prison grounds. Drugs, pussy, cable TV (on nineteen channels in languages I understood), tobacco, phonecards, coffee, writing materials, treats – basically everything else.

Private corporations hired prime floor space from the Crown at a hefty discount, and installed factories inside the prison complex. Us bandiete then worked in them for a real, commensurate salary. At the end of every month, fifteen percent was deducted from our wages. Ten percent of it was put into unit trusts outside – tax free and drawing interest in a real bank account. The other five percent was pooled and used to buy sports, gym, music and recreational equipment. It was also used to hire outside live entertainment and provided funds for treats like a Belgian chocolate for every bandiet in the mang on a Saturday night. They also funded computer classes and language classes – which I attended in a hopeless attempt to learn French.

All long-term prisoners came out with a huge wad of cash that had been saved down the years, as well as at least one or maybe even three working trades behind them. The bandiete in Leeuwen were mostly foreigners, and eighty percent were in for drug-related offences. We obviously didn't give a shit about rehabilitation, but for the native Belgians it seemed to work. I pestered the administration and got a job working for a German multinational called Eupen Kabels. My salary was around four and a half to five jimmys, which to me was screamingly funny because I was earning more than the average gatta in South Africa.

Michelline visited me every fortnight. No mean feat for a seventy-two-year-old lady. We became firm friends and she told me some of her life story. She had become a nun in her early twenties and had always felt a calling to work with prisoners. During the war against Hitler she had been down in the dungeons ministering succour to the Nazis' torture victims. In later conversations she revealed that it was a terrible decision forced upon *il Papa* at the time: because they stayed out of the war, Hitler let His Holiness' nuns and priests into certain prisons, camps and hospitals. It was that or nothing. The basement of Leeuwen is a sealed national monument and mausoleum to honour the dead. It brought with it a sense of history that made me roam through my mind at nights as I lay in my cell wondering how many inmates had been trapped in my particular crib and what their stories might be.

Its current inmate had a long time still to go, and to keep my mind active and my hands off my dick, I decided to take up two projects. I bought myself a very expensive watch after spending months cutting close to fifty kilometres of cable into twenty-five-centimetre lengths and soldering both ends.

And I made a pair of shorts.

We could buy sports kit from the canteen, and of course I bought myself the usual bandiet uniform – a good tracksuit and expensive takkies – but their shorts were fucking horrible. That's why I decided to make my own. The first thing I managed to do was pinch two black denim aprons from the steel foundry. I smuggled them through to the section tied around my body. Next, I bought a needle and some thread from Kareem and borrowed a pair of scissors from Jimmy. Yeah, I know, what kind of joint allows serial killers to keep scissors in their cells?

I told the ouens what I was planning and they all laughed like hell and told me I would never pull it off.

Hah.

I sat and looked at that material for two weeks and then started cutting. The pattern was in my mind. I cut them exactly like I wanted – with three pleats in the front, darts at the back, belt loops, a button-up fly, lekker deep pockets (from a pillowcase) and turn-ups just above my knee. Every stitch went in by hand. I even overlocked the outside seams manually. The boere were in on it too eventually, and never bust me for contraband or theft of Guvvie property. One night I nonchalantly strolled out onto the tier wearing the finished product. It even had a leather designer patch like a regular pair of jeans that I branded with— *Rooibaard Clothing*, using a soldering iron from work.

The other bandiete could not believe their eyes and accused me of being a closet tailor. Anyway, it served a purpose. It helped to take my mind off the pain of Christine. Heroin was not working, and although I had become a junkie, I still hated it. I hated the nausea, cramps and itchy skin that came from an overnight turk after lockdown. Smoking loads of hash didn't help either. I went through all the usual shit associated with smack. I got thin, I sold everything I could spare and still remained in shock, guilt and denial over her. The guilt came from knowing that if she had gone to that party with me, she would still be alive. But no, I had to be on the fucking run from gangsters and end up in the mang for pulling stupid moves. The gattas blamed poor Sam because I became a junkie and it wasn't his fault either – it was Jean's. And then, still, it wasn't Jean's fault either because I talked him into it against his will.

I did my time day by day until my release two and a half years after my arrest. I thought that, technically at least, that stretch was the easiest time I ever did. I mean in D-Section we ate steak, chips and ice-cream once a week, for fucksakes. I entertained the thought that it hadn't really affected me, but of course I was wrong.

It fucked me up big time.

26

Trouble in Paradise

I was released from Leeuwen Central Prison in May 1999 – and expelled from Belgium and the EU for ten years. Apparently I will be on parole until 2008 or something stupid. I left the prison with about 20 000 francs from my compulsory mang savings and my EU expulsion warrant, and was whisked off to the South African Embassy by one of the attachés, where they issued me a one-day passport.

After being dropped at my *pension*, which, incidentally, was right opposite the most famous tourist attraction in Brussels – *Het Plassende Jong*, the laaitie taking a slash – I cruised off on foot into the city in search of a bottle of Chivas and a ten-inch Cuban.

Thank fuck that was over!

I went back to my *pension*, cracked open the whiskey and rolled myself a fat joint from the 20g of primo Moroccan Canary that I'd smuggled out in my mouth. It made me talk a little funny but I said fuckall to the boere and they never noticed. Besides, when you fall off a horse, be sure to get back on quickly – so you don't lose your pluk.

Then I perched myself on the window sill and watched a busload of lady Japanese tourists giggling themselves silly while pretending to take a piss like the little statue downstairs – all the while shooting off reels of film.

I finished the spliff, poured another whiskey and lit my cigar. I needed to think.

What was going on in South Africa?

I had phoned Brother E two months before my release and he sent me a jimmy.

Sounded guardedly positive over the phone. Thing was, I didn't know if I wanted to stay in business with him.

I needed money and a gig.

Buying the compulsory plane ticket home and paying off my leech of an attorney had wiped out the 120k the Belgian gattas had confiscated after my arrest almost exactly to the cent. It was fixed but – hey – I was out, who fucking cared?

That's when I phoned Brother E, who sent me the jimmy ... way too late. One of the reasons I didn't want to stay in business with him.

I had two other offers.

My triad connections wanted to set me up as their man in South Africa, because, as they explained, they had a problem blending in, with their oriental features and all. I liked the idea of moving diamonds, but they also wanted me to distribute heroin for them. I balked at this, very politely, because I didn't want to piss them off or be responsible for starting a national crime wave and upping the HIV infection rate. The bad drugs like smack, tik-tik and rocks eat people alive. Chicks sell their bodies and okes suck cock or rob, hijack and steal – all just to keep the bad, bad back-monkey from biting. No. They also had too much of an easy penchant for murder. Triad outfits were one of the few responsible for a bad shootout in Amsterdam, and it is a free-trade city – the players don't tolerate that shit there. I was a budding long-term pro and couldn't have shit on my CV.

Then there was Ludwig. His operation was still running. He'd been running it from inside his cell on a cellphone – ha ha. He gave me an address and told me to send a self-addressed envelope. I would receive 25 000 dollars US, with which I was to buy a ticket to Zurich and book into a certain hotel. Here I was to stay and relax. Wait until his people contacted me. Then, on a certain day, I would be transported to another country, where we would pull off a six-hour operation. For this I would be paid a million Swiss francs. That would be the test to see how I shaped up. I really liked the idea, but I knew what Ludwig's crew got up to. They were the ones who did the eight-million-guilder job on that bank in Amsterdam. His bread and butter was car theft though – but they wouldn't smash windows and hotwire a set of wheels – they would hit a vehicle park with ten, fifteen low-bed trucks and steal the whole fucking lot. And they only went for Porsches, Mercedes and BMWs. These they transported across two borders and then dumped onto the market with perfectly falsified paperwork from the pencil-neck and IT-hacker part of the crew. My only problems with the idea were that I had no choice over the operations I would be involved in and most of them meant carrying a gun. Not that I had a problem with being armed – just not for another man. The choice to shoot had to be my own, not based on some other oke's bad judgement or shitty planning. Ludwig was an option, but most definitely the last one. I also didn't like the idea of having a boss. I was a boss myself, for fucksakes. It was the same as the triads, except with them I would be carrying a quarter ton of someone else's heroin in my pocket. Guess whose head the bullet goes through if something goes wrong?

So then, back to Brother and Sister E. Ludwig warned me about that. He reckoned if I was going to be a pro, then at least play the game in a country where prison was at best bearable should something go wrong. He had a bloody good point. Although the other D-Section freaks who preyed on women and children were not what I would like as long-term neighbours.

Of course, there was the other option.

Go straight.

No, don't giggle. I mean, being a professional criminal is a choice. The same applies to *not* being one. The shit I did as a kid was for kicks. Most of the other stupidity I got nailed for had booze in the middle of the equation somewhere. But, when I resigned from IT, it was to focus on my new career. And that was a cold-blooded choice to make my living as a criminal, and petty could never fit into that picture either. It was either for millions or nothing. No, I couldn't go straight. What? Where would I go to when I got back? Who would I go to? I'd burnt all my bridges. I had no friends because I was a boss – I was just a source of drugs. There was something else, too. In the beginning, when I did penny-ante shit with bankies of zol, I used to get ripped off by the punters because I was too soft. To remedy that, I started acting hard. It worked. I had rules, I didn't break them. I owned my share of our business outright. People never fucked with me. The problem was that I didn't know how *not* to act hard any more. I was avoiding the fact that I had *become* what I *acted*, and D-Section calcified it. I left that place with a pathological hatred for anyone who caused evil to befall women and children.

I liked to think of myself as a victimless criminal. Buying zol from people who grow it traditionally and smuggling it into a country where they smoke it legally seemed like a normal, almost mandated, business to me. The Dutch and the English stripped our country, so swopping green gold for real gold and ducking their tax systems was cool. Selling Ecstasy too. A pill made illegal because it had no medicinal purpose outside of being a party drug. Might as well make champagne or partying itself illegal.

What was happening in South Africa? I decided to have a look. I wish I never did.

*

Brother E's parents were waiting for me at the airport. They took me back to their house. I asked what was going on and they told me they had absolutely no fucking idea. All they knew was my flight number and instructions to give me a phone number. I walked down to the corner garage and called it.

My people. Welcome home boss. Where are you? We'll be there in twenty.

The boys picked me up, freaked at my long hair (I never cut it inside), and asked me what I wanted. A car, a phone and two jimmys scratch. They made calls, I got sorted. I decided to take a drive through to Stellenbosch just for old times' sake.

Christine my poor baby I miss you so much …

The boys hadn't been able to tell me anything, which put a smile on my face because it meant Brother and Sister E were keeping it sharp. Okay relax. I had supper at a good restaurant, and then cruised to De Akker. Same old, same old. It seemed strangely sane, almost distant. I met a whole bunch of old faces and soon had them all shitfaced. It was my first celebration after being released. I bought myself and an old mate Graham a cigar and we sat sipping Black Jack and talking kak. In the middle of it, a thought suddenly crossed my mind. Why don't I just pull into Stellenbosch, get a waiter or bar job again and forget about the rest of it?

I caught a plane the next morning and met up with Brother and Sister E. Our business was booming. We were running the entire eastern seaboard. In each town we had a main runner, just as Brother E and I had planned in detail. I was immensely pleased and very flattered, because when the three of us had had marathon planning sessions before my bust, it sometimes got heated as we argued the finer points. I sometimes thought Brother E didn't take my reasoning to heart. Whatever else he is, Brother E is sharp – as sharp as me. And together we made a scalpel. He had also managed to pull off the first half of the Swaziland operation that the two of us had still been planning very carefully days before my arrest.

Almost to the minutest detail.

I was just in time for the second half.

See, we didn't actually want to sell pills. We did because it raised capital fast and that capital all went into the zol side of the operation. That's why we spent so much money on logistics equipment. We were thinking long term from day one. We had set ourselves a target of five tons. We planned to build ourselves up until we landed it, and then stash the cash in offshore safety deposits. Our mafia friends would help us with the technicalities until we had learnt the fine art of money laundering for ourselves.

But to get there we had to start with what we could handle financially. That meant smallish at first. And it also meant buying it in the *land* ourselves.

I knew from my own years of buying in the 'Kei that we would need an interpreter. And it just so happened that I had a very good mate named Harry who spoke Swazi so fluently that he made real Swazis look at him suspiciously and ask him what the hell he was doing in a white man's skin. I had already introduced him to Brother E before my bust. See, Brother and Sister E ran the usual jols in and out of the Dam while I was butting, and built up enough tom for Brother E to do the op. There was one small problem though.

Harry.

Just after I got gaaned, he discovered crack. And turned into a king-sized fuckup overnight. Brother E used him to pull the move in the end but had to keep him handcuffed the whole time. Seriously. A week into the jol and somebody managed to fuck up. Harry stole a hired Gharry and ran away.

Anyway, the logistics and how he pulled it off.

From day one in our operations I had insisted on radios. I would never trust a cellphone with operational security. So, Brother E bought three. Two for the transport vehicles, and a running handheld set for on the ground. The Landcruiser and hired Gharry were used inside Swaziland, running in a long tandem to look out for boere, just as we planned it. Harry was still handcuffed to one of our boys, and he and our inside Swazi drove around finding all the good zol. Brother E bought about a hundred and fifty jimmys' worth. In the region of 300kg. It was all packed loosely into black bags and transported to our man's kraal. That's when Harry went AWOL. Without the handset, thank God. A terrible glitch that apparently left Brother E half nuts with rage.

A truck was hurriedly hired from a nearby town to replace the stolen Gharry and fitted with the spare radio in base camp. Base camp was a squat in a ruined house on a farm just outside a town near the border on the South African side. The farmer was unaware of them. Here the generators, scales, presses and vacuum machine were set up to begin packing. The other radio was in the Landcruiser. The two vehicles were then driven to the rendezvous point on the South African side of the border and parked as if the Landcruiser had stopped to do repairs on the stricken truck.

That night, twenty men went down to the kraal. Each one was issued with a couple of black bags with holes cut in them. These they put on like crude raincoats to cut their heat signatures. Then, led by the Swazi smuggler, they hefted the bulky bags of zol and began walking into the dead of night. The Swazi carrying the handset and counter-nightvision goggles – looking out for sloppy Interpol and DEA task-force agents.

Don't fuck around, china, they are active in all the agricultural and manufacturing narcotics hotspots, worldwide.

The men eventually appeared and the zol was loaded onto the truck. Ten jimmys changed hands to pay them. The zol was then taken to base camp and eventually packed into the usual twenty-five by twenty-five centimetre, kilo and half-kilo blocks, compressed to eight tons and then vacuum-sealed to 98 percent. The rock-solid bricks were then washed, packed into boxes, taped, labelled and put on the truck. They totalled about 300kg. Everything else was packed, and the short run to Joburg began.

The second half of the operation was getting the zol safely into the Cape from the centre of Joburg. That's where I came in.

I worked out how to calculate exact following distance when doing a hot run.

It's simple. You look out for a unique landmark and, as you pass it, you zero the trip meter on the speedometer. Then get on the radio and tell the ous behind you to sing out when they reach it. When they do, you check the trip meter and you can see exactly how far they are trailing and speed up or slow down accordingly. Our radios could handle thirty-five clicks in mountainous terrain and I insisted on a following distance of fifteen to avoid aerial surveillance. I reckoned gatta choppers wouldn't be able to put us together from the air at that distance, even with good cameras. Nobody could listen in on us unless they were fine-scanning frequencies, because we had our own dedicated crystals built into each set. I similarly insisted on codes and complete radio silence. It is an almost foolproof method, because the moment you hit a roadblock—everybody pulls off the road. And waits. Until the boere fuck off. I say almost, because when we ran that zol from the storage depot, something nearly went wrong.

For the move, we used a big 2.5-litre Kombi to carry the zol and a fuel-injected Golf as the chase car. Our run was completely clean all the way down to some dorpie in the Langeberg. I told our zol driver to pull off the road about ten kays out while we put petrol in the Golf. That done, we pulled ten kays out of town ourselves and told him to go in and juice up. The silly tit drove into town and managed to blow out the right-rear tyre against a pavement. Guess who came to his assistance? The gattas of course. The zol was in boxes labelled as if he were moving house: Kitchen Stuff, Books, Linen, etc. On top of this we tossed brooms and buckets and shit for camouflage. He had to look like an ou moving house.

It worked.

The boere helped him change the tyre, unpacking the boxes of zol to get at the spare wheel, while up on the hill outside of town, Brother E and I sat in cold silence sweating the possible loss of over a million bucks worth of zol.

The money seemed like everything I ever wanted. We had a beautiful barefoot water-ski boat with a two hundred horsepower 2.5 litre V6 two-stroke engine on the back, which we bought to hide a hundred jimmys and play with. We had enough cars for the business. We had three houses. One where we stashed the drugs, one where we invited everybody to come and party, and one where we slept. We had all the equipment we needed to do our zol runs. We had about ten thousand pills stashed in the jungle behind the kitchen. And of course the three hundred kilos of zol we'd dragged through the Karoo.

Thing was, I was tired of being paranoid.

SANAB somehow managed to find us. Not just fucking anywhere – in our sleeping pozzie! Nobody was supposed to know where the hell we fucking dossed.

As it happens, it was a big, beautiful beach house in Nature's Valley, where we stashed the boat and all the logistics equipment.

One morning I was lying in bed half-asleep, expecting our hairdresser. She was a close friend of Sister E's, trusted to keep her mouth shut, and came in by appointment to sort us out. I heard our German shepherd barking and didn't put my mind to it. Then I heard Brother E's footsteps, voices and someone walking towards my room. I looked up blearily and into the barrel of a gun pointed between my eyes.

– *Don't fucking move, Al. If you move I will shoot you. Now, slowly, very slowly, bring your right hand from under the covers. Now your left, slowly. Right, now lie there and don't fucking move* –

This was seriously dof. The mutherfucker sounded like something out of a very bad B-fliek, but the unfunny thing was that this fucker was serious. I picked up immediately that he was a high rank too, because when he spoke to me he did so in accentless English, but when he called out to his partners that he had me subdued, he spoke in natural Afrikaans. After skutting a pair of Levis on the floor he ordered me out of bed and told me to put them on. I did so.

I was taken into the lounge. Expressionless Brother E, three other boere, guns everywhere and a gatta showing me a search warrant issued from the Wynberg Bench. One watched us while the other three searched the house. The only articles they declared illegally in our possession were our zol presses and a half-bankie of zol from our rookstop lying in my wooden maaling-fish in the lounge.

Then they sat down and we had a chat. The officer who got me out of bed was doing most of the talking, while he rifled through my brief-case. Much older. I had him pegged as career Police Intelligence. Colonel probably. Turned out he was the boss of the Wynberg SANAB unit.

Way out of his jurisdiction.

The other three were ordinary SANAB pitbulls in his pen. Highest rank Inspector. Stupid, but so much like dogs on a bone or a bitch when it came to goeters. The Colonel mockingly asked if I had enjoyed Belgium and they all laughed like hell at that. Then they told us they knew we had zol and pills and that we were planning something soon, and began reeling off a list of houses, runners and operations going back about two years. At that point I not only realised that the fuckers were spot on in their intelligence, but the boss had my diary out! In it were lists of accounts: Caveman 1j, Deon 3j, Shane 7.5j ShaneD 30j, Wolf 8.5j, Hilton 15j, Clinton 15j, Steve 1.5j + coke scale ...

I went into full-blown panic. I had been clever enough to hide all the drugs but stupid enough to place myself in a position where all my business details were being read by a gatta. More than just a gatta, a senior narcotics detective. Okay, so he couldn't identify these individuals in a court and he couldn't know that 15j was my shorthand for fifteen jimmys, but he could know exactly what it was we were planning because I had it all written down. I could see it in my mind's eye. List of things to do:

Brother C. – Portugal side, open clean bank accounts, establish credit record, international drivers, character refs, buy police white sheet, passport, visa. Hire garage, rent bakkie, buy deep freezers. Open PO Box and install phone and fax.

Al and Brother E – this side – passport – Deon, polystyrene boxes, latex, beeswax, dog repellent bags, find Miguel, do Belgian mail drop, fish – sort out reliable vendors. Choose target airport (research Porta), set up accounting system. Search Internet for likely restaurants to supply fish with that side. E-mail and establish contacts for Brother C to follow up …

This stuff was the bones of our Portugal operation. We were planning to pack the *boom* in crates of fresh fish on ice and airfreight it to Porta. There we would have a real business operation supplying seafood restaurants. Because once we were in the EU, we were in a virtually borderless basket of countries, and all the zol went to Amsterdam so we wouldn't blip Portugal's Narcotics boere.

And here this vark was actually fucking reading it! What really scared me was he didn't bat an eyelid. He just read it all and put it back in my briefcase.

So, there it was. Out in the open.

The boere were not only on to us, they had good intelligence and they knew the general outline of some of our plans. I realised just how good he was when he said nothing. His more infantile colleagues would have pounced on it like gold and achieved nothing – but he let it slide. Clever poes. I liked the idea of knowing the gattas are watching – then you know exactly where they are and can happily keep them in your sights – but having them almost in your head is just plain scary.

Then Brother E did something that made me go pure fucking white with fear. He sat there in front of me and piemped an extremely dangerous player to them. That oke was the largest colossus I've seen anywhere. Very seriously connected in Cape Town. I never even spoke about the monkey behind his back, so hearing Brother E piemp him cold made my balls shrivel. Fuck, I didn't even like thinking about him. If he *ever* found out, he would peg me as part of it and do something messy and unpleasant to me for being Brother E's partner.

Brother E had shocked me to the core. Deeply.

Fuck, rule number one all the way from school was keep your fucking bek shut no matter if you got bust red-handed.

Keep your fucking bek shut!

We were both old school. That's why we were privy to that kind of intelligence. It was *understood* that there was no currency in trading with these mutherfuckers except on a bent payroll, so what Brother E did was madness. What if these cunts leaked what he told them and pinpointed their source?

Why?

Because if they couldn't stop us themselves, why not let our rivals take care of it? Huh? Fuck!

They picked up Brother E for the bankie of weed and drove him around the resort, pumping him for more info. I think they thought he might piemp other okes if I wasn't around. I put it down to me keeping my bek shut in Belgium but I think I let my raw shock show through. They returned very pissed off because they could smell I'd smoked a joint while they were gone. A few wild threats and they left.

Then about a week later we arrived home one morning from PE after being on the road with business for a couple of days. Our neighbours were the crew from the Storms River bungee jump and a couple of them came running over. Apparently a car full of very serious Moslems had been looking all over for us the previous day.

Oh, my sweet fuck. PAGAD. Now the serious shit had started. Had SANAB piemped us to PAGAD? They'd already killed two of our boys in Cape Town, and if they were picking off our staff they had to be *jags* for us. Sweet fucking shit. Two hours later and we were gone, with me debating the purchase of a Klakker.

With lots of ammo. On clips under the next bed I slept in.

Brother E agreed.

Okay, so now we had a fanatical terrorist organisation wanting to kill us, the gattas had us under a microscope and Brother and Sister E had broken up. I was told later that while I was in jail, he broke her nose beating her up. I knew they had fights but I didn't know he hit her. Like I said, I came out of D-Section hating men who hurt women and children spiritually, emotionally, physically and sexually. I had to spend two years with sick fucks like that.

It was a weird time. There was terrible tension between us as business partners. Sister E had begun working in nature conservation and didn't live with us any more. She had her own house and car. One morning we were driving to Plett for breakfast when Brother E turned to me and tuned me he was sorry for the shit he had given chicks and swore a pact with me that we would both never hit or hurt kinders again.

I was a bit – *what the fuck?* – and said so. I had learnt to put my temper to bed and use it only when necessary. And never on women.

Then there was my drinking. I was a raging alcoholic. Sister E told me that she had never met anyone who would start the day with a run on the beach, a fifteen-minute workout with weights, a bike ride, then a shower, followed rapidly by dropping two Es and nailing a bottle of Black Jack. It freaked Brother E out too. He once seriously asked me if I wanted to go to rehab. We had enough money to afford the best but it seemed like an absurd idea to me. Send a big drug dealer to rehab so that he can be more proficient at selling drugs. What a *lag*!

The two of us decided to take a breather in Amsterdam. Get away from the rat and snake race intent on buttfucking our lives. We bought tickets, taking a gamble with my visa application. We had decided to hit Amsterdam via France. There was a small glitch with our visas though. The Dutch Government cleared mine but Brother E was refused entry! What the fuck? I was supposed to be the one expelled from the EU. Anyway, we eventually got his visa from France.

We sent off two parcels of zol addressed to Brother E care of the Amsterdam Postmaster General.

Two days before we were supposed to fly, we went to a big party in Knysna and got smashed. Afterwards we cruised back to our new sleeping house. It was the one where the zol was stashed before we tossed it in the jungle.

I passed out, woke up hours later and noticed that Brother E was missing. He arrived an hour or two later, said nothing and I thought nothing more about it.

I should have thought though.

I really, really should have …

27

I Can See Your House from Here

I'm sitting on top of a horse. A great big Scania pulling a flatbed trailer below me on my left. In front of me is the E pier of Rotterdam harbour, and dancing on it— a quarter of a million people. The crowd is one huge living organism, heaving, pulsating and screaming in Ecstasy as the DJs ride the decks from a rig high above them on a stack of three cargo containers.

It's the Rotterdam Dance Parade. It started this morning at ten on the other side of the city, and me and Brother E are VIP guests. There are about thirty or forty twenty-two wheelers. I haven't been able to count exactly how many, this party is just way too big. Each truck represents one of the big clubs from The Netherlands, Belgium, France and Germany. There's even a couple from England. All the trailers have seven- to eleven-kay sound rigs, were done up during the night as funky floats and are currently being valiantly manned by dedicated crews of party animals. We are on The House Of Bounce – brother Max's outfit. He's the resident at The Grasshopper in Amsterdam and produces a couple of jockeys from Gatecrasher in Pomland.

Below me, the Rotterdam police are chasing a bunch of okes with a laughing-gas bottle they've been selling to people in balloons. The crowd is *not* assisting them in their efforts.

We arrived stupidly hung-over from partying in Amsterdam the night before, found our party truck and jumped on. They pulled out quietly at a normal walking pace from the Erasmus Bridge. We weren't allowed to play music on the bridge because apparently deep bass vibration from the sound rigs could cause structural damage. Imagine that. On the other side it was a different story. Each truck had its own DJs and they all mixed whatever they fancied.

Designated party beasts were dressed up to the nines and we went wild.

There are two fridges at the back of the trailer. One filled with Red Bull, Absolut and French champagne, the other with Belgian ice-cream. There's a punch that Max and his chick made with about a hundred pills or something ridiculous. Oh, did I mention – there's a bouncer too. Just to make sure that only VIPs get on and off. See, that was the fun part

– jumping off, running ahead, letting the parade go past, and jumping on again.

The whole of Rotterdam came out to see us. TV cameras were everywhere. Of course we were in all the shots because Brother E was waving a big, pink, plastic three-foot cock and balls around. I saw MTV, MCM and Viva channels all shooting us live and I kept wondering if anybody was watching who recognises me. Eventually we arrived on the pier at about two o'clock. The trucks all pulled into a massive laager and joined the rigs up by radio so that all of them are playing from the central DJ box. The crowd, of course, is inside this enormous sound arena and this is where we have been for the last six hours.

I've still got a gram of charles in my pocket, loads of zol and hash, at least ten pills and whatever's in the fridges – so I have no immediate narcotic needs. We have four, five thousand pills waiting at the flat in Amsterdam and about three hundred kilos of zol compressed, vacuum-sealed and hidden in the jungle in South Africa near our house in Nature's Valley. Money is not a problem – we have enough.

So why am I so unhappy? So lonely? So desperately sick of who I am and what I've become?

We arrived in Amsterdam for the Gay Games three weekends earlier, and it was the usual Amsterdammed for me, highlighted by being run over by a scooter, which was a total fuckup because I thought I had bust my ankle and we were supposed to go to the Dance Valley Festival in the Spaarnwoude the following Saturday. I was lucky, it was only bruised, and we eventually joined a totally mal party of sixty thousand mense. That Monday I found out I had made the Amsterdam daily newspaper *Het Parool*. There was a photo of me on page two dancing half-naked in the rain at the party.

Gee, my only legitimate claim to fame.

In the meantime we met up with all our usual shady associates and were offered deals.

Some Irish hard men told us they had an Ecstasy factory running in Tanzania because it was legal there. As a legitimate business concern they paid tax and employed personnel from the local population, so the government let them be. They wanted to supply us and reasoned that it would be far easier to ship overland through Africa than using airfreight like we were.

Fuck, airfreight worked. Why fix it?

Then we had a sit-down. A very serious one. For transport we had a taxi driver who was a friend and a player. Having a fast Merc Kompressor on call with a driver intimately acquainted with the city was a necessity for smoothing out business. He earned every cent we paid him. We would call him and establish a pick-up time. Then we would wander down to the Red Light District checking for tails. At a certain gay bar we would duck in, run through and duck out the other entrance into an adjacent street where our driver would be waiting. Pick up and gone within seconds.

Thing was – we were hot. And we knew it. Especially after our run-in with SANAB. So Interpol and/or Dutch Narcotics might very well be watching. The freaky thing is I found out they were. You know, I've been through so many crazy situations that seemed so surreal afterwards, I knew that if I told anybody they would laugh and tell me I have a diseased imagination.

A week prior to this sit-down I'm walking down the road from a pub on my way to a meeting of smugglers at another one. We used to get together as a loose fraternity, smoke, drink and talk shop for hours. Anyway, I'm stoned silly as per usual when I notice an ou standing in a shop doorway a little ways ahead. I wasn't specifically looking for him, but something in my Das sense went off. So I looked away and watched. Then, as he glanced at me, I saw his micro-expression of recognition go off. I thought, what the fuck? But let's remember – I'm stoned silly, so this could just be a good dose of spookgerookness. I reckon, c'mon Al, and keep going. Of course curiosity starts eating away at me, and I reckon, let's see if he's still there. I pop into a little shop, buy smokes and a big can of Heineken, and check. True's Bob the fucker has pulled off and is furiously scoping out some postcards in a shop behind me.

I'm standing there scheming that if I was acting in this as a movie, I would definitely have words to say to the scriptwriters about kitsch. But what the fuck, china – in for a penny in for a pound. I pop the top of the Heineken, light an entjie and start strolling aimlessly. Every once in a while I take a Das peek. Ja, still there. What a fucking *lag*. I've actually got a tail. Just like in the fucking books and movies. I start giggling wildly and other pedestrians start giving me strange looks.

Alright Al, be cool, so you've got a tail. China, get serious.

Seriouuus.

What you gonna do about it, brasso? Get rid of it of course. Ja makwera, but how? He doesn't know I've spotted him, and if he does he will pass me on to somebody else in their team and kick up my alert level so they will be three times as careful.

I have to neutralise him.

And there is only one way to do that.

I turned a corner, pressed against the wall, and waited. As he came round, his eyes widened in deep shock and I realised that it was totally forcheesie. He was tailing me. So I fell in step behind him – I mean, right behind him – until he could feel my warm, stoned-silly breath on his neck. Now he couldn't talk on his radio, which meant he was cut off from his team, and I was willing to bet twenty bucks to a lump of shit they never trained him for this kind of insane response. Eventually he scuttled off into a big hotel and I disappeared. But now we knew the need for extreme security was a necessity.

At that sit-down, held in a beautiful old Chinese hotel and restaurant on the border of the city, we were met by two okes dressed in Armani. We ordered lunch and chatted lightly. Afterwards we lit cigars, sipped Armagnac and started talking business.

They would fill our order. They gave us twenty samples to test. It came from an industrial lab that used to manufacture juice for the bodybuilding industry but then switched to MDMA for greater profits.

We discussed the hit.

Eighty mils was too light, one-twenty would knock the ordinary punter in a club on his arse, but a hundred would bring that same punter back twice in a night for ditto the price. Our samples were hundreds. And as per usual we could expect to kick the shit out of the market. I often wondered how come we always managed to find such good product when the infrastructure of our opposition was so much bigger than ours. I put it down to Brother E's history in Amsterdam and the fact that we kept the faith inside the city. They had no time for violent South African gangster-ouens.

Then these ous started talking seriously. They reckoned we had been watched. They didn't like my bust because it had blown my cover, but they wanted to recruit us into their organisation as distributors on the South African side. A million pills were on the table.

Pure MDMA.

Ecstasy is made up of four chemical precursors. Three of them are absolutely no trouble to obtain. The fourth is something called phenyl-methyl-ketone – PMK. It is a by-product of the petrochemical industry, commercially named Safrol Oil, and real E cannot be manufactured without it.

See, apparently the UN had a secret emergency meeting of the Security Council to discuss the massive advent of Ecstasy abuse worldwide. To curtail it, the dumb-assed twats decided to restrict the availability of PMK worldwide. This led to underground chemists cooking up tabs that had all sorts of weird stimulants, except MDMA, to handle the overwhelming demand.

My most shameful moment was when we once brought back a shipment of dark pink pills. They were in two batches marked with a V and an S. We street-named them Versaces and Strawberries. They were basically a mixture of amphetamine sulphate and ketamine (a veterinary drug). I cringed at the first batch I gave to my runners, but as true's Bob they loved it and I sold our entire shipment within three weeks.

The serious okes at the sit-down in Amsterdam were basically telling us they had a standard industrial lab and enough PMK.

We didn't need to land the million tabs they offered – their people would take care of that. The samples we had been given were just plain white pills, but they would make up batches of fifty thousand with a colour and a stamp of our choice. The chemists would also toss in a few extra harmless things per batch to piss about with the chemical signature so that forensics in Pretoria couldn't trace it back to a single cook. We told them we could hire a house in Sandton or Bishopscourt with twenty-four-hour armed security, set up an infrastructure and only deal with one source per city. And we would only work in the cities. Then they set down their prerequisites. Number one – we had to cut our hair and start wearing suits like them. Yeah, fucking right. Not after carefully growing it for years and spending a small fortune on haircare products and good hairdressers – but we didn't tell them that.

The one ou was a professional cage fighter who went off to Thailand once a year to fight in illegal tournaments. Only one oke leaves the cage in those barneys, and this ou always came back. We went into negotiations slowly. We told them that we had no time to take care of something as big as they were suggesting because we were so busy with the zol side of our business. But when we had landed our next shipment of zol, we would definitely be in contact. In spite of all my resolves it was just too tempting an offer. Way too tempting. Then they told us that if we wanted we could fill the order immediately – if we trusted them. We gave the nod.

Of course.

They made a call, they paid for lunch, and outside a car pulled up and delivered our order. We gave them the tom and cruised back into the city to drop off the pills. We chowed a couple, I put about eight into a bankie and we went for a jol and a splab about their offer. We were both tempted. But we knew, one fuckup and we were both dead. I had been in enough capers to know that the most important part of any plan is planning for the unplanned because, sure as popes and bears, things always go wrong. Then it's bullet-through-the-head time. But still, if we were careful …

We were heading for a mate named Johnny's coffeeshop. We still had a ways to go when a tiny rush and a shiver caught me unawares. Unconsciously, I said *eish*. Brother E looked at me, deeply suspicious:

– *I heard an eish. Was that an eish?* –

– *No, I don't think it was an eish. Not a real eish anyway … –*

– *I heard an eish, Al, c'mon that was an eish, right?* –

– *Just wait, maybe it was my imagination* –

[…]

– *Eish!* –

– *Hey! That was you eishing! That was an eish and it was a big eish too. I heard it* –

– *Ja, bra. Early indications definitely indicate extreme eishigeness* –

– *Eish, fuck eish! Here she comes* –

– *EISH!!* –

– *Double eish … –*

It was awesome E. Some of the very best Ecstasy we had ever bought. We arrived at Johnny's rushing off our tits.

Johnny was a chronically morose Jamaican who truly seemed to think that the reason the sky hadn't fallen on him yet was because Somebody was getting sick pleasure tormenting him with the suspense. I had made it a pet project to get him to laugh but had not succeeded yet.

We were sitting outside on the stoep when suddenly Brother E pointed out an oke coming over a bridge with two other mense about twenty metres away. He told me he was an American and we had to klap him. I stood up immediately and told Johnny to watch a professional South African street-fighter in action. I walked rapidly to the bridge and circled behind them. As the Yank reached the foot of the bridge he saw Brother E and went for him.

That's when I realised Brother E couldn't fight.

He had, in the meantime, run into the coffeeshop and found a thin aluminium rod that he tried to attack the oke with. This didn't work. Almost immediately he had Brother E on the deck and was trying to pull out his hair and klap him in the bek. I pulled the ou off, spun him around upwards and punched him three times. Full punches. He went down. Poleaxed. Cheekbone and jaw broken and his nose so shattered it split open as if he had been cut with a knife. Then I heard whistles and looked over my shoulder to see a crew of Amsterdam police running like hell towards me. I went straight down on my knees, locked my hands behind my head, winked at Johnny and, as he started laughing, lay down flat on the pavement waiting for them to arrive and hit me.

They did.

It was pointless making a noise about the cuffs being too tight. Or the lumps and grazes after. Rough arrest for me. The American had to wait for an ambulance, but they dragged us off to a van and then straight to Warmoesstraat police station for booking. On the way I managed to fish the leftover pills from my front jeans pocket. This was hampered by things like excruciating pain in my wrists and the cold gaze of the policewoman riding in the back with us. I got them out and managed to stuff them in the crack of my arse just as we arrived. Brother E providing distraction by flirting with the very pissed-off chick.

Cool.

As long as she didn't see me.

Inside we are placed in a narrow booth with a long bench. There are barred doors and a grilled window. They grab Brother E first. I fish the pills out of my buttcrack and try and toss them off the end of the bench. They plop down about a foot away from me. Fuck! I scoot my bum over and eventually nudge them off. Then scoot back, sigh, look up and see the bloody camera. Oh, sweet, shit. Did they see that?

Apparently they didn't because they brought Brother E back, grabbed me and took me for one of the most thorough body searches I've ever been subjected to. From the soles of my feet to the roots of my hair. Even that sweet spot where your nuts meet your nob, which is so distinctly lekker when your chick takes your hotrod to the lipstick carwash.

Even there.

Okay, so I was clean.

They took me back, and after picking up the pills and waiting a short while, we were booked. Our stories were down pat. They took our statements and I got to see First World policing in action. My photo was taken with a digital camera. My prints were taken with a digital scanner. My docket was computerised and I was presented with a printout. I had been charged with assault with intent to do grievous bodily harm.

Damned sure.

I spent that night in one of the freakiest jails I've ever been in. Amsterdam Central Prison. After an even more thorough body search I was shown to a cell. Brother E and I managed to slip the pills to each other so I still had about six or something and E is illegal in The Netherlands so it was a bit of a *sug*. Anyway, I was shown into this absolutely pristine cell. It was the only jail cell I've ever been in utterly devoid of graffiti. It had a bunk, and on the bunk, sealed in a plastic bag, was a fucking spotlessly laundered blanket and a pillow. Folded on this were disposable sheets and a pillowcase. There was also a spotless basin and toilet with paper and disposable razor, toothbrush and toothpaste.

And a camera.

Yeah, up in the corner of the ceiling was a camera behind plated glass. There were cameras everywhere throughout the place. Obviously no wanking unless you were really into that kind of porno. At any rate I eventually fell asleep and woke the next morning to the keys outside my cell. The door opened and outside were two screws. From the neck down they were identical in their uniforms, although one of them was a chick. The chick's a West Indian Rasta with major dreadlocks and the ou's a skinhead with a huge gold earring. The chick smiles:

– *Gooten morgen mijn heer, Wilt u Koffie of tee hebbe?* –

– *Koffie* –

– *Met suiker en melk?* –

– *Dank u* –

– *Astublieft, en wilt u witbrood of bruinbrood ete?* –

– *Wit* –

– Twee snijkies of vier –

– Vier –

– En u kant kies tussen kassensmeer, gronbonenbotter, chokalatsmeer –

– Chokalat en kassensmeer –

– Astublieft –

I was shocked. They gave you choices. All the chozz came in cater packs! Sealed and everything. I've stayed in backpackers in the Dam that were dirtier and they sure as shit didn't have service like that.

Later that morning we were taken back to the Warmoesstraat police station. We had all been charged. The American included. The Dutch are almost fanatical about non-violence. You could get caught with a kilo of coke and you'd be in a hell of a lot less kak than klapping some ou like I had. They arrested and charged everybody involved in public violence. Luckily our stories corroborated with the witnesses', even though the American obviously had a different account. We saw him later and fuck he looked terrible. I hit him much harder than I thought and never felt it because of the E.

The gatta in charge of the case told me that we were being released on our own recognisance to appear at a trial two months hence. I told him I had to be out of the country the following week and he said I wasn't to worry – I wasn't in the wrong because all the witnesses agreed that the American had run towards Brother E to attack him and I only jumped in to help. Phew …

I scared the crap out of Brother E, which to me was a good thing because he had never seen me fight and I was of the opinion that he set too much stock on making a noise. Because we had been kept separated most of the time, it was only after we were released that I found out the reason for the fight. Brother E had stolen a shipment of hash from him. That freaked me out. What the fuck?

I had just nearly faced up to eight years in a Dutch jail because Brother E stole from other players? He was my partner. He told me the ou was a problem and I took him out. I had to assume that it was righteous for our business. What the fuck??

*

That's where I found myself that afternoon, on the top of a truck, in a party of a quarter million people and desperately alone.

My erstwhile business partner and best friend was a police informer and a dangerous thief. What the fuck was the point of having professional scruples and alternative ethics if I was hooked up with an oke like this? And I was stuck with him. We were virtually joined at the hip. My poor girlfriend was dead and I'd never find another like her. Not with my lifestyle. I could pick up coke whores by the dozen but I needed to love somebody who would love me more than pink flake.

On top of this – I was on trial in The Netherlands, on parole in Belgium, expelled from the EU, splashed all over DEA computers, being followed by Interpol and/or Dutch Narcotics and back home SANAB and PAGAD were racing to take me out. Not to mention other gangsters.

I fucking hated my life.

Being an illegal drug smuggler is probably the toughest business arena in the world. I learnt everything about being a hard-nosed businessman inside it but it didn't make feel very good about myself and job security would have been a nice option to sleep on at nights.

Smuggling is just as cut-throat as dealing.

The chat shows we players enjoyed together were never about current operational intelligence. It was almost always about busts, busted methods and old scams that worked. If other ous knew you had a shipment in the air they would sommer piemp yours to protect the one they brought in behind you. Put sixteen mules on a plane and someone the bosses want to take out of circulation gets piemped cold to protect the others. Then of course there's the fighting and stealing. Not a very nice profession and a crap way to do business.

That night Brother E stayed in Rotterdam and I went home to Amsterdam. I was horribly depressed. I decided I had had enough, and did something I never thought I would ever do again. I went down on my knees and prayed with my head on the pills. I told God I was sorry, I didn't want to do this any more but I didn't know how to get out.

Please help me.

We dumped the pills into the post and a few days later found ourselves an hour from boarding our flight from Schiphol to Paris when two Dutch Narcotics detectives came up and arrested Brother E for the parcel of zol he'd posted to himself. He was charged with tax evasion and I caught the flight back home alone.

Two days later I phoned his mother and she told me the terrible news. Sister E had relayed to her what had happened when Brother E disappeared after the party in Knysna before we left for Amsterdam via France – the prologue to this book.

He'd driven to her house, forced his way in and raped and terrorised her for hours. She managed to escape eventually, and ran like hell for the house of an oke who worked with her and had a gun. She was utterly convinced Brother E was going to kill her. Brother E apparently ran around the house with a branch, screaming and raging like a demented animal. Sister E curled up in a foetal ball, wrapped in a duvet the ou with the gun had given her to cover her nakedness, while he ran from window to window following Brother E, scared shitless.

First I cried. Then I called Sister E. I told her I was back and said I was sorry. She told me it was okay, but I knew it wasn't. I've faced sexual assault and what I considered certain death, and it is not okay. It fucks you up for ages afterwards. I went to visit Brother E's parents, and on the drive down, the rage at what he'd done began hitting me. Sister E was one of my oldest and very closest girl friends, as well as being my business partner.

Fuck him. Rapist, piemp, thief.

I told his brother and parents that I was getting out. I refused to be a partner in crime to that type of sick fucking shit.

His parents and brother agreed.

Sister E and I went to Cape Town and collected all the pills. We divided them into three and I gave his share to his mense. I also gave them about twenty kilos of zol to cover their phone bill because Brother E was making international reverse-charge calls three times a day. I paid off the other okes on the payroll we still owed with zol, took my pills, dumped all Brother E's and took fifty kilos for myself. I fetched and dumped all of Brother E's stuff with his people. Then I moved to Jeffreys Bay.

I decided to kill him. It was the only way. This oke would never be able to see that what he'd done was nauseating. He would fly into one of his famous tantrums and blame everything and everyone except himself.

Okay, take him out. But how? Hire a hit? No, what if the moegoes fuck it up and the jol backfires?

I could booby-trap the zol left there with homemade claymores, but if he went there with someone else they would shred an innocent. Like the oke who went with me to fetch it. I had a sneaky feeling B wanted to help himself a little.

I would have to do it myself. Up close, technically quiet and very personal.

I bought a gun to kill him with. Then I hunted around for some very old connections who were still players and asked them to take care of Brother E in case he took me out first. One of my bras was actually going out with a chick whom Brother E had got his fists on. He needed no excuse. The girl had taken two years to get through the terror and tell him what had happened to her. Fuck that, they didn't even want to be paid.

I had nothing else to do except wait to kill him and follow him to hell, so I gave in to the black pain blindly and tried to drink myself to death.

Whatever came first …

I stopped fucking caring …

PART VI

Dreams

28

Noah's Curse

I prefaced this story of mine with a few verses from the greatest seafaring tale in the Bible. The one about the six-hundred-year-old drunken sailor whose youngest son walks in on him in his tent one day, only to find him stark bollocks naked and ripped to the tits. A direct result of his newly grown and *well-fermented* grapes – nurtured from the pips in raisins he carefully hoarded on the Ark no doubt.

The poor kid, getting a load of his old man and the oldest schlong ever to swing above The Great-Only-Ocean, obviously *Does Not Deal With This Situation Very Well* and runs out yelling his head off.

Some time later the old bugger wakes up with the world's one and only recorded six-hundred-year-old hangover and, after screaming in unholy pain and staggering off to drink what appears to be ALL of what is left of the Great Flood, he comes lurching back to interrogate everyone concerned, and determine in minute detail – EXACTLY what happened to him in that typical, ageless, booze-binge amnesia that always seems to accompany the monstrous frenzied hog-skinning that we have been observing.

Noah was not a man you would want to trifle with, so if he wanted to know EXACTLY what happened in the tent, you told him. Everybody did. This dude could HEAR God. You fucking tuned him alright. The story, when it all hurriedly came out, was that his two elder sons (*who simply couldn't bear the unthinkable idea of laying siege to their sanity with the sight of that six-hundred-year-old prong they had heard completely unprintable things about from their very unhinged sibling*) came running into the tent backwards with the nearest big blankety thing they could find, tossed it over their shoulders in his general direction and got the hell out of there.

The serious point of the story is that Noah then *used his Spiritual Authority as a prophet and head of their clan to curse his grandchild.*

Curse.

A kid who has absolutely nothing to do with his dad walking in on his oupa, while *his* OUPA was the one completely slaughtered, and yells at the little fucker to go fetch wood and water and skivvie for his brothers before he gets a good fucking clout. (*Rockspiders reckon that's how come we got darkies in the world somehow.*)

Nobody with a six-hundred-year-old hangover is nice.

My horribly abused township cat Bambutu could figure out there's a definitive nastiness in that simple story somewhere. Bambutu's seen the results of mad onshore intoxication and much worse – all at first hand. She was born into the detritus of mixed-blood slaves and cast-offs. People living in hovels and trying to kill their God-given humanity with cheap liquor and filthy drugs. Driven mad from numbed endurance of the chains and the white steel-capped boot, which crushed their necks and spat evil curses into their minds for so many generations. The very rich, loamy breeding grounds of newer and even more hideous crimes to spit back at the men who planted the cold seeds of hate there.

Bubu definitely knows that she was born into a dark, savage world that has been involved in a self-destructive, maniacal war with itself for endless generations. She's certainly tasted lots of the pain in it. A callously hurled brick crushed her back leg when she was a kitten and never received proper veterinary attention, so she is slightly crippled. A mean man, made mean like a mad dog, poured a pot of boiling water over her, leaving a terrible scar across her back and neck. The poor little beastie suffered crippling malnutrition from birth that retarded her emotions and stunted her growth. She has a constant hacking cough from breathing toxic burning garbage. When I first saw her, she was living on potato skins she skivvied in terror from a sewer heap made by the garbage rummagers and street people who live in a squatter settlement of twenty-four informal dwellings under the Kayamandi railway bridge in Stellenbosch.

I used to go there to smoke buttons and drink cheap wine with my mate Joey Evil. We would talk kak or pass out. Joey can't graft so lekker – he was in a car accident and has nerve damage, so now he walks with a wobbly limp that makes him look gesuip. His wife is in her fifties and supports him and their daughter whenever she can find char work. There is no running water, no clean fuel, no sanitation, hence the raw sewage that Bambutu lived on.

It hurt me beyond description watching this poor, defenceless, tiny and horribly damaged animal limping alone, soundlessly and patiently through that nightmare world. Trying only to survive and maybe find a tiny scrap of love, as she looked up terrified at the broken faces of her broken and poisoned masters. And she was merely an unwanted animal.

Then, in my own drunken mess, I would stagger back to the white part of town, to my filthy, empty squat. And I would lie there crying like I did all those years before as a missionary. Hating the pain and my weakness. Hating myself and raging at the hypocrisy of everything around me. Slowly drowning in a world of self-pity because I couldn't do anything about it. Nobody would listen to an ex-bandiet, buttonkop and poeswynsuiping kaffirboetie.

In time I abandoned my suicidal musings, left buttons and the filthy wine behind me for something and someone much better – but when I left, I took Bambutu with me. I bought her for the price of my very last button from a man named Pitte. I won't frighten you with the vet bill or how long it took to pay it off.

I decided to give her what she had never had, and I consciously let go of the inconsolable grief, anger and rage deep within myself. Before it destroyed me and those few real people trying to love me.

They say that the truly insane are convinced they are not. I *knew* I was mentally disturbed. That made it so much worse. Reality was sometimes so distant I had to fight with everything I had to try and reach it. And I was dying from alcoholism and drug addiction. Very slowly, but definitely dying.

I decided for myself that we would not die there. Not like that. My choice. I decided to be like my deeply hidden understanding of God to Bambutu, because by doing that, she would inadvertently teach *me* about the nature of unconditional love.

She still is …

It took ages for her to finally trust me completely. I gained it through patience and a constant gentle reaffirmation of my love for her – day in and day out, until eventually she stopped crying out in her sleep, started speaking in a tiny voice and came running when we called her. I knew what she needed and I provided it.

As time went by I allowed myself the magnificence of comparing her with my own spiritual identity. As I did so, things started unlocking and mental shackles began falling away. I began to realise that what Sister Michelline had told me in prison was true. So were all the things I believed in so strongly. I thought I had lost those beliefs but they had only hardened and become more tempered under the chains.

And memories of things I could not ignore started returning …

I was in my early thirties when I first began to appreciate and accept that what Wally and Denise did to me as a baby and a child was heinous and abhorrent – in the eyes of normal society, the Law and the eyes of God. It damaged me deeply in all the usual ways, drove me to the street and helped create the enraged adolescent and violent young adult I became.

Weirdly enough, I had to use cold logic to prove this as a fact that I could accept *emotionally*, by first asking myself a couple of very pertinent questions. You see, I truly believed it was *my* fault. It had to be. Bitch-born bastard. Until— until ... I started wondering ... *hypothetically*:

Did Audrey ever use her nails on Denise until she bled, or slam her head into the veranda until she was concussed? Did old Ma Goulding ever burn Wally when he was a baby? Thump him and send him to school dressed in a sack? Smash a radio to bits on his head? Put a gun in his mouth? Try to stab him to death? Brain him with a glass rock? Run him over with a car?

I don't fucking think so. No, I don't, and that means it was never my fault. And it wasn't Yvonne's fault either. She also had to suffer over-the-top shit, so those two sickos can't even blame it on me being a kid born bad. They were evil, not me.

Sandy never ever hit me, and not once did he ever humiliate or degrade me as a human being. It took many years for me to accept that my feelings for him were legitimate – as one should feel towards one who is a father to you. A man worthy of my love and honour. A father to the fatherless. A man I aspire to becoming.

Wally and Denise were abject child abusers and that about sums it up.

Of course that was the deepest and most painful aspect of my childhood and ultimately the most negative, but it was only the first element of the *triad* of destructive forces in my journey.

It took me even longer to realise that the shocking dismay and angry frustration I experienced in the church were also valid.

Destructive force number two. This time in my spiritual childhood.

Like millions, I had been subjected to pure spiritual abuse, something as abhorrent as burning babies. What made it particularly diabolical was that apartheid was perpetuated from the pulpit, and rebellious aberrations like me were a menace to the subliminal status quo, for naively asking too many awkward questions and rocking the boat. But it was way, way beyond that. It was way beyond politics and race. To me, it was supposed to be about *showing* love to everybody. Starting with the children. Doing stuff for poor indigent laaities who had nothing. Help the kids and *reach* the adults by rote. I hurt for those kids all the time and it seemed so bloody simple.

That, of course, drove me back into the soft, dark arms of my chemical predilections and self-battery. Ta-daaah! Bad shit number three. For a long time I believed Wally, Denise and the modern super-Pharisees, then self-medicated myself against the destruction of my self-worth and the compounded consequences.

When I have a drinkie-poo it should be poured from at least a full case of really cheap and nasty vodka, with any even cheaper and more socially insensitive sweet shit to kill the mildly motorsport-fuel taste that comes with that sort of a dop. Problem is, like a typical greedy fucking pig, I immediately want another. Only this time make it a double!

And then I want a spliff too, *immediately* – hopefully good Swazi, not the bloody majat used to smoke buttons with – and never jump on the china-white dragon's back again either, while we are on the ugly subject of lethal downers – but fuck it bra, you may certainly cut me a rail. Make it a few nice bosses china. And who's got good pills and candy?

Of course, as I have told you at length, this cheerfully insane way of reacting to things that hurt me emotionally and spiritually has landed me in a lot of jails around the world, and hospitals, and psychiatric emergency wards, loads of interesting rehabs of course, together with all the weird beds in weird places, with even weirder and similarly fucked bedfellows – the hands of good, kind and well-meaning folks, absolute fucking religious maniacs – the filthy shacks, hovels and ghettos that so many of our poor fucked-up people have to try and survive from; it has destroyed two marriages, ruined me financially about five times, screwed up every single one of my relationships and lost me almost all of my friends, together with the extreme resentment of the members of whatever goes as the ruins of my un-family. I'm not even going to *start* on the damage to all of my outraged major organs.

The glitz, glamour and money found in the narcotics industry is just gold for fairy dust. Sniff and it's gone. Or you're staring at the business end of a penitentiary's bars for years, or maybe drooling on your lap in an endless pyjama party organised by those fun people in State Mental Health. Then again, maybe you make a once-in-a-lifetime deal with an undertaker. Drugs are fun for a moment, but that moment is always frantically on the scuttle leeward, and life was designed to be more than a moment going around in vicious circles. And you're utterly fucked if you're taking drugs to make yourself feel better about who you are, or – even worse – to make other people like you in spite of the footprints of Cain in your veins. Rock bottom is when you take them to not feel yourself or other people at all any more.

Most of all – no, it is not just a cliché – crime actually doesn't pay. It *will* rip you off. I'm no deep sage or onion – I figured this out the hard way by doing it over and over until it penetrated my thick skull – jail just isn't fun.

My long sojourn from the ugly world of Wally and Denise, into Uncle Guvvie's brutally nurturing arms and beyond – swinging between the glittery violent world of drugs, the harsh loneliness of prison and the self-centred, pious insanity of the church, has often seemed to me the passing by of an utterly wasted life.

Finally, though, I began to realise that it was all a journey I needed to complete, and every milestone, place and memory – *perfect for its purpose.* If I looked carefully enough, I could find many angels in the architecture of my life.

God was not threatened by my rejection. I could not make Him love me more or *less* by any of my actions – either good or *bad.* Even if I compounded those mistakes by deliberately turning my back and returning to the easiest way to kill the ache of my perceived rejection. He did not go and sulk on a rock somewhere in a corner of heaven because I had decided to believe fools who lied and misrepresented everything He represents for their own purposes.

I managed to realise that I had no control over the abject abuse I suffered as a child. No child does. But as an adult I did. And in the absence of abuse I subconsciously created my own. Any half-assed cranial-reduction specialist will tell you that this is fairly normal abnormal behaviour – but realising it, making it *real,* and coming to terms with it – aaah, now that is a different fucking box of Smarties. I dunno where you're coming from, cousin, but if you've been through some or maybe more of the shit I've been through and you've managed to realise this *thing,* then you will agree with me – it is fucking hard. The hardest thing in the world.

When you believe you are going to hell, it tends to paralyse and fuck you up as a human being. Especially if you have a bad picture of hell like I did.

I've smashed bottles over my head and then cut an anarchy symbol in my chest with the broken ends. Slashed open my wrists and drunk the blood chased down with vodka and codeine – then painted crimson graffiti on walls with it. I've lain fighting on the floor for possession of a button pipe in the middle of a pitched firefight between gattas and gangsters, with bullets flying and ricocheting above our heads. Climbed up onto the top of a running Metro train, smashed on gin, to see if I could limbo under the live wire without frying myself. I used to walk out of an office where I was key personnel on a multibillion-rand project, get into my car, start driving, and as soon I hit one-sixty I would fire a creamed button pipe and make sure I did not prang during the rush. Pushing the envelope off the desk, straight through the fucking window and out into thin air sixty storeys up. Let's see if the bitch flies …

Why? Self-hatred is a terrible obsession. I was terrified of dying, but I wanted to so badly. As an adult I had become a very dangerous and damaged child – hurting many others and myself. Lying in a gutter or flying around the world. It was all the same thing. I needed to know what real love was all about.

I found it first by giving it to a very hurt little kitty.

And this made me realise something else. If I could give it in my fractured way to something as small, weak and utterly insignificant as a battered township cat – then I deserved it too. I needed to migrate from who I perceived and *projected* myself to be and into who I was created to be.

I legally changed my name to:

Al Lovejoy

Just that. I did it because I needed to kill the cacophonic echoes of all the labels I had carried.

Airport Alex, the ou formerly known as Acid Alex, also alternatively known as Skollie Papillon or secretly known as Alexander-Bitch-Born-Bastard-Blikkieskos-PuddlePirate-Asterix-Yster-Lix-Douglas-Goulding— needed to die.

My new name is perfect for its purpose.

I got rid of my gang past.

I went to two very talented tattoo artists in Cape Town who run a parlour called Wildfire. They are the oldest pros in town except for ancient Mr Adams who did my original gang stukas. Manuela did my arms and

Simon did my legs. Everything is a reflection of how I see myself. I have a tiki hanging under two stone totems with flanking lizards all in Marquesan style on my left arm to celebrate my spiritual protection. On my right I have an African wedding mask Manuela designed to celebrate my identity as an African. On my left leg I have the Borneo fire symbol of a warrior, in keeping with my star sign, and on my right a free-form tribal symbol of water – life.

I stopped committing crime.

I don't want to import or export drugs and I will never distribute them again.

By choice.

I will not carry a gun for another man, ever again. I am determined to try and live a life where I never need to be violent.

I am glad that no law enforcement agencies of any country want my gat any more.

Let's keep it that way.

And, please understand, I am not blaming Wally and Denise or the slimy bullshit pastors for my criminal career. It was my choice. But it was also my choice to stop. As far as I am concerned, that small fact is all that matters. I also think the fact that I chose to not kill Wally or Brother E makes me a far better man than either one of them.

I turned around, started walking and never looked back. Losing Brother E hurt like living hell. Hating him for what he did to Sister E hurt even worse. Killing him would have made it ten times more unbearable, because he was more of a brother than I've ever had. I truly loved him with all my heart. And I was stupid because I loved somebody who had no concept of the idea. Beating, raping and terrorising a defenceless girl means there is no love in the heart – only lust in the cock and shit in the head. A sick cowardly bully to the core. And if I capped Wally, it would make me just like him in the end. It's one thing to go into battle or to fight for your life, but the premeditated decision to play judge and executioner is a cold night not to be entered into lightly.

Was either one of them really worth an eternity of hell anyway?

I went through one nightmare of a fight with drugs, and especially alcohol. But this is not a twelve-step manual or a debate about drugs. It's my weird life, and I managed to fight off the big evils – Mandrax, heroin, ice and crack. And stay off them.

I tried twelve-stepping for a while, but getting up and saying in essence

– Hi, my name is Al, and I'm a cunt who's currently pretending not to be one just doesn't work for me, china. Besides, what I saw was the religion of addiction. Fuck that – I hate religion in all its forms. Don't get me wrong, one of the most sincere men I ever met, and one of the very few men I trust spiritually, is a champion of AA, but he has dedicated his life to treating addicts, so it's more the man than the method as far I'm concerned. I get horribly irritated with people who *Find the Light* and then set about forcing it down other people's throats using their brand new rituals, slogans and jargon – because my own insecurities used to drag me into those canned ways of thinking too quickly and I'd end up doing the whole song and dance myself – just for acceptance. Fuck rituals and slogans – I am a human being and so is everybody else.

I accept myself.

I've got nothing to say about narcotic addiction other than it is a drive, like hunger or sex, which resides in every one of us and causes us to want intoxication as a de-stressing mechanism. And, like any obsessive-compulsive disorder, it's only fucked up when the happy shit behind the drive is fucked up.

That friend I mentioned, the one I trust spiritually, he has a saying he loves:

When your horse dies— get off it.

I love that saying.

Cousin, I didn't hold back on my anger when I wrote about Wally, Denise, institutions and the church in this book. They hurt me badly and I punched back hard, *but* – and this a very big But – I could not, and will not, stay there in the ring with them. That can *all* stay right here, trapped between these pages. A darn good place for it all to be, if you ask me.

Forgiveness is a key.

When *any* one of us gets hurt mentally, emotionally, spiritually, our initial response is always one of denial. It will never happen to me, it is not happening to me, it never happened to me. I had to overcome that first. Get real. Then comes anger. Somebody is to blame. Is it me? Is it them? It must be them! Or am I just a fuckup? No, yes, it's them. Someone must pay! Getting stuck in this phase of resentment would make me a replica of the people I resented.

The next phase was very painful. I needed to grieve my past. Really grieve it. It was okay to cry because I thought God hated me for so long. It was okay to cry about the loneliness of always wanting to belong to real parents. It was okay to grieve the deeply damaged child and young adult. It was okay to mourn the long wasted years, lost in prison, crime and drug abuse.

It was okay to weep for Christine and my poor little dead girls.

But in due course the tears had to stop falling and I had to press on or it would turn into a self-pitying, snivelling whine.

The last phase is the path of acceptance. It is the path to the future. I had to begin attempting to see what I could contribute *to* life instead of seeing what I could get out of it. Surviving the roller-coaster like I had all those years made a moderately interesting tale but it was still second-class living at best. The reason why I fucked everything up was because I *refused* to look at what I was capable of. Tiny example – I didn't need to smuggle zol to Europe. I could have exported curios or live animals if I had so chosen. Yet, I saw myself as the anti-hero, always bucking the phantom Uncle Guvvie. It has also dawned on me that what other people do, accept or pay for in the name of God is their business. I need not defend God from them. Only their victims.

And I am happy.

Christ's disciples come to Him and ask Him what is the singular most important thing to believe in and do in the name of God. He calls a poor stranger's child over, places the mite before them and says – this child is the most important person to God. Whoever cares for this child loves Me. Whoever gives a simple cup of water to this laaitie has given it to Me. Whoever causes this child to suffer, become hard and turn into a vicious street criminal has done something so bad that it would have been better if that person were executed by a death penalty of strangulation and drowning.

It's that simple. Jesus loves the little children. Go love them too.

I am an orphan. I have no normal family, which means that everybody who has no normal family— *is my family*. We are the biggest family in the world. I have a life dream that we can re-gather our family and break the ancient curse …

I am going to greet you now, cousin. Thank you for listening to my story. In the wake of this long saga, I wish you well and leave you with—

A parable.

29

Blindness

Eksê.
What?
Are you awake?
Ja.
Hey, a man can't sleep eskê. I'm worried about my sentencing tomorrow.
Ja, me too. Only it's late bra, tomorrow is today already.
Fuck that's true.
Hey my broer, you skiem you also gonna get the death sentence?
Fuck bra, I don't wanna think about that.
Ja, me too my broer …
Hey, come on bra, tune me one of your mal stories again.
Have you still got that spliff we nipped china?
One time.
What you skiem my broer? The boere should only come around again on the four o' clock watch? Hey?
Ja I skiem so bra. These naaiers are too sleg to do anything extra.
Then toke it up bra and split it with me, and then I'll maybe tune …

Here's the spliff my broer, but c'mon tell me one of those stories china, and we forget about our klap tomorrow for a bit.
We get klapped today remember.
Okay, okay, so it's today, don't remind me again …
Okay kwaai. Once upon a twice, back in the olden days, there was this roeker who was mos blind. You make out?
One time.
Now this ou had been born like that. Very kak of course, but ja, no well, it happens. Anyway, so this roeker had to mos maar bedel to make a way because he couldn't see fuckall and so he obviously couldn't graft.
Ja, one time.
Anyway, remember this is mos now fucking long ago bra, and doer up in the land where the Slams ouens come from.
Ja.

So now their cities mos had walls around them and gates and everything and this ou sat at the gates bedeling.

Ja, one time.

Anyway, now skiem about it. The only way to get into this city was mos by the gate, and in their time all the lank important larnies used to park off there too. 'Cos they used to charge tax to the merchants coming in and out to smokkel with the mense what lived inside.

Ja, ja, kwaai.

Among these larnies were also the ouens who would like be the maggies of the city and they would collect tax and sort out kak between the mense. You make out?

Kwaai.

So you got ouens paying the maggies tax, other maggie-ouens sorting out who klapped who or slukked whatever first. More ouens doing business, wharrawharra, and in among all these bewegings there's this blind roeker.

Kwaai. One time.

Now there wasn't MTV and cellphones and all that kak in those times china. News could only travel as quick as the fastest horse. And then you had to hope that the mense didn't fuck up the story when they told it again. But the whole jol I'm trying to tune you is that there was this rumour going around. Like a really strong rumour. Like that last amnesty rumour, make out?

Ja, but that was kak and we're still stokkies, it don't count for us.

Ja I know, but this rumour was so strong the first time you'd hear it was from the ou standing next to you in the street— as you heard the mang's front door slamming behind you.

Fuck that's a strong rumour!

One time. Okay, so now check it out. This roeker's whole kop is in his ears because that's mos the only way he can make out what's going on around him.

Ja, ja.

So he listens. He probably can't sit too near these big larnies but close enough just to hear what's going for what.

Ja, I make out eksê. Skelm.

Ja, but the larnies' gedagte is mos different. In their eyes he was just a vuil old blind bergie.

Ja, one time.

Anyway my broer, so this rumour he hears is about a prophet. This prophet comes from some other spot and this ou's name is Yeshua ben Yosef. Which actually means that this ou is Yosef's laaitie.

Ja, kwaai.

Now he has heard lots of rumours and things, remember this ou has sat there bedeling for thirty years.

Mutherfucker! Thirty whole fucking years! Fuck bra, my last stretch was only six and a half.

Ja I know. Heavy hey. So anyway, what gets his motor running is he thinks there's a bewysstuk in this particular rumour about this ou, this Yosef's laaitie. He has listened to gossip and other mense all his life and he knows when he is hearing kak or not. You can mos work it out when you hear mense talk about a move a lot.

Ja one time.

And what makes him skiem that Yosef's laaitie is the makwera is that the ouens who were like the dominee-type ouens in that time, who he has heard talking about it – they don't smaak this Yosef's laaitie ou. But this roeker doesn't smaak these dominee ouens either because they are dik suinige naaiers. He's like a boemelaar and all these mense are the ous who he bedels from. Like his customers. Only the dominee ouens give him fuckall except once in a while so that the other mense will check them out as being kwaai ouens. You make out?

Ja, I make out.

Anyway, the rumours get stronger. Stuff about mense getting better and goeters from diseases and what-what. And the dominee ouens are getting a lot more befuck.

Ag, fuck them. Suinige twee-gevreet naaiers.

One time china. So now, check it out – one day, this roeker hears a crowd coming and the mense running in front are tuning everyone that it's this ou, Yosef's laaitie. So he skiems he has sat here for thirty years – he better not fuck up his one shot. The ou has to come past him to get into the city, and he might be blind but he knows how to yell. The crowd gets nearer and nearer, and then it's suddenly the crowd, and he starts yelling at Yosef's laaitie, begging and begging for mercy. He won't shut up – he just yells and yells and yells. Now the ouens walking with Yosef's laaitie, who were like his main bras and bizas – try and make this blind roeker shut the fuck up, but he just keeps on yelling louder! ... Then the crowd suddenly stops ... Goes quiet ... He hears some ou come up and kneel down in front of him ...

Yosef's laaitie!

Ja, zigzactly. But now listen to this. He hears them talking about him, the same ous what tried to make him shut him up, and a new voice, who must obviously be Yosef's laaitie because the other ous are calling him teacher and all those sorts of goeters. Anyway, so now they ask Yosef's laaitie who's to blame for this roeker being blind from birth and all that. Like did his parents cause major kak and this is their bad karma taken out on him or did he cause kak in a previous life or what? So Yosef's laaitie tunes his chinas, nooit, it's so that God can be seen in him.

What? But the ou is blind my broer, how can God be seen in him?

Wait bra. Now this blind roeker obviously can't see what's going on, out on the outside. All he sees is the black inside of his skull, but on the real outside Yosef's laaitie starts gobbing and gobbing. Big fat greenies. Dik fat ones in the dirt. Grrrrrrmmmphh, Grrrrmmmphhgrrgrg, Ptthooowwwat!

Fuck off broer, you making me naar.

No my broer, this is how it happened. Facts.

Ja, ja, but let's just be lekker, okay?

Anyway, so he puts his finger in it like this, and—

ARE YOU TOTALLY BEFUCK!?

Hey, ssssssht! You'll bring the boere down on us!

Nooit china, you know I don't smaak that naar kak.

Bra, I gotta tune you like it is because then I can only tune you what happened next.

What, he ate it or some sort of fucked-up kak?

Nooit bra, now you're being a naargat. Nooit, he made mud with it from the dirt and stuffed it in the holes where this roeker's eyes were supposed to be.

Fuck, serial hey?

Ja.

So then?

So now Yosef's laaitie tunes him, listen my broer, you must go to that fountain jol in the middle of the city and wash your eyes out. And don't spin out 'cos everything is going to be totally cool, you'll check. So he missions and washes his eyes and suddenly he's got eyes where the mud was and the ou can like see for real and everything.

Yoh-yoh!

Ja. Anyway, so he waais to his pozzie and his mense totally freak out and ask him, like what the fuck happened!?

They must have totally skiemed like What Da Fuck?

Ja, zigzactly. But now check this one out. The dominee ouens hear about it because this is like one of those front-door-of-the-mang-slamming-behind-you rumours. Everybody starts splabbing about it.

Fuck-ja.

So they like give this roeker a summons to come before them. So he waais. They tune this ou he must tune them exactly what happened. Okay so he tunes them like, you know, Yosef's laaitie – goeters in his eyes – he doesn't know what goeters, just goeters – washes his face and suddenly he doesn't have to walk into walls or donner down stairs any more.

Ha ha, fuck-ja.

Ja, so the dominee ouens start arguing about the whole jol and tuning like this Yosef's laaitie is like a devil or something and this is a lot of kak and cannot be from God and what-what. I mean, gobbing and spitting greenies and making mud and goeters – that just sounds siff. I mean, that's just plain vuil bra. You make out how delicate the larnies are. I mean check at you just now, and you mos kamstig a Holland joster.

Hey, fuck you bra, your poes.

Ja, ja, your auntie's blue one. So anyway, the dominee ouens call his mense in and they tune his toppie and tannie, is this like your laaitie eksê? So his mense tune ja, one time – but we don't know fuckall about what happened eksê. He just came home like that. You make out? Only they didn't actually say fuckall and goeters because they were like lank bang of the dominee ouens. These ous had a lot of mag. They were dominee ouens who were also like maggies of the church as well. You make out?

Fuck-ja, shit. Okay. Then?

So they put this ou on trial.

Fuck, nooit, you're talking kak. That's completely blind bra.

Nooit, s'true true china – njannies kappellas, they put this poor roeker on trial for his troubles. So he gets befuck, turns around and tunes these mutherfuckers, are you mense all totally fucking mal? Obviously not a good move, but my broer, in the circumstances, hey, fuck – you know what I'm saying?

Ja, fuck ja – me myself, I mean fuck it china, like what had the ou actually done wrong?

Zigzactly. Anyway, eventually these dominee ous find him guilty and throw him out their church.

What the fuck for?

Fuck knows. I don't skiem they even knew why. But it's not over yet. He's on his own, he's out of the church, which by the way, was a totally blind thing in those days because you could only get into heaven through the dominee ouens who had kicked him out – I mean, that was supposed to be those dominee ouens' main graft. Plus his parents don't want him to come around in case they also get into kak with the dominee ouens, and he can't bedel anymore because there is nothing wrong with him. So now what?

Ja, fuck, now what? What happened?

He goes looking, looking … for Yosef's laaitie. Only he doesn't know it, but Yosef's laaitie has already been looking for him, because Yosef's laaitie heard that this roeker was in the kak.

Fuck, that's majorly cool!

Ja, lekker hey. Anyway, so Yosef's laaitie finds him and asks him if he is stambula. This roeker tunes him ja, he's sterkbene. Some ou he had never been able to see made his eyes lekker but he got into kak because of it. He got thrown out the church and now it's like no more heaven for him. So Yosef's laaitie puts his hand on his shoulder, looks him straight in his new eyes, and asks him if he believes in the God of Heaven. This roeker tunes him, ja. So Yosef's laaitie tunes him, well my broer, the God of Heaven is looking at you …

Haai! Youse bandiete better keep your donnerse bekke shut! Go to sleep in there or I sommer give you bastards more charges!

Glossary

1 Mil: 1 Military Hospital

ag-en-twintig: twenty-eight (prison gang number)

alkies: alcoholics

ander: other

appie: apprentice

asgat pipe: a finished pipe (*literally* ash-arse)

AWB: Afrikaner Weerstand Beweging, Afrikaner Resistance Movement

baadjie (bloubaadjie): prison sentence over fifteen years (those convicts wore blue jackets)

baas: boss, master

baba: father, baby

baie: very, lots

bakkie: pick-up truck

balsak: Army kitbag (*literally* ballbag)

bandiet: prisoner

bandietklere: prison clothes

bang: scared

bankie: coin bag (of marijuana)

barmhartige krimineel: compassionate criminal

Baygon: insect repellent

beamptes: officials

bedel: beg

bedonnered: angry

bek(ke): mouth(s)

bene: legs (*literally*), strength

bergies: vagrants

bewegings: things happening

bewysstuk: proof, evidence

biza: blood brother

blikkieskos: tinned food

bliksem: hit

bloei baie: bleeding a lot

blouesaand: freshmen night (*literally* blue-arse night)

blougat: freshman (*literally* blue arse)

bly wakker: be alert, stay awake

BOB: Belgian Border Guards

boemelaar: beggar

boepbeker: prison mug

boep-chappies: prison tattoos

boepens: pot belly

boep radio: prison intercom radio

boere: police

boerestation: police station

boetie: brother

Bogart: joint hog

bokkies: girls

bokkos: vegetables (*literally* buck food)

bomas: thorn enclosures

bonehead: Afrikaner (*derogatory*)

boom: marijuana

boom-roeker: marijuana smoker

boomslang: tree snake

bosses: thick lines of cocaine

bozies: black people (*derogatory*)

bra: friend

braai: barbecue

braaivleis: barbecued meat

broer: brother

brown sugar: heroin

bughouse: cinema

bundu: bush

buttonkop: Mandrax addict

buttons: Mandrax

candy: LSD

casevac: casualty evacuation

Casspir: armoured police assault vehicle

chaff: chat up

charlie, charles: cocaine

check: see, newspaper

china: friend, mate

chommie: friend

chorb: pimple

chow: eat, food

chozz: eat, food

click: kilometre

daai: that
dagga: marijuana
DB: Detention Barracks
DBI: Detention Barracks Instructor
DEA: Drug Enforcement Administration
dertig: thirty (prison gang number for a foodie)
dieetstraf: dietary punishment
Diensplig: National Service
dik: fat, a lot
dik suinige naaiers: fat stingy fuckers
dikgerook: very stoned
dinges: thingy
disipliene: discipline
dissed: insulted
dixie: tin plate
doeke: scarfs
doen: do
doer: far
dof: stupid
dom: dumb
dominee: minister
donner: beat up
donnerse: bloody
doop: initiation
doos: cunt, arsehole
dop: drink
dorp: town
dorpie: little town
doss: sleep
drie maaltye: three meals (dietary punishment)
dronk: drunk
dros: escape
duckie: shirt
duime: thumbs
dwaal: delirium
eerste: first
eina: ouch
ek is 'n poes: I am a cunt
eksê: I say
Engelsman: Englishman
entjie: cigarette
etter: pus
familiemoordenaars: family murderers

flap: hit with cane
flics: police
fliek: film
foeitog: term of sympathy
fokken: fucking
fokkol: fuckall
fotoverhaal: photo story
G6: National Service discharge
gaan: bust, hurt or kill
Gaan haal die honde: Go get the dogs
gama: name
gammats: Cape Malays (*derogatory*)
gat: arse
gattas: police
gedagte: criminal intent, attitude, world view
geluk: gratuity
gemors: mess
gepantserde: armour-plated
gerook: stoned
gesuip: drunk
gevrek: stupid and lazy
giemba: obese person
gintu: sex worker
girrick: pipe filter
goeters: stuff (*lovely word! – author*)
gogga: insect
goofed: stoned
gooied: left
goonk: idiot
gou-gou: very quickly
graft: work
graunch: kiss
Groot Oom Kwaadraad: Vicious Big Uncle (pun on squared – *Afr.*)
Groot Trek: Great Trek
hamba gashle: go in peace
hosh: gang salute
hoerpoep: antiperspirant spray (*literally tart fart*)
hol-bunny: homosexual man
holhang: scrounge, beg
Holland joster: gang member who has killed
holnaai: anal sex
honk: work detail

Hotnots: Cape Coloureds (*derogatory*)
howzit: hello, how's it?
HSI: Hoof Staf Intelligensie/Chief of Staff Intelligence
imali: money
indota: initiated man
inkosi: I praise you
ja: yes
Ja Kolonel: Yes Colonel
jag: chase
jags: horny
Jakkalskoppe: Military Intelligence
jellyhead: drug user
jimmy: thousand
jippogat: malingerer
jol: party, thing, story, sex worker's client
jools: jewellery
jostermeid: female street gangster
joster-stroll: street gangster swagger
Jy gaan hel toe: You're going to hell
Jy met die oog! Wat is jou naam troep?: You with the eye! What's your name, troop?
kafee: café
kaffir: black person (*derogatory*)
kaffirboetie: non-racial white (*literally* kaffir brother)
kak: shit
kak gedagte: insidious thoughts
kakpotte: shit pots
kamer gereedfo' inspeksie: room ready for inspection
kamstig: apparently
kanonnies: friends
kap: crush or chop
kap vas: stop or arrest
kas: black location
kay: kilometre
keep skei: keep a lookout
Kei: Transkei
kêrels: police (*literally* the boys)
kerk: church
kerkpak: church suit
keuring: selection
key: kilogram
khaya: house
kiff: cool

kinders: girls
kitters: clothes
klaar: finished
klaarstaan: pre-dawn alert
klap: hit
klein: little
kleppie: thief
Klippies: brandy (Klipdrift)
knoesie: little bit (pinch)
koek: pussy
koffiemoffie: male flight attendant (*literally* coffee queer)
kom hier: come here
Kombi: minibus
kont: cunt
kop: head
kop-tiffy: Army psychiatrist
Koshuisraad: Hostel Council
kroon: money
krummelpap: crumbly maize porridge
kry sommer 'n paar lekker fat warm klappe: get a couple of nasty clouts
kwaai: cool
laager: enclosure
laaitie: child
laat waai: let's go
laatlammetjie: baby in an adult family
lag: laugh
Lala gashle madala baba: Sleep in peace old father
lammies: punch causing a small muscular knot, charley horse
lank: very
lappie: sniff inhalants with cloth patch
larney: posh guy
Leerlingraad: Learner's Council
lekker: nice
LMG: light machine gun
lokasie: location
lootie: lieutenant
los: leave
luss: bother
Maa'tha poes fokken witboernaaier! Djy gaan my nie naai nie: Your mother's cunt you white Afrikaner racist fucker, you aren't going to fuck me

Maak gebruik van jou kanse, seun: Make use of your chances, boy

maal: prepare marijuana

maaltye: meals

maar: but

maatjie: friend

mag: power

maggie: magistrate

mahala: free

majat: low-grade marijuana

makwera: boss

mal: mad

mallit: crazy person

mang: prison

mapuza: police

marchers: money

marrobaner: thief

meid: Cape Coloured woman (*derogatory*), cowardly

meidnaai: intercourse with a Cape Coloured woman (*derogatory*)

mejuffrou: miss

meneer: mister

mense: people

merting: dealing

mochie: girlfriend

moedertaal: mother tongue

moegoes: idiots

moela: money

Moenie vir my lag nie: Don't laugh at me

moer: beat up

moer-in: the hell in

moerse: huge

moffie: gay

mooi: good, pretty

Môre manne, klagtes en versoeke: Good morning men, complaints and requests

munt: black person (*derogatory*)

muti: medicine

naai: fuck

naaier: fucker

naar: nauseous

naargat: nauseating

nackerball: teacher's pet

nag: night or death

nchonalanga: prison gang lore

nee: no

NG Kerk: Dutch Reformed Church

njannies kappellas: as true's Bob

NLK: Northern Logistic Command

nogal: as well

nommers: prison gang numbers

nongalosh: prison gang that practises anal intercourse

nongie: homosexual, prison gang associated with homosexuality

nooit: no

nut: Mandrax tablet

nwata: fool

O fok nou kom daar kak: Fuck, now the shit's going to hit the fan

oke: guy

okie: little guy

onnie: teacher

oom: uncle

opkoms: confined to hostel

ops-tiffy: operations motor mechanic

opwarm: warm-up

ou: man

ouboet: oldest brother

ouen: guy

ouman: veteran

oupa: grandfather

ou-roeker: old marijuana smoker

padda: frog

padkos: packed lunch

PAGAD: People Against Gangsterism and Drugs

pak, pakkie: parcel

Papplaas: state rehabilitation centre

pastoor: pastor

PE: Port Elizabeth

peg: die

Peruvian flake: cocaine

PF: Permanent Force

picannin: black child

piel: penis

piemp: snitch, inform on

plaaswerkers: farmworkers

plank: Afrikaner (*derogatory*)

pluk: courage, drug trip

poephol: arsehole

poes: cunt

Poesbeker: cunt trophy

poesboekies: cunt photo comics

poeslap: sanitary pad (*literally* cunt rag)

Poesplaas: cunt farm

poeswyn: cunt wine

poizas: black warders

pomp: fuck, pump

pop: dupe

Porra: Portuguese

pozzie: place, home

raak wys: wise up

raas: noise

rail: line of cocaine

rand-baalle: marijuana sticks

regte: real

respek: respect

riempiesbank: leather thong bench

Ritmagtiging: route authorisation

roeker: marijuana smoker

rogue: bread

roller-skates: handcuffs

rondavel: round hut

Rooibaard: reddish marijuana strain

Rooinek: English South African

rookstop: a little marijuana to smoke

RTU: return to unit

SABC: South African Broadcasting Corporation

SADF: South African Defence Force

sadza: stiff, malleable porridge

Sammy: Sergeant Major

SANAB: South African Narcotics Bureau

sarmies: sandwiches

sawubona: hello

scab: newcomer

scale: steal

scaley: dodgy

schnaai: steal, defraud

screws: warders

ses-en-twintig: twenty-six (prison gang number)

shebeen: township tavern

shiv: sharp weapon

shot: thank you

siff: unhygienic (*literally* syphilitic)

sis: term of disgust

sjoe: phew

skaap: naive (*literally* sheep)

skates: handcuffs

skêbeng: steal

skel: scold

skelm: sly, thief

skiem: think

skiet: shoot

skievvie: servant

skimp: hint

skoffelling: shuffling

skoffelwerk: spade work

skollie: street gangster

Skollietaal: gangster language

skommel: masturbate

skoolgees: school spirit

skoolhoof: headmaster

skoon wit wyn: clean white wine

skraal: thin

skrik: fright, get frightened

skut: shake down, toss

skyf: marijuana

Slams: Moslems (Cape Malay slang)

slatwet: invoke gangster law

sluk: steal

smaak: like

smack: heroin

SMG: sub-machine gun

smokkel: smuggle

snoek: a barracuda-like fish

snor(re): moustache(s)

snotrag: handkerchief

snuif: sniff

sommer: because

sondaf: sunset (prison gang salute)

son'd op: sunrise (prison gang salute)

sonskynhoekie: lonely hearts column (*literally* sunshine corner)

SOP: standard operating procedure

Soutpiel: English South African (*literally* salty cock)

spiritsuiper: vagrant methylated spirits addict (*literally* spirits drinker) splab: talk

spookgerook: stoned to the point of paranoia

staan op: stand up

stambula: loyal, strong

States, the: South Africa

steamers: middle-aged alcoholics

steek taragoppie: stinging insect

sterk: strong

sterkbene: strong by success (*literally* strong legs)

stilte: quiet

stiltetyd: quiet time

stocks: girls

stokkie: awaiting-trial prisoner

stop(pe): marijuana stick(s)

Strafboek: punishment book

strafwerk: punishment work

Studenteraad: Student Council

sug: dangerous, sigh

suinige twee-gevreet naaiers: stingy two-faced fuckers

suip: drink

sukkel: struggle

swaai: roll, pack

swak: nothing, bad, slack

Swart Gevaar: Black Peril

taal: language

takkies: sneakers

tampon: doctor, medic

tampon tiffies: medics

tand: eat

tannie: aunty

tappies: cigarette butts

taragoppies: worms

teenwoordig: present

tiefchild: son of a bitch

tiekie: 3½ pence

tiekiebox: coin-operated phone booth

tiemied: ate

TK: Constantia School, Tokai

tog: after all

tom: money

toppie: old man

troep: troop

tune: tell

turk: withdrawal

twa: gun

twak: tobacco

twee maaltye: two meals (dietary punishment)

UCT: University of Cape Town

UNITA: Union for the Total Independence of Angola

vark: pig

vasbyt: persevere

vinnig: fast

Vlossie: Hercules military transport aircraft

volle samewerking: full cooperation

voorportaal: front hall

Voorregskaats: roller-skating privilege

vreet: eat

vrot: rotten

vuil: dirty

vuilgat: disgusting (*literally* dirty arse)

Vuilgatbeker: dirty arse trophy

vyf: five

waai: go

wakker: awake, alert

wallop: run away

weeshuislaaitie: orphan

whorejaer: sex worker's client (*literally* whore chaser)

windgat: arrogant

witbene: dead (*literally* white bones)

witboernaaier: racist white Afrikaner (*derogatory*)

wors: sausage

wys gedagtes: clever criminal intents

yster: iron

zanies: marijuana

zol: marijuana

Made in the USA
Lexington, KY
08 June 2011